MANAGING FINANCIAL RISK

The Institutional Investor Series in Finance

MANAGING FINANCIAL RISK

CLIFFORD W. SMITH, JR.

William E. Simon Graduate School of Business Administration
University of Rochester

CHARLES W. SMITHSON

Continental Bank

D. SYKES WILFORD

Chase Manhattan Bank

HarperBusiness
A Division of HarperCollins*Publishers*

International Standard Book Number: 0-88730-371-4

Library of Congress Catalog Card Number: 89-11080

Printed in the United States of America

Library of Congress Cataloging-in-Publication Data

Smith, Clifford W.
   Managing financial risk / Clifford W. Smith, Jr., Charles W. Smithson, D. Sykes Wilford.
     p. cm. – (The Institutional Investor series in finance)
   Includes bibliographical references and index
   ISBN 0-88730-371-4
   1. Business enterprises–Finance. 2. Risk management.
I. Smithson, C. W. (Charles W.) II. Wilford, D. Sykes. III. Title.
IV. Series.
HG4026.S58   1989
658.15–dc20   89-11080
                                          CIP

90 91 92 HC 9 8 7 6 5 4 3

To the officers of Chase Manhattan Bank . . .
. . . who helped to form the concept for this book

and

To Cindy . . .
. . . who helped to transform the concept to a book

Contents

PART II FORWARD CONTRACTS

PART III FUTURES

Preface

Financial engineering sounds like something you need a degree from MIT or CalTech to do. But, building innovative financial products with the financial building blocks is easy.

This book is the direct outgrowth of an education program the three of us taught for Chase Manhattan Bank from May 1985 to June 1987. We called the program the Advanced Financial Risk Analysis seminar (AFRA for short). In many ways the program was advanced. But, there was one message we continually stressed to the some 300 Chase officers who went through our program:

This stuff is not as hard as some people make it sound.

And that is the message we want you to pick up from this book. The financial markets have some complicated features but good common sense goes a lot further than the mathematical flash and dash.

Acknowledgments

As with any project of this size, we are indebted to a number of people who influenced our thinking, supported our work, and generally hounded us into getting this project completed.

In particular, we want to thank Lee Macdonald Wakeman of Chemical Bank. Lee was a coauthor of three papers with Cliff and Charles that form the foundation of our material on swaps. But, more than that, Lee had a profound influence on the way we look at these markets.

Don Chew, the editor of *The Journal of Applied Corporate Finance*, supported this project from its inception. Working with him helped us not only to clarify our thinking but also to get those thoughts on paper in a readable form.

Without our colleagues at the Chase Manhattan Bank, this book never would have existed. J. Richard Zecher, who is now president of Chase Investors, was the one who brought our group together and the one who stood behind our work in some rough times as well as the good. Robert D. Hunter, then the executive in charge of Chase Europe, along with Dennis Longwell, the present manager of Chase Europe, provided the support for the education program from which this book sprang. Bob and Dennis were some of our early believers, and we thank them. We also want to thank our colleagues, who worked with us to make the education program at Chase a success:

Mark Babunovic	Victor Barallat
Francisco J. Comprido	Nicholas deBoursac
Stefan Eckl	Cary Fieldcamp
Sharif Ghalib	Michael Hampton
Kacha Kastner	Ron Layard-Leisching
Lynn McFadden	Hilary Millar
Carol Moore	J. Nicholas Robinson
Tony Singleton	Bruce Smith
Kate Smith	Sandra Zimmer

Although the manuscript was basically complete before Charles joined

Continental, he was able to gain some insights from his experiences there, which added to this book. We wish to acknowledge the support of S. Waite Rawls III, the vice chairman; Joseph F. Schwaba, who managed the risk management products group; and Michael F. Fitzgerald, who dealt with the issues of marketing these products. And Charles sends his thanks to the people who designed, sold, and traded risk management products at Continental:

Marshall A. Blake	Thomas P. Brady	Judy A. Chan
Phillipe J. Comer	Marian deBerry	Robert Delarm
Jon F. Frye	Peter D. Hanson	Kevin Holme
Pamela G. Hudson	Nora Lee	Frederick T. Leiner
Nelda Mahady	John M. Mansueto	Karen K. Miller
Warren J. Naphtal	Steve A. Saratore	Scott Schweighauser
Ramon R. Uribarri		

We are also indebted to George Handjinicolaou (executive director, Interest Rate & Currency Management Products for Security Pacific Hoare Govett Limited), who read the preliminary drafts and provided particularly useful suggestions.

Finally, we owe our heartfelt thanks to Carol Franco and Carolyn Casagrande, who got this book started and had a great deal to do with the way it turned out.

PART I

An Overview

PART IV
An Overview

1

The New Financial Environment

Today financial price risk not only can affect quarterly profits, but it can determine a firm's very survival. Unpredictable movements in exchange rates, interest rates, and commodity prices present risks that cannot be ignored. It is no longer enough to be the firm with the most advanced production technology, the cheapest labor supply, or the best marketing team. *Price volatility can put even well-run firms out of business.*

Changes in exchange rates can create stiff competition where none previously existed. Similarly, commodity price fluctuations result in changes in input prices that can make substitute products—products made from different inputs—more affordable to end-consumers. Changes in interest rates have an impact on a firm's costs; for firms whose sales are inversely related to interest rates, rising rates can lead directly to financial distress as borrowing costs skyrocket while sales dry up.

Not surprisingly, the financial markets have responded to this increased price volatility. The past decade and a half have witnessed the evolution of a range of financial instruments and strategies that can be used to manage the growing exposure to financial price risk.

Financial instruments now exist to permit the direct transfer of financial price risk to some third party more willing to accept that risk. For example, through foreign exchange futures contracts, a U.S. exporter can transfer its foreign exchange risk to a firm in the opposite risk position or to a firm in the business of managing foreign exchange risk, leaving the U.S. exporter free to focus on its core business.

Moreover, the financial markets have evolved to the point that the financial instruments can be combined with debt issuance to separate financial price risk from the other risks inherent in the underlying capital-raising activity. For example, by combining bond issues with swaps, the issuing firm is able to decouple interest rate risk from traditional credit risk.

3

The World Became a More Risky Place

Underlying the demand for risk management products and financial engineering is the simple fact that financial prices have become more volatile. At the outset it is useful to ask why this instability exists. For an answer, we must trace the beginnings of and changes in the long-term increase in general price volatility, and then we must seek insight into its causes. To understand why the world is different, we have to look back to discover how the environment has changed. This requires taking a long look back, not just peeking over our shoulders to the last market crash or election.

Figure 1-1 provides some dramatic evidence of the change. This figure presents what must be regarded as a *long* price series: the price index for England from 1666 to the mid-1980s.

What is striking is that, from the seventeenth century until the late twentieth century, the price level in England was essentially stable. Prices did go up during wartime—the data series reflects conflicts such as the one the British had with that French person in the early nineteenth century—but fell back to pre-war levels once the conflict ended. However, the price history for the last half of the twentieth century indicates that the financial environment changed: for the first time, prices went up and stayed up. And this is not only an English phenomenon; a similar pattern for price levels in the United States (albeit, as our British colleagues point out, one with fewer data points) is illustrated in Figure 1-2.

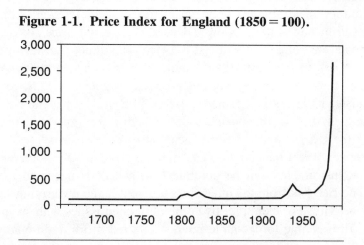

Figure 1-1. Price Index for England (1850 = 100).

Alternatively, we can study recent financial history by looking at inflation rates rather than price levels. As presented in Figure 1-3, the increase in prices over the last three decades is not quite as steady as is sometimes believed. Indeed, inflation was modest before the mid-1960s. Something happened during the 1960s that changed the rate of inflation. In 1965 prices started going up, a direction that continued through the 1970s. In addition to the unprecedented volatility, it is important to remember that the price changes were unexpected. Neither government officials nor financial pundits predicted the full scale of the inflationary explosion that characterized the 1970s.

It was not only inflation rates that became more volatile; similar increases in foreign exchange rates, interest rates, and commodity prices soon followed. It is important to understand that changes in these economic variables are interrelated. We must be prepared for changes in one market to affect the others.

There have been many suggestions as to the cause of the inflationary environment of the 1970s, for example, many have pointed to the OPEC oil price shocks. However, a more compelling answer is that inflation was a result of national and international monetary policy actions, the most important of which was the breakdown of the international fixed-exchange-rate system known as the Bretton Woods agreement. This system fixed the prices of the world's currencies in terms of the U.S. dollar *and* in terms of gold. Hence, the underpinning of the fixed-

Figure 1-2. U.S. Price Index, 1800–1985 (1967 = 100).

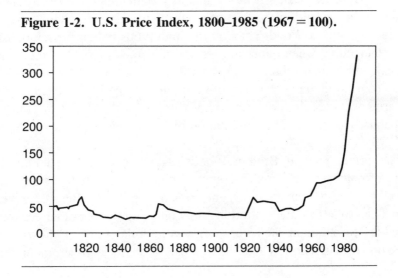

Figure 1-3. Inflation (CPI, two-year moving average, percent change).

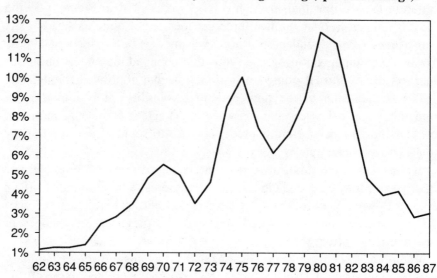

exchange-rate system—and of the stability it lent both to individual nations' domestic economies and to the global financial environment—was the fixed relation of the U.S. dollar to gold. The timing of the fluctuations in inflation presented in Figure 1-3 corresponds to the changing relation between the U.S. dollar and gold. The immediate cause of the breakdown of the system was the inability to maintain the fixed relation of the dollar to gold in the face of a worldwide glut of dollars. The first change to Bretton Woods came in the mid-1960s (when the relationship was changed between paper dollars and the stock of gold in the United States); subsequent changes to the rules of the system were made in 1968 (one gold price was established for the market and another for governments) and in 1971 (the convertibility of the dollar to gold was suspended), with the final dissolution of fixed exchange rates occurring in 1973.

The price rules of Bretton Woods, which once dictated monetary policy for the world's major countries, were eliminated, leaving governments free to pursue divergent monetary policies. Before, governments had to adjust their inflation rates, interest rates, or other economic variables to maintain their currency's gold/dollar price. Following the breakdown of Bretton Woods, if it chose to do so, a government could

manipulate these economic variables to support its fiscal policies and let the exchange rate fluctuate to "take up the slack."[1]

As uncertainty increased, prices in the United States went up and up, even as policymakers unveiled one anti-inflation plan after another.[2] Then, just when everyone was sure that inflation was here to stay — and was consequently adjusting business and financial plans to allow for it — the recession arrived. High inflation disappeared, but uncertainty did not.[3]

The most important point about the experience with inflation is that the inflation was not anticipated, nor was the subsequent disinflation. The only certainty about inflation is that we must be more humble in forecasting its future path.

---

1. For a discussion of fixed exchange rates, monetary policy rules, and the gold standard, see D. Sykes Wilford and Ronald A. Krieger, "Discretionary Monetary Policy and the Gold Standard," in *The Monetary Approach to International Adjustment*, ed. by Bluford H. Putman and D. Sykes Wilford (New York: Praeger, 1986), pp. 298–306. One point noted by most authors is that it is not clear that a new "Bretton Woods" system could be created, given the present financial structures, without a new gold standard and enforeceable rules.

Moreover, it is very unlikely that sufficient agreement could be obtained among the Group of Seven about which central bank would determine world policy. Each year the heads of state and financial policymakers of the seven largest Western economies (the United States, France, Japan, Germany, Britain, Italy, and Canada) meet to discuss policy. For six of these nations to agree to defer to the seventh, which would then be the one ruler of monetary policy, appears most unlikely. Only a major international crisis à la World War II or the Great Depression could force such an agreement.

2. Anti-inflationary programs were the norm during the 1970s in the United States. Unfortunately, none of them worked. Under Nixon, wage and price controls were tried. President Ford had a policy of "whip inflation now" — and even produced WIN buttons. Carter's administration, which would watch over the worst of the inflationary period, expounded on how it was committed to anti-inflationary policy.

3. One argument for the emerging inflationary spirals during the 1970s, as well as subsequent disinflationary spirals of the 1980s, centered around the monetary discipline, now absent, derived from the gold standard of Bretton Woods. For discussion of the gold standards and how they worked, see Donald M. McClosky and J. Richard Zecher, "The Success of Purchasing Power Parity: Historical Evidence and Its Implications for Macroeconomics," in *A Retrospective on the Classical Gold Standard 1821–1931*, ed. by Michael Bordo and Anna Schwartz (Chicago: University of Chicago Press, 1984, pp. 121–170.); Donald N. McCloskey and J. Richard Zecher "How The Gold Standard Worked, 1880–1913," in *The Monetary Approach to the Balance of Payments*, ed. by Jacob Frankel and Harry G. Johnson (Tampa: Financial Management Association, 1986), pp. 357–385.

The financial environment had thus changed: in contrast to the stable price levels of the past, developed economies began to experience unexpected price changes (increases); the financial markets were confronted with increased price uncertainty. The increased uncertainty about inflation was soon followed by uncertainty about foreign exchange rates, interest rates, and commodity prices.

Foreign Exchange Rates Became More Risky

Figure 1-4 provides data for the monthly percentage change in the U.S. Dollar/Japanese yen exchange rate, 1950–1988. This figure provides a very clear indication that the foreign exchange market has become more risky. The reason for the increased volatility in foreign exchange rates during the early 1970s is evident: the breakdown of the Bretton Woods system of fixed exchange rates.

Under the system of Bretton Woods, importers knew what they would pay for goods in their domestic currency, and exporters knew how much they would receive in their local currency. If the importer could sell at

Figure 1-4. Exchange Rate Volatility: Percent Change in U.S. Dollar/Yen Exchange Rate.

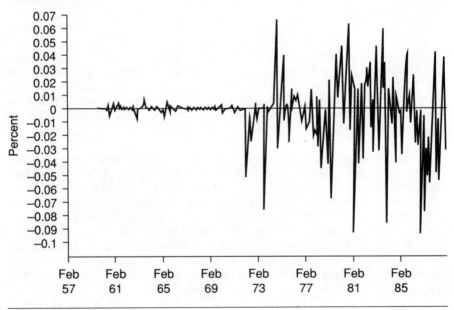

a profit to the consumer and the exporter's costs were below the export price, then gains from trade were had by all.

With the breakdown of Bretton Woods, the rules changed. Both sides to the transaction now faced exchange rate risk. Each party wanted to transact using home currency to avoid being "whipsawed" by the market. The importer's profit margin could, and often did, evaporate if the domestic currency weakened sharply, and the imported goods were priced in the exporter's currency.

Exchange rate volatility also affects domestic producers. Exchange rate risk occurs whenever the value of future cash flows is liable to change because of foreign exchange rate movements. With more volatile exchange rates, all market participants face greater risk.

In addition, the volatility of exchange rates affects the real return on domestic versus foreign financial assets. Adverse exchange rate movements may overshadow the interest payments or other income stream received on a foreign currency–denominated asset. Consequently, exchange rate volatility influences the currency distributions of global portfolios, as both borrowers and lenders try to diversify their foreign exchange risk by holding assets or liabilities in different currencies.

Interest Rates Became More Risky

Surprisingly, the increased volatility evident in the foreign exchange market did not initially spill over into the U.S. domestic money market. Indeed, vis-à-vis the late 1960s and early 1970s, interest rates actually stabilized in 1977 through 1979. As is shown in Figure 1-5, even though inflation rates went up and interest rates followed, interest rate volatility[4] actually *declined* under then chairman of the Federal Reserve Board Bill Miller. (Some have argued he paid for stable domestic interest rates with higher inflation and a weaker dollar.)

Uncertainty finally hit U.S. interest rates on October 6, 1979, when the newly appointed chairman of the Federal Reserve Board, Paul Volcker, initiated money supply targeting and abandoned interest rate targeting. Interest rates became extremely volatile: 90-day treasury bill interest rate volatility in the two years following October 1979 was five times greater than that of the prior two years. In the bond market, the

---

4. For exposition, Figure 1-5 is based on the monthly first difference in the rate rather than the percentage change or some other measure more closely related to volatility.

Figure 1-5. Interest Rate Volatility: First Difference in U.S. Treasury Yield (Five-Year Constant Maturity).

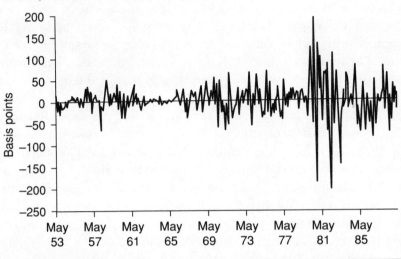

ratio was even higher. Unpredictability in bond prices, borrowing costs, and real returns became the norm.

The increase in interest rate risk had several major effects. First, financial institutions and their depositors became less willing to make long-term rate commitments. In the 1980s, savings banks in the United States were stuck with long-term, low-rate loans to homeowners that had to be financed with high-rate and volatile short-term funds. The savings banks experienced disintermediation as depositors put their funds into money markets through various new instruments. In response to interest rate volatility, passive attitudes toward investment disappeared, and investors moved to adjust to the new environment. Old rules were replaced with those geared for uncertainty. And as interest rate volatility appeared in conjunction with exchange rate volatility, it became more difficult for a market participant with a multicurrency portfolio to assess the expected real return or cost of transactions.

Commodity Prices Became More Risky

Volatility also increased in the commodity markets. In this context, the first commodity that comes to mind is oil. As part (a) of Figure 1-6 indicates, the price of petroleum products did become more volatile in the 1970s, but the same kind of behavior shows up for most basic

Figure 1-6. Commodity Price Volatility: (*a*) **Percent Change in Wholesale Petroleum Products Price Index.** (*b*) **Percent Change in Wholesale Metals Price Index.**

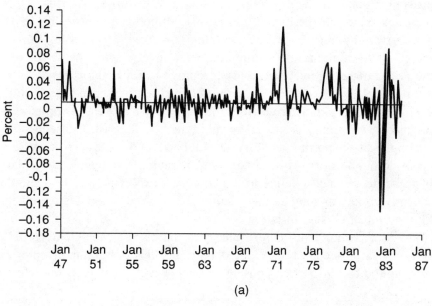

(a)

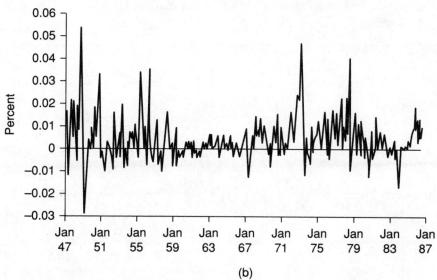

(b)

commodities. Part (*b*) of Figure 1-6 presents data on monthly volatility for metals.

Figure 1-7 provides another way of looking at commodity prices by providing data on the relative prices of commodities. As this figure indicates, much of the increase in basic commodity prices in the 1970s was driven by inflation. The declining purchasing power of dollars increased the demand for commodities as assets, with the result that the prices of real goods were bid up relative to financial assets.

In the 1970s commodity-exporting countries experienced a windfall: wealth was being transferred from the industrialized West to commodity producers, especially producers of oil in the Middle East. Consequently, a commodity-exporting country could become wealthy by recycling "petrodollars"—borrowing dollars and repaying the loan with dollars that had depreciated relative to the country's export prices. This simple scheme worked as long as the relative prices of commodities were kept high by unanticipated inflation.

However, when real interest rates rose sharply after the October 1979 shift in U.S. monetary policy, the opportunity cost of holding inventories of commodities also rose; consequently, the real value of commodities

Figure 1-7. Relative Prices of Commodities (Commodity Prices/Producer Price Index).

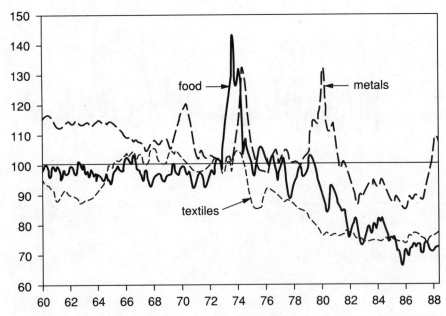

fell. Wealth was once again shifted, this time from the commodity producers to those holding floating-rate liens against those commodity assets. As Figure 1-7 indicates, the relative prices of commodities have fallen dramatically from the peaks reached in 1974 and 1979.

The Financial Markets Responded

For the financial community, the last decade and a half were particularly important because of the impact of the increased volatility on the financial markets and the demand for new financial instruments. The price environment is the key factor determining the success of a particular kind of financial instrument in the marketplace. Financial innovation is not the norm during periods of stable prices.

For example, in the late 1800s the most desirable financial instrument was the *consol* (a bond with a fixed interest rate but no maturity date; it lasted forever). Investors were quite happy to hold British government bonds with no maturity. Why? The bonds paid a steady real rate of interest, British sovereign credit was good, and expected inflation was nil. Confidence in price level stability led to a stable interest rate environment and therefore to long-lived bonds.

Stability didn't end with the nineteenth century. In the 1950s, price stability meant that banks were willing to lend on a fixed-rate basis. Until the 1970s, thirty-year fixed-rate mortgages (mortgages that were assumable with no prepayment penalty) were the norm. Floaters, CAPS, CMOs, etc.—the jargon of the mortgage business of the 1980s—were simply not needed. Indeed, because of the price history of Switzerland, long-term, fixed-rate mortgages are still the norm there.

Uncertainty in the global financial environment has caused many economic problems and disruptions, but it has also provided the impetus for financial innovation. Through financial innovation, the financial intermediaries were soon able to offer their customers products to manage or even exploit the new risk. Through this same innovation, financial institutions became better able to evaluate and manage their own asset and liability position.

The marketplace recognized early that the uncertainty about foreign exchange rates, interest rates, and commodity prices could not be eliminated by "better forecasting."[5] This recognition induced firms to begin

---

5. In some cases participants learned the futility of trying to forecast prices in efficient markets only through the expensive lessons provided by Benjamin Franklin's "hard school."

actively managing financial risk. The financial institutions—exchanges, commercial banks, and investment banks—have provided a range of new products to accomplish this risk management:

- In response to the increased foreign exchange rate risk, the markets provided forward contracts on foreign exchange, foreign exchange futures (in 1972), currency swaps (in 1981), and options on foreign exchange (in 1982).

- For managing interest rate risk, futures contracts were the first to appear (in 1975), followed by interest rate swaps (in 1982), interest rate options (in 1982), and finally, interest rate forwards—called "forward rate agreements" (in 1983).

- In addition to the existing forward contracts for metals and long-term contracts for petroleum, the onset of increased price volatility in the late 1970s led to the appearance of futures contracts for commodities (for oil in 1978 and for metals in 1983). These were followed by commodity swaps (in 1986) and commodity options (in 1986).

The products themselves are not new at all: forward contracts first appeared at medieval trade fairs in the twelfth century,[6] futures contracts first appeared in Japan (on rice) in the 1600s,[7] and even options appeared in Amsterdam as early as the seventeenth century.[8] However, in practice these markets are new; without price risk no one cared (the opportunity cost was too high) to use these "derivative products." It was not until prices became volatile that anyone felt the need to create modern versions of these contracting techniques.

Some Cases of Financial Price Risk

Financial price risk can be permanent or temporary; recognition of the difference is essential for choosing the proper risk management instrument. Temporary price exposures usually result from a particular

---

6. Richard J. Teweles and Frank J. Jones, *The Futures Game* (New York: McGraw-Hill, 1987).

7. Ibid.

8. *Futures and Options Trading in Commodity Markets* (Paris: International Chamber of Commerce, 1986).

transaction; for example, a corporation importing goods from Germany into the United States with the price denominated in deutsche marks has a temporary foreign exchange exposure. Foreign exchange forward markets have handled such problems for some time now. However, focusing only on the management of these familiar temporary exposures can obscure critical *permanent* economic exposures.

Permanent price exposures result from factors such as the location of manufacturing plants, the denomination of wages in one currency versus another, or regulations in a competitor's home country. For example, American factory workers want to be paid in U.S. dollars, whether the goods are going to be sold in dollars or in Japanese yen. Or it may be that the manufacturer's major competitor for U.S. sales is a Japanese corporation, whose prices in the United States are determined by movements in the yen/dollar rate. Thus, the firm faces a permanent price exposure to the yen/dollar exchange rate because its plant is located in the United States, and its competitor's plant is in Japan. This example is typical of the permanent price exposures that accompany exchange rate volatility. With the variance in exchange rates doubling over the past ten years, exchange rate risk has arrived on the American doorstep.

Permanent price exposure can also result from dramatic movements in a company's input/output prices: the more easily an asset (as a unit of output) can be replaced by other assets, the more volatile is its price in an unstable financial environment. Consider a gold mine. The value of the mine depends on the price of its output—gold. However, the prices of its inputs are not in gold. If labor is paid in dollars and the firm is leveraged with capital financed by floating-rate dollar debt, then the firm is extremely vulnerable to changes in the price of gold and in dollar interest rates. Unfortunately, gold prices may fall when interest rates rise, making the firm's overall risk even greater.[9]

---

9. Gold prices tend to be inversely related to real interest rates. If today's real interest rate equals today's nominal rate minus expected inflation, and if gold is a "sterile" asset, a rise in the real interest rate implies an increased real opportunity cost for holding gold. As real rates go up over time, investors tend to decrease the stock of gold by either decreasing the quantities they hold or bidding price down. Since gold is nonperishable and the stock adjusts slowly and predictably, the greatest adjustment may be expected to take place in the price. See D. Sykes Wilford and Ronald A. Krieger, "Discretionary Monetary Policy and the Gold Standard," in *The Monetary Approach to International Adjustment*, ed. by Bluford N. Putnam and D. Sykes Wilford (New York: Praeger, 1986), pp. 298–306.

The price of a commodity input can also introduce permanent price risk. A case in point is the aluminum industry. In addition to concerns such as exchange rates, bauxite prices, and smelting technology, the costs of producing aluminum also depend on the relative cost of energy. It is an energy-intensive business, so one would expect high energy prices to be a negative factor for profitability. This is not necessarily the case. Some smelters were set up as vehicles to "export energy." Companies set up operations in energy-rich areas to export the energy via the aluminum exports. (OPEC nations, for example, can utilize this as a way to manuever around quotas.) Aluminum smelting can thus be a way of exporting excess, nontransportable geothermal energy. As a result, many aluminum firms have found their value to be positively rather than negatively related to energy prices: as energy prices rose, the value of the aluminum smelter in an energy-rich location rose. Since the global industry's production takes place in both energy-rich and energy-poor countries, rising oil prices require energy-poor countries to pass along the increased energy costs to the aluminum company. This action changes the relative price of the aluminum supplied, energy-rich producers find themselves with a higher market share and higher prices. Of course, when energy prices fell in the mid-to-late 1980s the reverse became true. Because of price risk, today's best investment can become tomorrow's "dog" if not managed.

A final example shows how easily financial risk can sneak up on the unsuspecting.

Example

The U.S. S&Ls and interest rate risk

In the late 1970s the U.S. Savings and Loans (S&Ls) seemed to be money machines. Today S&Ls are anything but that.

The reason for this switch from money machines to money pits is found in the asset-liability structure of a typical S&L: Liabilities were short-term deposits that were repriced daily, monthly, or at most semiannually; assets were long-term mortgages. Given the difference that existed between the yield on the FSLIC-insured deposit on the liability side and that on a long-term mortgage on the asset side, S&L managers were paid handsomely. Figure 1-8 provides a stylized example.

Figure 1-8. U.S. S&Ls as Money Machines.

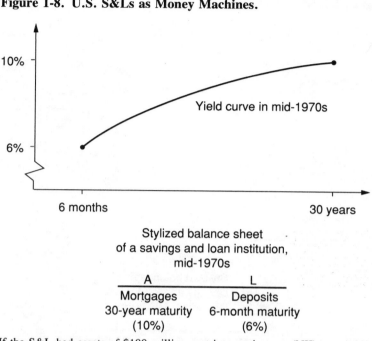

Stylized balance sheet
of a savings and loan institution,
mid-1970s

A	L
Mortgages	Deposits
30-year maturity	6-month maturity
(10%)	(6%)

If the S&L had assets of $100 million, net interest income (NII) was (10% − 6%) × $100 million, or $4 million. This yield curve spread, or gapping (owning a long-term asset funded with short-term borrowings), was typical for S&Ls.

This core business, however, created an incredible interest rate exposure.[10] As interest rates became highly variable in the early 1980s, short-term interest rates rose above long-term rates, presenting an inverted yield curve, something rarely seen during the 1960s. When the yield curve began to move significantly, these money machines turned into money pits, as shown in the stylized example in Figure 1-9. Although the core business risk was credit risk, changes in income resulted from interest rate risk.

Unfortunately, the interest rate risk left such firms bankrupt; jobs were lost, and investments became worthless. In 1977, when most of the mortgage portfolio still in place in 1981–82 was put on the books, who could have known that the overnight cost of funding would be more than 20% by the early 1980s? Or who would have guessed that the safe, below-market FSLIC-insured deposit

---

10. The interest rate exposure was additional to the credit risk the S&L accepted by making the mortgage loans, a risk that was not completely evident until the 1980s, when mortgage default led to a crisis in the S&L industry.

Figure 1-9. U.S. S&Ls as Money Pits.

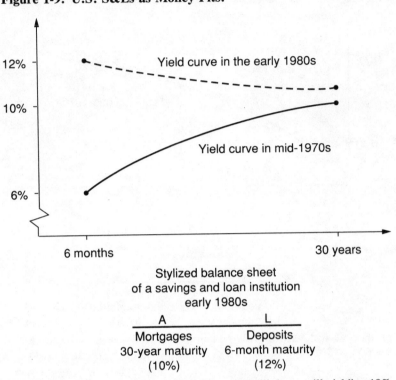

Stylized balance sheet
of a savings and loan institution
early 1980s

A	L
Mortgages	Deposits
30-year maturity	6-month maturity
(10%)	(12%)

The mortgages put on the book in the 1970s were still there, still yielding 10%. But with the new yield curve, deposits were yielding 12%. Hence, NII over this period was (10% − 12%) × $100 million, or −$2 million. NII swung from $4 million in the mid-1970s to −$2 million in the early 1980s simply because of the change in the yield curve.

of the 1970s would be disintermediated by the creation of the money market mutual fund in the 1980s. Those years of S&Ls being "money machines" by playing the funding gap (during a period of stable interest rates) came back to haunt them. From October 6, 1979, the day U.S. interest rate policy changed, interest rates would become highly volatile, turning old "safe" practices into new "dangerous" ones overnight.

Although the preceding examples of interest rate risk, foreign exchange risk, and commodity price risk have been general, real-world examples of these risks are all around us; both "living" and "no longer

living" examples abound. In the savings and loan industry, the list of FSLIC bailouts, takeovers, forced mergers, and liquidations seems endless.

On the commodity side, many of the debt crisis difficulties of Peru, Chile, Argentina, and Venezuela are the result of simultaneous falling commodity prices and high interest rates. Consequently, stockholders of large U.S. banks have had to learn about these risks the hard way, through lower earnings. And consider the case of Kennicott Copper, once regarded as the most technically advanced copper producer in the world. Today Kennicott does not exist as an independent entity; fluctuations in the price of copper put Kennicott in financial distress.

During the mid-to-late 1980s, the reverse was true for countries such as Portugal. Falling commodity prices combined with lower dollar borrowing costs and higher export revenues (they export primarily to the EEC) to create new wealth for Portugal.[11]

On the foreign exchange side, examples can be taken daily from the newspaper. Examples of wealth shifts away from the "rust belt" to the service and high-tech industries in the United States in conjunction with the rise in the dollar in the mid-1980s are common; but examples of reversals due to the falling dollar in 1986 and 1987 are just as common. The list of firms hit by exchange rate risk in the early 1980s is long: Caterpillar, Ford, General Motors, U.S. Steel, Kodak, etc. The other side of the coin is witnessed in the 1987 earnings of International Paper, General Electric, the U.S. Chemical Industry, and the revival of Caterpillar and Kodak.

---

11. Considering that Portugal had difficulty raising new funds in the syndicated loan market during the early 1980's, the February 10, 1988 Euromarket issue at a borrowing cost similar to Italy's demonstrates that you can get lucky with financial risk (just as you can get lucky at a casino).

2

Identifying and Measuring Financial Risk

Chapter 1 made it clear that the financial environment today is a lot riskier than it was prior to 1972. The variance—volatility—of interest rates, foreign exchange rates, and commodity prices is much greater today. The second message of Chapter 1 was that this increased volatility has had the effect of putting some otherwise well-managed firms into financial distress.

Although the CEO or CFO of a firm might find this discussion of the altered financial environment intellectually appealing, managers are usually more pragmatic, reacting with more specific questions: "Is *my* firm one of those that can be put out of business by this increased volatility? Is my firm exposed to interest rates? Foreign exchange rates? Commodity prices?"

It is these questions that this chapter addresses. We begin by describing the *risk profile,* a vehicle for summarizing the impact of financial price risk on a firm. Then we describe methods of actually measuring a firm's exposure, first looking at the special case of a financial institution's exposure to interest rate risk, and then broadening our scope to consider a general methodology.

The Risk Profile

In Chapter 1, U.S. Savings and Loan institutions were cited as classic examples of firms subject to—and, indeed, ultimately damaged by—interest rate risk. With assets that had long maturities (e.g., 30-year fixed-rate mortgages) and liabilities that were repriced frequently (e.g., passbook deposits), the value of the S&L was inversely related to interest

rates: as the interest rate rose—as the term structure shifted upward—the value of the S&L's assets declined significantly while the value of its liabilities changed little. The relation between interest rates and the value of the S&L is portrayed graphically in Figure 2-1. As interest rates rose ($\Delta r > 0$), that is, as actual interest rates, r, rose above the expected rates, r_e, the value of the firm declined ($\Delta V < 0$). The *risk profile* summarizes this relation.[1]

For the S&Ls, the exposure to interest rates was apparent in a firm's balance sheet; the exposure was due to a mismatch of maturities for assets and liabilities. However, a firm may have *economic exposures* that are not reflected in the balance sheet. For example, for a forest products firm, increases in interest rates decrease the demand for housing, thereby

---

1. In fact, the relation between the value of the firm and the interest rate is nonlinear. However, in this text we will, for simplicity of exposition, assume the relation to be linear; that is, we ignore the issue of convexity.

Figure 2-1. The Risk Profile for a U.S. S&L.

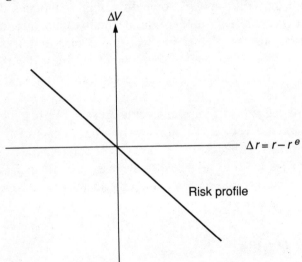

As actual interest rates, r, rise above expected sales, r_e ($\Delta r > 0$) the value of the S & L's assets declines relative to the value of its liabilities; thus the value of the firm declines ($\Delta V > 0$).

decreasing the demand for lumber. Thus, as cash inflows decline, the value of the forest products firm declines. However, this economic exposure, illustrated in Figure 2-2, will not appear on the firm's balance sheet.

We observe the same kind of relation in the case of foreign exchange risk. In some instances, the foreign exchange exposure is apparent. For example, the following is a case of a *transaction exposure*: A U.S. importer orders products from Germany, paying in deutsche marks (DM) when the products are delivered within 90 days. If, during that 90 days, the price of a DM rises (the value of the dollar declines), the U.S. importer will have to pay more for the product. In this case, illustrated in Figure 2-3, an increase in the price of the foreign currency leads to a decrease in the value of the importer.

Figure 2-2. The Risk Profile for a Forest Products Firm.

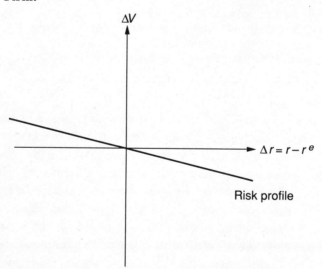

As actual interest rates, r, rise relative to the rate expected, r^e, the demand for housing declines. Consequently, housing starts decline and the demand for lumber drops. As cash inflows to the forest products firm decrease, the value of the firm decreases ($\Delta V > 0$).

Figure 2-3. The Risk Profile for a U.S. Importer.

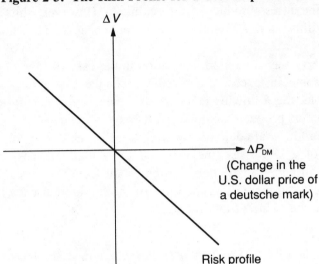

Risk profile

As the price of a deutsche mark rises, ($\Delta P_{DM} > 0$) the
dollar cost of the importer's order rises. With
rising cost, the importer's net cash flows decline,
thereby reducing the value of the firm ($\Delta V < 0$).

Firms with international operations have become adept at dealing both with these transaction exposures and with the *translation exposures* that result from the translation of overseas assets and liabilities into a company's domestic currency for accounting purposes. However, a more subtle problem is the recognition of a firm's economic exposures— also referred to as *competitive exposures*. For example, Eastman Kodak's exchange rate risk management policy is based on the recognition of its economic exposures.[2] When the value of the yen rises, Kodak film becomes more competitive with Fuji film in Japan, while Fuji becomes less competitive in Kodak's domestic market. This exposure is illustrated in Figure 2-4.

Not surprisingly, the same kinds of relations appear with respect to commodity price risk. In some cases, the exposures are apparent. For

---

2. This example is based on Paul Dickens, "Daring to Hedge the Unhedgeable," *Euromoney Corporate Finance* no. 45 (August 1988): 11–13.

Figure 2-4. Kodak's Risk Profile.

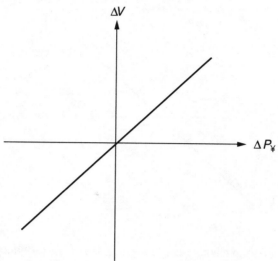

As the price of the yen rises ($\Delta P_{¥} > 0$), Kodak is able to market more effectively in Japan while Fuji is put at a disadvantage in the United States.

example, as the price of oil rises and revenues to oil producers rise,[3] the value of an oil producer rises (see Part (a) of Figure 2-5).[4] However, rising oil prices mean rising costs for an airline; rising oil prices are thus linked to falling firm values (see Part (b) of Figure 2-5).

Alternatively, the exposures can be subtle. Consider the aluminum production example introduced in Chapter 1. A primary input to aluminum production is electrical energy. Aluminum manufacturers in Iceland use electricity generated by that country's abundant geothermal energy. As the price of oil rises, the costs to competitors rise but the cost for Icelandic producers remain unchanged. Hence, as oil prices

3. This presupposes that the demand for oil is price-inelastic.
4. There is no doubt that the value of an oil-producing firm is positively related to the price of oil. However, we would be remiss if we failed to note indications that this positive relation may be becoming weaker. See, for example, Allanna Sullivan, "Restructured Oil Firms Suffer Little Hardships as Crude Prices Plunge," *The Wall Street Journal*, October 3, 1988, p. A1.

Figure 2-5 *(a)* **The Risk Profile for an Oil Producer.** *(b)* **The Risk Profile for an Oil User.**

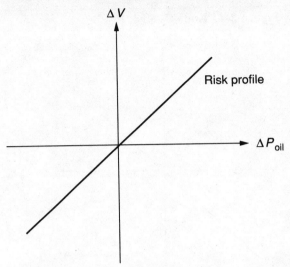

For an oil producer, rising oil prices ($\Delta P_{oil} > 0$) and rising revenues lead to an increase in the value of the firm ($\Delta V > 0$).

(a)

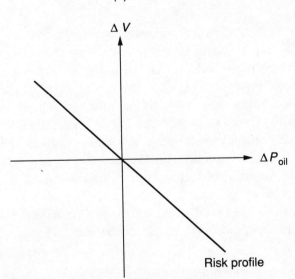

For an oil user, rising oil prices ($\Delta P_{oil} > 0$) mean increasing costs; so the value of the firm declines ($\Delta V > 0$).

(b)

rise, Icelandic producers' costs fall relative to those of their competitors; thus, the value of the Icelandic firms rises. It is when oil prices fall and their competitors' costs decline that the Icelandic aluminum producers worry[5] (see Figure 2-6).

For any financial price risk—interest rate risk, foreign exchange risk, or commodity price risk—the risk profile is a useful means of summarizing the exposure of the firm. The question to be answered is: How is the slope of the risk profile ($\Delta V / \Delta P$) determined? That is, does one estimate how much the value of the firm changes for a given change in the financial price? It is to this question that the remainder of this chapter is addressed.

_____

5. For this useful story about Icelandic aluminum producers, we are indebted to J. Nicholas Robinson of Chase Manhattan Bank.

Figure 2-6. Risk Profile for an Icelandic Aluminum Producer.

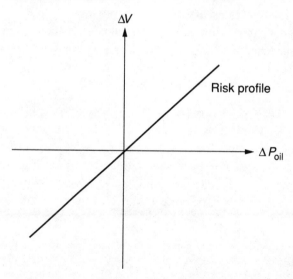

As the price of oil rises ($\Delta P_{oil} > 0$) the costs for firms competing with Icelandic aluminum procedures rise. Consequently, sales for the Icelandic firm increase, leading to an increase in the value of the firm ($\Delta V > 0$).

Quantifying Financial Price Risk: Interest Rate Risk for a Financial Institution

The S&L example is an extreme case—almost a caricature—of interest rate exposure for a financial institution. But because of the mismatches between the maturities of assets and the maturities of liabilities that occur as a normal course of business, all financial institutions face interest rate risk.

Maturity Gap

The method most financial institutions use to manage their exposure to interest rate changes is called the *maturity gap* approach.[6] The approach is so named because the procedure is to determine the "gap" between the dollar amounts of rate-sensitive assets (RSA) and rate-sensitive liabilities (RSL):[7]

$$\text{Gap} = \text{RSA} - \text{RSL} \qquad (2\text{-}1)$$

Changes in interest rates affect a financial institution via changing the institution's net interest income (NII). Hence, if the gap is known, the impact on the firm of changes in the interest rate is given by:

$$\Delta\text{NII} = \text{Gap} \times (\Delta r) \qquad (2\text{-}2)$$

To see how this works, consider the two hypothetical banks presented in Figure 2-7. Bank 1 is a "standard bank." Its assets are primarily business and mortgage loans with maturities of one year and longer; the bank's liabilities are primarily demand and savings deposits with maturities less than a year. Within the one-year gapping period, the assets that are rate-sensitive—those that will be repriced—are the three-

---

6. Our discussion of the maturity gap model is taken from Alden L. Toevs, "Measuring and Managing Interest Rate Risk: A Guide to Asset/Liability Models Used in Banks and Thrifts," Morgan Stanley Fixed Income Analytical Research Paper, October 1984. (An earlier version of this paper appeared in *Economic Review*, the Federal Reserve Bank of San Francisco, Spring 1983.) In this discussion, we consider only the basic model. For extensions of the model to the *periodic gap model* or *simulation models*, see the above-referenced work.

7. Assets and liabilities that are "rate-sensitive" are those that will be repriced during the gapping period.

Figure 2-7. Two Hypothetical Banks (all values in $ millions).

Assets		Bank 1	Liabilities	
3-month or less	100		3-month or less	400
6-month	100		6-month	300
12-month	400		12-month	200
Over 12-month	400		Over 12-month	100
	1,000			1,000

Assets		Bank 2	Liabilities	
3-month or less	100		3-month or less	100
6-month	100		6-month	100
12-month	400		12-month	300
Over 12-month	400		Over 12-month	500
	1,000			1,000

month assets ($100), the six-month assets ($100), and the twelve-month assets ($400); so RSA = $600. Within the one-year gapping period, the liabilities that are rate sensitive are the three-month liabilities ($400), the six-month liabilities ($300), and the twelve-month liabilities ($200); so RSL = $900. Hence, bank 1 has a gap of −$300 million:

$$\text{Bank 1:} \quad \text{Gap} = \text{RSA} - \text{RSL} = \$600 - \$900 = -\$300$$

Bank 2 has precisely the same distribution of assets but this bank has concentrated on funding itself with one-year and longer-term CDs. Consequently, RSA for this bank remains at $600 but the liabilities that are rate-sensitive during the one-year gapping period decline to $500– $100 in three-month liabilities, $100 in six-month liabilities, and $300 in twelve-month liabilities. Hence, bank 2 has a positive gap of $100 million:

$$\text{Bank 2:} \quad \text{Gap} = \text{RSA} - \text{RSL} = \$600 - \$500 = \$100$$

Once the gap is known, the impact of changes in the interest can be calculated directly using Equation (2-2). For instance, if interest rates increase by 1% (100 basis points), the NII for bank 1 will decrease by $3 million:

$$\text{Bank 1} \,|\, \Delta r = 0.01: \quad \Delta \text{NII} = -300 \times 0.01 = -3$$

and the NII for bank 2 will increase by $1 million:

$$\text{Bank } 2 \,|\, \Delta r = 0.01: \quad \Delta\text{NII} = +100 \times 0.01 = +1$$

If interest rates decrease by 1%, the NII for bank 1 will increase by $3 million, and the NII for bank 2 will decrease by $1 million.

These changes in NII for banks 1 and 2 are displayed in a *gap diagram* in Figure 2-8. A gap diagram shows the changes in NII that will occur for particular changes in interest rates (e.g., up 1% or down 1%) for various asset-liability structures (e.g., a negative gap of $300 or a positive gap of $100). The risk profile illustrated earlier shows the changes in the value of the firm with respect to changes in interest rates *for a given asset-liability structure*. In essence, the risk profile is like a "slice" of the gap diagram. For example, if we "slice" Figure 2-8 at the $-$300 million gap position, it is easy to see that an increase of 100 basis points in the interest rate will increase NII by $3 million, and a decrease of 100

Figure 2-8. A Gap Diagram.

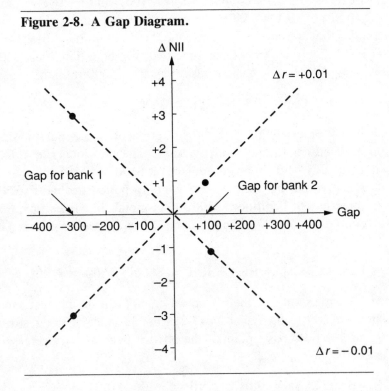

basis points in the interest rate will decrease NII by $3 million. This "slice" of the gap diagram—the interest rate risk profile for bank 1— is displayed in Figure 2-9. Hence, for the special case of interest rate risk for a financial institution, the question of this chapter— "How is the change in the value of a firm determined for a specified change in the financial price?—can be answered using the gap model.

Duration

Consider the bank balance sheet shown in Figure 2-10. We could examine this bank's exposure to interest rates by using the gap model to estimate the impact on NII of changes in interest rates, that is, Δ NII/Δr. Alternatively, we could use *duration analysis*.[8] In essence, the duration of a financial instrument provides a measure of when, on average,

---

8. Our discussion of duration is based on George G. Kaufman, "Measuring and Managing Interest Rate Risk: A Primer," *Economic Perspectives*, Federal Reserve Bank of Chicago.

Figure 2-9. Risk Profile for a Bank with a Gap of –$300.

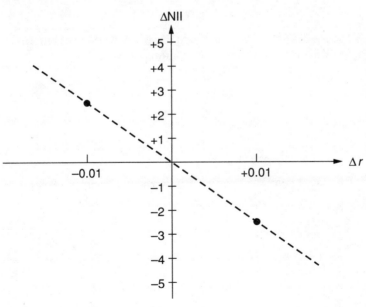

Figure 2-10. Bank Balance Sheet.

Assets		Liabilities	
Cash	100	1-year CD	600
Business loans	400	5-year CD	300
Mortgage loans	500	Equity	100
	1,000		1,000

the present value of the instrument is received. For illustration, we will look at the duration of two of the instruments on the bank's balance sheet: the five-year CD and the business loan, the cash flows for which are sketched in Figure 2-11.

The CD. The CD is simple. It is a zero coupon instrument so all of the value is received at maturity. Hence, the duration of the five-year CD is five years.

The Business Loan. Suppose that the business loan has a maturity of 2.5 years and is amortizing (has a sinking fund). As the cash flows in

Figure 2-11. (*a*) A Five-Year CD. (*b*) A $2\frac{1}{2}$-Year Amortizing Business Loan (with Semiannual Payments).

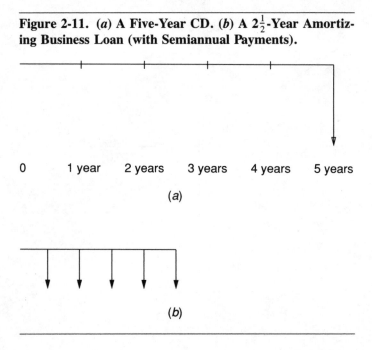

| 0 | 1 year | 2 years | 3 years | 4 years | 5 years |

(*a*)

(*b*)

Figure 2-11 illustrate, value is received prior to maturity; thus, it follows that the duration of the instrument is less than 2.5 years. To find out how much less, we can refer to Table 2-1. Columns 1–4 indicate the value of the bond. Column 1 gives the times that the cash flows in column 2 are paid. Using the discount rates[9] in column 3, the present values are determined (column 4), and the sum of these present values yields the $400 value of this loan. To determine when, on average, the present value is received, we need to calculate the weighted average time of receipt. Column 5 provides the weights; for example, at time 0.5 years, $86.70/400 = 0.22 of the total present value of the instrument is received. Multiplying these weights (column 5) by the times the cash flows are received (column 1) and summing gives the weighted average time of receipt—the duration of this business loan—as 1.45 years.

In algebraic form, the duration, D, as calculated above is

$$D = \sum_{t=1}^{T} \left(\frac{PV_t}{V} \right) \cdot t \qquad (2\text{-}3)$$

where PV_t is the present value of the cash flow received in time period t, and V is the market value of the instrument.

Duration effectively converts a security to its zero-coupon equivalent. In addition, duration provides a means of relating changes in interest

---

9. These discount rates are zero-coupon rates that include the risk premium appropriate for this instrument.

Table 2-1. Calculation of the Value and Duration of the Business Loan.

(1) Time to receipt (years)	(2) Cash flow	(3) Discount rate	(4) PV	(5) Weight	(6) Weight × Time
0.5	90	7.75%	86.70	0.22	0.11
1.0	90	8.00	83.33	0.21	0.21
1.5	90	8.25	79.91	0.20	0.31
2.0	90	8.35	76.66	0.19	0.38
2.5	90	8.50	73.40	0.18	0.45
			400.00		1.45

rates to changes in the value of the security. Specifically,[10]

$$D = -\frac{\Delta V}{\Delta r} \times \frac{(1 + r)}{V} \tag{2-4}$$

where D is the duration of the security as calculated above, V is the market value of the security, and r is the interest rate. Rewriting Equation (2-4), we can express the percentage change in the value of the security in terms of the percentage change in the discount rate, $(1+r)$, and the duration of the security:

$$\frac{\Delta V}{V} = -\frac{\Delta(1 + r)}{(1 + r)} \times D \tag{2-4'}$$

For example, if the discount rate increases by 1% (i.e., if $\Delta (1+r)/(1+r)$ = 0.01), the market value of the five-year CD will decrease by 5%:

$$\frac{\Delta V}{V} = -(0.01) \times 5.0 = -0.05$$

However, the same increase in the discount rate would decrease the value of the 2.5-year business loan by only 1.45%:

$$\frac{\Delta V}{V} = -(0.01) \times 1.45 = -0.0145$$

Hence, duration provides a method for relating the change in the value of the security to changes in interest rates.

Since duration is additive, the duration technique can be expanded to deal with the impact of changes in interest rates on the value of the entire firm. For a portfolio with n assets having market values V_i and durations D_i, the duration of the portfolio is

$$D_{portfolio} = \frac{\sum V_i D_i}{\sum V_i} \tag{2-5}$$

We can use Equation (2-5) to examine the duration of the assets of

---

10. Equation (2-4) holds only as an approximation. For true equality, we would have to replace our simple duration measure with "modified duration"—a level of detail finer than we wish here. For a development of this relation, the interested reader should see George G. Kaufman, G. O. Bierwag, and Alden Toevs, eds., *Innovations in Bond Portfolio Management: Duration Analysis and Immunization* (Greenwich, Conn.: JAI Press, 1983).

the bank in question. We already know that the duration of the business loan is 1.45 years. Suppose that the duration of the mortgage loans was calculated as 6.84 years. By definition, the duration of the cash is 0.0. Hence, the duration of the assets is

$$D_A = \frac{(100 \times 0.0) + (400 \times 1.45) + (500 \times 6.84)}{1,000} = 4.0$$

Likewise, we can examine the duration of the deposits. We have CDs with durations of one and five years so

$$D_D = \frac{(600 \times 1.0) + (300 \times 5.0)}{900} = 2.33$$

Combining the preceding results, we can calculate the duration of the equity: the elasticity of the value of the firm with respect to the discount rate, $(1 + r)$. Using Equation (2-5),

$$D_{equity} = \frac{(V_A \times D_A) - (V_D \times D_D)}{V_E}$$

$$= \frac{(1,000 \times 4.0) - (900 \times 2.33)}{100} = 19.03$$

Therefore, if the discount rate increases by 1%, the value of the equity of this firm will decline by 19.03%.

Duration provides an relation between interest rates and the value of the firm. Put in the context of our discussion so far, duration provides an alternative methodology for measuring the slope of the risk profile.

Quantifying Financial Price Risk: The General Case

Although gap and duration work well for financial institutions, these techniques break down in the examination of the interest rate sensitivity of a nonfinancial institution; and neither gap nor duration is of use in examining a firm's sensitivity to movements in foreign exchange rates or commodity prices. What is needed is a more general method for quantifying financial price risk—a method that can handle firms other than financial institutions and financial prices other than interest rates.

To get a measure of the responsiveness of the value of the firm to changes in the financial prices, we must first define a measure of the value of the firm. As with interest rate risk for financial institutions,

this value measure could be a flow measure (gap analysis uses net interest income) or a stock measure (duration uses the market value of the portfolio).

Flow Measures

Within a specific firm, estimation of the sensitivity of income flows is an analysis that can be performed as part of the budgeting/planning process. The trade press notes that firms have begun using simulation models to examine the responsiveness of pretax income to changes in interest rates, exchange rates, and commodity prices.[11] Beginning with base-case assumptions about the financial prices, the firm obtains a forecast for revenues, costs, and the resulting pretax income. Then the firm considers alternative values for an interest rate, an exchange rate, or a commodity price and obtains a new forecast for revenues, costs, and pretax income. By observing how the firm's forecast sales, costs, and income move in response to changes in these financial prices, the managers of the firm are able to trace a risk profile similar to those illustrated in Figures 2-1 through 2-6.

In the accomplishment of such an estimation, two inherent problems confront the analyst: (1) This approach requires substantial data, and (2) it relies on the ability of the researcher to make accurate, explicit forecasts for sales and costs under alternative scenarios about the financial prices. Hence, such an approach is generally possible only for analysts within a specific firm.

Stock Measures

Given the data requirements just noted, analysts outside the firm generally rely on market valuations, the most widely used of which is the market value of the equity. Using a technique similar to that by which analysts obtain the firm's "beta," it is possible to measure the historical sensitivity of the equity value to changes in interest rates, foreign exchange rates, and commodity prices.

In Part (a) of Figure 2-12, we have drawn a general risk profile, relating deviations in the value of the firm from the expected value ($V - V_e$) to deviations in the financial price from its expected value.[12] In Part

---

11. See, for instance, Paul Dickins. op. cit.
12. In the context of the financial prices we are examining, this expected price is the *forward price*.

Figure 2-12. (*a*) **A Risk Profile in**
$(\Delta V, \Delta P)$ **Space.** (*b*) **A Risk Profile in**
(V, P) **Space.**

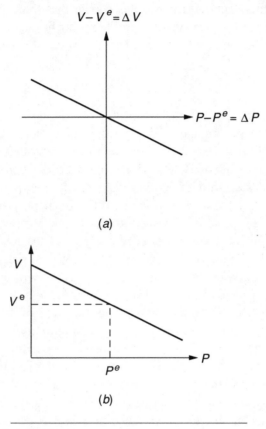

(*b*), we have transferred this risk profile from (ΔV, ΔP) space to (V, P) space; that is, the point (ΔV $= 0$, ΔP $= 0$) in Part (*a*) is at ($V = V^e$, $P = P^e$ in (*b*).

Figure 2-12(*b*) suggests a simple methodology for estimating the slope of the risk profile for any firm: Use the firm's share price as the measure of the value of the firm (i.e., define $S_t = V_t$). Using time series data on the firm's share price and on the financial price, estimate via linear regression the equation:

$$S_t = \alpha_o + \alpha_1 P_t \qquad (2\text{-}6)$$

In Equation (2-6) the parameter α_1 is the slope term, $\Delta V / \Delta P$; thus, it appears that the estimate of α_1 would provide the slope estimate we seek. There are, however, two problems with this simple methodology.

First, modern corporate finance has shown that share price follows a random walk.[13] Empirically, this problem can be dealt with by using rates of return in place of prices. That is, we could change Equation (2-6) to

$$R_t = a + b(\Delta P/P)_t \qquad (2\text{-}6')$$

where R_t is the rate of return in period t for holding the share of stock, and $\Delta P/P$ is the percentage change in the value of the financial asset; for example, if we wished to estimate the sensitivity of the value of the firm to six-month LIBOR, $\Delta P/P$ would be the percentage change in the value of a six-month Eurodollar deposit. The parameter b measures the responsiveness of firm value to the financial price, that is, the elasticity of share price with respect to the financial price.

Second, financial price risk is only one part of the total risk a shareholder faces. In the jargon of corporate finance, total risk can be divided into market risk and diversifiable risk. And, as we will discuss in depth in Chapter 18, financial price risk is a *diversifiable* risk: the risk to the shareholder that arises from interest rate changes, or from changes in foreign exchange rates, or from changes in commodity prices is one that can be eliminated by holding a well-diversified portfolio of securities. Equation (2-6') has in effect attributed total risk (the variance in R_t) only to diversifiable risk (the variance in $\Delta P/P$). Market risk must be added to this equation; that is, we must decompose the total variance in R_t into the variance attributable to the variance in $\Delta P/P$ as well as the variance attributable to variance in the market returns.

The market risk of a security is measured by the responsiveness of share returns to the returns on the market portfolio. The so-called market model is $R_t = \alpha + \beta R_{M,t}$ where $R_{M,t}$ is the return on the market portfolio and β measures market risk. Consequently, expanding Equation (2-6') to reflect market risk gives

$$R_t = \alpha + \beta R_{M,t} + b(\Delta P/P)_t \qquad (2\text{-}7)$$

---

13. That share price follows a random walk derives from *efficient financial markets*. A review of the efficient markets proposition and of the empirical evidence is contained in any corporate finance text; see, for example, Chapter 13 Richard Brealey and Stewart Myers, *Principles of Corporate Finance*, 2d ed (New York: McGraw-Hill, 1984).

where β reflects the market risk of security j, and b reflects the responsiveness of the return on share j to changes in the financial price.

Using a more concrete illustration, suppose we wish to determine the sensitivity of a firm to:

- the one-year T-bill interest rate
- the deutsche mark/dollar exchange rate
- the pound sterling/dollar exchange rate
- the yen/dollar exchange rate
- the price of oil

Using Equation (2-7), this can be done by estimating the regression equation

$$
\begin{aligned}
R_t = \alpha &+ \beta R_{M,t} \\
&+ b_1(\Delta P_{TB}/P_{TB})_t \\
&+ b_2(\Delta P_{DM}/P_{DM})_t + b_3(\Delta P_{\pounds}/P_{\pounds})_t + b_4(\Delta P_{\yen}/P_{\yen})_t \\
&+ b_5(\Delta P_{oil}/P_{oil})_t
\end{aligned}
$$

where R_t is the rate of return for holding a share of the firm's stock; $R_{M,t}$ is the rate of return for holding the market portfolio; $\Delta P_{TB}/P_{TB}$ is the percentage change in the price of a one-year T-bill; $\Delta P_{DM}/P_{DM}$, $\Delta P_{\pounds}/P_{\pounds}$, and $\Delta P_{\yen}/P_{\yen}$ are the percentage changes in the dollar prices of the three foreign currencies; and $\Delta P_{oil}/P_{oil}$ is the percentage change in the price of crude oil.[14] The estimate of b_1 provides a measure of the sensitivity

---

14. The approach we propose has its roots in a number of earlier studies: Kenneth R. French/Richard S. Ruback/G. William Schwert, "Effects of Nominal Contracting on Stock Returns," *Journal of Political Economy* 91, no. 1 (1983) (on the impact of unexpected inflation on share returns); Mark J. Flannery/Christopher M. James, "The Effect of Interest Rate Changes on Common Stock Returns of Financial Institutions," *Journal of Finance* 39, no. 4 (September 1984); and William L. Scott/Richard L. Peterson, "Interest Rate Risk and Equity Values of Hedged and Unhedged Financial Institutions," *Journal of Financial Research* 9, no. 6 (Winter 1986) (on the impact of interest rate changes on share prices for financial firms); and Richard J. Sweeney/Arthur D. Warga, "The Pricing of Interest Rate Risk: Evidence from the Stock Market," *Journal of Finance* 41, no. 2 (June 1986) (on the impact of interest rates on share prices for nonfinancial firms). Our experiences to date with this model suggest that it exhibits the problems of measuring the reaction of firm value to changes in exchange rates that have been discussed by Donald R. Lessard, "Finance and Global Competition: Exploiting Financial Scope and Coping with Volatile Exchange Rates," *Midland Corporate Finance Journal* 4, no. 3 (Fall 1986): pp. 6–29.

of the value of the firm to changes in the one-year T-bill rate; b_2, b_3, and b_4 estimate the sensitivity to the exchange rates; and b_5 estimates the sensitivity to the oil price.[15]

Example

Estimation of financial price risk

To illustrate the kind of results the preceding technique would yield, we looked at three examples: an industrial, Caterpillar; an oil company, Exxon; and a bank, Manufacturers Hanover. For the period January 6, 1984, to December 2, 1988, we calculated weekly (Friday close to Friday close) share returns and the corresponding weekly percentage changes in the price of a one-year T-bill; the dollar prices of a deutsche mark, a pound sterling, and a yen; and the price of West Texas Intermediate crude. Using these data, we estimated the regression equation, Equation (2-8). The resulting estimates of the firm's beta and the sensitivities to the price of the T-bill, the foreign exchange rates, and the oil price are displayed in Table 2-2.

Caterpillar appears to have a positive exposure to the one-year T-bill rate; the negative parameter estimate indicates that increases in the one-year T-bill rate

---

15. These coefficients actually measure elasticities. Furthermore, had we used the percentage change $(1 + \text{one-year T-bill rate})$ instead of the percentage change in the price of the one-year T-bill, the coefficient b_1 could be interpreted as a "duration" measure (specifically, a measure of "the duration of equity").

Table 2-2. Betas and Exposures to Interest Rate, Foreign Exchange Rates, and Oil Prices

	Caterpillar		Exxon		Manufacturers Hanover	
	Parameter estimate	*t* value	Parameter estimate	*t* value	Parameter estimate	*t* value
Beta	1.25**	13.02	0.60**	9.51	0.94**	9.92
Sensitivity to:						
Price of 1 yr T-bill	−4.45**	3.14	0.76	0.81	2.27*	1.62
Price of DM	0.228	0.92	−0.122	0.75	−0.485*	1.97
Price of sterling	−0.126	0.61	0.225*	1.65	0.365*	1.81
Price of yen	0.227	1.06	−0.190	1.34	−0.086	0.41
Price of WTI crude	−0.010	0.23	0.099**	3.28	0.129**	2.84

* Significant at 90%

** Significant at 95%

(decreases in the price of the T-bill) lead to increases in the value of the firm. Somewhat more surprising, in the context of much that has been written about Caterpillar, is the lack of any significant exposure to the yen. This result is more understandable if we decompose this five-year span and look at Caterpillar's sensitivity to the price of the yen year-by-year:

	1984	1985	1986	1987	1988
Parameter estimate for percentage change in price of yen	1.14	0.27	−0.23	−0.42	−0.49
t value	1.23	0.62	0.51	0.58	1.17

The data reflects the fact that as Caterpillar has moved its production facilities, the firm changed from being positively exposed to the yen (an increase in the value of the dollar would harm Caterpillar) to being negatively exposed to the yen (an increase in the value of the dollar helps Caterpillar).

Exxon does not appear to have a significant exposure to the interest rate (at least to the one-year T-bill rate). Exxon does exhibit the anticipated exposure to the price of oil: increases in the price of crude oil are linked to increases in the value of Exxon. Also, as has been reported in the trade press, if we look at the sensitivity to oil price over time, our estimates suggest that Exxon's exposure to the price of oil has been declining—in magnitude and, generally, in significance:

	1984	1985	1986	1987	1988
Parameter estimate for percentage change in price of oil	0.80	0.17	0.09	0.12	0.05
t value	4.05	0.97	3.44	1.13	0.68

Given its international production and distribution, as well as its international portfolio of assets, Exxon also exhibits exposures to foreign exchange rates. Our estimates suggest that Exxon benefits from an increase in the value of the pound (and there is some indication that it may be harmed by an increase in the value of the yen).

Given the tendency for a bank to accept short-date deposits to fund longer-dated assets (loans), it is not surprising that our estimates for Manufacturers Hanover indicate a marginally significant inverse exposure to interest rates; the positive parameter estimate indicates that an increase in the one-year T-bill rate (a decrease in the price of the T-bill) will lead to a decrease in the value of the bank. Although this is interesting in and of itself, more information may be gleaned if the analyst compares this parameter estimate with those of other firms in the same industry. In the following table, we can compare the

estimated sensitivity of Manufacturers Hanover to the one-year T-bill rate to that of other banks:

Bank	Estimated sensitivity	*t* value
Bank of America	2.2	1.13
Bankers Trust	1.1	0.88
Chase	1.6	1.15
First Chicago	2.0	1.22
Manufacturers Hanover	2.3	1.62

In addition to the anticipated interest rate exposure, our estimates suggest that Manufacturers Hanover also is exposed to other financial price risks. Our estimates indicate significant foreign exchange risk, due perhaps to foreign lending or foreign operations.[16] It appears that this bank is also exposed to oil price risk: a rising oil price is linked to an increase in the value of Manufacturers Hanover.[17]

16. Our estimates suggest that Manufacturers Hanover is benefited by increases in the value of the pound and harmed by increases in the value of the deutsche mark. We obtained generally the same estimates for Chase Manhattan Bank.

17. We obtained similar results for Chase Manhattan and Bank of America.

3

Tools for Managing Financial Risk: A "Building Block" Approach[1]

As we described in Chapter 1, the increased economic uncertainty first evident in the 1970s has altered the way financial markets function. As foreign exchange rates, interest rates, and commodity prices have become more volatile, corporations have discovered that their value is subject to various financial price risks in addition to the risk inherent in their core business.

To illustrate the effect of changes in a given financial price on the value of a company, we again use the concept of a risk profile, introduced in Chapter 2. Figure 3-1 presents a case in which an unexpected increase in financial price, P (e.g., the treasury bill rate, the price of oil, or the dollar price of a yen), decreases the value of the firm, V. The difference between the actual price and the expected price is shown as ΔP, and ΔV measures the resulting change in the value of the firm. Had ΔP remained small, as it did prior to the 1970s, the changes in firm value would have been correspondingly small. But, for many companies, the increased volatility of exchange rates, interest rates, and commodity prices (large ΔPs) in the 1970s and 1980s has been a major cause of sharp fluctuations in share prices (large ΔVs). With this greater potential for large swings in value, companies have begun exploring new methods for dealing with financial risks.

For companies confronted with the increased volatility of financial prices, the first and most obvious approach was to try to forecast future

---

1. This chapter is adapted from Charles W. Smithson, "A LEGO Approach to Financial Engineering: An Introduction to Forwards, Futures, Swaps, and Options," *Midland Corporate Finance Journal* 4, no. 4 (Winter 1987): 16–28.

Figure 3-1. A Risk Profile.

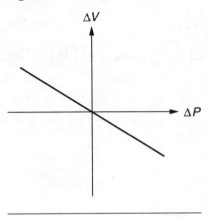

prices more accurately. If changes in exchange rates, interest rates, and commodity prices could be predicted with confidence, then companies could avoid unexpected swings in value. In the context of Figure 3-1, if the actual price could be anticipated, ΔP would equal zero and the value of the firm would thus remain unchanged. Because of the efficiency of the financial markets, however, attempts to outpredict the market are unlikely to be successful. (Indeed, many economists trying to outforecast the market learned that lesson the hard way.)

Because forecasting cannot be relied upon to eliminate risk, the remaining alternative is to manage the risks. Financial risk management can be accomplished by using on-balance-sheet transactions. For example, a company could manage a foreign exchange exposure resulting from foreign competition by borrowing in the competitors' currency or by moving production abroad. However, on-balance-sheet methods can be costly and, as firms such as Caterpillar have discovered, inflexible.[2]

Alternatively, financial risks can be managed with the use of off-balance-sheet instruments: forwards, futures, swaps, and options. When we first began to examine these financial instruments, we were confronted by what seemed an insurmountable barrier to entry: Participants in the various markets and the trade publications seemed to possess specialized expertise applicable in only one market, to the exclusion of all the others. Adding to the complexities of the individual markets themselves is a welter of jargon: "ticks," "collars," "strike prices,"

---

2. See "Caterpillar's Triple Whammy," *Fortune* 114 (October 27, 1986): 91–92.

"straddles," and so forth. Indeed, it looks to the novice like a Wall Street version of the Tower of Babel, with each group of market specialists speaking a different language.

In marked contrast to this specialist approach, we will in this text take a generalist approach, treating forwards, futures, swaps, and options not as four unique instruments and markets, but rather as four instruments for dealing with a single problem—managing financial risk. Indeed, we are going to show how the off-balance-sheet instruments are like those plastic building blocks children snap together: They can be built from one another (or combined into larger creations).

Forward Contracts

Of the four instruments considered in this chapter, the forward contract is the oldest and, perhaps for this reason, the most straightforward. A forward contract obligates its owner to buy a given asset on a specified date at a price (known as the "exercise price") specified at the origination of the contract. If, at maturity, the actual price is higher than the exercise price, the contract owner makes a profit; if the price is lower, the owner suffers a loss.

In Figure 3-2, the payoff profile for buying a forward contract is superimposed on the original risk profile. If the actual price at contract maturity is higher than the expected price, the inherent risk will lead to a decline in the value of the firm; however, this decline will be offset by

Figure 3-2. Payoff Profile for Forward Contracts.

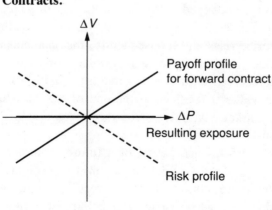

the profit on the forward contract. Hence, for the risk profile illustrated, the forward contract provides a perfect hedge. (If the risk profile were positively instead of negatively sloped, the risk would be managed by selling instead of buying a forward contract.)

In addition to its payoff profile, two features of a forward contract should be noted. First, the default (or credit) risk of the contract is two-sided. The contract owner either receives or makes a payment, depending on the price movement of the underlying asset. Second, the value of the forward contract is conveyed only at the contract's maturity; no payment is made either at origination or during the term of the contract.

Futures Contracts

Although futures contracts on commodities have been traded on organized exchanges since the 1860s, financial futures are relatively new, dating from the introduction of foreign currency futures in 1972. The basic form of the futures contract is identical to that of the forward contract: a futures contract obligates its owner to purchase a specified asset at a specified exercise price on the contract maturity date. Thus, the payoff profile for the purchaser of a forward contract presented in Figure 3-2 could equally well illustrate the payoff to the holder of a futures contract.

Like the forward contract, the futures contract has two-sided risk. But, in marked contrast to forwards, credit or default risk can be virtually eliminated in a futures market. Futures markets use two devices to manage default risk. First, instead of conveying the value of a contract through a single payment at maturity, any change in the value of a futures contract is conveyed at the end of the day in which it is realized. Look again at Figure 3-2. Suppose that, on the day after origination, the financial price rises and, consequently, the financial instrument has a positive value. In the case of a forward contract, this value change would not be received until contract maturity. With a futures contract, this change in value is received at the end of the day. In the language of the futures markets, the futures contract is "cash-settled," or "marked to market" daily.

Because the performance period of a futures contract is reduced via marking to market, the risk of default declines accordingly. Indeed, since the value of the futures contract is paid or received at the end of each day, it is not hard to see why Fischer Black likened a futures contract to

"a series of forward contracts. Each day, yesterday's contract is settled, and today's contract is written."[3] That is, a futures contract is like a sequence of forwards in which the "forward" contract written on day 0 is settled on day 1 and is replaced, in effect, with a new "forward" contract reflecting the new day 1 expectations. This new contract is itself settled on day 2 and replaced, and so on until the day the contract ends.

The second feature of futures contracts that reduces default risk is the requirement that all market participants—sellers and buyers alike[4]—post a performance bond called the *margin*. If a futures contract increases in value during the trading day, this gain is added to the margin account at the day's end. Conversely, if the contract loses value, this loss is deducted from the margin account. If the margin account balance falls below some agreed-upon minimum, the holder is required to post additional bond; that is, the margin account must be replenished or the holder's position will be closed out.[5] Because the position will be closed before the margin account is depleted, performance risk is eliminated.[6]

Note that the exchange itself has not been proposed as a device to reduce default risk. Daily settlement and the requirement of a bond reduce default risk, but the existence of an exchange (or clearinghouse) merely serves to transform risk. More specifically, the exchange deals with the two-sided risk inherent in forwards and futures by serving as the counterparty to all transactions. If a party wishes to buy or sell a futures contract, he or she buys from or sells to the exchange and, hence, needs to evaluate only the credit risk of the exchange, not the credit risk of some specific counterparty. The primary economic function

---

3. See Fischer Black, "The Pricing of Commodity Contracts," *Journal of Financial Economics* 3 (1976): 167–179.

4. Keep in mind that buying a futures contract means taking a long position in the underlying asset. Conversely, selling a futures contract is equivalent to taking a short position.

5. When a contract is originated on the U.S. exchanges, an "initial margin" is required. Subsequently, the margin account balance must remain above the "maintenance margin." If the margin account balance falls below the maintenance level, the balance must be restored to the initial level.

6. Note that this discussion has ignored daily limits. If there are daily limits on the movement of futures prices, large changes in expectations about the underlying asset can effectively close the market. (The market opens, immediately moves the limit, and then is effectively closed until the next day.) Hence, there may be an instance in which the broker desires to close out a customer's position but is not able to do so immediately because the market is experiencing limit moves. In such a case, the statement that performance risk is "eliminated" is too strong.

of the exchange is to reduce the costs of transacting in futures contracts. The anonymous trades made possible by the exchange, together with the homogeneous nature of the futures contracts—in terms of standardized assets, exercise dates (four per year), and contract sizes—enables the futures markets to become relatively liquid. However, as was made clear by the recent experience of the London Metal Exchange, the existence of the exchange does not in and of itself reduce default risk.[7,8]

In sum, a futures contract is much like a portfolio of forward contracts. At the close of business of each day, in effect, the existing "forward" contract is settled and a new one written.[9] This daily settlement feature combined with the margin requirement allows futures contracts to eliminate the credit risk inherent in forwards.

Swap Contracts[10]

Because they were publicly introduced in 1981,[11] swaps are commonly portrayed as one of the latest financing innovations. However, a swap contract is in essence nothing more complicated than a series of forward

7. In November 1985, the "tin cartel" defaulted on contracts for tin delivery on the London Metal Exchange, thereby making the exchange liable for the loss. A description of this situation is contained in "Tin Crisis in London Roils Metal Exchange," *The Wall Street Journal* (November 13, 1985), p. 1.

8. From the point of view of the market, the exchange does not reduce default risk; that is, the expected default rate is not affected by the existence of the exchange. However, the existence of the exchange can alter the default risk faced by an individual market participant. For a futures contract bought from a specific individual, the default risk is determined by the default rate of that specific counterparty. If the same futures contract is bought through an exchange, the default risk depends on the default rate of the entire market. Moreover, to the extent that the exchange is capitalized by equity from its members, the perceived default risk is further reduced because the participant has a claim not against some specific counterparty, but against the exchange. Therefore, trading through the exchange is in a sense purchasing an insurance policy from the exchange.

9. A futures contract is *like* a portfolio of forward contracts; however, a futures contract and a portfolio of forward contracts become identical only if interest rates are "deterministic," that is, known with certainty in advance. See Robert A. Jarrow and George S. Oldfield, "Forward Contracts and Futures Contracts," *Journal of Financial Economics* 9 (1981): 373–382; and John A. Cox, Jonathan E. Ingersoll, and Stephen A. Ross, "The Relations between Forwards Prices and Futures Prices," *Journal of Financial Economics* 9 (1981): 321–346.

10. This section is based on Clifford W. Smith, Charles W. Smithson, and Lee M. Wakeman, "The Evolving Market for Swaps," *Midland Corporate Finance Journal* (Winter 1986): 20–32.

11. The currency swap transaction between IBM and the World Bank in 1981 is normally marked as the public introduction of swaps.

contracts strung together. The credit risk attending swaps is somewhat less than that of a forward contract with the same maturity, but it is greater than that of a comparable futures contract.

As implied by its name, a swap contract obligates two parties to exchange, or swap, specified cash flows at specified intervals. The most common form is the interest rate swap, in which the cash flows are determined by two different interest rates.

Figure 3-3 (*a*) illustrates an interest rate swap from the perspective of a party who is paying out a series of cash flows determined by a fixed interest rate ($\bar{R}$) in return for a series of cash flows determined by a floating interest rate ($\tilde{R}$).[12] Figure 3-3 (*b*) serves to illustrate that this

---

12. Specifically, the interest rate swap cash flows are determined as follows: The two parties agree to some notional principal, P. (The principal is notional in the sense that it is used only to determine the magnitude of cash flows; it is not paid or received by either party) At each settlement date 1, 2, . . . , T, the party illustrated makes a payment $\bar{R} = \bar{r}P$, where $\bar{r}$ is the T-period fixed rate that existed at origination. At each settlement, the party illustrated receives $\tilde{R} = \tilde{r}P$, where $\tilde{r}$ is the floating rate for that period (e.g., at settlement date 2, the interest rate used is the one-period rate in effect at period 1).

Figure 3-3. (*a*) An Interest Rate Swap. (*b*) An Interest Rate Swap as a Portfolio of Forward Contracts.

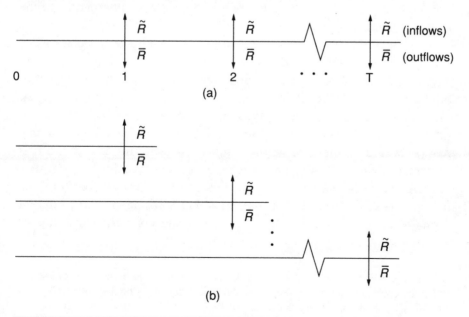

swap contract can be decomposed into a portfolio of forward contracts. At each settlement date, the party to this swap contract has an implicit forward contract on interest rates: the party is obligated to sell a fixed-rate cash flow for an amount specified at the origination of the contract.

In terms of our earlier discussion, this means that the solid line in Figure 3-2 could also represent the payoff from a swap contract. Specifically, this line would be consistent with a swap contract in which the party illustrated receives cash flows determined by P (say, the U.S. treasury bond rate) and makes payments determined by another price (say, LIBOR). Thus, in terms of their ability to manage risk, forwards, futures, and swaps all function in the same way.

Identical payoff profiles notwithstanding, the instruments differ with respect to default risk. The performance period of a forward is equal to its maturity; and because no performance bond is required, a forward contract is a pure credit instrument. Futures both reduce the performance period (to one day) and require a bond, thereby eliminating credit risk. Swap contracts use only one of these mechanisms to reduce credit risk: they reduce the performance period.[13] This point becomes evident in Figure 3-3. Although the maturity of the contract is T periods, the performance period is generally not T periods but a single period. Thus, given a swap and a forward contract of roughly the same maturity, the swap is likely to impose far less credit risk on the counterparties to the contract than the forward.

At each settlement date throughout a swap contract, the changes in value are transferred between the counterparties. To illustrate this in terms of Figure 3-3, suppose that interest rates rise on the day after origination. The value of the swap contract illustrated has thus risen. This value change will be conveyed to the contract owner not at maturity (as would be the case with a forward contract) nor at the end of that day (as would be the case with a futures contract). Instead, at the first settlement date, part of the value change is conveyed in the form of a "difference check" paid by one party to the other. Thus, the performance period is reduced from that of a forward, but it is not so short as that of a futures contract.[14] (Keep in mind that we are comparing instruments with the same maturity.)

---

13. There are instances in which a bond has been posted in the form of collateral. As should be evident, in such a case the swap becomes very like a futures contract.

14. We will show in Chapter 9 that unlike futures, for which all change in contract value is paid/received at the daily settlements, swap contracts convey only part of the total value change at the periodic settlements.

At this point we should stop to reinforce the two major points made so far. First, a swap contract, like a futures contract, is similar to a portfolio of forward contracts. Therefore, the payoff profiles for these three instruments are identical. Second, the primary difference among forwards, futures, and swaps is the amount of default risk they impose on counterparties to the contract. Forwards and futures represent the extremes, with the swap being the intermediate case.

It is important to note that swaps do impose some credit risk. For this reason it is not surprising that commercial banks have become increasingly active in a market that was initiated, for the most part, by investment banks. It is also not hard to understand the underlying cause of the sharp difference of opinion that has arisen between commercial and investment banks over the "most advisable" evolutionary path for the swap market to follow. Because investment banks are not in the business of extending credit, they would much prefer swaps to become more like futures, that is, an exchange-traded instrument with bonded contract performance. Commercial banks, by contrast, stand to benefit if swaps remain a credit instrument; accordingly, they would prefer the credit risk to be managed by imposing capital requirements on the financial institutions arranging the swaps.

Option Contracts

As we have seen, the owner of a forward, futures, or swap contract has an *obligation* to perform. In contrast, an option gives its owner a *right*. An option giving its owner the right to buy an asset—a *call option*—is illustrated in Figure 3-4. (Here, once again, the financial price P could be an interest rate, a foreign exchange rate, the price of a commodity, or the price of some other financial asset.) The owner of the contract illustrated has the right to purchase the asset at a specified future date at a price agreed upon today. Consequently, if P rises, the value of the option also goes up. But because the option contract owner is not obligated to purchase the asset, the value of the option remains unchanged (at zero) if P declines.[15]

The payoff profile for the owner of the call option is repeated in part (*a*) of Figure 3-5. In this case, the contract owner has bought the right to

---

15. For continuity, we continue to use the ΔV, ΔP convention in figures. To compare these figures with those found in most texts, treat ΔV as deviations from zero ($\Delta V = V - 0$), and remember that ΔP measures deviations from expected price ($\Delta P = P - P^e$.)

Figure 3-4. The Payoff Profile of a Call Option.

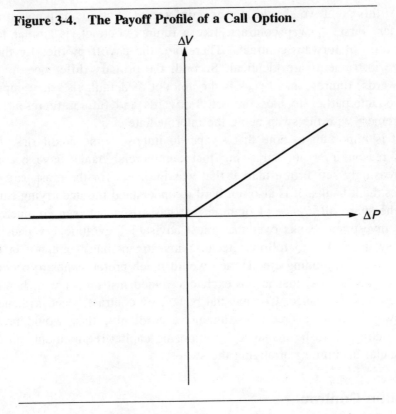

buy the asset at a specified price—the exercise (strike) price. (In Figures 3-4 and 3-5, the exercise price is implicitly equal to the expected price.)

The payoff profile for the party who sold the call option (also known as the call *writer*) is shown in part (*b*) of Figure 3-5. Note that the seller of the call option, not the buyer, has the obligation to perform. For example, if the owner of the option exercises his or her option to buy the asset, the seller of the option is obligated to sell the asset.

Besides the option to buy an asset, there is also the option to sell an asset at a specified price, known as a *put option*. The payoff to the buyer of a put is illustrated in part (*c*) of Figure 3-5, and the payoff for the seller of the put is shown in part (*d*).

In many instances, jargon does more to confuse than to clarify, and this is particularly true in the "buy/sell," "call/put" jargon of options. Suppose a party is exposed to rising interest rates; that is, an increase in interest rates reduces his or her wealth. As illustrated at the top of Figure 3-6, this party could eliminate the downside exposure by buying a call

Figure 3-5. Payoff Profiles of Puts and Calls. (*a*) Buy a call. (*b*) Sell a call. (*c*) Buy a put. (*d*) Sell a put.

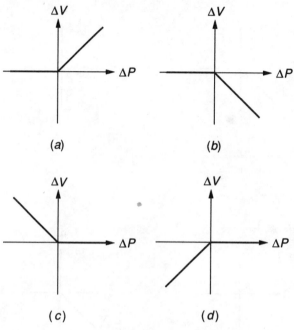

on the interest rate (an interest rate "cap"). In terms of bond prices, the proper strategy for hedging this exposure is to buy a put on bonds. As Figure 3-6 illustrates, a call on interest rates is equivalent to a put on bonds. The same thing occurs in the foreign exchange market: a put on DM/$ is equivalent to a call on $/DM. (There have been times when two people have argued about whether something was a put or a call when, in fact, they were both right.)

So far we have considered only the payoffs for the option contracts. Figures 3-4 through 3-6 assume, in effect, that option premiums are neither paid by the buyer nor received by the seller. By making this assumption, we have sidestepped the thorniest issue: the valuation of option contracts. It is to this we now turn.

The breakthrough in option pricing theory came with the work of Fischer Black and Myron Scholes in 1973.[16] Conveniently for our pur-

---

16. Fischer Black and Myron Scholes, "The Pricing of Options and Corporate Liabilities," *Journal of Political Economy* 81, no. 3 (May–June 1973): 637.

54

Figure 3-6. Hedging Exposures with Options.

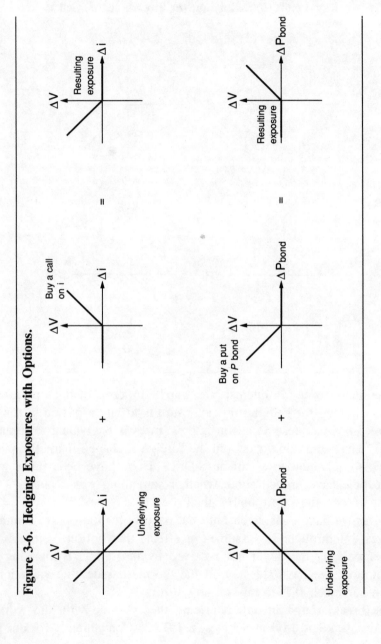

poses, Black and Scholes took what might be described as a "building block" approach to the valuation of options. Look again at the call option illustrated in Figure 3-4. For increases in the financial price, the payoff profile for the option is that of a forward contract. For decreases in the price, the value of the option is constant—similar to "riskless" security such as a treasury bill.

The work of Black and Scholes demonstrated that a call option can be replicated by a continuously adjusting ("dynamic") portfolio of two securities: (1) forward contracts on the underlying asset and (2) riskless securities. As the financial price rises, the "call option–equivalent" portfolio contains an increasing proportion of forward contracts on the asset. Conversely, the portfolio contains a decreasing proportion of the asset as the price of the asset falls. Because this portfolio is effectively a synthetic call option, arbitrage activity should ensure that its value closely approximates the market price of exchange-traded call options. In this sense, the value of a call option—and, thus, the premium charged its buyer—is determined by the value of its option-equivalent portfolio.

Part (a) of Figure 3-7 illustrates a call option payoff profile that includes the premium. This figure (like all of the option figures so far) illustrates an *at-the-money* option: an option for which the exercise price is the prevailing expected price. As parts (a) and (b) of Figure 3-7 illustrate, an at-the-money option is paid for by sacrificing a significant amount of the firm's potential gains. However, the price of a call option falls as the exercise price increases relative to the prevailing price of the asset.

Alternatively, an *out-of-the-money* option, illustrated in part (c) of Figure 3-7, may be considered. As shown in part (d), the out-of-the-money option provides less downside protection, but the option premium is significantly less. The lesson to be learned here is that the option buyer can alter the payoff profile simply by changing the exercise price.

For the purposes of this discussion, the most important feature of options is that they are not as different from other financial instruments as they might at first seem. Options do have a payoff profile that differs significantly from that of forward contracts (or futures or swaps). But, option payoff profiles can be duplicated by a combination of forwards and risk-free securities. Thus, we find that options have more in common with the other instruments than was apparent. Futures and swaps, as we saw earlier, are in essence nothing more than portfolios of forward

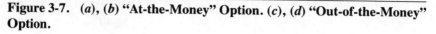

Figure 3-7. (*a*), (*b*) "At-the-Money" Option. (*c*), (*d*) "Out-of-the-Money" Option.

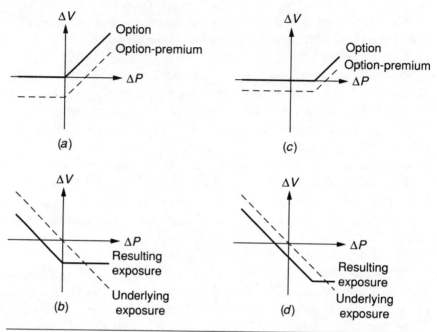

contracts; and options, as we have just seen, are very much akin to portfolios of forward contracts and risk-free securities.

This point is reinforced if we consider ways in which options can be combined. Consider a portfolio constructed by buying a call and selling a put with the same exercise price. As the top of Figure 3-8 illustrates, the resulting portfolio (long a call, short a put) has a payoff profile equivalent to that of buying a forward contract on the asset. Similarly, the bottom portion of Figure 3-8 illustrates that a portfolio made up by selling a call and buying a put (short a call, long a put) is equivalent to selling a forward contract. The relationship illustrated in Figure 3-8 is known formally as *put-call parity*. The special importance of this relationship in the present context is the "building block construction" it makes possible: two options can be "snapped together" to yield the payoff profile for a forward contract, which is identical to the payoff profile for futures and swaps.

In summary, although options differ from forwards, futures, and swaps in many ways, we have discovered two "building block" relations between options and the other three instruments: (1) Options can be

Figure 3-8. Put-Call Parity.

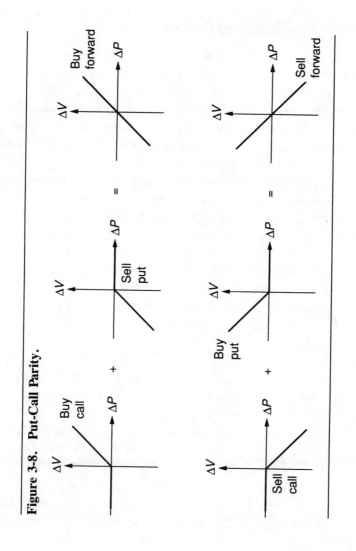

simulated by "snapping together" a forward, futures, or swap contract and a position in risk-free securities; (2) Calls and puts can be "snapped together" to become forwards.

The Financial Building Blocks

Forwards, futures, swaps, and options—to the novice, they look very different from one another. And if you read the trade publications or talk to the participants in the four markets, the apparent differences among the instruments are likely to seem even more pronounced. It looks as if the only way to deal with these financial instruments is to pick one and become a specialist in that market, to the exclusion of the others.

However, it turns out that forwards, futures, swaps, and options are not really unique constructions but resemble those plastic building blocks that children snap together into complex creations. To understand the off-balance-sheet instruments, you don't need a lot of market-specific knowledge; you just need to know how the instruments can be linked. As we have seen: (1) Futures are built by "snapping together" a package of forwards. (2) Swaps are similarly built by "snapping together" a package of forwards. (3) Options can be built by "snapping together" a forward and a riskless security. (4) Options can be "snapped together" to yield forward contracts; conversely, forwards can be "unsnapped" to yield a package of options.

Figure 3-9 characterizes each of the four instruments we have been discussing according to the shapes of their payoff profiles. It also serves as a reminder of the put-call parity between options and forwards, futures, or swaps. Figure 3-9 thus provides, in effect, the "instruction manual" for our box of financial building blocks. A quick look shows that although there can be many pieces in the box, there are only six basic shapes to be concerned with. The straight pieces come in three colors; we can obtain a forward payoff profile with either forwards (the red ones), futures (the yellow ones), or swaps (the blue ones). The kinked pieces are all the same color (white) because options can be combined to simulate a forward, a future, or a swap.

In the next fourteen chapters we look at the individual instruments in detail. Chapters 4 and 5 deal with forwards. Chapters 6–8 describe futures. Swaps are discussed in Chapters 9–12, and Chapters 13–16 describe options. Although it is beneficial to have detailed information about how each instrument and the market within which it is traded

Figure 3-9. The Financial Building Blocks.

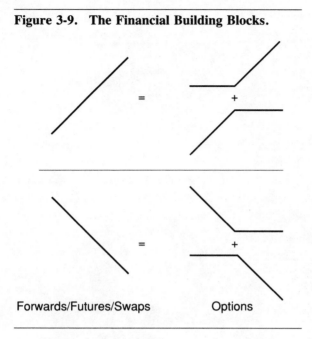

Forwards/Futures/Swaps   Options

work, it is important not to lose sight of the "building block" nature of these financial instruments. Indeed, after a discussion of the reason a firm hedges, in Chapter 17, we conclude this book with a chapter that could actually best be described as "construction using the building blocks"—we are going to show how complicated financial instruments, the so-called hybrid securities, are constructed using the building blocks.

PART II

Forward Contracts

4

The Forward Contract

As indicated in Chapter 3, the forward contract is the fundamental building block of the financial instruments. It forms the basis for the risk management instruments both from a conceptual standpoint and with respect to their introduction and use in the financial markets. Most notable are foreign exchange forward contracts, the contracts with which banks, corporations, governments, and some individuals manage their exposure in the $½ trillion foreign exchange markets (estimated daily volume during peak periods).

Simply put, a forward contract is a contract made today for the delivery of an asset in the future. The buyer of the forward contract agrees to pay a specified amount at a specified date in the future in order to receive a specified amount of a currency, a specified amount of a commodity, or a specified coupon payment from the counterparty. The specified future price is the *exercise price* of the contract.[1]

To make this definition of a forward contract more concrete, we have provided some illustrations in Figure 4-1. Part (*a*) illustrates a foreign exchange forward. The party illustrated has agreed to pay, at time T, Y in order to receive £X . Part (*b*) illustrates a commodity forward contract. The party illustrated has agreed to pay, at time T, Y in order to receive X barrels of oil. Part (*c*) illustrates an interest rate forward contract. The party illustrated has agreed to pay a fixed-rate coupon, $\overline{R}$, at time T, to receive a floating-rate coupon, $\tilde{R}$.

At contract origination, the net present value of an at-market forward contract is zero. The exercise price of the contract is set at the expected future price, so neither the buyer nor the seller of the forward will

---

1. The forward contract may stipulate that only the difference between the exercise price and the spot price prevailing at the future date be exchanged.

Figure 4-1. Some Illustrative Forward Contracts. (*a*) **A Foreign Exchange Forward.** (*b*) **A Commodity Forward.** (*c*) **An Interest Rate Forward.**

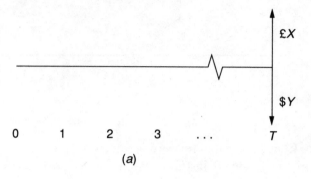

(*a*)

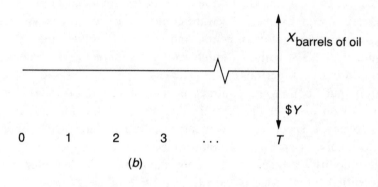

(*b*)

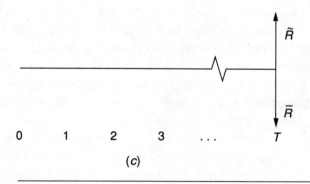

(*c*)

obtain value unless the exchange rates, commodity prices, or interest rates differ from expectations. Thus, the exercise price set is the price that equates the buyer's expected cash flow to the seller's expected cash flow.

Since the net present value of the contract at origination is zero, why do parties enter into forward contracts? The contract must certainly have value for both the buyer and the seller; otherwise they would not enter into the contract. The value exists because one party desires to reduce risk or has a view on the future movement of the underlying price series that differs from the market's; or the value may exist because the forward contract allows creation of something valuable (e.g., synthetic assets).

In the main, participants in the forward markets are those who wish to fix future transaction costs. For example, a car importer knows today's cost of a particular model of car in both the domestic and the foreign currency. The importer also knows what the car purchased today will sell for upon delivery in domestic currency. What is uncertain is how much the car will cost in domestic currency when it arrives, since it must be paid for in a foreign currency at that time. To eliminate this uncertainty, the importer today can contract the price of exchange between domestic currency and foreign currency for this future date using a forward contract.

The automobile importer also provides a more down-to-earth example. When an importer sells a car, it is unusual that cash is paid and the keys are handed over simultaneously. In most auto sales, the purchaser agrees to pay and the seller agrees to deliver at some date in the future (the completion date of the sale) at the agreed-upon price. That price will be paid on the completion date but is agreed upon now, and it will not change regardless of what happens to auto prices in the interim. The contract covering the period from agreement to completion is, in fact, nothing more than a forward contract. If the time to completion of the sale is one week, no one really gives the forward nature of this contract much consideration; but if the time to completion is several months, car prices could change significantly. In such a circumstance, the forward contract is a valuable way of reducing price risk for both parties. Forwards, in this sense, are a part of everyday life.

The number of people interested in using forward contracts is therefore determined by the number who face uncertainty about future prices. Since a great number of people are exposed to this kind of uncertainty, why isn't there a forward contracting agent on every street corner con-

tracting in every commodity and every consumer good? As we will see, the answer lies in the potential for default.

Forward Contracts and Default

In a world of no transaction costs, with all parties always paying their debts, there might indeed be a forward contracting agent on each street corner. Unfortunately, not all parties to contracts fulfill their responsibilities without coercion. Moreover, the act of contracting itself entails a cost. Thus, the forward contract exhibits both performance risk and transaction costs. Since transaction costs for a forward contract are usually small,[2] we concentrate our attention on performance risk—or, in bankers' terms, "credit risk."

Forward contracts are, by definition, credit instruments. Suppose today you contract to deliver the difference between (1) a specified ratio of dollars per deutsche mark and (2) the market ratio of dollars per deutsche mark one year in the future, multiplied by some specified number of dollars. Say the exercise price of exchange is 3.00 DM/$ (the dollar price of a DM is $0.33). If at contract maturity the exchange rate has risen to 4.00 DM/$ (the price of a DM has fallen to $0.25), you are now richer. You can buy deutsche marks for $0.25 and then sell them for $0.33—a profit of $0.08 per DM. Your counterparty—the party who agreed to buy the DM—is now poorer by the same amount. If the buyer decides to abrogate the contract, you are out a sum of money, just as would be the case if a loan were reneged upon. In this sense, a forward contract is a credit instrument.

The fact that forward contracts entail credit risk is important in determining who uses them. Individuals, institutions, corporations, and governments with access to credit lines are able to use forward contracts. Those for whom the costs of creating credit lines are high relative to the benefits of using the forward contract will not participate in the market. Realistically, then, the forward market is not appropriate for the individual, the sole proprietorship, or the small corporation. It is a market for

---

2. Transaction costs are small as a percentage of the forward contract amounts normally seen in the market. Transacting has a high fixed-cost component and very low marginal costs. Thus, a $100 and a $10,000,000 forward foreign exchange contract have nearly the same transaction cost. Logically, for a $10,000,000 transaction, the transaction cost component is of much less importance than for a $100 transaction.

large corporations, governments, and other institutions—both financial and nonfinancial—that have access to credit lines as a regular part of their business.

A Foreign Exchange Forward Contract

The Contract[3]

Foreign exchange spot markets and foreign exchange forward markets are liquid, efficient, and sophisticated. The movement of these markets is therefore largely regulated by the legal contract under which they operate and by the enforceability of that contract.

As was just noted, forward contracts entail performance risk. Therefore, the forward contract is written to address this risk. In this sense, the contract is similar to that of a loan or a line of credit. For example, the contract defines payment responsibility following contract expiration. Continuing our example of the previous section, suppose the contract stipulates that the price of future delivery is at a rate of DM 3.00 per dollar. If the price of dollars is DM 2.00 at contract maturity, the party selling deutsche marks for dollars at DM 3.00 would have an incentive to break the contract by not delivering. Consequently, the forward contract is written in such a way that nonperformance amounts to not making a payment on a loan.

Agreeing on an exercise price is left to the two parties, but a forward contract is clear about how the price is referenced. In the case of foreign exchange forwards, the contract reference is a set amount of one currency for a set amount of another—a forward rate of exchange. The contract specifies the spot rate at the maturity date as the average of the bid and asked prices quoted by a specified bank for the spot purchase and spot sale, respectively, of the contract currency in exchange for U.S. dollars at a prescribed location (usually New York, London, or Tokyo) at a prescribed time (usually 11 A.M. local time).

The process of setting the exercise price and settlement date of the contract (with written confirmation) is an essential part of forward contracting. The settlement date of a contract is the date at which a

---

3. We would like to thank our colleagues at the Chase Manhattan Bank, particularly Sandra Zimmer and Richard Zecher, for providing us with specific information on the terms of a forward contract.

contract is actually payable. For example, if on March 1 a three-month forward is agreed on, the maturity date would be June 3, but the settlement date would be two days later.[4] These dates, as well as the date of origination of the contract, are stipulated in a confirmation telex exchanged between the contracting parties.

Most foreign exchange forward contracts specify that neither party is obligated to actually deliver one currency against another. Rather, the amount payable is determined by the difference between the spot price and the exercise price at contract maturity. The payoff profile for forward contract positions is illustrated in Figure 4-2. Part (a) shows the payoff profile for the buyer of the forward contract—the individual who is long the forward contract. At contract maturity, the buyer is obligated to buy the asset at the price agreed to at contract origination, P_0^F. If the spot price at maturity, P_T, exceeds the exercise price, the forward contract owner will be able to buy the asset at the lower exercise price and sell at the higher spot price, making a profit of $P_T - P_0^F$ per unit. Hence, the profit for the owner of the forward contract is

$$\text{Profit} = (P_T - P_0^F) \times (\text{Number of units contracted}) \qquad (4\text{-}1)$$

Conversely, the seller of the forward contract profits when the spot price at maturity is less than the exercise price: the seller can buy at the cheaper spot price and sell at the higher exercise price. The profit for the seller of the forward contract is

$$\text{Profit} = (P_0^F - P_T) \times (\text{Number of units contracted}) \qquad (4\text{-}2)$$

Because the foreign exchange forward contract is settled on the difference between the spot exchange rate at T and the contracted exchange rate, the foreign currency itself does not have to be delivered; the contract can be settled in U.S. dollars. Exactly as in any loan agreement, if one party is late in delivery of funds, a penalty interest cost is incurred on the outstanding balance.

Not surprisingly, the clauses of a contract that concern pricing and settlement comprise the minority of the forward contract; the bulk of the documentation is involved with the credit issues just mentioned. Events

---

4. The reason for this is that spot currency transactions are dealt two days forward (with the exception of Canadian dollars for U.S. dollars), and forwards are always quoted from spot. Thus, a March 1 spot quote is for March 3, so a three-month forward would be March 3 to June 3.

**Figure 4-2. The Payoff for Forward
Contract Positions. (*a*) The Profile
for the Buyer (the Long Position).
(*b*) The Profile for the Seller (the
Short Position).**

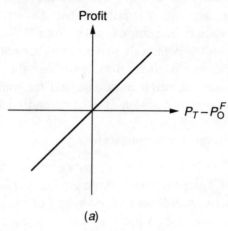

(*a*)

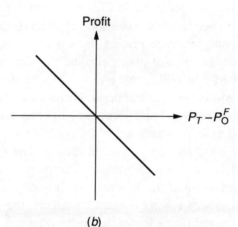

(*b*)

At contract maturity (time $= T$), the profit
to the buyer of a forward contract is equal
to the difference between the spot price at T
and the exercise price agreed to at contract
origination ($P_T - P_0^F$) times the size of the
forward contract. The profit to the seller of
the contract is the reverse.

of default receive particular attention, underscoring the credit nature of the contract.

The essence of a forward contract is the fact that the maturity date (the date on which the contract period ends) is the only date that is relevant in calculating the amount one party will owe the other upon settlement. That is, the legal agreement stipulates that the settlement flows are based on the deviation in contract price from the spot price *on the maturity date*. From the contract's perspective (but not necessarily from the contractors' perspectives) the time path that the foreign exchange rate follows between the origination date and the maturity date (when the settlement payment is calculated) is of no consequence.

The Forward Foreign Exchange Rate

We turn next to the pricing of a foreign exchange forward contract—the determination of the forward foreign exchange rate. This section is intended not only to provide an understanding of the pricing of foreign exchange forwards but also to illustrate the basic concepts of a forward contract. At origination, an at-market forward contract has a net present value equal to zero. Given this condition, alternative market constraints can be used to create arbitrage pricing models for a forward contract.

Forwards are traded in most major currencies, with bid-asked spreads quoted in standard maturities of one, two, three, six, nine, and twelve months.[5] Moreover, for the major currencies—sterling, yen, and deutsche mark—quotes on four, five, etc. months are also available. On a negotiated basis, forwards are also available in major currencies for odd dates (also referred to as *broken dates*). The extent to which a currency forward is available depends on exchange controls, the depth of alternative markets, and the monetary policy of a country. Because of regulatory differences among domestic markets, the reference market used to price a forward (set a forward rate for a currency) is usually the Euromarket.

The easiest way to price a foreign exchange rate forward contract is to determine the future foreign exchange rate that could be created synthetically. The technique used to do this is called *covered arbitrage*. (Alternatively, one could think of this technique as the methodology of

---

5. Longer-term contracts do exist, in which case the bid-asked spreads are subject to negotiation.

creating a forward rate that guarantees that the contract's net present value is zero.) For clarification, think of a forward contract as a pair of zero-coupon loans.

This concept is illustrated in Figure 4-3. Part (*a*) illustrates the cash flows of a party who has agreed to buy deutsche marks forward (or, conversely, sell dollars forward). This contract obligates the party to pay, at period T, a set number of dollars in return for a set number of deutsche marks. Part (*b*) compares the cash flows in part (*a*) to a pair of zero-coupon loans. At time zero (i.e., at contract origination) the party illustrated borrows in dollars, $Q, and simultaneously lends the same amount in deutsche marks, DM R. That is, given the spot exchange

Figure 4-3. A Forward Contract as a Pair of Loans.

A Forward Contract

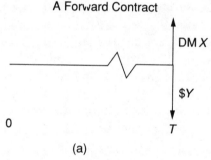

(a)

can be thought of as a pair of zero-coupon bonds

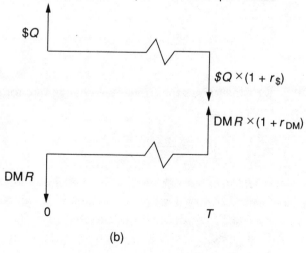

(b)

rate at time zero between dollars and deutsche marks, S_0, Q dollars is equivalent to R deutsche marks: DM $R = \$Q \times S_0$. At maturity (time T) the party will have to pay back $Q \times (1 + r_\$)$ dollars, where $r_\$$ is the U.S. dollar interest rate for maturity T, and will receive $R \times (1 + r_{DM})$ deutsche marks, where r_{DM} is the T-period rate for a deutsche mark borrowing. If the two cash flow diagrams in part (b) were combined into a single cash flow diagram, the result would be the forward contract illustrated in part (a), where

$$\text{DM } X = R \times (1 + r_{DM}) \qquad \text{and} \qquad \$Y = Q \times (1 + r_\$)$$

Consequently, a forward contract for foreign exchange can be priced as if it were a pair of zero-coupon loans; the bullet repayments plus interest are netted against the future spot foreign exchange rate on the maturity date. Thus, on a purely mechanical pricing basis, the spot rate at origination (S_0) times the amount of the domestic currency ($\$Q$) fixes the amount of foreign currency to be lent. And with knowledge of the two relevant interest rates, $r_\$$ and r_{DM}, the amounts of the two cash flows to be exchanged at T are determined.

Therefore, the forward exchange rate at contract origination, F_0, can be obtained by dividing one cash flow at T by the other:

$$F_0 = \frac{R \times (1 + r_{DM})}{Q \times (1 + r_\$)} \tag{4-3}$$

Since R deutsche marks is equal to Q dollars times the spot exchange rate at contract origination ($R = Q \times S_0$), it follows that the forward rate is:

$$F_0 = S_0 \left(\frac{1 + r_{DM}}{1 + r_\$} \right) \tag{4-4}$$

Generalizing, we can express the forward exchange rate for currencies 1 and 2 at time t as

$$F_t = \frac{S_t(1 + r\,2_t)}{1 + r\,1_t} \tag{4-5}$$

where the forward and the spot rates are defined at time t as the number of country 2 units per country 1's currency units (i.e., if country 2 is West Germany, F_t and S_t are defined in deutsche marks per dollar).

Alternatively, Equation (4-5) can be written in the form often referred to as *interest rate parity*:

$$\frac{F_t}{S_t} = \frac{1 + r2}{1 + r1}$$

That is, the ratio of the forward rate to the spot is a reflection of the interest rates in the two countries. If the interest rate in country 2 is higher than that in country 1, then the forward rate is greater than the spot—or country 2's currency is weaker in the forward market than country 1's. Returning to dollars and deutsche marks, if the dollar interest rate is lower than the DM interest rate, the forward DM/$ rate is greater than the spot; an alternative way of saying this is that the dollar is selling at a premium to the deutsche mark (or the DM is selling at a discount to today's spot rate).

Example

Calculating a forward exchange rate

Foreign exchange and interest rates as of March 15, 1988, were as follows:

Spot DM per dollar	1.6685
U.S. LIBOR (1 year)	0.0730
DM LIBOR (1 year)	0.0357

Using Equation (4-5), we can calculate the one-year forward rate as 1.6105. The spot rate minus the forward rate is called the premium if positive and the discount if negative. If the forward is less than the spot, the DM is anticipated to be stronger in the future. If the forward is greater than the spot, the DM is anticipated to be weaker in the future. In this example, the premium is 0.0580. Consequently, as of March 15, 1988, the DM is expected to be stronger against the dollar in one year than at present.[6]

Bid-Ask Spreads and Forwards

In the preceding calculations of the forward rate from arbitrage conditions between markets, we used what are commonly referred to as *mid-rates*. The problem is that buyers must pay an amount such that the sellers will earn enough to cover the transaction costs of creating the synthetic forward contract. After all, who would want to spend their

---

6. The use of the word *expected* might imply to some readers a theory of exchange rate determination. We do not intend it to be utilized thus. Rather, we wish to convey that the forward rate is contracted in such a way, given existing market forces, to imply a stronger future DM spot price.

time providing a market for forwards unless they were paid to do so? A market exists to bring different parties together to trade, but the provider of the market must be compensated.

The way the foreign exchange market compensates the banks providing this service is through the bid-ask spread. A market participant specializing in making prices in a particular contract—a market maker—will quote one price to a person if that person buys and another price if that person sells. This bid-ask spread compensates for the cost involved in providing the service of contracting.

In the foreign exchange market, prices are usually quoted in units of foreign currency per dollar.[7] Prices are quoted to the fourth decimal point for deutsche marks, sterling, Canadian dollars, etc. and to the first or second decimal place for currencies such as Italian lira (trading at 1,275.6 per dollar on March 16, 1987) and yen. The bid-ask spread on the major currencies in the spot market is very small. For example, on spot deutsche marks, the bid-ask spread is usually as low as 5 to 10 "pips" (a pip is 1/10,000 of a DM). Thus, on March 15, 1988, at 11:12 GMT Chase Manhattan Bank was showing a quote of "DM/\$ 1.6680/90" or "DM/\$ 1.6680–1.6690."

The interest rate markets (the money markets) also operate on this bid-offer concept.[8] For example, on March 16 at 10:11 GMT the twelve-month Eurodollar deposit rate was $7\frac{3}{16}$ to $7\frac{5}{16}$, and the Euro deutsche mark deposit rate was $3\frac{1}{2}$ to $3\frac{5}{8}$. Given this information, we can look again at the forward rate and the forward premium described in the last example; but this time, instead of using mid-rates, we calculate the relevant bid-ask forward rates.

Example

Recalculating a forward exchange rate

On March 15, 1988 the relevant bid-ask spreads were

Spot DM per dollars	1.6680–1.6690
U.S. Libor (1 year)	0.071875–0.073125
DM Libor	0.035000–0.036250

---

7. The exceptions to this rule are the pound sterling and the ECU (European Currency Unit), which are usually quoted in dollars per unit of sterling or ECU.

8. In this case we refer to the Euromoney markets, for example, the Eurodollar and Euro deutsche mark markets.

Utilizing Equation (4-5), we calculate the forward rate as 1.6087–1.6135.

To obtain the twelve-month bid rate for the forward, we divided $(1 + r_{DM}$ bid) by $(1 + r_{\$}$ ask) and then multiplied by the spot bid. The reverse was done to obtain the forward ask rate. Let's walk through the logic. Since we are attempting to create a future buying rate, we want to pay a rate less than the rate at which we would sell. Thus, we take the buying rate today as our base—the bid spot rate. We must then invest deutsche marks for one year while borrowing dollars. Since we are investing deutsche marks, we can only get the buying rate—the bid rate—and since we are borrowing dollars, we get stuck with having to pay the higher rate. To calculate the ask rate, we reverse the process.

In this example we calculate the premium as 0.0593–0.0555. Note that the premium is quoted with the higher number first. Usually the foreign exchange forward market quotes the spot and then the forward premium or discount. If the currency is at a premium to the dollar, as in this case (DM interest rates are lower), then the higher figure is quoted first; this will indicate that the numbers are subtracted from the spot bid-ask spread.

To give some idea of how these prices actually appear in the market, Figure 4-4 provides the spot and forward rates for Chase Manhattan Bank foreign exchange trading operations from around Europe as they appeared on Reuters on March 16, 1988.[9]

Forward Contracts on Interest Rates

As noted in Chapter 1, on October 6, 1979, the Federal Reserve shocked the financial system by raising the discount rate 200 basis points and starting to target the money supply. From this date, interest rate volatility became the norm, providing the impetus for forward contracts on interest rates, referred to as *forward rate agreements* (FRAs). The market

---

9. Note in Figure 4-4 that the quote of the forward premium for deutsche marks differs slightly from the calculations in the preceding example. The reason is that the interest rates used in the example were obtained one hour earlier than this table was obtained. This illustrates that to actually do an arbitrage, one must be able to move quickly, before someone else in the market does it. There is another reason why arbitrage situations don't exist all the time: the bid-ask spread in the forward market will likely be narrower than the arbitrage range spread. This is because the credit risk inherent in the forward contract is less than that implied in the actual borrowing and deposit of funds that would be necessary to perform the arbitrage.

Figure 4-4. Prices in the Foreign Exchange Market, Quoted on March 16, 1988 (Taken from Reuters Screen CMBX).

Location US/	Spot Rate Spot	Forward Rates 1Mo	2Mo	3Mo	6Mo	12Mo
1058 LDN STG	1.8500/10	32/30	62/60	95/92	182/176	328/31
1112 FFM DMK	1.6680-90	49-44	97-92	147-142	290-280	590-57
1027 FFM SFR	1.3800/10	61/58	117/114	174/171	327/321	615/59
0953 PAR FFR	5.6680/00	62/72	130/140	120/245	420/440	710/75
1035 BRU BFC	34.91/92	2.7/2.2	4.7/4	7/6	15/13	36/30
1039 MLN LIT	1237.75-25	470/520	9/960	1325/14	25/26	4450/4
1119 LDN DFL	1.8700/10	44-42	87-85	133-130	264-259	545-53
1113 LDN YEN	127.32/37	25/23	53/50	82/79	169/165	365/35
1043 LDN AUD	.7311/16	26/24	50/58	74/72	150/146	318/30

Key:

STG	=	Pounds sterling
DMK	=	German marks
SFR	=	Swiss francs
FFR	=	French francs
BFC	=	Belgian francs
LIT	=	Italian lira
DFL	=	Dutch guilders
YEN	=	Japanese yen
AUD	=	Australian dollars

Note that currencies are quoted as units of foreign currency to dollars, except for sterling, which is quoted in dollars per pound sterling. Prices are for Chase Manhattan Bank European branche and are representative of transaction prices for each location at the represented hour. For example Italian lira quotes are for the Chase Milan Branch at 10:39 A.M. in Italian lira.

Source: Reprinted by permission of REUTERS.

for FRAs exists in various currencies, the key ones being U.S. dollars, pounds sterling, deutsche marks, Swiss francs, and Japanese yen. However, given the volatility in the dollar and sterling interest rates, these two currencies have the largest volume. Although the market is truly global, most of the business is done in London. Within the sterling and dollars markets, quotes are two-way, with a bid-offer spread rate presented to the customer. This is, of course, similar to any actively traded securities market, and it closely parallels the forward foreign exchange market.

The Contract

Although each institution that deals in forward rate agreements has its own "terms and conditions," the British Bankers Association (BBA) terms and conditions have become the industry standard.[10] Consequently, much of our discussion will refer to these terms and conditions.

Key to a forward rate agreement is the fact that it is a forward contract on interest rates, not a forward commitment to make a loan or take a deposit. Consequently, a key clause of any FRA agreement underscores the point that neither party to the contract has a commitment to lend or to borrow the contract amount (i.e., the principal of the contract). Furthermore, all FRA contracts contain a clause referring to normal banking practice, which commits the parties to specific performance. If the performance commitment is not met, this clause makes the outstanding net cash value of the contract subject to the same conditions that would apply to a loan not performed upon. Such a clause illustrates that: (1) an FRA, like a foreign exchange forward, is essentially a credit instrument; and (2) just as with a foreign exchange forward, no front-end cash transaction takes place; all value is conveyed at maturity.

Dealing on an FRA is done by phone or telex (or by letter). Given the nature of the transaction, most firms stipulate that dealing will be done only if the counterparty allows the firm to tape an oral agreement. However, confirmation must be made in the form of a telex registered letter.

The formula as stated by the BBA for calculating the settlement of a forward contract is:[11]

> Wherever two parties enter into an FRA the Buyer will agree to pay to the seller on the settlement date (if the Contract Rate exceeds the BBA Interest Settlement Rate), and the Seller will agree to pay to the Buyer on the settlement date (if the BBA Interest Settlement Rate exceeds the Contract Rate) an amount calculated in accordance with the following formula:
>
> (a) when L is higher than R
>
> $$\frac{(L - R) \times D \times A}{(B \times 100) + (L \times D)}$$

10. British Bankers Association, Forward Rate Agreements ("FRABBA" terms), London, August 1985.
11. *Ibid.*, section D, p. 8.

or

(b) when R is higher than L

$$\frac{(R - L) \times D \times A}{(B \times 100) + (L \times D)}$$

where

L = BBA Interest Settlement Rate

R = Contract Rate

D = Days in Contract Period

A = Contract Amount

B = 360 or 365 days according to market custom

Examining the preceding formula, we can see why it makes sense. One party to the contract agrees with the other on the future interest rate at which they are willing to contract (R). Upon settlement—in three months, twelve months, or whatever—the actual rate is observed in the market. That rate is L and is determined as the 11:00 A.M. London rate in the interbank market. Knowing L, we know the difference between L and R. Depending on whether you were the buyer or the seller, your gain or loss is this difference times the number of days in the contract period times the contract amount, divided by the term $(B \times 100)$ (which adjusts the days to the correct basis) plus the appropriate interest rate discounting the original contract $(L \times D)$.[12] To obtain an intuitive feel for these calculations, let's consider an example.

Example

Using a FRA

Suppose a party entered into a FRA contract with Citicorp (CITI). Neglecting bid-ask spread considerations, the contracting party wants to be paid (to receive) income on a contract amount of $100 million (U.S.) if, in three months, three-month LIBOR is more than what is expected given today's yield curve (the three-month rate in three months). If the three-month forward rate is 10%, CITI

---

12. This formula has to be changed for FRAs of duration greater than twelve months. This formula is modified to create a series of one-year values for the contract period, which are then discounted appropriately.

would agree to pay if the settlement rate were above 10% and would agree to receive if the rate were below 10%.

Let's assume that the parties agree to the contract on March 15 for a June 15 spot date for determining the settlement rate, with actual transference of funds occurring two business days later—June 17 (the settlement date). What happens if on June 15 the rate is exactly 10%? Nothing. Neither our contracting party nor CITI receives or pays. However, suppose that June 15 arrives and the three-month LIBOR rate determined by the reference bank in the contract is 11%. CITI must pay on June 17 to the contracting party. How much does CITI pay? Before resorting to the formula, let's think it through logically. The notional amount is $100 million; the difference in settlement and contract rates is 1.0%; and the contract was for 92 days. First, we need to know how much 92 days of interest differential is worth for $100 million:

$$(100,000,000) \times (0.01) \times (92/360) = 255,555.56$$

This is the value after holding another three months; however, the payments are going to be made at settlement, so this amount must be discounted by the three-month LIBOR in effect:

$$\frac{255,555.56}{1 + [0.11 \times (92/360)]} = 248,568.03$$

We get precisely the same answer if we utilize the formula provided by the BBA:[13]

$$\frac{(L - R) \times D \times A}{(B \times 100) + (L \times D)} = \frac{(11.00 - 10.00) \times 92 \times 100,000,000}{36,000 + (11.0 \times 92)}$$

$$= \frac{9,200,000,000}{37,012} = 248,568.03$$

The Forward Interest Rate

In the previous discussion we took as given the contract rate—the forward interest rate. The fact is, however, that the forward interest rate, like the forward foreign exchange rate, can be derived from an arbitrage

---

13. Logically our intuitive approach could be written as:

$$\frac{A \times \frac{(L-R)}{100} \times \frac{D}{B}}{1 + \frac{L-R}{100} \times \frac{D}{B}}$$

which, when manipulated algebraically, equals the BBA formula.

condition. We will first illustrate with an example and then generalize the arguments.

Example

Deriving a forward rate

Suppose you are faced with a tough decision. You have $100 to invest for two years. Should you invest for one year then take the proceeds and invest for another, or should you invest for two years? Is there any difference?

From the newspaper you obtain interest rates for one-year and two-year investments. One-year investments yield 7%, and two-year investments yield 8%. Is the fact that the two-year rate exceeds the one-year rate sufficient information for you to make your decision?

No. To compare the two investments, you not only need to know the rates for one and two years, but you also need to know what investment rates you can expect in one year's time. You need to know the market expectation of that one-year reinvestment rate in one year's time.

How can you calculate the rate expected by the market? That is, how can you calculate the one-year rate that will prevail one year hence—the *forward rate*?[14] Remembering the lesson from the forward foreign exchange market that the foreign exchange forward rate is the one that eliminates arbitrage profit, you seek an arbitrage condition to guide you. At contracting time, conditions must be such as to eliminate arbitrage. The forward rate, f, must be such that borrowing or lending for one year and then rolling over the borrowing or lending for a second year [$100(1 + 0.07) \times (1 + f)$] is expected to be equivalent to the borrowing or lending for two years [$100(1 + 0.08)^2$]. Using this arbitrage relation,

$$(1 + f) = \frac{\$100(1 + 0.08)^2}{\$100(1 + 0.07)}$$

---

14. Our discussion of these yield curve calculations is standard and is covered in many texts. See, for instance, Richard Brealey and Stewart Myers, *Principles of Corporate Finance*, 2nd ed. (New York: McGraw-Hill, 1984), Chap. 21.

15. Alternatively, we can look at the future values of the two strategies. If you invest for one year and roll over at the end of the first year, the future value is

$$FV = 1.07 \times 100 \times 1.09009 = 116.64$$

If you invest for two years, the future value is

$$FV = 1.08^2 \times 100 = 116.64$$

The future value is the same. Of course, if it were not, then the forward rate we calculated would not be the arbitrage rate, and one strategy would dominate the other.

So $f = 9.009\%$.[15]

The decision to invest for one year and then reinvest for the second year versus investing for the full two years can now be made. The "market" expects the one-year reinvestment rate to be 9.009%. If you expect the one-year rate in one year to be higher than 9.009%, then invest for one year with plans to reinvest for one year at the end of the first year. If, however, you expect the one-year rate in one year to be below 9.009%, then invest for two years today.

To generalize the formula for one-year investments, we recognize that the forward rate is implicit in the yield curve itself. For example, if we wish to know the one-year rate one year from today ($t = 0$), we solve the equation

$$(1 +_0 R_1)(1 +_1 R_2) = (1 +_0 R_2)^2$$

where

$_0R_1$ = the one-year interest rate today

$_0R_2$ = the two-year interest rate today

$_1R_2$ = the forward interest rate for one year between years 1 and 2

If we wish to know the forward rate from year j to year k, we solve

$$(1 +_0 R_j)^j(1 +_j R_k) = (1 +_0 R_k)^k$$

For periods less than one year, the equation must be modified. For instance, if we want to know the forward rate from month j to month k and if the interest rates are quoted as simple rates, we solve for $_jR_k$ in

$$[1 + (j/12)_0R_j] \times \{1 + [(k - j)/12]_jR_k\} = [1 + (k/12)_0R_k]$$

If, however, the interest rates are quoted compounded, the appropriate form is

$$(1 +_0 R_j)^{j/12}(1 +_j R_k)^{(k-j)/12} = (1 +_0 R_k)^{k/12}$$

Bid-Ask Spreads

Just as foreign exchange forwards grew out of parallel borrowing and depositing, FRAs evolved from *forward forward* contracts. A forward forward is an obligation in which one financial institution agrees to deposit money at another institution at a specified future date, at a specified interest rate (set at contract origination). Here the credit risk

is obvious; physical deposits are to be made. The FRA was developed to strip the deposit risk from the interest rate risk. With an FRA only the cash flows need be exchanged, so the credit risk is reduced.

The language of the FRA market reflects this evolution. The bid-ask spread is called deposit-borrow spread. On a Reuters screen the FRA rate might be quoted as $11-10\frac{7}{8}$. This means you can *borrow* at 11 or deposit at $10\frac{7}{8}$. Of course, since FRAs are forwards, there is no actual borrowing or depositing as would be the case for forward forward contracts.

As with foreign exchange forwards, the deposit-borrow spread is circumscribed by the actual cost associated with the physical depositing and borrowing that would occur as an alternative to using the FRA. FRAs are priced, then, as if they were actual deposits (and borrowings) for different maturities, but the bid-offer spread is narrower than for actual borrowings and deposits because the credit risk of the transaction has been reduced significantly. (There is, as pointed out earlier, still residual credit risk similar to that inherent in a forward foreign exchange rate contract.)

Figure 4-5 illustrates the bid-offer spreads inherent in a FRA contract. This screen presents FRAs for three months' duration commencing in

Figure 4-5. Prices in the Forward Rate Agreement Market, Quoted on June 21, 1988 (Taken from Reuters Screen FRAS).

Dates	Dollars	Dates	Sterling
3M V 6M	7.93–7.87	3M V 6M	9.96–9.88
4M V 7M	8.10–8.04	4M V 7M	9.99–9.91
5M V 8M	8.20–8.14	5M V 8M	10.02–9.94
6M V 9M	8.35–8.29	6M V 9M	10.03–9.95
9M V 12M	8.49–8.43	9M V 12M	10.04–9.96
3M V 9M	8.20–8.14	3M V 9M	10.12–10.04
4M V 10M	8.30–8.24	4M V 10M	10.13–10.05
5M V 11M	8.41–8.35	5M V 11M	10.14–10.06
6M V 12M	8.49–8.43	6M V 12M	10.12–10.04

Key:
The date 3M V 6M refers to three months' money in 3 months; 4M V 7M refers to three months' money in 4 months and so on.

Source: Reprinted by permission of REUTERS.

three months' time, four months' time, etc.; also shown are six-month FRAs. Again, the language used—3 vs. 6 or 5 vs. 8—is a holdover from the forward forward contract days. The indicative rates quoted reflect the forward rates from the zero-coupon LIBOR curves for dollars and sterling.

Example

Booking a FRA

Suppose Banco Lar of Brazil wants to lock in its U.S. dollar LIBOR borrowing costs for three months, six months from now.

Banco Lar's trader, having established that credit lines exist, calls Barclays Bank in London. Since the yield curve slopes upward, he knows that the quotes will be well above today's three-month LIBOR. (He has unraveled the yield curve to get the forward interest rate, $_3R_6$. But when he calls for a quote, he is not going to let Barclays know whether he is going to deposit or borrow.) The Barclays trader quotes 8.49–8.43 for "$10" ($10,000,000 notional principal). Both parties understand that FRABBA terms apply (they have already exchanged master forward agreements). The Banco Lar trader says no; his quote is for "$12." The Barclays trader requotes 8.49–8.43—exactly the same conditions. (For a very large amount, say, $100,000,000, the bid-offer spread could change.)

The Banco Lar trader takes the 8.49 borrowing rate. Banco Lar has now fixed its borrowing rate—though not the physical borrowing—for a three-month period in six months.

5

Using Forwards to Manage Risks

Forward contracts exist to permit an individual, a firm, or a government to separate financial price risk from an underlying position and to transfer that price risk to another party. The individual who manages his or her exposure to foreign exchange rates by using a forward foreign exchange contract transfers the exposure to the party who buys or sells the forward contract.

Consider a firm subject to foreign exchange risk. For example, suppose a financial institution has a one-year exposure to the dollar/deutsche mark exchange rate. Specifically, suppose that the value of a particular financial institution is positively related to the value of the dollar in relation to the DM; if the value of the dollar rises, the value of the financial institution will rise. The risk profile for this firm is illustrated in Figure 5-1.

From Chapter 4, we know that the financial institution could manage this exposure by buying a forward contract on deutsche marks. For illustration, we repeat the following data from Chapter 4:

Spot DM per dollar	1.6685
Dollar LIBOR (1-year)	7.3%
DM LIBOR (1-year)	3.57%

Given these data, the financial institution would agree to buy deutsche marks in one year at a rate of 1.6105 DM/$, that is, a price per DM of $0.62. As illustrated in Figure 5-2, if the value of the dollar in one year falls, the inherent decline in the value of the firm will be offset by an increase in the value of the forward contract and vice versa.

The result of using the forward contract is that the financial institution has transferred its foreign exchange risk to the seller of the forward

Figure 5-1. An Illustrative Risk Profile.

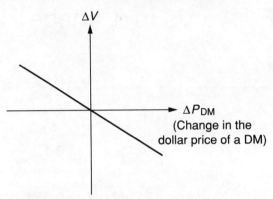

As the value of the dollar rises, P_{DM} falls and the value of the firm rises. As the value of the dollar falls, P_{DM} rises and the value of this firm falls.

contract. The financial institution that bought a forward contract on deutsche marks has neutralized its exposure to DM/$ movements. As illustrated in Figure 5-3, the exposure now resides with the seller of the forward contract.

However, the same result for the financial institution could be obtained on its balance sheet. As we know from Chapter 4, the long position in the forward contract on exchange rates can be created synthetically by borrowing dollars, buying deutsche marks (spot), and investing in a DM-

Figure 5-2. Hedging with a Forward Contract.

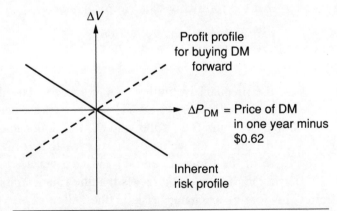

Figure 5-3. The Exposure of a Seller of a Forward Contract.

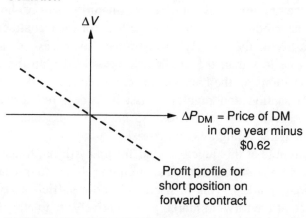

ΔV

ΔP_{DM} = Price of DM in one year minus $0.62

Profit profile for short position on forward contract

denominated financial asset. In the context of the financial markets, the balance sheet of the financial institution would look like:

Assets	Liabilities
1-year Euro deutsche mark deposit: 10 million at 3.7%	1-year Eurodollar deposit: 5.993 million at 7.3%

Since the alternative of using the balance sheet to manage risk is available, why does the forward market exist? The answer is performance risk—default risk. If the firm uses its balance sheet, the financial institution has accepted the credit risk of the institution or individual to whom it lent the Euro deutsche mark deposit. (By the same token, the individual creating the Eurodollar deposit with the financial institution has also incurred the credit risk of that institution.)

The forward contract does not eliminate the credit risk inherent in the on-balance-sheet hedge, but the risk is reduced substantially since actual deposits are not created in the transaction. The credit risk remaining for the forward is the performance of one party relative to the deviation in the contract's value from zero. If spot prices continually mirror the forward prices at contract origination, there is negligible credit risk for the forward contract. On the other hand, if spot prices are extremely

volatile, then there is greater performance risk in a forward contract because there is, ex ante, a greater probability of one party to the contract owing a large amount to the other at the maturity date of the contract.[1]

Hence, the credit risk associated with a forward contract increases as the volatility of the underlying instrument increases. Nonetheless, it will always be less than the credit risk associated with the creation of offsetting positions on the balance sheet. Since credit risk is not costless (ease of transaction and regulatory issues aside), the forward market creates a less expensive alternative to back-to-back loans (the deposit route) for hedging foreign exchange risk.

We should note at this juncture that, for many firms, transaction costs associated with the deposit arbitrage are high relative to transaction costs in the forward market. This in itself may be a sufficient condition for the existence of the forward market. Alternatively, regulatory issues may be important in determining which method of hedging risk is used. For example, where exchange controls exist, offsetting back-to-back loans between parents and subsidiaries can sometimes be utilized to accomplish the task normally left to the forward market. These regulatory constraints will become more relevant as we discuss other instruments for risk management.

The incentive to use forward contracts results from a variety of factors:[2] response to regulatory constraints, accounting, synthetic asset creation, control of agency problems, straightforward risk reduction, tax arbitrage, etc. However, always underlying the demand for the forward is uncertainty about the future spot price. Without uncertainty — volatility — there would be no reason to use the forward market.

The Markets

We concentrate on the forward markets for foreign exchange and interest rates (money and bond markets) — FX forwards and FRAs. However, other forward markets do exist, especially for commodities such as gold and oil. These other markets are of great importance and are becoming an

---

1. This point will be stressed when we look at the credit risk characteristics of a swap in Chapter 12.
2. We will address the rationale for using risk management instruments in Chapter 18.

increasing part of the trading operations of major financial institutions.[3] Also, there are forward contracts traded outside traditional interbank markets, for example, the forward contracts on primary metals traded on the London Metal Exchange.

In the foreign exchange market, volume figures compiled by the Bank of England suggest a 1986 daily volume of $200 billion, with forwards making up about 30% of total volume in the foreign exchange market. It is estimated by market makers that total 1988 activity in the foreign exchange markets will hit some $400 billion per day, with forwards taking 25–30% of the market.[4] Trading continues to be dominated by DM/$, £/$, and yen/$, followed by SF (Swiss francs)/$ and various non-dollar-to-nondollar deals.

Trading in foreign exchange is concentrated in London, New York, Hong Kong, and Tokyo, but the market is truly global. Major dealing centers can be divided by time zones. Books are moved around the clock:

London → New York → Tokyo → Hong Kong → London

The major time zones can be divided into trading centers and sub-centers, depending on currency:

Far East	Middle East	Europe	Americas
Tokyo	Bahrain	London	New York
Hong Kong		Paris	Chicago
Singapore		Zurich	Toronto
Sydney		Geneva	San Francisco
		Frankfurt	

Other centers, operating on much smaller scales, include Brussels, Luxembourg, Madrid, Milan, Amsterdam, Munich, Hamburg, Kuwait, Kuala Lumpur, Los Angeles, Montreal, and Johannesburg.

Many currencies can be dealt either directly or indirectly in the FX forward markets:

---

3. Of particular interest are gold forwards, which are vehicles for institutions holding gold to create active returns on previously "sterile" (non-interest-bearing) assets.
4. Data from the Bank of England and Federal Reserve Bank of New York, "Foreign Exchange Market Survey," March 1986; and various interviews with market makers.

U.S. dollar
Pound sterling
German mark
Swiss franc
French franc   Traded with ease
Canadian dollar
Japanese yen
Dutch guilder

Danish krone
Irish pound
Italian lira
Finnish markka
Belgian franc
Spanish peseta
Austrian schilling
Australian dollar
Singapore dollar
Hong Kong dollar   Less liquid, but
Kuwaiti dinar   quotes are
New Zealand dollar   readily available
Malaysian ringgit
South African rand
Portuguese escudo
Thai baht
Saudi riyal
Swedish krona
Norwegian krone
ECU
SDR

The FRA market is also growing. Annual turnover in 1988 was estimated to be $300 to $500 billion, up from only $50 billion in 1985. Growth has been primarily in the interbank market, where FRAs are used as an effective tool for asset and liability management. But FRAs are becoming more widely used by corporate treasurers to manage interest rate risk. Although less than 10% of all FRA transactions now involve nonfinancial corporations, it is expected that the percentage will rise to 20% as the market develops.

Average sizes of forward rate agreement transactions are $5 million to $20 million, although contracts to $100 to $200 million are not unusual. The most liquid markets are in dollars and sterling, but deutsche marks are becoming more important daily; they threaten to overtake the leaders as the most traded currency.[5]

Most trading continues to be done in London, with over 150 traders said to be trading FRAs.[6] Considering the close relationship between FRAs and swaps, one would expect New York to dominate trading, at least in dollar FRAs, but this has not happened. Indeed, just as with the development of the forward foreign exchange market, London continues to dominate trading. Markets for both FRAs and FX forwards tend to be more liquid, with finer bid-ask spreads in London trading hours.

With FRAs and forward FX markets growing, new product derivations are beginning to appear. Two of these are "forward exchange agreements" (FXAs) and "exchange rate agreements" (ERAs).[7] FXAs and ERAs are both *forward* foreign exchange agreements.[8] Whereas a traditional foreign exchange forward contract sets a rate in the future for the spot exchange of currencies, the FXA sets the rate at which a forward exchange can be fixed in the future. Thus, just as the FRA allows one to fix a three-month borrowing or lending rate three months from now, the FXA allows one to fix the three-month forward foreign exchange rate three months from now. The FXA differs from the forward foreign

---

5. Estimates are from Paul Dickins, "Fast Forward with FRAs," *Euromoney Corporate Finance* no. 41 (April 1988): 27–32; and Izabel Grindal, "Flexible Risk Control and Arbitrage," *Futures and Options World* no. 205 (June 1988): 47–51. Volume figures are estimates, and disputes about which currencies are most liquid abound. Indeed, one set of survey results found that sterling FRAs had 60% of the London market in 1987. Moreover, the domestic French franc market has developed considerable steam and provides an alternative to MATIF for risk management.

6. This estimate was developed from various sources by the authors.

7. ERAs were developed by Barclay's Bank and FXAs by Midland Bank in 1987. Volumes are small but growing, and the British Bankers Association is drawing up rules of exchange for the market.

8. In the parlance of the foreign exchange market, foreign exchange agreements are also referred to as "foreign exchange swaps." However, this agreement is not the same as the swap we will discuss in Chapters 9–12. A foreign exchange swap is an exchange of one currency for another on one day, matched by a reverse exchange on a later day. The swap rate is the difference between the rates of exchange on the two days, set today. Of course, the rate will be the forward premium or discount, just as in a forward foreign exchange contract (referred to as the *outright forward*). This premium is called the *swap rate* or *swap points*.

exchange contract in that spot exchanges of the underlying currencies are never made; rather, only the forward rate is set.[9] The ERA is similar to the FXA. It fixes the relevant forward premium (as does a forward forward or an FXA), but it does not fix the actual forward rate. In the ERA contract, no adjustment is made for changes in the spot rate, only for the premiums in the relevant forward contracts. (To put it another way, the interest rate differential is fixed, but the spot rate of exchange is not.)

As the preceding discussion suggests, firms are moving rapidly to redeploy the forward concept as events dictate. Better risk management tools are being developed to lessen the risk of contracting. FXAs and ERAs are natural extensions of FRAs and outright foreign exchange forwards. Finer (and less expensive) hedging contracts can be created as these markets grow and develop greater liquidity.

The Trading Room: Unwinding Risk

Trading forward contracts can be done on a matched basis, a matched book basis, a synthetic basis, a single product book basis, a portfolio basis, etc. Indeed, the trading room gives rise to many different ways in which forward contracts can be dealt.

Foreign Exchange Forward Trading

The most common method for trading FX forwards is to trade them in conjunction with the spot foreign exchange desk and the deposit desk.

---

9. The formula for the FXA (taken from Paul Dickins, *Euromoney Corporate Finance*, no. 42 (May 1988): 18, is:

$$np \times \left\{ \left[\frac{(sd - sc) + (fd - fc)}{\dfrac{r \times days}{100 \times year}} \right] - (sd - sc) \right\}$$

where

np = notional principal
sd = outright exchange rate (forward rate)
sc = settlement spot rate
fd = contract forward points (premium)
fc = settlement forward points (premium)
r = LIBOR (interest rate)
days = number of calendar days in period of contract
year = 360 (days)

This allows the risk to be broken apart and reassembled into different forms. The following example illustrates this.

Example

Laying off an FX forward

George trades FX forwards at the London branch of XYZ bank of Hong Kong. He makes a market in DM/$ forwards and is responsible for managing the risk of his position. Available to him on the trading room floor are the related markets: spot foreign exchange, Euro deposits, foreign exchange "swaps" (spot combined with outright forwards), FRAs, etc.

On July 5, 1988, he received a call from BHZ Co. of Birmingham, a firm he has dealt with on a regular basis for several years.

BHZ: George, how's the dollar?

George: DM/$1.6800–1.6810, with the deutsche mark trading lower (weaker) in active trading.

BHZ: I am worried about these orders I have at spot DM/$1.67. Let's cover for 50 dollars ($50 million) for twelve months outright, if we get a bounce (if the dollar gets stronger.)

George: OK, the premium now for 12 months is 355/345, so at spot DM/$1.6700, if the forward premium holds, trading should be at DM/$1.6345–$1.6355.

BHZ: Call me back in about an hour.

It is one hour and twenty minutes later, and spot has moved against BHZ. The DM has weakened and is now trading at DM/$1.6900/10 spot—a full 2 pfennigs away from BHZ's target. George calls BHZ with the bad news.

BHZ: Hello, George? OK! That's awful.

George: No sign of intervention in Frankfurt, but the SNB (Swiss National Bank) has done a FX swap for $120 million against Swissie for three months.

BHZ: What's an FX swap?

George: This is a forward outright with a spot transaction. It's designed to push interest rate differentials and soak up francs simultaneously. The Swiss are trying to break the strength in the dollar. Odds are the Bundesbank will be in later, but I'm not sure the FED is committed. We'll have to watch when New York opens.

BHZ: OK, call me if the FED comes in by 3:00 P.M. (GMT).

George calls BHZ at 4:00 P.M.

George: BHZ? OK, the FED's in, and the midpoint spot has retreated to DM/$1.68 flat. I think you should cover now.

BHZ: OK, I'll cover. I want to sell DM against dollars, twelve months forward for a size equal to $50 million.

George: Fine, done at DM/$1.6445 for $50 million.

Now George has a problem. How does he lay off the position he just accepted? What are his alternatives?

First, George could try to find the other side of the transaction. Having bought DM at DM/$1.6445, he can attempt to sell DM at DM/$1.6465, thereby earning the 20 pips $(1.6465 - 1.6445)$ difference. Of course, this would mean being lucky enough to find someone needing this position for $50 million.

However, since George sits next to the DM money market desk, he knows that the DM money market trader is particularly aggressive and is willing to lend at an attractive rate.[10] Moreover, George knows that the dollar money market desk at his bank currently wants to attract deposits. George decides to "arbitrage" these two desks.

To see if this arbitrage is possible, George takes the forward premium (1.6800 minus 1.6445), divides it by the spot, and calculates the "swap yield" as a percentage:

$$0.0355/1.6800 = (0.0211) = 2.11\%$$

Adding this to the Euro deutsche mark borrowing rate of 5.89%, George gets a synthetic dollar rate of 8.00%. George must deliver $50 million in twelve months, for which he will receive DM 82.225 million. Thus, he must borrow today the present value of DM 82.225 million for one year, convert to spot dollars, and reinvest at the dollar deposit rate. If that dollar deposit rate is greater than his synthetic dollar borrowing rate of 8.00%, then George is able to arbitrage his desks. Indeed, the rate his desk will pay is 8.0005%. George locks up the spread of 0.0005% on $50 million for one year, or $25,000.

Did he do well? It's not all that clear. If he could have made the bid-ask spread on the forward of 20 pips, George would have made:

$$(1.6465 - 1.6445) \times \$50 \text{ million} = \$100,000$$

In the preceding example, our trader used the "typical" way of synthetically creating a hedge for his forward position. There are others. He could have closed the spot leg and left open the deposit by putting the dollars in an overnight account, or he could have used a three-month deposit with a three- versus twelve-month FRA if this were more

---

10. A real-life George may have had an aggressive DM lending rate to utilize because the bank had unmatched DM yield curve positions being managed in their Frankfurt office.

convenient, etc. (Indeed, due to volatility of the spot rates, most traders are likely to close this leg first and then worry about the other prices of the transaction.)

What is important to remember is that forwards, deposits, FRAs, ERAs, etc. can all be broken down into their component parts or put together to create alternative instruments that can be used to close or open positions. The trader must constantly be opening and closing legs in a way that allows him to earn the bid-ask spread (on average) on his position.

FRA Trading

Like foreign exchange forward trading, FRA trading is driven by arbitrage. Here it is the arbitrage of taking and placing deposits for mismatched dates; the FRA is a vehicle to move up and down the yield curve while leaving the balance sheet intact.

Trading FRAs is best illustrated by another example. This time we will begin with a user of FRAs and turn our user into a trader.

Example

Gobi Bank

Gobi Bank is a $5 billion (assets) bank located in the U.S. Midwest. It deals primarily with small corporations and directly with the public as the area's premier consumer bank.

Gobi Bank has just entered into a syndication with the New York branch of a Swiss bank and a major U.S. investment bank. In this syndication, Gobi Bank agreed to provide $200 million on a two-year fixed-rate basis.

Gobi's asset-liability management committee has been convened to discuss the increased exposure the bank now has to interest rates. Before the transaction, the bank had a "square" (matched maturity) asset-liability position. With the syndication, Gobi has increased its assets by $200 million. This increase is currently being funded on an overnight basis in the federal funds market. To replace the federal funds borrowing, Gobi expects that it can increase its placings of six-month CDs with the state pension fund.[11] The asset-liability committee decides to issue the CDs—Gobi's cheapest form of funding. However, funding the two-year syndication with six-month CDs leaves Gobi with a mismatched maturity.

---

11. The pension fund buys the CDs in $100,000 amounts, thereby getting a FDIC-guaranteed instrument at a higher rate than other government paper; Gobi Bank is not considered an investment-grade risk without the guarantee.

It is now three months later. The CDs will be rolled over in three months. The loans have one year and nine months to go and the bank is worried about interest rates going up. Indeed, with elections coming up during the CD rollover period, they are extremely concerned about a spike in rates just when these new CDs are issued. The managers of Gobi tell their treasurer to "get them through" this period.

The treasurer has a dilemma. He needs to get through the upcoming refunding. Does he issue new CDs now and seek out short-term assets? Does he issue new CDs and place three months in the Euromarket? In either of these cases he must "blow up" (increase) his balance sheet by an extra $200 million for three months. Given the new drive by the state banking authorities to set minimum capital adequacy ratios (which his firm is barely meeting), he decides instead to manage his exposure off balance sheet.

He calls his interbank contact at DDF Bank in New York. After a short discussion, he decides to leave his position funded on a six-month basis but to lock in today his borrowing costs in three months' time using an FRA. On the Reuters screen, three-month vs. nine-month FRAs are being quoted as 8.20–8.14. That is, the expected six-month rate three months from now is about 8.17. The bid-offer spread is 3 basis points around the midpoint (the expected rate). The treasurer is taking at 8.20.

Having learned about this technique of managing his interest rate risk, the treasurer decides that FRAs are a better way to manage interest rate risk than actual takings and placings. Consequently, he hires an FRA trader to manage his risk. The trader will work closely with Gobi's funding desk to shift the balance sheet's risk profile. One result for this treasurer will be that he can finance assets now with the "cheapest" source of funds relative to the market (such as the aforementioned CD) and use FRAs to restructure his interest rate risk, depending upon asset maturity mixes. No longer does he have to be as active in all different instruments on the liability side—from Federal Funds to bonds—merely to shift interest rate risk.

For the bank in the preceding example, the function of the FRA trader is to help the bank manage its own interest rate risk. In this case, the trader is constantly working off of the Bank's position. Bid-offer spreads will be adjusted away from midpoint, depending upon the bank's inherent position as a taker or a placer of funds in the three-month, six-month, etc. ranges. Open positions will be covered in the funding book and vice versa. The FRA trader is an integral part of the bank's treasury operation.

However, FRAs need not be traded in conjunction with a natural position. The trader can run a book on a matched or open basis using

only that market to lay risk into. It is more likely that FRAs will be traded with an underlying instrument, that is, by a swaps trader or a futures trader. FRA positions can be substituted (or hedged) in these other markets as well. Integration of risk across markets and exploitation of natural positions are the keys to a company's success as a FRA trading entity.

Using Forwards: Some Illustrations

Managing Foreign Exchange Risk

The easiest way to describe the problems involved in the use of foreign exchange forwards is with an example.

Example

SSW Imports

Consider a car importer. Suppose SSW of North America, Inc. decides to open for business as a subsidiary of a major German firm. It will import and distribute SSW cars manufactured in Bavaria. It decided to enter the U.S. market in 1984, when the dollar averaged DM 2.84. At that level, SSW could sell its product in the United States and have a profit margin of 20% on each automobile imported.

Recognizing that the firm was in for the long haul, SSW brought capital into the United States and converted it into dollars. It contracted to hire Americans and distribute its autos through American-owned and -operated outlets. SSW prices its cars in dollars, and with the dollar at DM 2.8 it would be able to sell 50,000 autos per year. If it is able to sell only 20,000 cars, its profit margin, at the same price per car, becomes severely negative. The key to its strategy is to ensure that it can sell at least 50,000 cars per year.

As the firm approached 1985, the dollar had strengthened to over DM 3.0, and the profit outlook for SSW of North America was bright. When the time came to import the cars for sale in 1985, the dollar was so strong against the DM that SSW would have a profit margin of 30% if it could achieve its sales goal of 50,000 units. The chief executive officer sees a large bonus in the offing if these profit targets are actually hit.

With visions of the large bonus in mind, the CEO calls in the treasurer of SSW and instructs her to hedge all of the foreign exchange risk for 1985. Realizing that there is a well-functioning market for foreign exchange forward contracts, the treasurer turns to this instrument to accomplish her task. But how much does she hedge, and how?

Within SSW of North America, dollars are coming in on each car (with a 30- to 60-day delay), and deutsche marks are going out. The lag from importation

to sales is fairly predictable. The treasurer knows what each car will sell for and has a good idea how many cars will be imported per month during the year. Given the forward foreign exchange rates from the Telerate monitor, the treasurer is ready to deal.

But *how* does she deal? *Where* does she deal? She might first call her local banker, but odds are that the banker will have no idea what the treasurer is talking about. The local banker might respond, "In this area we don't get too many requests for foreign exchange forwards" and refer the treasurer to a money center bank.

After listening to the treasurer's request, the account officer at the money center bank responds that there is "no problem." (The treasurer knows from many years of experience in this business that whenever someone says "no problem," there usually is one.) The account officer passes the treasurer on to the dealing desk, where the problems begin. The traders seem to be speaking another language. When the treasurer asks for a price, they respond with: "Ten dollars at big figure 80/90." The account officer provides a translation: ten dollars means $10 million and big figure means the closest pfennig.

It turns out that there are more questions: Does the treasurer want to hedge the DM purchase price in dollars on a monthly basis, weekly basis, yearly average, or what? Will the DM import price vary over the year?

Suppose that, once these questions are fully answered, the conclusion is reached that SSW wants to hedge DM 187,500,000 per month, with the first delivery beginning three months from now. But how does the treasurer implement the hedge? She knows that in each month, commencing in one month she will have to come up with DM 187.5 million. But how?

The banker says that the answer is "obvious" (this is almost as good as "no problem"): SSW will have to enter into a set of twelve forward contracts. The first contract is for one month, the second is for two months, etc., on out to twelve months. Each contract is for the present value of DM 187.5 million. Relieved, the treasurer of SSW instructs the banker to implement the hedge.

It looks finally over. Wrong again. The banker calls back and says that eight-, ten-, and eleven-month forwards are not "standard"; these will be a little more difficult and therefore more expensive to do. Since she has gone this far, the treasurer responds, "OK, do it."

After a week of dealing with this, the treasurer thinks she can return to her job of managing lines of credit and investing excess corporate cash; finally, she can forget about foreign exchange exposure. But the banker calls again: "Sorry, but you have not signed a master foreign exchange forward agreement, so the back office at the bank rejected the forward order you placed yesterday." Too tired and busy to start over, the treasurer says to send out the document, and she will have SSW's lawyers go over it.

It is now January. The lawyers have spent two weeks looking over the document. The treasurer of SSW North America signs it and places the order (adjusting for the time lost during the discussions) for twelve forward contracts.

Yet it is still not quite over. The banker calls back and says that, because of the firm's low credit rating, SSW of North America will have to provide collateral. Getting angry, the treasurer points out that SSW's debt is guaranteed by its AAA-rated German parent. Realizing that SSW is ready to do business elsewhere, the banker backtracks and goes to the credit chain of the bank for a foreign exchange credit line for SSW of North America, noting that it is guaranteed by the parent company in Germany.

The order is placed. The order is executed. SSW is set for the year. The treasurer can see the CEO and report that everything is OK.

In the meantime, 1985 has arrived, the dollar has strengthened even more, and the treasurer looks like a genius for taking so long to put on the hedge, thereby increasing the firm's profit margin. The CEO is happy. But just before the treasurer leaves on vacation, the CEO shows up with a question: "Which way do you think the dollar will go from here? Shouldn't we take profit now?"

Managing Interest Rate Risk

Think once more about the example of a savings and loan firm during the late 1970s, which was first introduced in Chapter 1. Consider the asset-liability structure of a typical 1970's S&L. As illustrated in Figure 5-4, liabilities were short-term deposits that would be frequently repriced—daily, monthly, or semiannually—whereas the S&L's assets were long-term mortgages. The difference between the interest paid on the government-insured, short-term deposit on the liability side and the interest earned on the more lucrative, long-term mortgage on the asset side is the net interest income.

In the mid-1970s, short-term deposit rates were in the neighborhood of 6%, and long-term mortgage rates were in the neighborhood of 10%. Thus, net interest income (NII) on assets of $100 million was $4 million. This "yield curve spread" or "gapping" (owning a long-term asset funded with short-term borrowings) was typical for S&Ls. Indeed, the managers of S&Ls were at one time considered ultimately conservative bankers.

However, when the yield curve started shifting after 1979, the position of the S&Ls changed dramatically. By 1982, long-term rates had risen to the neighborhood of 11%, but short-term average deposit rates had made a dramatic leap to 12%. Let's assume that the S&L stayed at the same size—$100 million—and that one quarter of its mortgage loans had matured and had been replaced with new mortgage loans at the higher rates. Interest earned was

$$10\% \times \$75 \text{ million} + 11\% \times \$25 \text{ million} = \$10.25 \text{ million}$$

Figure 5-4. A Stylized Balance Sheet for a S&L in the Mid-1970s.

Assets	Liabilities
Mortgages	Government-insured deposits
	Equity

However, the S&L was still supported by short-term deposits, so interest paid was

$$12\% \times \$100 \text{ million} = \$12 \text{ million}$$

Hence, NII was *negative* $1.75 million.

As a result of interest rate volatility, NII swung from $4 million to a minus $1.75 million. If an instrument had been available to manage that interest rate risk, it would have certainly helped.[12] For the moment, let us assume that a market in interest rate forward contracts—such as forward rate agreements—had existed.

Suppose that the manager of the S&L decided in 1979 to use a forward rate agreement to hedge interest rate risk. Given the balance sheet in Figure 5-4, he knows he needs to adjust his cash flows so that if short-term rates rise, he will be protected against a rise in his cost of funding. Utilizing the forward market in interest rates, he can neutralize these liabilities costs with respect to future, unanticipated changes in rates.

The risk profile for this S&L is illustrated in Figure 5-5. If interest rates rise, the firm could be forced into bankruptcy. Conversely, if rates fall, the S&L would make more profit. If rates remain as predicted by current forward rates, the corresponding expected profit is considered satisfactory. Consequently, the manager of the S&L decides to hedge, thereby neutralizing the effects of a volatile money market on his portfolio.

How does the S&L manager create this hedge? He needs the hedge to throw off a neutralizing cash flow with the same periodicity as the

---

12. Indeed, an instrument was introduced during this period and was used by many managers: financial futures. This instrument will be discussed in Chapters 6–8.

Figure 5-5. The Risk Profile for the S&L.

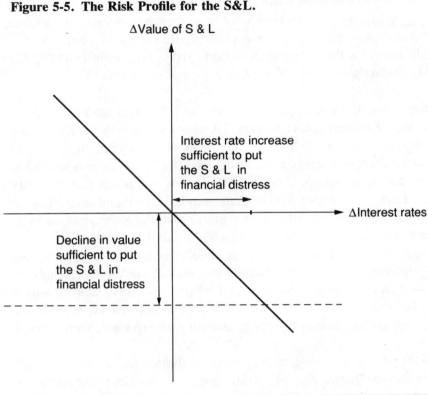

ΔValue of S & L

Interest rate increase
sufficient to put
the S & L in
financial distress

ΔInterest rates

Decline in value
sufficient to put
the S & L in
financial distress

repricing of his liabilities, say, every three months. He must construct a forward position such that if future interest rates are greater than expected, he will receive income; and if they are less, he pays. He must construct the position so that the cash flows are thrown off every three months. Thus, he must construct a *set* of FRAs, with one expiring every three months for the next, say, three years.

As illustrated in Figure 5-6, the FRAs would offset the cash flows on the $100 million short-term deposits. Hence, the notional principal of each FRA would be $100 million. The contract terms of the FRAs would state that if a reference interest rate, say, three-month LIBOR, is above what was expected—the forward interest rate at contract origination—then the S&L would receive the difference in interest rates times the $100 million notional principal. Of course, as with all forwards, the reverse would also hold true.

The only problem with such a hedge is that FRAs, like all forwards, are credit instruments. And twelve of these forward contracts, the longest of which has a maturity of three years, could use up all of this S&L's credit lines. (A three-year FRA is fairly risky, and, even in 1979, this S&L would likely not be a AAA risk.)

Other Uses of FRAs. The main use of FRAs continues to be management of interest rate exposures. For example, an insurance company must keep much of its assets in the form of short-term, highly liquid money market or treasury instruments. But the insurance company often finds that, in doing so, it has mismatched its assets and liabilities. By using FRAs, the institution can continue to hold the liquid assets it needs while moving the interest rate risk further out along the yield curve to better "duration-match" or "gap-match" its liability structure.

Suppose a bank wants to create assets. Instead of simply buying only floating-rate notes or floating-rate bonds to match its floating-rate funding, it might find it useful to have a "synthetically created" floating-rate instrument via a set of FRAs. The point is that the existence of the FRA allows institutions to change interest rate exposures without huge cost.

Also, portfolio managers may wish to shorten the duration of their fixed-income portfolios. FRAs are one tool available for doing so. Indeed, the future may witness an ever-expanding use of FRAs.

Figure 5-6. The Hedged S&L's Risk Profile.

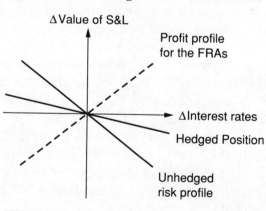

Example

Using FRAs in an insurance company

George Demitri is asset manager for ADS Insurance Company of New York. ADS writes life insurance policies in San Francisco, Los Angeles, and, through its Japanese subsidiary, Tokyo. As with any insurance company, his portfolio is designed to match the duration of expected benefit payments (retirement, death, and so forth). In general, these liabilities—payments—are of long-term duration. His assets are, too, except for one portion of his assets, which is concentrated in money market instruments, including T-bills. The ADS balance sheet is as follows:

	Assets	Liabilities	
	2 billion	100 million	
	19 billion	2 billion	
		18.9 billion	

(left axis label: Increasing maturity)

However, George has a problem. His boss has announced that he needs to see a higher yield on the short-term portfolio. George is told to (1) maintain liquidity and (2) increase yield. George knows that to maintain liquidity he must stay in very liquid, short-dated, low-yielding U.S. treasuries. Liquidating a billion dollars of paper to get cash in an emergency—such as when an earthquake hits San Francisco or Tokyo—is not all that easy if it is tied up in junk bonds, real estate, mortgage-backed securities, or Australian bonds.

George must maintain liquidity but pick up yield. First he notes that the yield curve is upward-sloping, so instruments of longer duration increase his yield. Three-month rates are around 12% and the five year rate is over 14%. If he could invest long-term while maintaining liquidity, he could pick up yield. And he can. He can keep his short-term portfolio in place but use an FRA to "synthetically" construct a longer-term instrument.[13]

George decides to try to "extend the maturity" of $100 million in six-month Euro deposits to three-years. His six-month deposits are yielding 12%. George wants to lock in the premium of the three-year yield relative to the 12% six-month yield. What does he do?

George needs to know the six-month rate in three years. He then must get

---

13. Is this risky for ADS? No. At present, the asset maturities are "too short" (due to the need to maintain liquidity) relative to the liabilities.

banks to bid on an FRA of this duration. The forward interest rate is not readily available on a Reuters screen, but it can be calculated using the spot yield curve for three years. The spot yield curve (Eurodollar) currently is as follows:

	Yield
6-month	12.0
12-month	12.5
18-month	12.75
24-month	13.00
30-month	13.10
36-month	13.25
42-month	14.00

From this yield curve, George calculates the six-month rate in thirty-six months, $_{36}R_{42}$:

$$(1 +_0 R_{36})^3 (1 +_{36} R_{42})^{1/2} = (1 +_0 R_{42})^{3.5}$$

$$(1.1325)^3 (1 +_{36} R_{42})^{1/2} = (1.14)^{3.5}$$

$$(1 +_{36} R_{42})^{1/2} = \frac{1.5819}{1.4525} = 1.0891$$

$$_{36}R_{42} = (1.0891)^2 - 1 = 18.61\%$$

George then called his bankers and had them bid on the deal. George knew that a thirty-six-month vs. forty-two-month FRA was nonstandard, so he expected to pay something for the FRA. Indeed, he will likely have to give up 5 to 10 basis points to do the deal.

George locked in the premium implied in the yield curve for the six-month instrument he owns in three years. His yield is secure for that three month period. But what about the other four repricings?

George needs an FRA for each of those six-month Euros—a strip of FRAs, one for each rollover date:

$$6 \text{ mo. vs. } 12 \text{ mo.}$$
$$12 \text{ mo. vs. } 18 \text{ mo.}$$
$$18 \text{ mo. vs. } 24 \text{ mo.}$$
$$24 \text{ mo. vs. } 30 \text{ mo.}$$
$$36 \text{ mo. vs. } 42 \text{ mo.}$$

Hence, George must now calculate the implied forward rate for each period, package it, and convince the bankers to bid on the "strip" of FRAs.[14] This will

---

14. George, like you, is probably wondering if there is another contract that will accomplish the same trick for him—something that will look like a "strip" of FRAs but will not entail signing so many contracts. The answer is swaps, an instrument we will discuss in Chapters 9–12.

guarantee a cash flow to him at the rollover dates as long as six-month LIBOR is below the agreed FRA rate. If rates are higher, George is OK because he has picked up a higher yield upon rollover.

Forward contracts can be used for synthetic asset creation, as in the previous example. The synthetic position can offer interesting risk characteristics. The following example, combining a forward, a bond, and short-term dollar funding, shows how forwards can be used to implement portfolio strategies.

Example

Long Pesetas, Short DM, and Long Bonds[15]

Spain as a Member of Europe

Spain joined the European Economic Community (EEC) in 1986, having established itself as a dynamic growing economy capable of competing within the rules of the common market.[16] To secure its position within the EEC, in 1986 Spain undertook a program of both liberalizing its capital markets in anticipation of future reforms and controlling the economy to achieve the stability necessary to join the European Monetary System (EMS).[17]

Spain's membership in the EMS requires: (1) a stable inflation rate in line with the EMS average and (2) a stable DM/Pta (deutsche mark/peseta) exchange rate.

The Exchange Rate. Traditional weakness and instability of the DM/Pta exchange rate (see Figure 5-7) required correction as the Bank of Spain sought to establish Spain's credentials for entry into the EMS. The authorities recognized that the peseta must behave like an EMS currency.

Since early 1987, foreign exchange reserves at the Bank of Spain had been increasing at a rate of $0.5–$1.0 billion a month as the bank bought foreign exchange, especially dollars (see Figure 5-8), to stabilize the peseta. This intervention had been deemed necessary for Spain to avoid the potentially negative impact of short-term capital inflows.

Stabilizing the peseta against the EEC currencies was a high priority of the authorities in anticipation of EMS membership. To be successful in the long run, however, this requires getting control over inflation.

---

15. This example is an actual strategy created during 1987 by Sykes Wilford for Drexel Burnham Lambert.

16. The EEC's goal is to achieve, by 1992, a single European market with unrestricted flows of capital and goods.

17. The EMS (European Monetary System) is a semifixed-exchange-rate system that includes the currencies of Belgium, Germany, France, the Netherlands, Denmark, and Ireland.

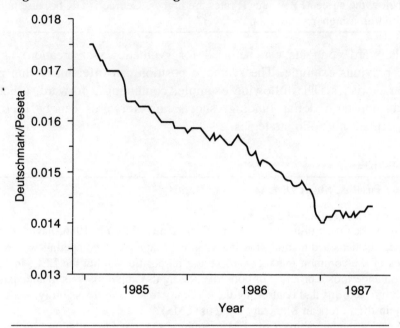

Figure 5-7. DM/Pta Exchange Rate: 1985 to Mid-1987.

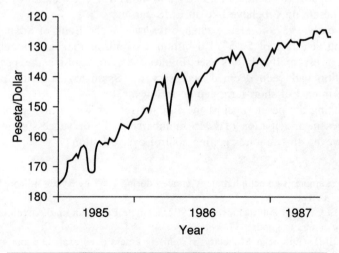

Figure 5-8. $/Pta Exchange Rate: 1985 to Mid-1987.

Inflation. In the first half of 1987, Spanish inflation fell to 6.2% from 8.8% in 1986. However, this was still twice the EMS average of 3%. Figure 5-9 illustrates that the inflation differential was still too large, particularly compared with that between Germany and other EMS members.

To control inflation, the Bank of Spain sought to control the growth in the money supply. This occurred within an environment characterized by: (1) a large fiscal deficit (5.2% of GDP in 1986, compared with 5.3% in the United States) and (2) in the face of a rising peseta, intervention in the foreign exchange markets to sell pesetas. Both of these factors led to upward pressures on money growth (see Figure 5-10).

A Window of Inconsistent Policies

The attempt to control both money supply and exchange rates has created a vicious circle, which may be characterized as follows:

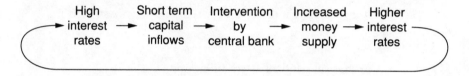

Figure 5-9. Inflation Rates in the EMS and Spain: 1985 to Mid-1987.

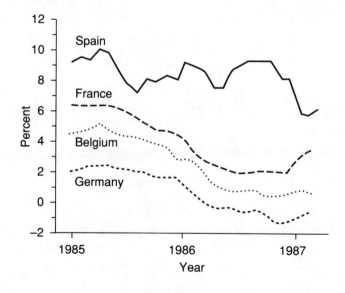

The policies of the central bank revolved around subduing inflation to gain the credibility necessary to join the EMS. Thus, high interest rates were likely to win out over exchange rate targets. However, the inverted yield curve suggested that inflation expectations and short-term rates were in conflict; inflation was too low (and was likely to fall further) to sustain the rate levels.

The Strategy
1. Take advantage of high interest rates.
2. Use Spanish bonds as a vehicle to capture capital gains.
3. Fund in deutsche marks because of low borrowing costs.
4. Synthetically create the deutsche marks funding via a forward

Today:
1. Buy pesetas at spot rate.
2. Buy with the pesetas a peseta bond.
3. Sell DM forward against the dollar for settlement in six months.

In six months:
1. Sell the peseta bond.
2. Convert pesetas into dollars at prevailing spot.

Figure 5-10. Growth in Three-Month MIBOR.

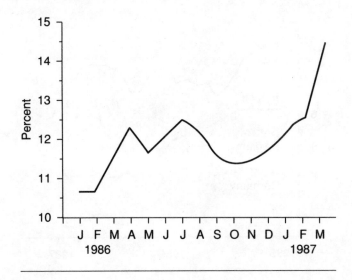

3. Receive dollars at the forward rate to settle the forward.
4. Convert sufficient dollars at the spot to settle the DM forward.

Assets	Liabilities	
13.5% Peseta bond	Dollars⎫ DM/$ ⎭	4% DM borrowing

Thus, the interest differential is 9.5%. But there are two risks:

1. Interest rates in Spain may change.
2. The Pta/DM exchange rate may change.

In this example, had the risk factors remained the same, the investor would have earned a spread of 9.5% per year on the investment. If the peseta declined (rose) against DM, he would have lost (gained) money depending on the percentage of the change in the Pta/DM rate from spot. If bond rates rose, he would have lost on the value of the bonds, and vice versa if it fell.

Many investors felt comfortable with those risks. What happened? Interest rates in Spain fell, and the peseta strengthened against the DM. The investor made a yield several times higher than 9.5%.

Was the forward contract critical for the investor? If the investor had access to German mark borrowings or was based in DM, it was not. However, for Drexel's American clients, the forward was the easiest way to synthetically create the DM borrowing.

Did the forward increase or decrease risk for the American investor? In this example, it was risk-reducing. The Pta/DM exchange rate was much more stable than the Pta/$ exchange rate, given the stated government policy to position the peseta to join the EMS.

Forward contracts can and are used by portfolio managers to create the positions they want. One final example further illustrates this point.

Example

Deutsche marks, pounds, dollars and yield curves

Jim Davis, a portfolio manager, decided to go short dollars and long the mark. But he also liked longer-term instruments, since he was expecting long rates to fall globally. In early 1988 he saw his opportunity.

- He was dollars-based.
- He wanted to be long DM bonds.
- He wanted to pick up yield over the DM bond and have sterling/dollar FX risk.

When Margaret Thatcher and Nigel Lawson had a public row over monetary policy and the lid on the DM/£ exchange rate came off, Jim moved quickly by calling Diane, a leading trader at a major U.S. dealer in London:

Jim: I want to get long against the DM, but I don't want gilt risk (gilts are U.K. government sterling-denominated bonds).

Diane: Fine. How about the following strategy:

1. Buy DM spot with dollars.

2. Purchase a DM bond, ten years, yielding 6.04% per year.

3. Do a one-year sterling forward against DM, picking up the premium of another 6%.

4. We run it two months and unwind.

You make money if spot DM strengthens against dollars, if spot sterling strengthens against dollars, or if DM bond interest rates fall. And you have a "yield curve arbitrage tool."

Jim: What do you mean by "yield curve arbitrage tool"?

Diane: Look at the relative shapes of the yield curves. The sterling yield curve is flat out to ten years, with ten-year gilts at about 10% (one-year was also about 10%), while ten-year DM bonds are at 6% and the one-year rate is 3.5.

Jim: Maybe I should change my mind about the sterling risk and just buy gilts.

Diane: No way! Gilt rates are three times as volatile as DM bond rates; besides, over the carry period you pick up yield over the gilt rate through the differently shaped yield curve.

Jim: Sketch me the position and fax it over.

Diane's Fax arrives:

	Assets		**Liabilities**	
			Dollars	7.0%
6.5%	+£ −DM	1 year		
6.0%	DM bonds			

Jim: Diane? Good. Do it for the equivalent of $25 million.

Diane: OK; let's confirm:

1. *Buy £ one year forward against DM.*

2. *Convert U.S. $ spot to DM.*

3. *Buy DM Bonds.*

Jim: Right. Do it.

Diane: Fine. Your rates are...

Epilogue. Jim did well. DM/£ went from 3.00 to 3.17. The dollar declined, with little change in DM bonds. Jim unwound on Diane's advice and was promoted.

Forwards allow creativity. Using them to manage all types of risk, to take new risks, or to adjust old risks is commonplace today. The creation of even more liquid foreign exchange markets, in various currencies, is allowing even more interesting investment strategies to be created, unavoidable business risks to be managed, and mismatched structures to be matched synthetically. The preceding illustrations are just a few examples of how forwards can be creatively packaged to service the needs of the financial, corporate, and governmental communities.

PART III

Futures

6

The Futures Contract

A futures contract is a legally binding commitment to make or take delivery of a given quantity of a given asset/commodity at a given time in the future.[1] The price paid to take delivery or received to make delivery is determined by the price at which that specific futures contract trades. Futures contracts are traded on organized exchanges, the oldest of which is the Chicago Board of Trade.[2] The mechanism of futures trading is "open outcry"; that is, buyers and sellers announce their intentions in an open trading "pit."[3] Trading in futures contracts in the United States is regulated by the Commodity Futures Trading Commission (CFTC).

The range of available futures markets and contracts is extremely wide. As illustrated in Table 6-1, futures contracts are actively traded on twenty-nine exchanges in twelve countries.[4]

For assistance in developing this section, we wish to acknowledge particularly the assistance provided by Ira G. Kawaller, Director, Chicago Mercantile Exchange.

1. As Ira Kawaller of the Chicago Mercantile Exchange pointed out, this definition is well suited for futures on commodities or assets where physical delivery is possible, but it is less suitable for futures contracts that are cash-settled such as stock index futures or of Eurodollar futures. He proposed an alternative definition of a futures contract as a price-fixing mechanism involving a margining system.

2. The Chicago Board of Trade is the oldest operating futures exchange, opened in 1842. However, as noted in Chapter 1, futures contracts were traded much earlier—as early as the seventeenth century, in Japan.

3. This "open outcry" auction stands in marked contrast to the specialist system for trading equities.

4. Our data on futures exchanges and contracts is taken from "The World's Futures and Options Contracts," a guide that appeared in *Global Investor* (March 1988). This article omitted the Brazilian commodity exchanges and the Japanese commodity exchanges, where forward contracts are traded on commodities such as red beans, potato starch, and silk cocoons. Although the contracts traded on the London Metal Exchange are more like forward contracts than like the futures contracts described in Chapters 6–8, they were included.

Table 6-1. Futures Exchanges

North America	Europe	Far East and Australasia
United States	*United Kingdom*	*Hong Kong*
Chicago Board of Trade	Baltic Futures Exchange	Hong Kong Futures Exchange
Chicago Mercantile Exchange	International Petroleum Exchange	*Australia*
Coffee, Sugar & Cocoa Exchange	London Futures and Options Exchange	Sydney Futures Exchange
Kansas City Board of Trade	London International Financial	*Japan*
MidAmerica Commodity Exchange*	Futures Exchange	Tokyo Stock Exchange
Minneapolis Grain Exchange	London Metal Exchange	*Malaysia*
New York Commodity Exchange	*France*	Kuala Lumpur Commodities
(Comex)	Compagnie de Commissionnaires	Exchange
New York Cotton Exchange	Agrées	*New Zealand*
New York Futures Exchange	Lille Potato Market	New Zealand Futures Exchange
Philadelphia Stock Exchange	MATIF	*Phillipines*
	Netherlands	Manila International Financial
Canada	Amsterdam Pork and Potato Exchange	Futures Exchange
Toronto Futures Exchange		*Singapore*
Winnipeg Commodity Exchange		Singapore International Monetary
		Exchange

*Merged with Chicago Board of Trade

Source: *Global Investor*, a *Euromoney* publication, March 1988. Used with permission.

In addition to the agricultural commodities for which the futures markets are best known—corn, oats, soybeans, pork bellies, etc.— futures contracts are traded on precious metals:

Gold
Silver
Platinum

and on industrial commodities:

Aluminum	Copper
Lead	Nickel
Heating oil	Propane
Gasoline	Crude oil

Of primary concern here, futures contracts are also traded on a number of financial assets, including foreign exchange:

Swiss francs	Australian dollars
Deustche marks	Canadian dollars
British pounds	Japanese yen
French francs	ECU

interest-bearing securities:

T-bills	T-notes and bonds
Gilts	Bank bills
Eurodollar deposits	GNMA securities
Muni bond index	Corporate bonds

and stock indexes:

Standard & Poor's 500 index	Value Line index
Major Market index	Institutional Index
NYSE Composite index	Russell indices
National OTC index	Toronto Stock Exchange index
Financial Times index	Hang Seng index
All-Ordinaries index	Barclays index
Nikkei index	

Table 6-2 details the individual futures contracts currently traded, showing the exchange on which the contract is traded, the size of the contract, the tick size (i.e., the minimum price movement recognized under the rules of the contract), expiration months for the contract, the

Table 6-2. Exchange-Traded Futures Contracts.*

United States

Chicago Board of Trade

Commodity	Size	Tick Size	Months	Hours	Delivery
Corn	5,000 bu	$12.50	Mar May Jul Sep Dec	9.30–13.15	Physical
Oats	5,000 bu	$12.50	Mar May Jul Sep Dec	9.30–13.15	Physical
Soyabeans	5,000 bu	$12.50	Jan Mar May Jul Aug Sep Nov	9.30–13.15	Physical
Soyabean Oil	60,000 lbs	$6.00	Jan Mar May Jul Aug Sep Oct Dec	9.30–13.15	Physical
Soyabean Meal	100 tons	$10.00	Jan Mar May Jul Aug Sept Oct Dec	9.30–13.15	Physical
Wheat	5,000 bu	$12.25	Jul Sep Dec Mar May	9.30–13.15	Physical
Gold	1 kilo	$3.22	Nearest 3 months	7.20–13.40	Physical
Gold	100 troz	$10.00	Nearest 3 months	7.20–13.40 and (Sun–Thur only) 17.00–20.30	Physical

118

Silver	1,000 troz	$1.00	Nearest 3 months	7.25–13.25	Physical
Silver	5,000 troz	$5.00	Nearest 3 months and Feb Apr Jun Aug Oct Dec	7.25–13.25	Physical
Major Market stock index	$250 × index	$12.50	Monthly	8.15–15.15	Cash
Institutional index	$500 × index	$25.00	Monthly	8.15–15.15	Cash
U.S. T-notes	$100,000	$31.25	Mar Jun Sep Dec	8.00–14.00 and (Sun–Thur only) 17.00–00.30	Physical
U.S. T-bonds	$100,000	$31.25	Mar Jun Sep Dec	8.00–14.00 and (Sun–Thur only) 17.00–00.30	Physical
Muni bond index	$1,000 × index	$31.25	Mar Jun Sep Dec	8.00–14.00	Cash
GNMA(CDR)	$100,000	$10.00	Mar Jun Sep Dec	8.00–14.00	Physical
GNMA(cash)	$100,000	$31.25	Mar Jun Sep Dec	8.00–14.00	Cash
Corporate bonds	$500 × index	$31.25	Mar Jun Sep Dec	8.00–14.00	Cash

*This table is adapted from tables that appeared in *Global Investor*, a *Euromoney* publication, March 1988. Used with permission.

Table 6-2. (Continued)

Chicago Mercantile Exchange

Commodity	Size	Tick Size	Months	Hours	Delivery
Feeder Cattle	44,000 lb	$11.00	Jan Mar Apr May Aug Sep Oct Nov	9.05–1.00	Cash
Live Cattle	40,000 lb	$10.00	Feb & alt months	9.05–1.00	Physical
Live Hogs	30,000 lb	$7.50	Feb Apr Jun Jul Aug Oct Dec	9.10–1.00	Physical
Pork Bellies	40,000 lb	$10.00	Feb Mar May Jul Aug	9.10–1.00	Physical
Random lumber	130,000 ft	$13.00	Jan & alt months	9.00–1.05	Physical
Gold (N.Y.)	100 troz	$10.00	Jan Mar May Jul Sep Dec	7.20–14.00	Physical
S&P 500 stock index	$500 × index	$25.00	Mar Jun Sep Dec	8.30–15.15	Cash
Eurodollars*	$1,000,000	$25.00	Nearest 1 and Mar Jun Sep Dec	7.20–14.00	Cash
U.S. T-bills	$1,000,000	$25.00	Mar Jun Sep Dec	7.20–13.00	Physical
Swiss Francs	Sfr125,000	$12.50	Nearest 1 and Jan Mar Apr Jun Jul Sep Oct Dec	7.20–13.16	Physical

Australian Dollars	A$100,000	$10.00	Nearest 1 and Jan Mar Apr Jun Jul Sep Oct Dec	7.20–13.18	Physical
Deutsche marks*	DM125,000	$12.50	Nearest 1 and Jan Mar Apr Jun Jul Sep Oct Dec	7.20–13.26	Physical
Canadian dollars	C$100,000	$10.00	Nearest 1 and Jan Mar Apr Jun Jul Sep Oct Dec	7.20–13.26	Physical
British pounds*	£25,000	$12.50	Nearest 1 and Jan Mar Apr Jun Jul Sep Oct Dec	7.20–13.24	Physical
Japanese yen*	¥12,500,00	$12.50	Nearest 1 and Jan Mar Apr Jun Jul Sep Oct Dec	7.20–13.22	Physical
French francs	Ffr250,000	$12.50	Nearest 1 and Jan Mar Apr Jun Jul Sep Oct Dec	7.20–13.28	Physical
Ecu	Ecu25.00	$12.50	Mar Jun Sep Dec	7.10–13.30	Physical

*The CME Eurodollar, British pound, Deutsche mark and Japanese yen contracts are listed on a mutual offset link with Simex in Singapore.

Table 6-2. (Continued)

Coffee, Sugar & Cocoa Exchange

Commodity	Size	Tick Size	Months	Hours	Delivery
Coffee C	37,500 lbs	$3.75	Mar May Jul Sep Dec	9.45–14.28	Physical
No. 11 Sugar	50 tons	$11.20	Jan Mar May Jul Sep Oct	10.00–13.43	Physical
No. 14 Sugar	50 tons	$11.20	Jan Mar May Jul Sep Nov	10.00–13.45	Physical
Sugar (white)	50 tons	$10.00	Jan Mar May Jul Oct	9.45–13.43	Physical
CPI-W inflation	$1,000 index	$10.00	Jan Apr Jul Oct	9.30–14.30	Cash

Kansas City Board of Trade

Commodity	Size	Tick Size	Months	Hours	Delivery
No. 2 red wheat	5,000 bu	$12.50	Mar May Jul Sep Dec	9.30–13.15	Physical
Value Line stock index	$500 × index	$25.00	Mar Jun Sep Dec	8.30–15.15	Cash
Mini Value Line	$100 × index	$5.00	Mar Jun Sep Dec	8.30–15.15	Cash

122

MidAmerica Commodity Exchange

Corn	1,000 bu	$1.25	Mar May Jul Sep Dec	9.30–13.30	Physical
Oats	1,000 bu	$1.25	Mar May Jul Sep Dec	9.30–13.30	Physical
Soyabeans	1,000 bu	$1.25	Jan Mar May Jul Aug Sep Nov	9.30–13.30	Physical
Soyabean Meal	20 tons	$2.00	Jan Mar May Jul Aug Sep Oct Dec	9.30–13.30	Cash
Wheat	1,000 bu	$1.25	Mar May Jul Sep Dec	9.30–13.30	Physical
CRCE cotton*	50,000 lbs	$5.00	Mar May Jul Oct Dec	9.30–14.00	Physical
CRCE rice*	2,000 cwt	$10.00	Jan Mar May Sep Nov	9.15–13.30	Physical
Cattle	20,000 lbs	$5.00	7 consecutive	9.05–13.15	Physical
Hogs	15,000 lbs	$3.75	Feb Apr Jun Jul Aug Oct Dec	9.10–13.15	Physical
Copper	55,000 lbs	$27.50	Current 3 and Jan Mar May Jul Sep Dec	7.50–13.30	Physical
Gold	33.2 troz	$3.32	7 consecutive	7.20–13.40	Physical

*The Chicago Rice and Cotton Exchange is an affiliate of the MidAmerica Commodity Exchange. Only the rice contract is currently trading.

Table 6-2. (Continued)

MidAmerica Commodity Exchange (Continued)

Commodity	Size	Tick Size	Months	Hours	Delivery
Platinum	25 troz	$2.50	Current 3 and Jan Apr Jul Oct	7.20–13.40	Physical
Silver	1,000 troz	$1.00	15 consecutive	7.25–13.40	Physical
U.S. T-bonds	$50,000	$15.62	Mar Jun Sep Dec	7.30–15.15	Physical
U.S. T-bills	$500,000	$12.50	Mar Jun Sep Dec	7.20–14.15	Cash
British pounds	£12,500	$6.25	Mar Jun Sep Dec	7.20–13.34	Physical
Deutsche mark	DM62,500	$6.25	Mar Jun Sep Dec	7.20–13.30	Physical
Japanese yen	Y6,250,000	$6.25	Mar Jun Sep Dec	7.20–13.32	Physical
Swiss francs	Sfr62,500	$6.25	Mar Jun Sep Dec	7.20–13.26	Physical
Canadian dollars	C$50,000	$5.00	Mar Jun Sep Dec	7.20–13.26	Physical

Minneapolis Grain Exchange

Commodity	Size	Tick Size	Months	Hours	Delivery
Hard red spring wheat	5,000 bu	$6.25	Mar May Jul Sep Dec	9.30–13.15	Physical

Comex

Commodity	Size	Tick Size	Months	Hours	Delivery
Aluminum	40,000 lbs	$2.00	Nearest 3 and Jan Mar May Jul Sep Dec	9.30–14.10	Physical

	Contract size	Tick	Contract months	Hours	Settlement
Copper	25,000 lbs	$12.50	Nearest 3 and Jan Mar May Jul Sep Dec	9.25–14.00	Physical
Gold*	100 troz	$10.00	Nearest 3 and Feb Apr Jun Aug Oct Dec, up to 23 months out	8.20–14.30	Physical
Silver	5,000 troz	$5.00	Nearest 3 and Jan Mar May Jul Sep Dec	8.25–14.25	Physical
Corporate bond index	$500 × index		Mar Jun Sep Dec	9.00–15.00	Cash
New York Cotton Exchange					
U.S. Dollar index	$500 × index	$5.00	Mar Jun Sep Dec	8.20–14.40	Cash
Ecu	Ecu100,000	$10.00	Mar Jun Sep Dec	8.20–14.40	Physical
U.S. T-notes	$100,000	$15.625	Mar Jun Sep Dec	8.20–15.00	Physical
Cotton	50,000 lbs	$5.00	Mar May Jul Oct Dec	10.30–15.00	Physical
Orange juice	15,000 lbs	$7.50	Jan Mar May Jul Sep Nov	10.15–14.45	Physical

*The Comex gold contract is listed on a mutual offset link with the Sydney Futures Exchange.

Table 6-2. (Continued)

New York Futures Exchange

Commodity	Size	Tick Size	Months	Hours	Delivery
NYSE Composite stock index	$500 × index	$25.00	Mar Jun Sep Dec	9.30–16.15	Cash
Russell 3000 stock index	$500 × index	$25.00	Mar Jun Sep Dec	9.15–16.10	Cash
Russell 2000 stock index	$500 × index	$25.00	Mar Jun Sep Dec	9.15–16.10	Cash
CRB commodity price index	$500 × index	$25.00	Mar May Jul Sep Dec	9.00–15.30	Cash

New York Mercantile Exchange

Commodity	Size	Tick Size	Months	Hours	Delivery
No. 2 Heating oil	42,000 gals	$4.20	Nearest 15 months	9.50–15.05	Physical
Propane	42,000 gals	$4.20	Nearest 15 months	9.40–15.05	Physical
Unleaded gasoline	42,000 gals	$4.20	Nearest 15 months	9.50–15.05	Physical
WTI Crude oil	1,000 bbl	$10.00	Nearest 18 months	9.45–15.10	Physical
Platinum	50 troz	$5.00	Jan Apr Jul Oct	8.20–14.20	Physical
Palladium	100 troz	$5.00	Jan Apr Jul Oct	8.10–14.20	Physical

Philadelphia Stock Exchange

Australian dollars	A$100,000	$10.00	Mar Jun Sep Dec	8.00–14.30 and (Sun–Thur only) 19.00–23.00	Physical
British pounds	£25,000	$12.50	Mar Jun Sep Dec	8.00–14.30	Physical
Canadian dollars	C$100,000	$10.00	Mar Jun Sep Dec	8.00–14.30	Physical
Deutsche marks	DM125,000	$12.50	Mar Jun Sep Dec	8.00–14.30 and (Sun–Thur only) 19.00–23.00	Physical
French francs	Ffr250,000	$12.50	Mar Jun Sep Dec	8.00–14.30	Physical
Japanese yen	¥12.5 bn	$12.50	Mar Jun Sep Dec	8.00–14.30 and (Sun–Thur only) 19.00–23.00	Physical
Swiss francs	Sfr125,000	$12.50	Mar Jun Sep Dec	8.00–14.30	Physical
Ecu	Ecu125,000	$12.50	Mar Jun Sep Dec	8.00–14.30	Physical
National OTC stock index	$500 × index	$25.00	Nearest 2 and Mar Jun Sep	9.30–16.15	Cash

Table 6-2. (Continued)

Canada

Toronto Futures Exchange

Commodity	Size	Tick Size	Months	Hours	Delivery
Canadian T-bills	C$1,000,000	C$24.00	Nearest 4 and Mar Jun Sep Dec	9.00–15.15	Physical
Canadian T-bonds	C$100,000	C$31.25	Mar Jun Sep Dec	9.00–15.15	Physical
TSE 35 stock index	C$500 × index	C$10.00	Nearest 3 months	9.15–16.15	Cash

Winnipeg Commodity Exchange

Commodity	Size	Tick Size	Months	Hours	Delivery
Barley (Alberta)	20 tonnes	C$2.00	Sep Nov Feb Apr Jun	9.30–13.15	Physical
Barley (domestic)	20 tonnes	C$2.00	Oct Dec Mar May Jul	9.30–13.15	Physical
Flaxseed	20 tonnes	C$2.00	Oct Dec Mar May Jul	9.30-13.15	Physical
Oats (domestic)	20 tonnes	C$2.00	Oct Dec Mar May Jul	9.30–13.15	Physical
Rapeseed/canola	20 tonnes	C$2.00	Sep Nov Jan Mar Jun	9.30–13.15	Physical

Rye	20 tonnes	C$2.00	Oct Dec Mar May Jul	9.30–13.15	Physical
Wheat (domestic)	20 tonnes	C$2.00	Oct Dec Mar May Jul	9.30–13.15	Physical
Gold	20 troz	US$2.00	Mar Jun Sep Dec	10.00–13.25	Physical
Silver	200 troz	US$2.00	Jan Apr Jul Oct	10.00–13.25	Physical

United Kingdom

Baltic Futures Exchange

Barley	100 tonnes	£5.00	Jan Mar May Sep Nov	11.00–12.30 and 14.45–16.00	Physical
Sea-freight index	$10.00 × index	$5.00	Jan Apr Jul Oct	10.15–12.30 and 14.30–16.15	Cash
Live cattle	5,000 kg	£5.00	Jan Feb Apr Jun Aug Oct Nov	10.00–12.00 and 14.15–15.45	Cash
Pigs	3,250 kg	£3.25	Feb Apr Jun Aug Oct Nov	10.00–12.00 and 14.15–15.45	Cash

Table 6-2. (Continued)

			Baltic Futures Exchange (Continued)		
Commodity	Size	Tick Size	Months	Hours	Delivery
Potatoes (main)	40 tonnes	£4.00	Feb Apr May Nov	11.00–12.30 and 14.45–16.00	Physical
Potatoes (cash)	40 tonnes	£4.00	Mar Jul Aug Sep	11.00–12.30 and 14.45–16.00	Cash
Soyabean meal	20 tonnes	£2.00	Feb Apr Jun Aug Oct Dec	10.30–12.30 and 14.45–16.45	Physical
Wheat	100 tonnes	£5.50	Jan Mar May Jul Sep Nov	11.00–12.30 and 14.45–16.00	Physical
			International Petroleum Exchange		
Gasoil	100 tonnes	$25.00	Current and 9 consecutive	9.15–12.15 and 14.30–17.15	Physical
Heavy fuel oil	100 tonnes	$25.00	Current and 9 consecutive	9.30–12.10 and 14.40–17.05	Physical
Leaded gasoline	100 tonnes	$25.00	Current and 9 consecutive	9.40–12.05 and 14.40–16.35	Physical

London Futures and Options Exchange

Robusta coffee	5 tonnes	£5.00	Jan Mar May Jul Sep Nov	9.45–12.32 and 14.30–17.02	Physical
No. 6 Cocoa	10 tonnes	£1.00	Mar May Jul Sep Dec	10.00–12.58 and 14.30–16.45	Physical
No. 5 Sugar	50 tonnes	$5.00	Mar May Aug Oct Dec	9.45–19.10	Physical
No. 6 Sugar (fob)	50 tonnes	$10.00	Mar May Aug Oct Dec	10.30–12.30 and 14.30–19.00	Physical

London International Financial Futures Exchange

FTSE 100 index	£25 × index	£12.50	Mar Jun Sep Dec	9.05–16.05	Cash
Eurodollars	$1,000,000	$25.00	Mar Jun Sep Dec	8.30–16.00	Cash
3-month Sterling	£500,000	£12.50	Mar Jun Sep Dec	8.20–16.02	Cash
Short gilt	£100,000	£15.625	Mar Jun Sep Dec	9.05–16.20	Physical
Medium gilt	£50,000	£15.625	Mar Jun Sep Dec	8.55–16.10	Physical
Long gilt	£50,000	£15.625	Mar Jun Sep Dec	9.00–16.15	Physical
US T-bonds	$100,000	$31.25	Mar Jun Sep Dec	8.15–16.10	Physical
Japanese T-bonds	¥100 m	¥10,000	Mar Jun Sep Dec	8.10–16.05	Cash

Table 6-2. (Continued)

London International Financial Futures Exchange (Continued)

Commodity	Size	Tick Size	Months	Hours	Delivery
British pounds	£25,000	$12.50	Nearest 3 and Mar Jun Sep Dec	8.32–16.02	Physical
Deutsche mark	DM125,000	$12.50	Mar Jun Sep Dec	8.34–16.04	Physical
$/Deutsche marks	$50,000	DM5.00	Nearest 3 and Mar Jun Sep Dec	8.34–16.04	Physical
Japanese Yen	¥12.5 m	$12.50	Mar Jun Sep Dec	8.30–16.00	Physical
Swiss francs	Sfr125,000	$12.50	Mar Jun Sep Dec	8.36–16.06	Physical
London Metal Exchange					
Aluminum 99.5%	25 tonnes	£0.50	Daily to 3 months, then monthly to 12 months	11.50–11.55 12.50–12.55 15.35–15.40 16.15–16.20	Physical
Aluminium high-grade 99.7%	25 tonnes	$1.00	Daily to 3 months, then monthly to 12 months	11.55–12.00 15.40–15.45 12.55–13.00 16.20–16.25	Physical
Lead	25 tonnes	£0.25	Daily to 3 months, then monthly to 12 months	12.05–12.10 12.40–12.45 15.20–15.25 16.00–16.05	Physical

Commodity	Lot size	Tick	Delivery	Prices	Trading
Copper grade A	25 tonnes	£0.50	Daily to 3 months, then monthly to 12 months	12.00–12.05 12.30–12.35 15.30–15.35 16.10–16.15	Physical
Copper standard	25 tonnes	£0.50	Daily to 3 months, then monthly to 12 months	12.00–12.05 12.35–12.40 15.30–15.35 16.10–16.15	Physical
Nickel	6 tonnes	$1.00	Daily to 3 months, then monthly to 12 months	12.15–12.20 13.00–13.05 15.45–15.50 16.25–16.30	Physical
Silver	10,000 troz	£0.001	Daily to 3 months, then monthly to 12 months	11.45–11.50 13.05–13.10 15.50–15.55 16.30–16.35	Physical
Silver	2,000 troz	$0.001	Daily to 3 months, then monthly to 12 months	11.45–11.50 13.05–13.10 15.50–15.55 16.30–16.35	Physical
Zinc	25 tonnes	£0.25	Daily to 3 months, then monthly to 12 months	12.10–12.15 12.45–12.50 15.25–15.35 16.05–16.10	Physical

Table 6-2. (Continued)

France

Compagnie des Commissionaires Agrées

Commodity	Size	Tick Size	Months	Hours	Delivery
Cocoa beans	10 tonnes	Ffr50	Mar May Jul Sep	10.30–13.00 and 15.00–18.30	Physical
Robusta coffee	5 tonnes	Ffr50	Jan Mar May Jul Sep Dec	10.15–13.00 and 15.00–19.00	Physical
No. 2 Sugar	50 tonnes	Ffr50	Mar May Aug Oct Dec	10.45–13.00 and 15.00–19.00	Physical

Lille Potato Futures Market

Commodity	Size	Tick Size	Months	Hours	Delivery
Potatoes	20 tonnes	Ffr5.00	Nov Feb Apr May	11.00–12.45 and 15.00–16.30	Physical

Marché à Terme des Instruments Financiers (MATIF)

French T-bonds*	Ffr500,000	Ffr250	Jun Sep Dec Mar	10.00–15.00	Physical
French T-bills	Ffr 5 millions	Ffr125	Jun Sep Dec Mar	10.00–15.00	Physical

Netherlands

Amsterdam Pork and Potato Exchange

Pork	10,000 kg	Dfl 0.05	12 forward	10.30–11.30 and 13.30–16.15	Physical
Potatoes	15,000 kg	Dfl 0.01	Feb Mar Apr Nov	10.45–12.45 and 14.00–16.00	Physical

*An identical contract to the MATIF T-bond future is also traded on an over-the-counter basis outside exchange hours and is cleared and guaranteed by the clearing house.

135

Table 6-2. (Continued)

Hong Kong

Hong Kong Futures Exchange

Commodity	Size	Tick Size	Months	Hours	Delivery
Gold	100 troz	HK$10.00	Nearest 3 months	9.00–12.00 and 14.30–17.30	Physical
Soyabeans	30,000 kg	HK$1.00	Monthly	9.50–10.50 and 12.50–14.50	Physical
Sugar	112,000 lbs	$11.20	Jan Mar May Jul Sep Oct	10.30–12.00 and 14.25–16.00	Physical
Hang Seng stock index	HK$50 × index	HK$50	Nearest 3 months	10.00–12.30 and 14.30–15.30	Cash

Australia

Sydney Futures Exchange

Commodity	Size	Tick Size	Months	Hours	Delivery
Gold*	100 troz	$5.00	Nearest 3 and Feb Apr Jun Aug Oct Dec up to 23 months out	9.00–16.00	Physical

Wool	2,500 kgs	A$25.00	Feb Apr Jun Aug Oct Dec	10.30–12.30 and 14.00–16.00	Cash
Live Cattle	10,000 kg	A$10.00	Nearest 12 months	10.30–12.30 and 14.00–16.00	Physical
All-Ordinaries stock index	A$100 × index	A$10.00	Mar Jun Sep Dec	9.30–12.30 and 14.00–15.45	Cash
90-day bank bills	A$500,000	A$11.00	Nearest 6 and Mar Jun Sep Dec up to 2 years out	9.00–12.30 and 14.00–16.30	Physical
Eurodollars*	$1,000,000	$25.00	Mar Jun Sep Dec	6.00–18.00	Cash
Commonwealth T-bonds	A$100,000	A$30.00	Mar Jun Sep Dec	9.05–12.30 and 14.00–16.30	Cash
U.S. T-bonds*	$100,000	$31.25	Mar Jun Sep Dec	6.00–18.00	Physical

*The SFE gold contract is listed on a mutual offset link with Comex in New York, and the Eurodollar and U.S. T-bond contracts are fungible with Litte in London.

Table 6-2. (Continued)

Japan

Tokyo Stock Exchange

Commodity	Size	Tick Size	Months	Hours	Delivery
10-yr Japanese bonds	¥100m	¥10,000	Mar Jun Sep Dec	9.00–13.00 and 13.00–15.00	Cash

Malaysia

Kuala Lumpur Commodity Exchange

Commodity	Size	Tick Size	Months	Hours	Delivery
Crude palm oil	25 tonnes	M$25.00	Nearest 6 and alternate for 1 year out	11.00–12.30 and 15.30–18.00	Physical
Palm kernel	10 tonnes	M$10.00	Nearest 5 and alternate for 1 year out	10.45–12.00 and 16.00–17.30	Physical
Rubber RSSI	25 tonnes	M$0.10	Nearest 12 months	10.00–13.00 and 16.00–18.00	Physical
Rubber SMR 20	20 tonnes	M$0.25	Nearest 9 months	10.00–13.00 and 16.00–18.00	Physical

Tin	1 tonne	US$0.01	Nearest 3 and alternate for 1 year out	12.15–13.00 and 16.00–18.00	Physical

New Zealand

New Zealand Futures Exchange

Crossbred wool	2,500 kgs	NZ$25.00	Jan Mar May Aug Oct Dec	9.30–15.45	Physical
Barclays stock index	NZ$20 × index	NZ$20.00	Nearest 3 and quarterly	8.05–17.00	Cash
Bank bills	NZ$500,000	NZ$11.00	Nearest 3 and quarterly	8.50–15.55	Cash
N.Z. T-notes	NZ$100,000	NZ$31.00	Nearest 3 and quarterly	8.00–17.00	Physical
U.S. dollars	US$50,000	NZ$5.00	Nearest 3 and quarterly	8.15–16.45	Cash

Table 6-2. (Continued)

Philippines

Manila International Futures Exchange

Commodity	Size	Tick Size	Months	Hours	Delivery
Cane sugar	112,000 lbs	0.20¢	Nearest 6 months	Sessions at 9.15,10.15 13.15,14.15	Physical
Soyabeans	30,000 lbs	0.50¢	Nearest 6 months	Sessions at 9.45,10.45 13.45,14.45	Physical

Singapore

Singapore International Monetary Exchange

Commodity	Size	Tick Size	Months	Hours	Delivery
Gold	100 troz	US$10	Feb Mar Apr Jun Aug Sep Oct Dec	9.30–17.15	Physical
Nikkei stock index	¥500 × index	¥2,500	Nearest 1 and Mar Jun Sep Dec	8.00–14.15 and (Sat) 8.00–10.15	Cash
Eurodollars*	US$1,000,000	US$25	Nearest 1 and Mar Jun Sep Dec	8.30–17.20	Cash

U.S. T-bonds	US$100,000	Mar Jun Sep Dec	7.30–17.00	Physical
British pounds*	£25,000	Nearest 1 and Mar Jun Sep Dec	8.25–17.15	Physical
Deutsche marks*	DM125,000	Nearest 1 and Mar Jun Sep Dec	8.20–17.10	Physical
Japanese Yen*	¥12,500,000	Nearest 1 and Mar Jun Sep Dec	8.15–17.05	Physical

*The Simex Eurodollar, British pound, Deutsche mark and Japanese yen contracts are listed on a mutual offset link with the Chicago Mercantile Exchange.

daily trading hours, and whether the contract is cash-settled or physical assets are delivered.[5]

Commodity futures have been traded on the Chicago Board of Trade since the 1860s.[6] In marked contrast, the first financial futures contract introduced was the foreign currency futures contract, introduced in 1972 on the International Monetary Market of the Chicago Mercantile Exchange. The foreign currency futures were followed by GNMA futures in 1975, T-bill futures in 1976, T-bond futures in 1977, and so on. Figure 6-1 summarizes the introduction dates of some of the more familiar financial futures contracts.

Institutional Features that Reduce Credit Risk

The futures contract is like a forward contract in that it is a means of contracting for delivery at a future date at a price agreed upon today. However, as was pointed out in Part II, forward contracts have the significant limitation of being a pure credit instrument.[7] A futures contract is designed to deal directly with the credit risk (default risk) problem; it is structured and traded so as to reduce substantially the credit risk borne by the contracting parties. Moreover, the institutional features of the futures market are designed to provide for a liquid secondary market.

In the discussion to follow, we will highlight those institutional features of the futures contract that reduce the credit risk. In the final section of this chapter, we will look at those features of the contract and of the market that provide liquidity.

There are three institutional features of the contract and the market that interact to lower the credit risk for a futures contract: *daily settlement, margin requirements,* and the *clearinghouse.* At the end of this section

---

5. Some contracts were eliminated by *Global Investor* when this guide was compiled because, although the contract is officially "listed," no actual trading takes place on the contract.

6. A concise history of the futures markets in the United States is contained in "Futures: The Realistic Hedge for the Reality of Risk," Chicago Board of Trade (1988). This booklet noted that when the Chicago Board of Trade opened in 1842, it was trading forward rather than futures contracts. Futures contracts first appeared in 1865.

7. The Chicago Board of Trade publication noted in footnote 6 points out that the move to futures contracts was made because "many merchants were not fulfilling their forward commitments, causing bitter disputes between buyers and sellers."

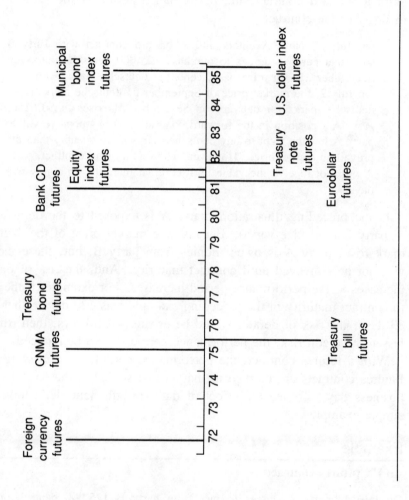

Figure 6-1. The Advent of Financial Futures.

we will consider another feature of some futures markets, *price limits*, to see how this feature affects the credit risk of a futures contract.

Daily Settlement

With a forward contract, the performance period is the same as the maturity of the contract:

> On July 1, party A enters into a forward contract with Party B such that party A agrees to purchase 125,000 deutsche marks on September 21 at a price of 61 cents per deutsche mark ($0.6100). On July 2, the market price of September 21 deutsche marks (i.e., deutsche marks for delivery on September 21) rises to $0.6150. Party A's position in the forward contract now has positive value: party A has the right to buy deutsche marks more cheaply than the prevailing market price. However, with this forward contract, party A will not receive the value until contract maturity, in eighty-two days.

In the preceding illustration, party A is exposed to the default risk of party B (and vice versa). Because the market price of the deutsche mark rose, party A is owed monies from party B; but, these monies will not be conveyed until contract maturity. And, the risk of default increases as the performance period increases. For example, if the time to contract maturity in the preceding example was 120 days rather than 83 days, the risk of default would be greater. It follows, then, that to lessen the credit risk, the performance period should be reduced.

With a futures contract, the performance period is *one trading day*. Futures contracts are marked to market and settled at the end of every business day. To see the effect of daily resettlement, let's look at a simple example.

Example

An FX futures contract

On July 1, party A agrees to buy from party B 125,000 deutsche marks for delivery on September 21 at a price of $0.6100 per deutsche mark.[8] At origination, both parties agree that $0.6100 per DM is the prevailing

---

8. In the parlance of the futures market, party A is "long" since she has executed a "buy" trade.

price for September 21 deutsche marks, so the net present value of the contract is zero.

Suppose that, on July 2, the price of a September 21 deutsche mark rises to $0.6150. (Such a rise is the result of changes in the demand for and supply of deutsche marks, both in the spot and futures market. However, let's simplify the situation and propose that the rise is the result of a third party, C, entering the market demanding September 21 deutsche marks.)

Since party A has agreed to buy an asset for $0.6100 per unit that is now worth $0.6150 per unit, the value of party A's position has risen. In marking the contract to market, party A's contract now has a net present value of $625,:

$$125,000 \times (\$0.6150 - \$0.6100) = \$625$$

Conversely, the market value of the contract to party B is negative $625.

The contract is resettled by party B making a payment to party A in the amount of $625. After the resettlement, the net present value of the contract is again equal to zero.

Hence, when a futures contract is marked to market and settled daily, the performance period is reduced to only one day. In the preceding example, the maturity of the contract is eighty-three days; however, the performance period is not eighty-three days but only one business day. With the reduced performance period, default risk declines accordingly.

Moreover, the preceding example clearly illustrates a point we alluded to in Chapter 3:

> In effect, a futures contract is like a bundle of forward contracts. Each day, the forward contract originated on the previous day is settled and replaced with a new contract, such that the new contract has a delivery price equal to the settlement price for the previous day's contract.[9]

In this vein, the futures contract described in the example can be viewed as follows: On July 1 a forward contract was entered into with a

---

9. This statement is adapted from William F. Sharpe, *Investments*, 3d ed. (Englewood Cliffs, NJ: Prentice-Hall), p. 527. There are subtle, theoretical differences between a futures contract and a bundle of forward contracts, which are discussed in Kenneth R. French, "A Comparison of Futures and Forward Prices," *Journal of Financial Economics* 12, no. 3 (November 1983): 311–342. However as Professor French noted at the conclusion of his article, the significant differences between forwards and futures are found in the contracts rather than the prices.

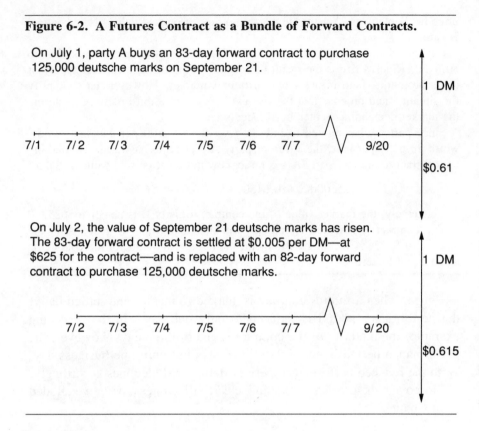

Figure 6-2. A Futures Contract as a Bundle of Forward Contracts.

On July 1, party A buys an 83-day forward contract to purchase 125,000 deutsche marks on September 21.

On July 2, the value of September 21 deutsche marks has risen. The 83-day forward contract is settled at $0.005 per DM—at $625 for the contract—and is replaced with an 82-day forward contract to purchase 125,000 deutsche marks.

maturity of eighty three days and a delivery price of $0.61 per deutsche mark. On July 2, the July 1 forward contract was settled at a price of $0.6150 per deutsche mark and was replaced with a new forward contract with a maturity of eighty-two days and delivery price of $0.6150 per deutsche mark. This view of a futures contract as a bundle of forward contracts is illustrated in Figure 6-2.

Margin Requirements

Daily settlement reduces the performance period to one day; however, even for this one-day period, there is still the possibility that the counterparty will default. (In the context of our earlier example, there is the possibility that on July 2 party B will not make the necessary $625 payment.)

The surest way to deal with this day-to-day credit risk is to require the contracting parties to post a *surety bond* and that is precisely what is done. In the futures market, this bond is referred to as the *margin*. To buy or sell a futures contract, the individual must post the specified bond—the margin—to guarantee contract performance. The amount of the margin is determined by the exchange itself.

At the time the contract is bought or sold, the trader posts the *initial margin*. The initial margin varies with the type of futures contract but is approximately equal to the maximum observed daily price fluctuation for the contract in question. That is, the amount of the surety bond required is enough to cover the maximum change in the value of the contract that has occurred to date.

The range of initial margin requirements is wide. The initial margin can be as little as 0.1% (for instance, the initial margin on a futures contract to purchase $1,000,000 worth of treasury bills is $1,000) or as much as 15% (for the Standard & Poor's index contract). However, for most contracts, the initial margin is 5% or less.[10]

In futures markets in the United States, margin can be posted in the form of cash, a bank letter of credit, or U.S. treasury instruments. If margin is posted in the form of securities, the trader continues to earn the interest accrued while the security acts as margin.

On each trading day, monies are added to or subtracted from the trader's margin account—in cash—as the futures trader's position increases or decreases in value. In the context of our example, on July 2 $625 would be transferred from party B's margin account to Party A's margin account; this $625 is referred to as the *variation margin*. If, as a result of the value of the trader's position declining, the balance in the margin account goes below a specified level, referred to as the *maintenance margin*, the trader is required to replenish the margin, that is, return it to its initial level. If the trader whose margin account

---

10. The relatively small magnitude of the margin for futures contracts versus the margin requirement for stocks, and the fact that margins for futures are set by the exchange rather than some regulatory authority, elicited considerable attention following the events of October 19, 1987. However, one must keep in mind that a "margin" in the futures market is very different from a "margin" in an equity market such as the NYSE. In the stock market, the investor buys stock or credit; the margin is the down payment, with the remainder of the share price borrowed from the broker. In the futures market, the margin is a performance bond guaranteeing that the trader will make required payments if the price of the asset or commodity changes.

has fallen below the maintenance level fails to replenish the margin account, his position is closed out.[11] To see how this works in practice, let's return to our example.

Example

An FX futures contract—Continued

Continuing our simplistic example, let's suppose that parties A and B have somehow agreed that the initial margin for a contract on 125,000 deutsche marks will be $2,500 and that the maintenance margin will be 80% of the initial margin, $2,000.[12]

On July 1 the futures contract between party A and party B is originated, so both parties will be required to post the initial margin of $2,500.

On July 2, the price of September 21 deutsche marks rises from $0.6100 to $0.6150. Consequently, at the close of business on July 2, $625 is transferred from the margin account of party B to that of party A. Party A now has a margin account balance of $3,125; and party B has a margin account balance of only $1,875.

Party B's margin account is now below the maintenance margin, so party B will be requested to replenish his margin account, returning the balance to the initial margin: he will be asked to add $625 to the margin account to restore the balance to $2,500.

If party B replenishes the margin account, the contract continues. If on July 3 the price of September 21 deutsche marks again rises, monies will again be transferred from party B's margin account to party A's account; and, if the price increase is great enough, party B will once again be required to replenish the margin. (The reverse will occur if the price of September 21 deutsche marks falls on July 3.)

If, however, party B does not add the required $625 to the margin account, party B's position is closed out. Party B will no longer have the futures position, and the balance of $1,875 in the margin account will be returned to him. If party A still wants to buy deutsche marks for September 21 delivery, he will have to find another party to accept the sell position.[13]

---

11. In the discussion so far we have pretended that the contracting is done directly: party A contracts directly with party B. However, the contracting process actually goes through a broker—a futures commission merchant. Consequently, credit risk is further reduced by the fact that the broker endorses the contract, thereby accepting performance risk.

12. These were the actual margins for deutsche mark contracts on the International Monetery Market on February 25, 1988.

13. In truth, party A will not actually have to search for a counterparty. As will be explained, the clearinghouse will take care of this.

As indicated by this example, if the contract is marked to market daily and the initial and maintenance margins are set appropriately, the probability of loss from a default is effectively eliminated.[14]

The Clearing House

As just noted, daily settlement and the margin requirement can effectively eliminate default-induced losses in a futures contract. However, this is not to say that the costs associated with default are zero. Two sources of costs due to credit risk remain.

First, given the manner in which we have set up our example, parties A and B would have to exchange monies directly with one another so they would necessarily expend resources evaluating each other's credit risk. Thus, one cost associated with default is the cost of evaluating the credit risk of the parties with whom you trade.

> Party A buys September 21 futures contracts on 125,000 deutsche marks from parties B, C and D. Party A must evaluate the credit risk of each of the three counter-parties.

Second, if a trader's counter-party defaults, the trader is protected against direct losses but, is subject to an opportunity loss in the sense that the contract is closed out. Thus, the remaining cost associated with credit risk is the cost of replacing a contract if a counterparty defaults.

> Party A has purchased one September 21 futures contract on deutsche marks from each of the parties B, C, and D. If the price of September 21 deutsche marks rises and party C drops out (by not replenishing the margin account), party A will not lose monies directly. However, party A must either search for a replacement counterparty or live with one fewer deutsche mark futures contract.

The clearinghouse handles these two problems by breaking apart and depersonalizing agreements. The clearinghouse does not take a position in any trade but interposes itself between all parties to every transaction. Hence, the equity of the clearinghouse provides a bond for the parties contracting for futures contracts through the clearinghouse.

---

14. What, then, was the problem on October 19 and 20, 1987, when default risk was certainly not eliminated and a large number of futures contracts were defaulted? Clearly, the margin levels were not set "appropriately." Ex post, it was clear to an observer that the margin levels were lower than necessary.

The manner in which the clearinghouse functions is illustrated in Figure 6-3. Part (*a*) illustrates the futures contract we have described so far: Party A agrees to buy 125,000 deutsche marks from Party B at a price of $0.6100 per Deutsche Mark. Part (*b*) illustrates the same transaction, but with the clearinghouse interposed between the two parties: Party A agrees to buy 125,000 deutsche marks at $0.61 each from the clearinghouse and party B agrees to sell 125,000 deutsche marks to the clearing house at $0.61 per DM. At this point, the *open interest* is 125,000 deutsche marks—the value of one contract.

Figure 6-3. Operation of the Clearinghouse.* (*a*) **The Futures Contract.** (*b*) **The Futures Contract with the Clearinghouse Interposed.** (*c*) **Day 2: The Price Rises and the Contract is Marked to Market.**

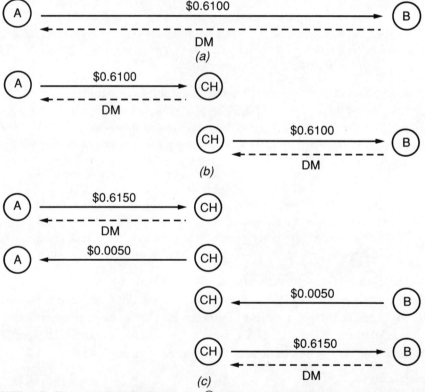

William F. Sharpe, INVESTMENTS, 3e, © 1985, pp. 525–526. Adapted by permission of Prentice Hall, Inc., Englewood Cliffs, New Jersey.

Part (c) illustrates what happens when the futures price of the DM rises and the contract is marked to market. Suppose that, as a result of changes in the demand for or supply of deutsche marks, the futures price of September 21 DM rises to $0.6150. This price change requires a payment of $0.0050 per DM ($0.0050 × 125,000 = $625) from party B to the clearinghouse and the same payment from the clearinghouse to Party A.

Figure 6-3(c) again illustrates how a futures contract is like a bundle of forward contracts. On day 2, the eighty-three-day forward contract is settled via a payment of $0.0050 per DM and is replaced with an eighty-two-day forward contract with a price of $0.6150 per DM.

Part (c) also illustrates the marking to market. What if, (as was the case in our example) that the marking to market requires that party B replenish the margin account? If party B returns the margin balance to the initial level, the format of Figure 6-3 would remain unchanged. However, if party B fails to replenish the margin account, party B's position is closed out.

Figure 6-3 (d) illustrates the case of party B's failure to meet a margin call. When party B is unable to restore the margin account to the initial level, the clearinghouse enters into a reversing trade with party B—the clearinghouse contracts to sell 125,000 September 21 DM to party B at a price of $0.6150 per DM—thereby netting out (closing out) the position.[15] However, party A's position is still open; the clearinghouse is still obligated to deliver the September 21 DM. The clearinghouse covers this obligation by matching party A with another contract, one to purchase September 21 DM from party C at a price of $0.6150.

The effect of closing out party B's contract is displayed in part (e). Note that the open interest is still only one contract.

Price Limits

In the aftermath of the "crash" of October 19, there has been considerable discussion of imposing price limits on financial futures contracts. More common for futures contracts on commodities than for financial futures, a price limit has considerable intuitive appeal:

---

15. In the example at hand, the reversing trade locks in party B's loss of $625 from July 1 to July 2, a loss that has already been paid out to the margin account. The remainder of the margin account would be returned to party B.

Figure 6-3. (*d*) Party B Fails to Replenish the Margin Account, and the Position Is Closed Out. (*e*) Net Positions After Party B Is Closed Out.*

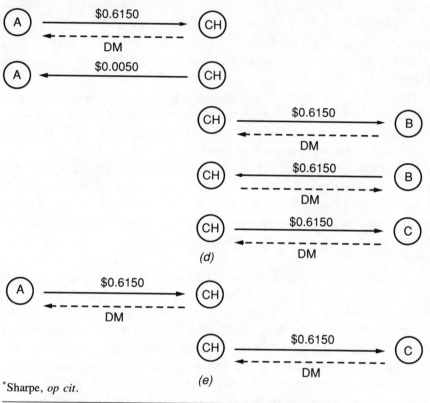

(d)

(e)

*Sharpe, *op cit.*

With daily resettlement and the margin account mechanisms in place, the problem of default risk arises only when the futures price moves "too much" in a single day. Therefore, to "solve" this problem, we will institute a rule that the price can move only so much in a single trading day.

More specifically, the rule would dictate that if the futures price for a specified contract moves beyond the limit during a trading day, trading is then halted on that contract for the remainder of the day.

However, this kind of reasoning has a fatal flaw. William Sharpe provided the best exposition of the flaw when he told the story of a farmer:

> Tired of the violent fluctuations in temperature that occur from one
> day to the next in the American great plains (and the consequences
> on his crops), this farmer decided to "eliminate" this problem by
> having his thermometer altered so that it could move no more than
> five degrees in either direction from the previous day's reading.[16]

The point of this anecdote is that the problem of volatility in futures
prices can no more be "solved" by imposing price limits than the volatility in temperatures can be "eliminated" by altering the thermometer.
Modification of the thermometer does nothing to change climatic or
meteorological conditions; the price limit does nothing to change the
economic factors underlying the volatility in the futures prices.

However, it has been argued that price limits could reduce the credit
risk problem, to the extent that the price limit substitutes for margin.[17]
The reason this occurs is that price limits *could* reduce the amount of
information available to the traders in the futures market. To see how
this works, let's return to our example.

> Suppose that on July 2, world economic conditions are altered such
> that the value of the dollar declines dramatically relative to the
> deutsche mark.

If there are no price limits on the DM/$ futures contract, the futures
prices could fully reflect the altered conditions:

> On July 2, the futures price of September 21 deutsche marks rose
> from $0.6100 to close at $0.6325.

With such a dramatic move, credit problems and "reneging" are likely
to occur:

> In marking the contract to market, party B owes $2812.50 (and
> party A is owed the same amount). However, party B's margin
> account balance is only $2,500. Party B will face a margin call of
> $2,812.50 (to leave the margin account balance at $2,500). Given
> the $0.0225 change in the price of a DM—a change of 3.6% in
> one day—party B is unwilling to meet the margin call. Party
> B reneges on the futures contract. The contract will be closed

---

16. The anecdote is adapted from Sharpe, op cit., p. 534.
17. This discussion is adapted from Michael J. Brennan, "A Theory of Price Limits in
Futures Markets," *Journal of Financial Economics* 16, no. 2 (June 1986): 213–234.

out but party B's broker—or the clearinghouse[18]—will suffer a loss of $2,812.50 minus $2,500 = $312.50.

Suppose, however, that a price limit had been in effect for the DM/$ futures contract. Suppose that the daily price limit for the DM/$ futures had been set at $0.0100 per DM: if the price of DM rises or falls by as much as one cent, trading is suspended for that day. Such a rule would limit the amount that could be lost on a DM/$ futures contract to $1,250 per day.

> On July 2, the price of September 21 deutsche marks immediately begins to rise from $0.6100; but, with the price limit, it can rise no higher than $0.6200.
>
> Party B's contract must be marked to market at the end of the trading day. Consequently, party B has lost $1,250, and the margin account balance has dropped below the maintenance margin to $1,250. Party B faces a margin call of $1,250.

With this limit on how much party B can lose in a day, the ability of the futures market to convey information to the traders is reduced. Hence, the probability that the party will renege on the contract is altered.

> Party B knows that the $0.6200 is not an equilibrium price. Party B knows that the equilibrium price is higher than $0.6200 but not how much higher. If party B thought the equilibrium price was only a little above this level, say at $0.6210, party B might be willing to meet the margin call of $1,250 to restore the margin account balance to $2,500. Suppose he replenishes his account.

The price limits might alter the amount of information available to the trader, but they cannot alter the underlying economic conditions.

> On July 3, the market opens and immediately moves the limit. The price of September 21 deutsche marks rises to $0.6300 and trading is suspended.
>
> Party B has lost another $1,250 and his margin account balance is down to $1,250. He is again faced with a $1,250 margin call. He might make this margin call, or he might renege. Let's suppose he reneges.

---

18. As Ira Kawaller pointed out, the loss would accrue to the clearing member before it accrued to the clearinghouse itself.

On July 5, equilibrium is finally reached. The market opens and the price of September 21 deutsche marks immediately goes to its equilibrium price, $0.6325. Party B's broker closes out the contract. The loss on the contract on July 5 is $312.50, which is taken out of party B's margin account, leaving a balance of $1,250 − $312.50 = $937.50, which is returned to party B.

In the preceding example, the price limit reduced the credit risk to the broker and the exchange: without the price limit, the broker/exchange lost $312.50; with the price limit, the broker/exchange did not suffer a loss. However, this change was solely the result of the trader getting "tricked"; with the price limit in place, the trader's perception of what the equilibrium price would be was different from the market-determined equilibrium price. If the trader cannot be tricked, the effect disappears. Note that this implicitly assumes that the futures price is the only source of the trader's information. To the extent that the trader has alternative sources of information about the equilibrium price, the potential for being tricked—the effectiveness of the price limit—declines.

Institutional Features that Promote Liquidity

In addition to the three features that reduce default risk, there are two features of the futures contract and market that enhance the liquidity of the market: *standardized contracts* and the *organized exchange*.

Standardized Contracts

For a market to be liquid, the commodity/asset being traded in the market must be homogeneous. To attain this homogeneity, contracts traded in the futures market are standardized. The contract specifies a standardized asset and a standardized maturity date.

Consider again the deutsche mark futures contract we have been using as an illustration in this chapter. On the International Monetary Market (IMM) of the Chicago Mercantile Exchange (CME), the DM contract specifies a contract size of 125,000 deutsche marks with maturities occurring on the third Wednesdays of March, June, September, or December.

Moreover, in a futures contract, the mechanism for delivery is com-

monly standardized.[19] For example, on the IMM, the T-Bill futures requires the delivery of T-bills having a face value of $1,000,000 and a time to maturity of ninety days at the expiration of the futures contract. The T-bond futures contract permits latitude with respect to the specific bonds to be delivered: the contract specifies the delivery of $100,000 worth of T-bonds that have at least fifteen years remaining to maturity or to their first call date.[20]

Furthermore, the price of the futures contract is also standardized to the extent that the minimum price movement—the "tick size"—is specified. For example, the "tick size" for the deutsche mark contract we have been using as an illustration is $0.0001 per DM ($12.50 per contract).

Organized Exchanges

To bring together buyers and sellers, the futures market is organized into exchanges, with each exchange trading particular futures contracts. This is in marked contrast to a forward market, which has no physical location for making the trades.

The oldest of the currently functioning futures exchanges is the Chicago Board of Trade (CBOT). Most of the futures exchanges are organized similarly to the CBOT. Membership on the CBOT is by individuals and provides the right to trade on the exchange and to have a voice in its operation. (Although only individuals can be members, brokers such as Merrill Lynch are permitted to trade on the exchange.)

---

19. This delivery specification is particularly important for commodity futures. For example, in the case of wheat futures on the Chicago Board of Trade, only certain kinds of wheat are acceptable for delivery (No. 2 soft red, no. 2 hard red winter, no. 2 dark northern spring, or no. 1 northern spring), and delivery may be accomplished only via warehouse receipts issued by warehouses approved by the exchange.

20. The deliverable bonds will have a wide range of coupons maturities. Consequently, there will be a range of prices for the deliverable bond; thus at any point in time there will be one bond that is cheapest to deliver.

To avoid the problem of the sellers of the futures contracts all wanting to deliver this one cheapest—and the consequent "market corners" or "squeezes"—the Chicago Board of Trade uses a "conversion factor" that adjusts the delivery values of the different bonds to eliminate the effects of the differing coupons and maturities. The conversion factor is determined by the value of the specific deliverable bond having a $X\%$ coupon and Y years to maturity relative to a "normal bond" having an 8% coupon and 20 years to maturity.

Memberships are traded like any other asset and can be purchased from the current owner or leased.

Although the CBOT has at times been likened to a "club" a nonprofit organization of its members—it is probably more fruitful to think of the futures exchanges as *for-profit* "partnerships." The members of these exchanges have strong private incentives to form careful rules for running the exchange that will maximize the value of their memberships.[21] An anecdote might help to illustrate this point. When a trade is made in the "pit," there is always the possibility of an error; the buyer and the seller might write down different amounts or prices. On the Chicago Mercantile Exchange and other exchanges, the rule for settling such errors is for the two parties to split the loss.[22] Because the traders want to maximize their own profit, each trader has the incentive to maximize accuracy. Also, perhaps more importantly, traders will be unlikely to buy or sell contracts from a trader who has an abnormally high error rate. Such rules work to maximize the value of a membership on the exchange and simultaneously to maximize the liquidity on the exchange.

---

21. Although the rules of operation are set by the exchange, they are subject to the approval of the Commodity Futures Trading Commission.
22. This is the case only if direct methods of correcting the error have been unsuccessful.

7

Futures Prices

At maturity—on the delivery date—the futures contract can be converted directly to the underlying asset. Therefore, at maturity, the price of the futures and the cash price of the asset must be the same. Prior to maturity, the cash price and the futures price need not be the same. But because the futures price must converge to the cash price at maturity, we know that there must exist some systematic relation between the two prices. The relation between cash and futures prices is the subject of this chapter.

Futures Prices and the Cost of Carry

To examine the relation between cash and futures prices, let's begin by looking at some illustrative prices. In Figure 7-1 we provide data on the cash prices—the spot prices—of some grains and feeds on Thursday, March 3, 1988. Figure 7-2 provides data on corresponding futures prices on the same day.

Look, for instance, at wheat prices. The spot price of no. 2 soft red wheat is $2.935 (293.5 cents) per bushel in St. Louis. But the price on a futures contract on the Chicago Board of Trade that is deliverable in no. 2 soft red wheat and will mature in only thirteen days—on the third Wednesday in March—is 304.5 cents per bushel. Moreover, as Figure 7-2 indicates, the futures price of wheat in May is higher than that in March the futures price of wheat in July is higher than that in May and so on. Hence, the data on wheat prices demonstrate two important characteristics of futures prices:

Figure 7-1. Spot Prices.

CASH PRICES

Thursday. March 3, 1988

Quotations as of 4 p.m. Eastern Time

GRAINS AND FEEDS

	Thurs	Wed	yr. ago
Barley, top-quality Mpls., bu	2.10-.15	2.10-.15	1.95
Bran, wheat middlings, KC ton	76.00	74.00	50.00
Corn, no. 2 yel. Cent-Ill., bu	bp1.92	1.92½	1.41½
Corn Gluten Feed, Midwest, ton ...	95.-120.	95.-120.	98.50
Cottnsd Meal, Clksdle, Miss. ton ..	137½-140	142.50	126.50
Hominy Feed, Cent-Ill. ton	68.00	68.00	45.00
Meat-Bonemeal, 50%pro. Ill. ton .	240.00	240.00	185.00
Oats, No. 2milling, Mpls., bu	1.93-.95	1.96-2.00	1.46
Sorghum, (Milo) No. 2 Gulf cwt ...	3.80	3.84	3.28
Soybean Meal,			
Decatur, Illinois ton	189½-191½	191.-194.	146.00
Soybeans, No. 1 yel Cent.-Ill. bu ...	bp6.07	6.14	4.70½
Sunflwr Sd No. 1 Duluth/Supr cwt ..	8.40	8.40	7.10
Wheat, Spring 14%-pro Mpls. bu ...	3.11½	3.12½	3.22½
Wheat, No. 2 sft red, St. Lou. bu ...	2.93½	2.93½	3.09½
Wheat, No. 2 hard KC, bu	3.11¼	3.13	2.92

bp: Country elevator bids to producers

1. The futures price of a commodity or asset, F, is greater than the spot price, P.[1]

2. The futures price, F, rises as the time to maturity increases.[2]

These characteristics reflect the *cost of carry* for a futures contract and illustrate a critical arbitrage relation. To see how this works, an example will be most useful.

Example[3]

Cost of carry

Suppose the spot price of no. 2 red wheat in a Chicago warehouse is 300 cents per bushel, the yield on a one-month T-bill is 6%, and the cost of storing and insuring one bushel of wheat is 4 cents per month. Given these data, what can be said about the price today for a one-month futures contract, that is, the price of a futures contract that has one month to maturity?

Instead of buying a futures contract on wheat, one could buy wheat today and store it for one month. In one month, the total cost of this transaction to the buyer is the cost of using the money for one month (the forgone interest) and the cost of storing and insuring the wheat:

---

1. In our wheat example, this will be true even after we adjust for the transportation cost between St. Louis and Chicago.
2. We will ignore any seasonality, such as that evident in the futures price of oats.
3. This example is adapted from Sharpe, *op. cit.*

Figure 7-2. Futures Prices.

FUTURES PRICES

Thursday, March 3, 1988.

Open Interest Reflects Previous Trading Day.

	Open	High	Low	Settle	Change	Lifetime High	Lifetime Low	Open Interest
—GRAINS AND OILSEEDS—								
CORN (CBT) 5,000 bu.; cents per bu.								
Mar	201½	202¼	200½	200¾	– 1¼	222¾	171	13,253
May	207	207¾	206	206½	– ½	225½	174	6,343
July	210¾	212	210	210½	– ½	226½	180	41,822
Sept	212¾	214¼	212½	212½	– ¼	223	180¾	7,082
Dec	216¼	219	215¾	216½	– ¼	222¾	184	26,952
Mr89	223	226	222½	223½	– ¼	229½	193½	1,547
May	226¾	230	226¾	227	– ¼	232¾	207½	236
Est vol 23,000; vol Wed 27,225; open int 155,235, 518.								
OATS (CBT) 5,000 bu.; cents per bu.								
Mar	192½	192½	186	186	– 7½	205½	129½	1,617
May	178½	179¼	173¾	173¾	– 7¼	194½	150¾	451
July	172	172¼	169½	169½	– 3¾	177	144	1,264
Sept	170	170½	169	169	– 2¾	173¼	143	1,300
Dec	177	177½	176½	176½	– 2	180	162	463
Est Vol 2,000; vol Wed 1,323; open int 8,095, +239.								
SOYBEANS (CBT) 5,000 bu.; cents per bu.								
Mar	630	631¼	622½	623	– 7½	645	474	7,863
May	636	637½	628	629	– 7½	656	476	42,190
July	644	645¼	637	637¾	– 7¾	663½	488½	35,382
Aug	646¾	647	640½	640½	– 5½	665	512	4,786
Sept	646	647	641½	641½	– 4¼	663	503	3,183
Nov	654½	656	648	648½	– 6½	666	499¼	30,476
Ja89	662	662½	657	657	– 5	672	553	1,573
Mar	670	670	662½	663½	– 6½	676	579	199
Est vol 48,000; vol Wed 38,818; open int 125,663, +763.								
SOYBEAN MEAL (CBT) 100 tons; $ per ton.								
Mar	189.50	189.90	188.20	188.60	– 1.50	205.00	135.00	4,424
May	188.00	188.50	186.50	187.10	– 1.70	199.00	148.00	25,016
July	188.30	188.70	186.50	187.10	– 2.10	198.00	148.10	16,471
Aug	188.50	189.00	187.50	187.70	– 2.20	198.00	148.00	5,395
Sept	190.00	190.50	188.00	188.00	– 2.50	192.00	153.00	3,236
Oct	190.80	191.00	189.50	189.70	– 2.40	193.00	159.00	2,050
Dec	193.00	193.50	191.50	192.00	– 1.00	196.00	159.00	5,311
Ja89	....	....	....	193.20	– 2.00	196.00	177.00	231
Est vol 14,000; vol Wed 15,641; open int 62,211, +461.								
SOYBEAN OIL (CBT) 60,000 lbs.; cents per lb.								
Mar	20.60	20.82	20.50	20.60	– .05	23.55	16.29	5,807
May	21.01	21.20	20.86	20.90	– .11	23.70	16.50	36,725
July	21.32	21.53	21.21	21.24	– .09	23.90	16.65	23,738
Aug	21.47	21.60	21.35	21.35	– .07	23.90	16.71	5,283
Sept	21.60	21.70	21.40	21.42	– .13	23.77	16.55	4,202
Oct	21.60	21.75	21.46	21.46	– .14	23.65	17.25	3,037
Dec	21.75	21.90	21.60	21.61	– .05	23.75	18.30	7,703
Ja89	21.75	21.90	21.65	21.65	– .05	23.30	21.45	381
Est vol 17,500; vol Wed 21,755; open int 86,879, 448.								

	Open	High	Low	Settle	Change	Lifetime High	Lifetime Low	Open Interest
WHEAT (CBT) 5,000 bu.; cents per bu.								
Mar	306	308	304	304½	– 2¼	339	253	2,053
May	313½	316	312¼	312½	– 1¾	339	263	15,041
July	318¼	321	317¼	317½	– 1¾	335¼	253½	16,588
Sept	325	326¾	323	323	+ 1¾	340	272	1,932
Dec	334½	337¼	334	334	– 2	351	289	2,132
Mr89	340	340	338	339	– 2	354	330	119
Est vol 9,000; vol Wed 13,559; open int 37,850, 628.								
WHEAT (KC) 5,000 bu.; cents per bu.								
Mar	309½	309½	307½	307½	– 2¾	326¾	262½	2,053
May	311½	314	311	311½	– 1¾	326	262¼	11,343
July	317	318½	316	316	– 1¾	328¾	272	7,881
Sept	321	323½	321	321	– 1¾	333¼	313	331
Dec	327½	329	326½	326½	– 2½	339	301½	134
Est vol 5,670; vol Wed 7,838; open int 21,742, 641.								
WHEAT (MPLS) 5,000 bu.; cents per bu.								
Mar	293	295½	293	293½	– 1	324	266	1,859
May	297½	298½	295¾	296¼	– 2	315	286½	4,168
July	305	305¼	302¾	303½	– 1½	312	300	595
Sept	305	307	305	305	– 316	300	173	
Est vol 1,725; vol Wed 1,614; open int 6,816, +198.								
BARLEY (WPG) 20 metric tons; Can. $ per ton								
Mar	70.60	70.80	70.40	70.80	+ .10	87.00	67.10	846
May	73.30	73.40	73.30	73.40	– .30	83.80	69.00	8,224
July	75.30	75.30	75.10	75.20	– .10	80.30	71.00	6,235
Oct	79.30	79.30	78.70	78.90	– .40	82.90	75.00	3,715
Nov	79.00	79.00	79.00	79.00	– .30	81.70	79.00	811
Dec	....	....	....	79.30	– .40	83.10	79.70	730
Est vol 1,100; vol Wed; open int 20,561, +222.								
FLAXSEED (WPG) 20 metric tons; Can. $ per ton								
Mar	220.50	221.20	220.50	221.20	+ 1.10	252.50	208.10	218
May	226.50	227.00	226.40	227.00	+ 1.00	260.00	214.00	4,085
July	232.20	232.80	232.20	232.80	+ 1.00	264.10	229.70	1,183
Oct	....	....	....	240.80	+ 1.70	272.50	237.20	219
Est vol 640; vol Wed 1,007; open int 5,785, +189.								
RAPESEED (WPG) 20 metric tons; Can. $ per ton								
Mar	301.50	301.70	298.40	298.40	– 3.60	315.80	231.50	1,606
June	297.50	297.70	295.90	295.90	– 2.60	321.30	252.90	14,941
Sept	297.50	297.50	296.30	296.40	....	318.50	259.80	6,328
Nov	296.00	296.00	294.80	295.40	– 2.60	316.50	261.80	7,909
Ja89	301.50	301.50	299.80	300.50	– 2.20	311.90	299.80	1,287
Est vol 3,920; vol Wed 3,665; open int 32,071, 422.								
RYE (WPG) 20 metric tons; Can. $ per ton								
Mar	....	....	....	105.60	– 2.30	112.80	91.10	351
May	108.50	108.50	108.20	108.20	– 2.30	111.00	99.50	1,573
July	107.50	107.50	107.50	107.50	– 2.50	111.00	101.00	898
Est vol 125; vol Wed 480; open int 2,855, 15.								

CBT: Chicago Board of Trade
KC: Kansas City Board of Trade
MPLS: Minneapolis Grain Exchange
WPG: Winnipeg Commodity Exchange

$$300.0[1 + (30/360)0.06] + 4.0 = 305.5$$

Hence, 305.5 cents per bushel is the maximum that should be paid for the one-month futures contract. If the futures contract were priced at 306, a party could sell futures contracts, buy wheat today, store it for one month, and make a riskless profit—an *arbitrage* profit.

The point of our wheat example is that the futures price must be related to the spot price through the cost of carry, c, for the futures contract in

question. As shown in the preceding example for commodity contracts, arbitrage guarantees that the futures price will be less than or equal to the spot price plus the cost of carry:

$$F \leq P + c \qquad (7\text{-}1)$$

We saw in the example that if $F > P + c$, a trader could make a riskless profit by taking a long position in the asset and a short position in the futures contract. If $F < P + c$, the aribtrage strategy would be to buy the futures and sell the commodity short but short sales of a physical commodity are difficult.[4]

However, it is with futures on financial assets that we will be concerned and short selling is possible for financial assets. In this case, if $F < P + c$, a trader can make an arbitrage profit. Hence, with the financial futures, the principle of no arbitrage requires that Equation (7-1) be a strict equality:

$$F = P + c \qquad (7\text{-}2)$$

In Figure 7-3, we provide data on financial futures for the same date (March 3, 1988) that was used to illustrate futures prices for commodities. We have annotated the data for the Eurodollar futures contracts to show how these data are interpreted.

The cost-of-carry relation holds for financial assets as it does for commodities. The only difference is in the things that make up the cost of carry. For commodities, the cost of carry is simply the cost of storing and insuring the commodity. For financial assets, the cost of carry refers to the *net* financing costs (coupon income minus financing costs). Put another way, the cost of carry is the difference between the opportunity cost of holding the asset (the short-term interest rate — the financing cost) and the yield earned from holding the financial asset (e.g., the coupon payments received in the case of holding bonds).

Moreover, Equation (7-2) is particularly useful for considering what is referred to as *basis* in a futures contract. Basis is defined as the difference between the futures price and the spot price:

$$\text{Basis} = F - P \qquad (7\text{-}3)$$

---

4. However, in the context of the preceding wheat example, if one had a large enough inventory of wheat, the strategy could be accomplished by reducing inventory (selling wheat on the spot market) and buying futures.

Figure 7-3. Financial Futures Prices.

FUTURES PRICES

Thursday, March 3, 1988.

Open Interest Reflects Previous Trading Day.

	Open	High	Low	Settle	Change	Lifetime High	Lifetime Low	Open Interest
BRITISH POUND (IMM)–25,000 pounds; $ per pound.								
Mar	1.7670	1.7685	1.7665	1.7675	+.0010	1.8845	1.5870	36,470
June	1.7560	1.7585	1.7555	1.7570	+.0010	1.8780	1.5280	6,833
Sept	1.7450	1.7474	1.7406	1.7456	+.0018	1.8702	1.6992	199
Dec	1.7388	1.7388	1.7358	1.7386	+.0018	1.8652	1.6980	102
Est vol 3,465; vol Wed 10,595; open int 43,604, 755.								
CANADIAN DOLLAR (IMM)–100,000 dlrs.; $ per Can $								
Mar	.7968	.7977	.7962	.7971	+.0021	.7977	.7052	14,454
June	.7934	.7946	.7929	.7939	+.0022	.7946	.7325	6,627
Sept	.7900	.7912	.7898	.7907	+.0023	.7912	.7307	1,198
Dec	.7868	.7884	.7868	.7875	+.0024	.7884	.7390	325
Est Vol 4,723; vol Wed 4,315; open int 22,659, 1,079.								
JAPANESE YEN (IMM)–12.5 million yen; $ per yen (.00)								
Mar	.7737	.7750	.7737	.7748	+.0019	.8320	.6672	48,143
June	.7786	.7798	.7783	.7796	+.0020	.8390	.6735	13,059
Sept	.7835	.7850	.7835	.7850	+.0021	.8485	.7075	782
Est Vol 11,363; vol Wed 41,726; open int 62,099, +358.								
SWISS FRANC (IMM)–125,000 francs; $ per franc								
Mar	.7128	.7138	.7116	.7126	.0021	.7955	.6450	27,286
June	.7215	.7224	.7200	.7210	.0022	.8040	.6580	4,560
Sept	.7305	.7305	.7280	.7294	.0023	.8120	.6950	185
Est Vol 16,323; vol Wed 22,685; open int 32,061, +5.								
W. GERMAN MARK (IMM)–125,000 marks; $ per mark								
Mar	.5900	.5907	.5897	.5903	+.0003	.6426	.5359	35,257
June	.5951	.5955	.5945	.5951	+.0002	.6494	.5410	11,776
Sept	.6004	.6007	.5997	.6002	....	.6555	.5609	624
Dec		....	....	.6057	....	.6610	.5705	103
Est Vol 12,309; vol Wed 21,095; open int 47,760, +77.								
EURODOLLAR (LIFFE)–$1 million; pts of 100%								
Mar	92.20	93.22	93.18	93.19	....	93.67	90.00	13,704
June	93.08	93.09	93.06	93.07	....	93.39	89.89	11,419
Sept	92.84	92.85	92.83	92.84	....	93.13	89.74	5,763
Dec	92.57	92.58	92.57	92.57	....	92.93	89.80	1,581
Mr89	92.33	92.33	92.33	92.33	+.01	92.33	90.86	502
June	92.10	92.10	92.10	92.11	+.01	92.10	91.99	108
Est Vol 4,682; vol Wed 5,176; open int 33,101, +30.								
STERLING (LIFFE)–å500,000; pts of 100%								
Mar	90.75	90.76	90.73	90.76	+.03	91.70	88.60	12,466
June	90.65	90.65	90.60	90.63	+.03	91.54	89.28	16,410
Sept	90.54	90.54	90.53	90.55	+.01	91.27	89.26	3,512
Dec	90.44	90.44	90.42	90.45	+.01	91.12	89.22	2,011
Mr89	90.32	90.32	90.32	90.35	+.02	90.83	89.25	1,510

	Open	High	Low	Settle	Change		Lifetime High	Lifetime Low	Open Interest
U.S. DOLLAR INDEX (CTN) 500 times USDX									
Mar	90.93	90.93	90.83	90.84	–	.04	102.05	86.07	2,274
June	91.25	91.28	91.12	91.14	–	.10	101.20	86.60	1,866
Sept	....	....	....	91.55	–	.08	92.96	87.42	1,506
Est vol 600; vol Wed 1,849; open int 5,653, +807.									
The index: High 90.90; Low 90.80; Close 90.81 .05									
CRB INDEX (NYFE) 500 times index									
Mar	225.70	226.55	224.40	225.00	–	0.95	242.25	210.00	1,068
May	224.70	225.80	223.55	224.00	–	0.95	237.50	217.10	355
July	225.00	225.00	222.50	223.50	–	1.00	235.90	218.50	626
Sept	224.50	224.50	223.00	223.50	–	0.95	236.70	221.50	263
Est vol 954; vol Wed 638; open int 2,412, 415.									
The index: High 226.06; Low 224.36; Close 224.50 1.45									
TREASURY BONDS (CBT)-$100,000; pts. 32nds of 100%									
Mar	95-03	95-10	94-30	95-06	+	5	8.505	.017	101,138
June	94-03	94-09	93-29	94-05	+	5	8.618	.017	187,518
Sept	93-06	93-10	92-31	93-06	+	5	8.726	.018	13,267
Dec	92-09	92-11	92-03	92-10	+	5	8.825	.018	4,828
Mr89	91-15	91-17	91-12	91-16	+	5	8.918	.019	3,598
June	90-19	90-25	90-19	90-24	+	5	9.006	.018	3,128
Sept	....	....	....	90-01	+	5	9.090	.019	338
Dec	....	....	....	89-12	+	5	9.169	.018	130
Mr90	....	....	....	88-25	+	5	9.240	.019	136
Est vol 200,000; vol Wed 333,837; op int 314,111, 5,964.									
TREASURY NOTES (CBT)-$100,000; pts 32nds of 100%									
Mar	98-24	98-31	98-22	98-28	+	4	8.167	.018	22,421
June	98-02	98-08	97-31	98-05	+	4	8.275	.019	51,091
Sept	97-09	97-14	97-09	97-12	+	4	8.393	.019	895
Est vol 10,000; vol Wed 33,433; open int 74,409, 679.									
5 YR TREAS NOTES (CTN) $100,000; pts. 32nds of 100%									
Mar	101-12	01-125	101-11	101-10		....	7.68	....	2.413
June	00-255	00-265	100-24	100-24		....	7.82	....	5.001
Sept	100-08	100-08	100-06	100-06		....	7.95	....	1,650
Est vol 1,500; vol Wed 1,635; open int 9,064, 102.									
TREASURY BONDS (MCE)-$50,000; pts. 32nds of 100%									
Mar	95-03	95-10	95-00	95-05	+	1	8.508	.003	1,159
June	94-00	94-09	93-29	94-04	+	1	8.621	.004	2,795
Est vol 4,000; vol Wed 6,300; open int 3,996, +302.									
TREASURY BILLS (1MM)-$1 mil.; pts. of 100%									
	Open	High	Low	Settle	Chg		Discount Settle	Discount Chg	Open Interest
Mar	94.37	94.37	94.35	94.37	+	.02	5.63	.02	6,379

Contract delivery months that are currently traded

Prices represent the open, high, low, and settlement (or closing) price for the previous day

One day's change in the settlement price

	Open	High	Low	Settle	Change	Yield Settle	Chg	Open Interest
EURODOLLAR (IMM)–$1 million; pts of 100%								
Mar	93.19	93.20	93.18	93.18	....	6.82	....	100,492
June	93.08	93.08	93.03	93.05	....	6.95	....	123,448
Sept	92.84	92.84	92.80	92.82	....	7.18	....	46,824
Dec	92.57	92.58	92.54	92.55	....	7.45	....	22,728
Mr89	92.32	92.34	92.30	92.30	....	7.70	....	16,316
June	92.11	92.11	92.08	92.08	....	7.92	....	12,938
Sept	91.91	91.92	91.88	91.89	....	8.11	....	10,509
Dec	91.75	91.76	91.72	91.73	....	8.27	....	7,578
Mr90	91.61	91.62	91.59	91.59	....	8.41	....	10,114
June	91.49	91.50	91.47	91.47	....	8.53	....	9,937
Sept	91.39	91.40	91.37	91.37	....	8.63	....	6,683
Dec	91.30	91.31	91.28	91.28	....	8.72	....	5,282
Est Vol 38,497; vol Wed 72,618; open int 372,849, +3,663.								

The number of contracts still in effect at the end of the previous day's trading session. Each unit represents a buyer *and* a seller who still have a contract position

One day's change in the futures' interest rate – equal and opposite to change in the settlement price

The interest rate implied by the settlement price, e.g., 100 – 93.18 = 6.28

The total of the right column, and the change from the prior trading day

IMM: International Monetary Market
LIFFE: London International Financial Futures Exchange
CTN: New York Cotton Exchange
NYFE: New York Futures Exchange
CBT: Chicago Board of Trade
MCE: MidAmerica Commodity Exchange

From Equation (7-2) it follows that some movements in the basis for a particular asset are predictable movements, based on the cost of carry of the asset.

The first of these predictable movements is the convergence of the futures price to the price implied by the cost-of-carry relation. We must keep in mind that the cost-of-carry model is an equilibrium model. As the futures price strays from the price implied by Equation (7-2), the arbitrage forces will act to bring the futures price back to that predicted by the cost-of-carry model. Thus, over the tenor of the futures contract, futures prices will tend to converge toward the price implied by the cost-of-carry relation.

The second predictable movement is the convergence of the futures price to the cash price at expiration of the futures contract. As the time to delivery becomes shorter, the cost of carry declines. Storage and insurance costs decrease along with the time for storing the commodity; also, the shorter the holding period, the lower the opportunity cost for holding an asset. Hence, as specified by Equation (7-2), as the time to delivery becomes shorter and the cost of carry, c, becomes smaller, the futures price, F, converges to the cash price, P.

Futures Prices and Expected Future Spot Prices

We have seen that the price today for a futures contract specifying delivery at period T is related to the *prevailing* spot price via the cost of carry. However, a more important question is how the price today for a futures contract specifying delivery at period T is related to the *expected* spot price at period T.

The expectations model states that the current futures price is equal to the market's expected value of the spot price at period T:

$$F_t = E(P_T)$$

If this model is correct, a speculator can expect neither to win nor to lose from a position in the futures market; expected profits are zero:

$$E(\text{profit}) = E(P_T) - F_t = 0$$

Put another way, if the expectations model is correct, the speculator can expect to earn only the riskless rate of return. This somewhat counterintuitive idea can best be understood through an example.

Example

The expectations model

Suppose that, at time period 0, a speculator purchases a futures contract at a price of F_0 and posts 100% margin in the form of riskless securities. At contract maturity, at time T, the value of the margin account will have grown to

$$F_0(1 + r_f)$$

where r_f is the risk-free rate of return for a period equal to the maturity of the futures contract.

At maturity, the value of the futures contract itself will be

$$P_T - F_0$$

The actual rate of return the speculator will earn is

$$r = \frac{(1 + r_f)F_0 + (P_T - F_0)}{F_0} - 1 = r_f + \frac{(P_T - F_0)}{F_0}$$

The expected rate of return the speculator will earn is

$$E(r) = r_f + \frac{(E(P_T) - F_0)}{F_O}$$

Hence, if the expectations model is correct, the expected rate of return is

$$E(P_T) = F_0 \rightarrow E(r) = r_f$$

Proponents of the expectations model argue that, in a market with rational traders, the expectations model simply has to work. The argument behind this position goes something like this:

> If a majority of the traders expected the spot price at maturity to be above the prevailing futures price, they would buy futures, thereby forcing the futures price up. Conversely, if these rational traders expected the spot price in the future to be below the current futures price, they would sell futures, lowering the futures price. Hence, the only price that will give an equilibrium is for the futures price to be equal to the expected spot price at maturity.

Cost of Carry versus Expectations

We have presented conflicting views of the way in which futures prices are formed. Suppose the expected future price does not change over the maturity of the futures contract: price expectations remain constant. The

expectations model would yield a constant futures price, as illustrated by the horizontal line in Figure 7-4.

John Maynard Keynes was among the first to take exception to such a model.[5] He looked at commodity futures and argued that the futures contract provides a mechanism to transfer risk from the hedgers (the commodity producers, who have natural long positions in the commodity) to speculators. To accomplish this transfer of risk, the equilibrium in the futures market would be such that hedgers would be (on net) short commodity futures contracts (to offset their natural long positions), while speculators would be long commodity futures contracts. Consequently, to get the speculators to buy the commodity futures contracts—to hold the long positions in futures—the expected rate of return for holding futures would have to exceed the risk-free rate. For the expected rate of return on the futures position to exceed the risk-free rate, the futures price would have to be less than the expected spot price and rise as the

---

5. John Maynard Keynes, *Treatise on Money* (London: Macmillan, 1930.)

Figure 7-4. Futures Prices over Time with Constant Future Price Expectations.

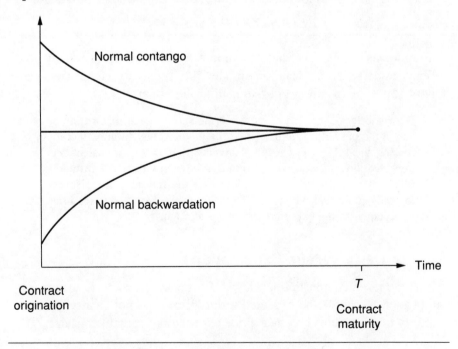

contract maturity approaches. This relation, referred to by Keynes as *normal backwardation*, is illustrated as the rising line in Figure 7-4.

Conversely, if equilibrium is achieved through hedgers, on net, being long futures contracts, the speculators would have to be enticed to hold short futures positions—to sell futures contracts. In this case the futures price would have to begin above the expected spot price and fall as contract maturity approaches. Referred to by Keynes as *normal contango*, this relation is illustrated by the falling line in Figure 7-4.

Example

Backwardation and contango in bond futures

Consider again the construction of a synthetic futures position, this time a futures position on bonds. A party borrows (at the short-term rate) and uses proceeds to purchase bonds (yielding the long-term rate).

The cost of this synthetic bond futures contract is the rate that must to be paid on the short-term borrowing minus the rate earned from the coupons received on the long-term bonds. Through arbitrage, the futures price in a standard contract must be equal to the cost of this synthetic futures.

If the yield curve is positively sloped, the cost of this synthetic futures is negative: the long-term yield received exceeds the short-term yield paid. Hence, the expected return to the holder of the long futures position is positive. This is normal backwardation: the futures price is less than the expected future spot price, and futures prices are lower for contracts whose delivery dates are further in the future. Look again at Figure 7-3—specifically, at the treasury bond futures traded on the Chicago Board of Trade. The further in the future is the delivery date, the lower is the futures price:

March	95.06
June	94.05
Sept.	93.06
Dec.	92.10
March 89	91.16
June 89	90.24
Sept. 89	90.01
Dec. 89	89.12
March 90	88.25

If the yield curve is inverted—negatively sloped—the reverse holds true. The cost of the synthetic futures is positive, so bond futures prices would have exhibit normal contango.

Stephen Figlewski argues that it is the cost-of-carry model, rather than the expectations model, that explains the manner in which futures prices are determined.[6] He argues that the expectations model fails to take into account arbitrage. His argument can be paraphrased as follows:

> If an individual is holding treasury bonds that could be delivered against a treasury bond futures contract, and if the futures price is equal to this individual's expectation of the future spot price of treasury bonds, an arbitrage is possible: He could sell futures against his cash position, thereby eliminating all of the risk in his position, but his expected return would be the same as it would had he held the risky bond position unhedged. This means that the expected return he is earning exceeds the risk-free rate: he is earning a risk premium without bearing the risk. Such a situation would attract other investors, and as more people tried to buy bonds and sell futures, the cash price would be bid up and the futures price bid down until the cost-of-carry relation is reestablished.

However, this should not be taken to mean that the cost-of-carry relation ignores expectations; it does not. The market's expectation of the future spot price of the asset is implicit in the current spot price. In an efficient market—and everything we have seen suggests that these financial markets are efficient—the price today incorporates all available information, including information about what the asset will be worth in the future. Following Figlewski, "the point of the cost of carry model is that given the current cash price [which incorporates a forecast for future spot prices], expectations about the cash price at expiration should not have any *independent* effect on futures prices."[7]

Futures Prices and the Cost of Hedging: Basis

Given what we have said about hedging in general, it follows that, as long as futures are priced according to the cost-of-carry relation, the total return to the holder of a fully hedged position should be the risk-free rate of return. The cash position in the underlying asset is a risky position, so the market return for holding this position would be made up of the risk-free rate of return plus a risk premium. By selling a futures contract against the underlying exposure, the hedger has transferred the riskiness of the asset to the buyer of the contract, so the buyer should

---

6. Stephen Figlewski, *Hedging with Financial Futures for Institutional Investors: From Theory to Practice* (Cambridge, Mass.: Ballinger, 1986), p. 68.
7. Ibid. p. 69.

earn the risk premium. Hence, the person who holds the asset and has hedged completely by selling a futures contract against the asset is left with the riskless rate of return.

The problem is that the underlying cash position may not be fully hedged; the return to the futures contract may not be exactly equal to the risk premium on the underlying asset. The hedger has a long position in the asset and a short position in the futures contract and has consequently invested in the difference between these two assets. Hence, the return to the hedged portfolio is determined by the what happens to the difference between the spot and the futures prices—which is what we defined earlier as the *basis*:

$$\text{Basis} = F - P$$

The hedger, the person with the long position in the asset and the short position in the futures contract, profits if the basis gets smaller and loses if the basis gets larger. The reverse is true for the speculator.

Hence, the hedger has not eliminated all risk but has instead replaced price risk with basis risk. The reason that hedgers use the futures market is that basis risk is potentially more manageable than price risk. But managing the basis risk requires understanding the sources of this risk.

Basis risk results from unpredictable movements in the basis— unpredictable differences between the futures price and the spot price.[8] Although these unpredictable movements in the basis arise from various sources, there are four primary sources of basis risk: changes in the convergence of the futures price to the cash price, changes in factors that affect the cost of carry, mismatches between the exposure being hedged and the futures contract being used as the hedge, and random deviations from the cost-of-carry relation.[9]

The Convergence of the Futures Price to the Cash Price. A "normal" pattern of convergence of the futures price to the cash price is illustrated in Figure 7-5. Part (*a*) illustrates the spot and futures prices

---

8. Predictable movements in basis—such as the convergence of the basis toward the cost of carry during the tenor of the futures contract and the convergence of the basis to zero at contract maturity, which were discussed earlier in this chapter—are incorporated into the expected return at the hedged position.

9. Another way of looking at this is to say that the basis for financial instruments is affected by six factors: the cost of carry, the time until delivery, the deliverable supply, the cost of delivery, changes in cash instruments (e.g., coupon and maturity), and price expectations.

themselves, and Part (*b*) illustrates the basis—the difference between these two prices. At contract maturity, the futures price and the cash price merge; thus, for a hedge in which the futures contract is held to maturity, the return on the futures position will be equal to the return on the asset itself. However, if the futures position is unwound prior to contract maturity, the return from the futures position could differ from the return on the asset due to the basis risk. And, as is obvious from Figure 7-5, the basis is in large part determined by the rate and path of convergence of the futures price to the spot price. Moreover, the convergence determines the behavior of the margin account. For the case illustrated, the futures price rises smoothly over time. Thus, there would be a gradual flow of margin from the account of the party who sold the futures contract to the account of the buyer of the futures contract.

Suppose that the path of convergence was different from that in Figure 7-5. If the futures price converged more rapidly than is illustrated, the basis would decline toward zero more quickly and would consequently be smaller at any point in time. In this case, the flow of margin from the futures seller to the futures buyer would occur more rapidly.[10]

---

10. Regardless of the speed of convergence, the total amount of margin that moves from the seller of the contract to the buyer of the contract is the same; the only difference is in the timing of the cash flows. The slower the futures price converges to the spot price, the slower are the transfers of the margin. Consider an extreme situation, where the spot price moves as before, but the futures price does not move at all until just before maturity:

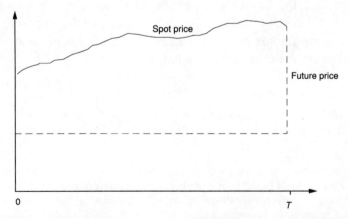

With the convergence as illustrated, no monies are transferred from the contract seller to the contract buyer until just before contract maturity. In such a case the futures contract would behave essentially like a forward contract.

Figure 7-5. Convergence of the Future Price.

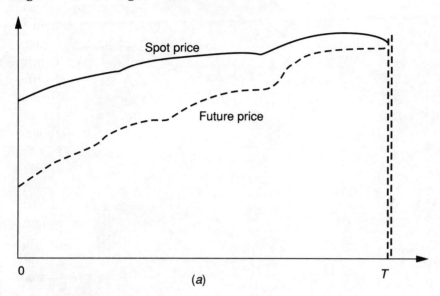

Spot price

Future price

0   (a)   T

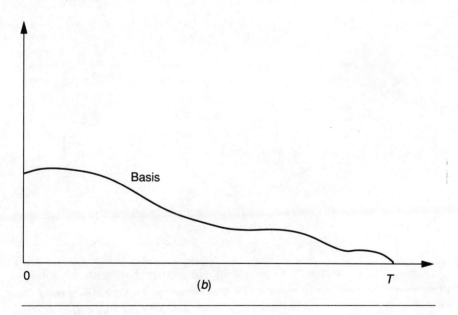

Basis

0   (b)   T

Figure 7-6. Convergence of the Futures Price.

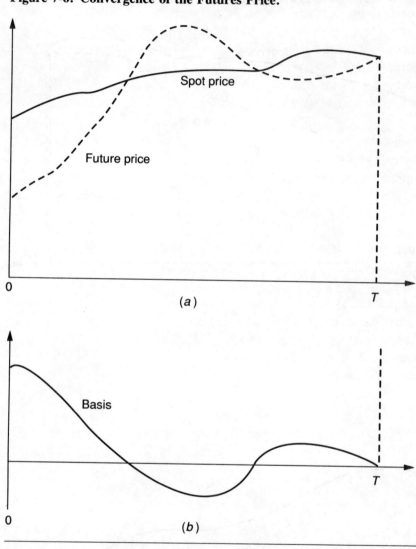

Alternatively, suppose, as illustrated in Figure 7-6, that the futures price overshot its equilibrium. In this situation, the basis would be negative for a time. Margin would first move from the seller of the futures contract to the buyer, then from the buyer to the seller, then again from the seller to the buyer.[11]

---

11. However, since the starting and ending points for the futures price are the same, the total margin that changes hands is the same.

Changes in Factors Affecting the Cost of Carry.   Clearly, as the cost of carry changes, the basis on a futures position changes. For commodity futures, the cost of carry includes storage and insurance costs; changes in either of these cause the basis to change. However, the most significant determinant of the cost of carry is the interest rate. As the interest rate increases, the opportunity cost of holding the asset rises, so the cost of carry—and therefore the basis—rises.

Mismatches between the Exposure Being Hedged and the Futures Contract Being Used as the Hedge.   So far, we have implicitly been examining situations in which the exposure being hedged is the same as the futures contract, for example, hedging an exposure to a movement in the deutsche mark dollar exchange rate with a deutsche mark futures contract, or hedging an exposure to the U.S. treasury bill interest rate with treasury bill futures. However, situations exist in which the position being hedged does not match the deliverable asset/commodity for any futures contract, and the hedger will have to rely on a *cross-hedge*.[12] For example, a deutsche mark futures contract might be used as a cross-hedge for an exposure in Swedish krona, or a treasury bill futures contract might be used as a cross-hedge against an exposure to the U.S. commercial paper rate.

In a cross-hedging situation, there is an additional source of basis risk. Basis results not only from differences between the futures price and the prevailing spot price of the deliverable asset, but also from differences between the spot prices of the deliverable asset and the exposure being hedged:

$$\text{Basis}_{\text{cross-hedge } x \text{ for } y} = (F_x - P_x) + (P_x - P_y)$$

For example, for an exposure to the U.S. commercial paper rate hedged with a treasury bill futures, basis could result from (1) differences in the futures and spot prices of treasury bills, and (2) differences in the spot treasury bill and commercial paper interest rates. Let's define the latter contribution to basis risk as the *cross-hedge basis*. As will be shown in Chapter 8, the "normal" cross-hedge basis can be determined by the correlation between the spot price of the asset being hedged and the spot price of the deliverable product in the futures contract being used as the

---

12. We will spend a considerable amount of time talking about the way a cross-hedge is constructed and managed in the next chapter.

hedge. Stephen Figlewski[13] has argued that there are three important factors responsible for variation in the basis for a cross-hedge:

1. *Maturity mismatch*: The maturity of the underlying instrument for the futures contract may be different from the maturity of the asset underlying the exposure. For example, the exposure of the S&L we have alluded to may be to thirty-year mortgage interest rates, and the hedge may be constructed using treasury bond futures, for which the underlying instrument has a maturity of fifteen years.[14]

2. *Liquidity differences*: Suppose the asset being hedged is traded in a market that is illiquid in comparison to the market for the deliverable asset in the futures contract. In such an instance, the price fluctuations for the asset being hedged would be likely to be large relative to the fluctuations in the price of the deliverable asset, implying that basis would increase. Hence, the basis is inversely related to the liquidity for the asset being hedged.

3. *Credit risk differences*: An example provided by Figlewski is the use of treasury bond futures to hedge a portfolio of corporate bonds. Put another way, changes in the quality spread show up in the basis for a cross-hedge.

Random Deviations from the Cost-of-Carry Relation. The final source of basis risk is the catchall component. From day to day and from minute to minute, the basis on a futures position will change for reasons not understood; however, over longer periods, this random, "white noise" component of basis risk will cancel itself out.

---

13. Figlewski, *op. cit.* pp. 77–78.
14. As noted in the preceding chapter, the bond to be delivered against a T-bond futures must have at least fifteen years remaining to maturity.

8

Managing Risks with Futures

As noted in Chapter 6, financial futures are a recent addition to the financial toolbox. Nonetheless, they have come to be widely used as a means of hedging exposures to foreign exchange, interest rate, and commodity price risk. To illustrate the expansion in the use of futures, Table 8-1 and Figures 8-1 through 8-4 trace the growth in the trading volume for some of the more familiar futures contracts—deutsche marks, treasury bonds, Eurodollars, and crude oil—over the period 1977–87.

The logic of using futures to hedge an underlying exposure, illustrated in Figure 8-5, is simple: If the firm has an inherent short position in a financial asset (i.e., increases in the price of the asset will decrease the value of the firm), the hedge will be constructed by buying the appropriate number of the appropriate futures contract for the appropriate expiration month. Combining the inherent position with the hedge, the exposure is neutralized. For the firm that has an inherent long position, the reverse is true: the hedge is constructed by selling the appropriate number of the appropriate futures contract for the appropriate expiration month.

The problem for the hedger is, of course, to determine those "appropriate" values—the appropriate futures contract, the appropriate expiration month, and the appropriate number of contracts. To demonstrate how the hedger determines what is "appropriate," it is easiest to use an example. For the discussion to follow, we chose to look at a firm with an interest rate exposure, but the logic is the same for foreign exchange and commodity exposures.

Table 8-1. Futures Contract Volumes, 1977–87.

	Contracts Traded			
	Treasury Bonds*	Eurodollar**	Deutsche Mark**	Crude Oil***
1987	66,841,474	20,416,216	6,037,048	14,581,614
1986	52,598,811	10,824,914	6,582,145	8,313,529
1985	40,448,357	8,900,528	6,449,384	3,980,867
1984	29,963,280	4,192,952	5,508,308	1,840,342
1983	19,550,535	891,066	2,423,508	323,153
1982	16,739,695	323,619	1,792,901	—
1981	13,907,988	15,171	1,654,891	—
1980	6,489,555	—	922,608	—
1979	2,059,594	—	450,856	—
1978	555,350	—	400,569	—
1977	32,101	—	134,368	—

*Chicago Board of Trade
**Chicago Mercantile Exchange
***New York Mercantile Exchange
Source: "1977–1987 Volume of Futures Trading," Futures Industry Association, Washington, DC.

Figure 8-1. Deutsche Mark Futures Contract Volumes, 1977–87.

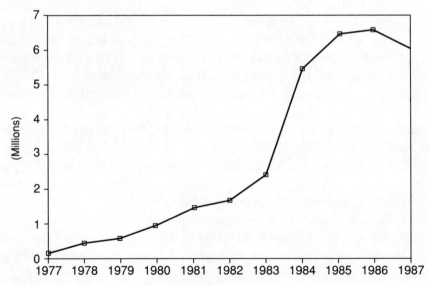

Figure 8-2. T-Bond Futures Contract Volumes, 1977-87.

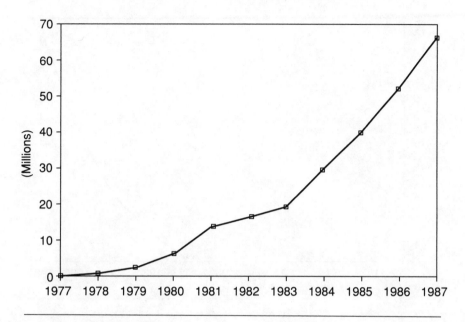

Figure 8-3. Eurodollar Futures Contract Volumes, 1977–87.

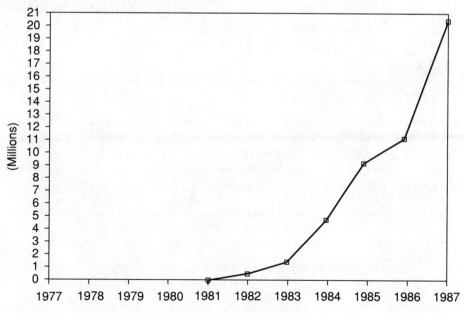

Figure 8-4. Crude Oil Futures Contract Volumes, 1977–87.

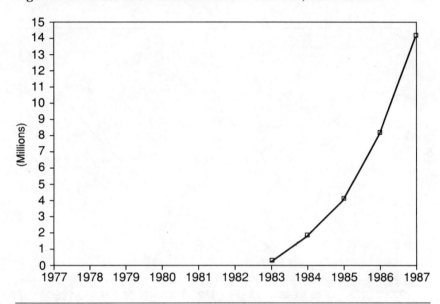

Using Futures to Hedge an Underlying Exposure

To illustrate how a futures contract can be used as a hedge, it is probably best to begin at the beginning, with the simplest case.[1]

Example

The naive case: no basis risk

At the beginning of 1989, the treasurer of Ajax Enterprises knows that, due to seasonal variations in sales and in the production of inventory for Christmas sales, the firm will require a three-month, $1 million bank loan on June 19. The treasurer knows that the contractual rate Ajax will have to pay on the loan will be the three-month Eurodollar rate (LIBOR) plus 1 percent. Hence, the treasurer is concerned about increases in three-month LIBOR since every 1 percent (100 basis points) increase in LIBOR increases Ajax's borrowing costs by $2,500.

---

1. This case and some of those that follow have been adapted from *Using Interest Rate Futures and Options*, a 1986 publication of the Chicago Mercantile Exchange.

Figure 8-5. The Logic of the Futures Hedge. (*a*) **A Long Hedge.**
(*b*) **A Short Hedge.**

If the firm has an inherent short
position

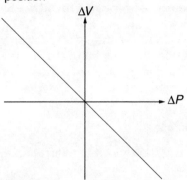

If the firm has an inherent long
position

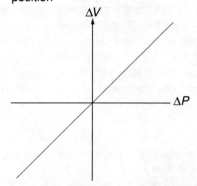

the hedge will be created by buying
the appropriate number of the
appropriate futures contract

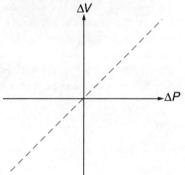

the hedge will be created by buying
the appropriate number of the
appropriate futures contract

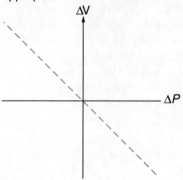

to neutralize the exposure.

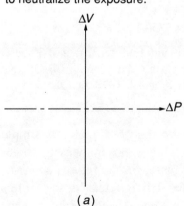

to neutralize the exposure.

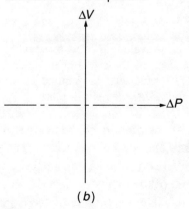

(*a*)

(*b*)

Using the Eurodollar futures contract traded on the Chicago Mercantile Exchange, the treasurer can achieve a perfect hedge. The treasurer can lock in the Eurodollar borrowing rate given by the implied forward LIBOR rate by selling one June Eurodollar futures contract.

Suppose that, on January 2, the three-month LIBOR rate was 9.25%. Suppose further that the implied forward LIBOR rate from the June Eurodollar futures contract was 9.55%. Given that Eurodollar futures are quoted as 100 minus the interest rate, this means that the price of the June Eurodollar futures contract on January 2 is

$$100 - 9.55 = 90.45$$

The treasurer of Ajax sells one June futures at 90.45 to lock in a three-month rate of 9.55%.

Suppose that the treasurer's fears are realized, and by the time he needs to borrow, three-month LIBOR is up. Although this would be extreme, let's suppose that, precisely on June 19, the three-month LIBOR rate rises from 9.25% to 11.00%. This 175-basis-point increase in LIBOR means that Ajax's borrowing costs have increased by $1.75 \times \$2,500 = \$4,375$. Conversely, the increase in the interest rate means that Ajax has earned monies on the futures position, which can be used to offset some of this increase in the borrowing cost. In 1989, June 19, is the last trading day/delivery date for the June Eurodollar futures contract. Hence, on June 19, as the futures contract expires, the futures rate and the spot rate must merge; thus, the price of the June futures contract on June 19 must be

$$100 - 11.00 = 89.00$$

Hence, the price of the futures contract has declined by 1.45, or 145 "ticks." The price movement per tick is $25, so Ajax's profit on the futures contract is $145 \times \$25 = \$3,625$.

Combining the preceding amounts, Ajax's net increase in its borrowing cost is

$$\$4,375 - \$3,625 = \$750$$

which is equivalent to an increase in the three-month Eurodollar rate of 30 basis points. That is, the effect of the hedge is to lock in a three-month LIBOR rate of 9.55%, precisely the implied forward three-month LIBOR rate that existed when the hedge was put in place.

The construction of the hedge in the preceding example was simple because everything matched. The underlying exposure was to three-month LIBOR, the same as the deliverable asset for the futures contract. The end of the exposure exactly matched the delivery date for the futures contract. The magnitude of the exposure was equal to the amount of the futures contract.

Moreover, the price movement in this case was such that no monies were transferred into or out of the margin account during the life of the contract. Consequently, Ajax neither earned additional interest income (in its margin account), nor did it forgo interest on monies paid out of its margin account.

In the real world, the exposure doesn't exactly match the characteristics of the futures contract. And it's virtually a sure bet that the price changes will not all occur on the final day of the futures contract. As we will demonstrate in the remainder of this section, these factors have an impact on the way in which the hedge should be constructed.

Mismatches on Maturities: Basis Risk

In the preceding example, there was no basis risk. The period of the exposure matched precisely the period covered by the futures contract; consequently, the futures price and the spot price were the same when the futures hedge was removed. Were this not the case, basis risk would result.

Example

Basis risk

Suppose that Ajax required the $1 million loan not on June 19 but on June 1, a little more than two weeks before maturity for the futures contract. The treasurer of Ajax would still hedge the exposure by selling one June futures contract on January 2 at 90.45, trying to lock in a three-month Eurodollar rate of 9.55%.

To keep the numbers simple, suppose that on June 1, three-month LIBOR rises to 11.00% (as it did on June 19 in the preceding example).[2] So, as before, the increased borrowing cost for Ajax will be $4,375. With this increase in the spot interest rate, the futures interest rate will also rise, so the price of the futures contract will fall. However, since June 1 is not the expiration date for the contract, there is no guarantee that on June 1 the futures and spot rates will match. Let's suppose that they do not, and that on June 1 the futures price does not fall to 89.00 but only to 89.25. The futures price has moved 120 ticks, so Ajax's profit on the futures position is $120 \times \$25 = \$3,000$.

The result is that Ajax's net increase in its borrowing cost is

$$\$4,375 - \$3,000 = \$1,375$$

---

2. For now, we continue to suppose that the price change occurred only on June 1; LIBOR remained at 9.25% from January 2 to May 31, so the margin account was unaffected.

an amount equivalent to a 55-basis-point increase in the three-month LIBOR rate. Hence, the treasurer did not end up with the 9.55% rate he went out to get but instead ended up with a rate of 9.80%; the difference of 25 basis point is the result of the basis of 25 basis points that existed when the futures contract was closed out.[3]

In this example, the basis went against the treasurer, and the hedge was less than 100% effective. However, the basis could go for the hedger; for example, if the price of the futures contract on June 1 had been 88.75, the rate Ajax would have ended up with would have been 9.30%, and the hedge would have been more than 100% effective.

The situation illustrated in the preceding example is more normal. Due to basis, the hedge can be more or less than 100% effective. Since there is nothing the hedger can do about the underlying causes of basis, which were discussed in Chapter 7, the only thing the hedger can do is to try to line up exposure dates—in the preceding example, loan pricing dates—with the maturity dates for the futures contract.

Mismatches on Maturities: Strip and Rolling Hedges

So far we have considered single exposures such that the maturity for the exposure fits a single futures contract. However, a hedger might have more than one maturity to hedge.

Example

A strip hedge

The treasurer of Beta Manufacturing is also faced with uncertainty about future borrowing costs. Like Ajax, Beta uses three-month borrowing, for which it pays a rate linked to three-month LIBOR; but, unlike Ajax, Beta borrows not simply once per year but rather throughout the year. On January 2, the treasurer of Beta expects the following borrowing pattern over 1989:

March 1	$15 million
June 1	$45 million
September 1	$20 million
December 1	$10 million

---

3. When the futures contract was closed out, the spot interest rate was 11.00%. The rate implied by the futures price was

$$100 - 89.25 = 10.75\%$$

Hence, the basis was 25 basis points.

To hedge the resulting exposure to the three-month Eurodollar rate, the treasurer of Beta would, on January 2, sell a *strip* of futures. Beta would sell fifteen March Eurodollar futures contracts, forty-five June contracts, twenty September contracts, and ten December contracts.

On March 1, Beta would close out the hedge on its first borrowing by buying fifteen March contracts. Likewise, on June 1, Beta would buy forty-five June contracts; on September 1, Beta would buy twenty September contracts; and on December 1, Beta would buy ten December contracts. As was illustrated in the last example, the effectiveness of the hedge would depend on the basis existing on the dates at which the contracts were closed out.

The preceding strategy works well as long as there is sufficient liquidity in the most distant futures contract. However, if the more distant futures contracts do not have sufficient liquidity, or if the maturity of the exposure exceeds the most distant futures contract, the hedger can resort to a *rolling hedge*. A rolling hedge can achieve the same result as a strip hedge.

Example

A rolling hedge

Were the treasurer of Beta concerned about the liquidity of more distant futures contracts, she could hedge the exposure to the three-month Eurodollar rate by rolling the hedge:

January 2	Sell 90 March Eurodollar futures contracts
March 1	Buy 90 March Eurodollar futures contracts Sell 75 June Eurodollar futures contracts
June 1	Buy 75 June Eurodollar futures contracts Sell 30 September Eurodollar futures contracts
September 1	Buy 30 September Eurodollar futures contracts Sell 10 December Eurodollar futures contracts
December 1	Buy 10 December Eurodollar futures contracts

By doing this, the treasurer can take advantage of the liquidity in earlier contracts.

A rolling hedge can also be effective where a strip hedge is not possible.

Example

Another rolling hedge

At the beginning of 1989, the treasurer of Beta continues to have the following expectations about borrowings in 1989:

March 1	$15 million
June 1	$45 million
September 1	$20 million
December 1	$10 million

So, on January 2, the treasurer implements the rolling hedge detailed in the preceding example:

January 2   Sell 90 March Eurodollar futures contracts

However, suppose that by the time March 1 arrives, the treasurer has developed her forecast for Beta's borrowing needs for March 1, 1990, as $20 million. To hedge this revised borrowing schedule, the transactions done by Beta on March 1 are as follows:

March 1   Buy 90 March Eurodollar futures contracts
Sell 95 June Eurodollar futures contracts

In the last example, Beta's remaining borrowing needs were for $75 million. Now, with the addition of the forecast $20 million borrowing in March of 1990, Beta's borrowing needs—the amount it needs to hedge—is $95 million; thus, Beta will sell ninety-five, rather than seventy-five, June futures contracts.

Continuing in the same manner, suppose that by the time June 1 arrives, the treasurer is forecasting a borrowing requirement of $60 million for June 1, 1990. Hence,

June 1   Buy 95 June Eurodollar futures contracts
Sell 110 September Eurodollar futures contracts

By buying the 95 June contracts, Beta is closing out the hedge for its June 1989 borrowing.[4] At the same time, it sells 110 contracts to hedge its September 1989 borrowing (20 contracts), its December 1989 borrowing (10 contracts), its March 1990 borrowing (20 contracts), and its June 1990 borrowing (60 contracts).

The treasurer can continue this system without end. On September 1, she closes out the hedge for the September borrowing by buying the 110 September contracts and sells December 1989, March 1990, June 1990 and September

---

4. The effectiveness of the hedge again depends on the basis between the spot three-month LIBOR rate and the implied rate from the futures price on June 1.

1990 contracts sufficient to hedge her anticipated borrowing needs in December 1989, March 1990, June 1990, and September 1990. On December 1, she buys December contracts to close out the hedge for the December borrowing and sells March 1990, June 1990, September 1990, and December 1990 contracts to hedge borrowing needs in March, June, September, and December 1990. On March 1, 1990, ...

By "stacking" the contracts, futures can be used to hedge an exposure that extends beyond the end of the longest available contract. However, the stacking approach does have some drawbacks.[5] First, more contracts must be bought and sold as the hedge is rolled forward, thereby increasing the transaction cost of the hedge. Second, since the prices for futures contracts not yet traded are uncertain, there is an additional source of basis risk.

Mismatches in the Asset: Cross-Hedging

To this point, we have considered only cases in which the underlying exposure was to the same financial price that determines the price of the futures contract. In our examples so far, the firm was exposed to three-month LIBOR, precisely the same financial price that determines the price of the Eurodollar futures contract. However, it is often the case that the exposure is not precisely matched by a traded futures contract. In such cases, the hedger will have to resort to a cross-hedge and will be faced with two questions: (1) What futures contract should be used to hedge the exposure? (2) How many contracts will be needed to hedge the exposure?

The answer to the first question is simple. To establish the "best" cross-hedge, use the futures contract that is most closely correlated with the underlying exposure. To see how this works, let's look again at Ajax.

Example

A cross-hedge: selecting the appropriate futures contract

At the beginning of 1989, the treasurer of Ajax Enterprises again expects that it will be necessary for Ajax to borrow on June 1. However, let's change

---

5. Mark Drabenstott and Anne O'Mara McDonley, "Futures Markets: A Primer for Financial Institutions," *Economic Review,* Federal Reserve Bank of Kansas City, November 1984.

the parameters of this expected borrowing. First, instead of $1 million, let's suppose the forecast borrowing is $36 million. Second, instead of a three-month bank borrowing tied to LIBOR, let's suppose that the treasurer has decided to issue one-month commercial paper.

Nonetheless, the treasurer remains concerned about rising interest rates and wishes to hedge his interest rate exposure. But (as is evident in Table 6-2) there is no futures contract in one-month commercial paper. To select the "best" contract to hedge the exposure to commercial paper rates, the treasurer looks at the correlations between the one-month commercial paper rate and several interest rates for which there are traded futures contracts available.

Futures Contract	Interest Rate	Correlation with One-Month CP Rate[6]
U.S. T-bills	90-day T-bill Rate	0.908
Eurodollars	90-day LIBOR	0.964
U.S. T-bonds	15-year T-bond Rate	0.622

The high correlation between the ninety-day LIBOR rate and the one-month commercial paper rate, depicted graphically in Figure 8-6, leads the treasurer to select the Eurodollar contract as the most appropriate futures contract.

As the preceding example illustrates, the "appropriate futures contract" for instituting a cross-hedge is normally selected as that futures contract most highly correlated with the underlying exposure. However, this simple decision rule may need to be modified if the futures contract so selected has insufficient liquidity. If the futures contract is illiquid, a large order could have a discernible effect on the price. To the extent that the hedger's buy order triggers a price increase and the sell order triggers a price decrease, the cost of constructing a hedge would be increased. Moreover, in an illiquid market, the bid-ask spread will usually be large, leading to an increase in the overall cost of the hedge. Consequently, concerns about the liquidity of a particular contract could result in the hedger shifting to another futures contract that has higher liquidity but a lower correlation.

---

6. The correlation coefficients displayed were calculated using data for the period 1/2/87 through 1/13/89.

Figure 8-6. Three-Month LIBOR versus One-Month Commercial Paper.

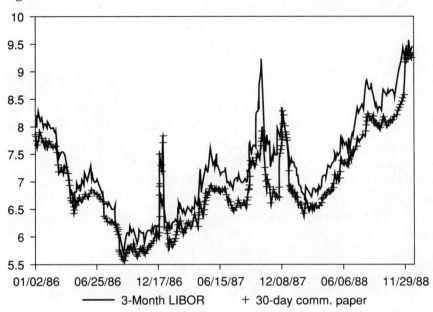

Once the appropriate futures contract is selected, the hedger must answer the second question: How many contracts will be needed to hedge the exposure? The answer to this is made up of two parts. The hedger must first consider the relation between movements in the underlying exposure and the price of the futures contract being used as a hedge. Since the financial price being used in the hedge is not the same as the financial price responsible for the firm's underlying exposure, there is no guarantee that there will be one-for-one movements in the two financial prices. What the hedger needs to know is how these two prices move with one another. For example, in the case of interest rate risk, if the rate in the hedge changes by X basis points, how much will the rate to which the firm is exposed change? Although there are many ways to answer this question, the simplest and most straightforward method is to use a linear regression. The analyst will regress the financial price to which the firm is exposed on the financial price imbedded in the futures contract being used as the hedge, $P_{futures}$:

$$\text{Exposure} = a + bP_{futures}$$

Or, in the case at hand, where the financial prices are interest rates, the regression equation would be

$$r_{exposure} = a + b(r_{futures})$$

where $r_{exposure}$ is the interest rate to which the firm is exposed and $r_{futures}$ is the interest rate imbedded in the futures contract. The estimate of b tells how the interest rate to which the firm is exposed moves in relation to the interest rate imbedded in the futures contract. For example, if the estimate of b turns out to be 0.5, it means that the rate to which the firm is exposed moves only half as much as the rate in the futures contract; so, all other things equal, only half as many futures contracts would be needed to hedge the exposure. Conversely, if the estimate of b turns out to be 2.0, the rate to which the firm is exposed moves twice as much as the rate in the futures contract; so, all other things equal, twice as many futures contracts would be needed to hedge the exposure.

Example

A cross-hedge: selecting the appropriate number of contracts (Part 1)

The treasurer of Ajax has decided to hedge his June 1 exposure to the one-month commercial paper rate with June Eurodollar futures contracts—priced off three-month LIBOR. To determine how these two rates move in relation to one another, he used monthly data for 1986–88 to estimate the relation

$$r_{exposure} = a + b(r_{futures})$$

The estimate of b obtained from a regression of the data was 0.75.

Hence, *considering only the relation between the one-month commercial paper rate and the three-month LIBOR rate*, the treasurer knows that to hedge his $36 million exposure, he would need to sell $36 \times 0.75 = 27$ June Eurodollar contracts.

In determining the number of futures contracts needed to hedge an exposure, the second thing the hedger must consider is the effect of a one-unit change in the financial price on the underlying exposure versus the effect of this one-unit change in financial price on the value of the futures contract. For the case at hand, an increase in the interest rate need not have the same effect on the underlying exposure as it does on the value of the futures contract. If a given change in the interest rate has a larger impact on the underlying exposure than on the value of the futures contract, fewer futures contracts will be needed to hedge the position, and vice versa.

Example

A cross hedge: selecting the appropriate number of contracts (Part 2)

As we know, the treasurer of Ajax has decided to hedge a $36 million June 1 one-month commercial paper borrowing with June Eurodollar futures, that is, with three-month LIBOR.

However, a 1 basis-point movement in the interest rate does not have the same impact on a one-month borrowing as it does on the three-month futures contract. A 1 basis-point movement changes the value of a one-month $1 million borrowing by

$$\$1,000,000 \times 0.0001 \times 30/360 = \$8.33.$$

But, as we have already seen, a 1 basis-point movement changes the value of the $1 million futures contract by

$$\$1,000,000 \times 0.0001 \times 90/360 = \$25$$

The response of the futures contract is three times that of the underlying exposure—the one-month borrowing.

Hence, *considering only the difference in the way the borrowing and the futures contract respond to a given change in the interest rate,* the treasurer of Ajax knows that he would need only one-third as many futures contracts to hedge the exposure. That is, to hedge a $36 million one-month exposure, he would need to sell twelve rather than thirty-six three-month futures contracts.

In summary, the construction of a cross-hedge requires that the hedger do the following:

1. *Determine the appropriate futures contract to use as the hedge.* In general, the appropriate futures contract is the one that is most closely correlated with the underlying exposure. However, an alternate futures contract may be selected if there is insufficient liquidity in the preferred contract.

2. *Determine the appropriate number of futures contracts.* The appropriate number of futures contracts is determined by (1) the relation between movements in the underlying exposure and the price of the futures contract being used as a hedge, and (2) the effect of a one-unit change in the financial price on the underlying exposure versus the effect of this one-unit change in the financial price on the value of the futures contract.

To see how this is accomplished, let's put the two parts of our example together:

Example

A cross-hedge

At the beginning of 1989, the treasurer of Ajax Enterprises expects that it will be necessary for Ajax to borrow $36 million on June 1 via an issue of one-month commercial paper. Concerned about rising interest rates, the treasurer wishes to hedge the firm's interest rate exposure. Since there is no futures contract in one-month commercial paper, the treasurer selected the "best" contract to hedge the exposure by finding the futures contract interest rate that has the highest correlation with the one-month commercial paper rate, which turned out to be three-month LIBOR. Hence, the appropriate futures contract is the June Eurodollar futures contract.

To determine the appropriate number of June Eurodollar futures to use to hedge the $36 million one-month commercial paper exposure, the treasurer first used monthly data for 1986–88 to estimate the relation

$$r_{\text{exposure}} = a + b(r_{\text{futures}})$$

and obtained an estimate of b of 0.75. Second, the treasurer noted that a 1 basis-point movement changes the value of a one-month $1 million borrowing by $8.33, but a 1 basis-point movement changes the value of the $1 million futures contract by $25. Hence, the response of the futures contract is three times that of the underlying exposure—the one-month borrowing. Putting this together, the number of contracts necessary to hedge the exposure is

$$36 \times 0.75 \times 0.33 = 9$$

Consequently, on January 2, the treasurer of Ajax would sell nine June Eurodollar futures contracts.

Once the cross-hedge is implemented, the degree to which it will actually hedge the underlying exposure is determined, as before, by the basis. However, in the case of the cross-hedge, the hedger is using a futures contract in financial price X to hedge an exposure to financial price Y, so there are two distinct sources of basis risk. First, the cross-hedge is subject to the normal basis: when the hedge is removed, the spot price for X need not be equal to the futures price of X.[7] The second source of basis risk is in deviations between the spot price of X and the spot price of Y.[8] To see how this occurs, let's look at how our cross hedge worked.

---

7. As we have shown, the spot price and futures prices are guaranteed to be equal only at expiration of the futures contract.
8. As Ira Kawaller pointed out, this second source of risk is the risk that the ex post relation between X and Y (the parameter b in our equation) turns out to be equal to the ex ante estimate of the relation from the regression equation.

Example

The results of the cross-hedge

On January 2 three-month LIBOR is 9.25%, and the price of June Eurodollar futures is 90.45—implying a June futures LIBOR rate of 9.55%. On January 2 the spread between the spot LIBOR rate and the commercial paper rate is 50 basis points, so the one-month commercial paper rate is 8.75%.

In preceding examples, Ajax was hoping to lock in the futures rate of 9.55%; that is, Ajax was trying to lock in an increase in three-month LIBOR of 30 basis points. We saw that the treasurer of Ajax estimated the relation between changes in three-month LIBOR and changes in the one-month commercial paper rate to be 0.75. In other words, an expected of 30-basis-point increase in three-month LIBOR would result in an expected increase of $0.75 \times 30 = 22.5$ basis points in the one-month commercial paper rate. Hence, the one-month commercial paper rate Ajax is trying to lock in is 8.75% + 22.5 basis points = 8.975%.

Precisely on June 1 the three-month LIBOR rate rises to 11.00%,[9] and the price of June futures falls to 89.25. Ajax's profit on each futures contract is $3,000, so the profit on the nine contracts is $27,000.

If the estimated relation between three-month LIBOR and one-month commercial paper holds, the 175-basis-point increase in three-month LIBOR (11.00% − 9.25%) should result in an increase of $0.75 \times 175 = 131.25$ basis points in the one-month commercial paper rate. Hence, the one-month rate the treasurer would expect is 8.75% + 131.25 basis points = 10.0625%. However, let's suppose that on June 1 the one-month commercial paper rate rose to 10.20%. The increase in Ajax's borrowing costs due to the increase in the commercial paper rate is

$$\$36,000,000 \times (0.1020 - 0.0875) \times 30/360 = \$43,500$$

Combining the increase in the borrowing cost with the profit on the hedge position, Ajax's net increase in its borrowing cost is

$$\$43,500 - \$27,000 = \$16,500$$

An increase in the borrowing cost of $16,500 is equivalent to an increase in the one-month rate of 55 basis points. Hence, Ajax's final one-month borrowing rate was 8.75% + 55 basis points = 9.30%.

The difference between the final rate Ajax will pay on its borrowing, 9.30%, and the rate the treasurer tried to lock in, 8.975%, is 32.5 basis points. The difference is again due to basis risk, but in this case there are two sources of the basis:

---

9. We are still presuming that the price change occurs only on June 1; from January 2 through May 31, LIBOR remained at 9.25%.

1. On June 1, the spot LIBOR rate of 11.00% differed from the LIBOR rate implied by the futures price, $100 - 89.25 = 10.75\%$, by 25 basis points. Since the relation between the three-month LIBOR rate and the one-month commercial paper rate has been estimated to be 0.75, the basis of 25 basis points for three-month LIBOR translates to a basis of $0.75 \times 25 = 18.75$ basis points for one-month commercial paper.

2. On June 1, the expected one-month commercial paper rate was 10.0625%, but the actual commercial paper rate was 10.20%. This difference resulted in a basis for the one-month commercial paper hedge of $10.20\% - 10.0625\% = 13.75$ basis points.

Combining the two sources of basis,

$$18.75 + 13.75 = 32.5 \text{ basis points}$$

we obtain the total basis for this one-month commercial paper hedge.

Adjusting for the Margin Account: "Tailing" the Hedge

So far, we have looked at the construction of a hedge considering only the gain or loss on the futures position at the end, when the hedge is removed. However, as we know from our discussions in Chapter 6, profits and losses accrue to a futures contract over the life of the contract as monies are transferred into or out of the hedger's margin account. Since the monies in the margin account earn interest, monies that flow in early are more valuable than those that flow in later, and the value of the hedger's position is higher if monies flow out of the margin account late rather than early.

For purposes of illustration, suppose a firm has sold a futures contract to hedge an underlying position; gains on the hedge will be used to offset losses on the underlying position. Figure 8-7 illustrates the effect of the timing of cash flows into the margin account. In all three parts of the figure, the gain to the hedger, independent of the margin account, is equal to the difference in the beginning and ending futures prices times the size of the futures contract, $(F_0 - F_T)FC$; however, the accrued interest for the margin account is very different for the three cases displayed in parts (a) through (c). First compare parts (a) and (b). Part (a) is much like the situation we have been using so far: the futures price remains constant until just at the end of the hedge period. In part (b) monies flow into the hedger's margin account smoothly over the duration of the hedge. For the situation illustrated in part (a), there is essentially no interest earned; for that illustrated in part (b), the hedger earns interest on the increas-

Figure 8-7. The Effect of the Timing of Cash Flows into the Margin Account.

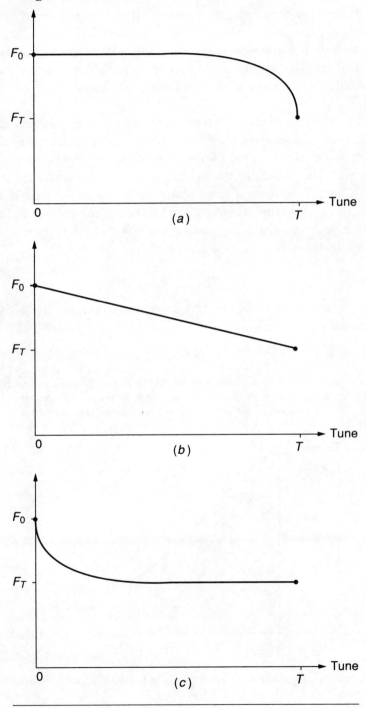

es in the margin account. Consequently, if the futures price behaves as in part (*b*) rather than part (*a*), the number of futures contracts necessary to hedge a given position is smaller. If futures prices behave as in the situation illustrated in part (*c*), the hedge position can be even smaller, since more of the monies flow in early during the hedge period.[10]

The upshot of all of this is that the number of futures contracts needed to hedge an exposure must be adjusted for the effect of the margin account. In the jargon of the futures market, this is referred to as *tailing the hedge*. The object of the tail is to adjust the number of futures contracts so that the *present value* of the hedge is just sufficient to offset the underlying exposure. Hence, if the number of contracts to be sold to hedge a given exposure is N, ignoring the effect of the margin account, the tailed hedge is

$$e^{-rT} \times N$$

where T is the maturity of the hedge and r is the appropriate riskless interest rate.

---

10. For purposes of illustration, we have presumed that monies flow in only one direction during the duration of a hedge. This is certainly not necessary. As illustrated below, monies could first flow out of the margin account from period 0 to period t_1,

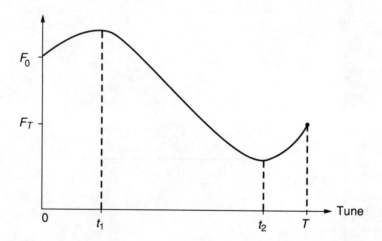

then flow into the margin account from period t_1 to t_2, and then flow out of the margin account again from period t_2 to T.

Example

A tailed hedge

Cassa Manufacturing, like Ajax, expects that it will have to issue one-month commercial paper in the future. However, Cassa is expecting to issue $400 million in fifteen months.

The treasurer of Cassa wants to hedge this exposure using futures contracts. Using what we have seen for Ajax, it appears that the appropriate contract is the Eurodollar futures; and, ignoring the effect of the margin account, the appropriate number of contracts to sell would be

$$400 \times 0.75 \times 0.33 = 100$$

However, if the margin account is considered—if the hedge is "tailed"—the number of Eurodollar futures contracts to be sold is

$$e^{-rT} \times 100$$

where T is 15 months. Thus, if we suppose that the corresponding riskless interest rate is 8.2%, the treasurer of Cassa will sell ninety Eurodollar futures contracts:

$$e^{-(0.082)(15/12)} \times 100 = 90.25$$

Managing a Futures Hedge

Once the hedge has been established, it is essential that it be monitored. As observers of the futures market note, placing a hedge and then forgetting it amounts to imprudent hedging.[11]

Margin calls and the daily marking to market require the hedger's attention. In many cases, the funds needed to meet the margin calls must be obtained from sources other than the underlying position itself. For this reason, a successful hedging program must provide an optimal-size source of these funds. Clearly, the hedger does not want to have too small a source of funds to meet margin calls; if the funds are not available, the hedge will be closed out. On the other hand, the hedger does not want to keep too large a pool of liquid funds available for meeting margin calls, since he or she thus forgoes interest that could otherwise be earned.[12]

---

11. Drabenstott and McDonley, *op. cit.*
12. In Chapter 7 of *Hedging with Financial Futures for Institutional Investors* (Cambridge, Mass.: Ballinger, 1986), Stephen Figlewski provides a methodology for determining the optimal pool of liquid funds available to meet margin calls.

Moreover, the hedger needs to monitor the rate at which funds are moving into and out of the margin account. If funds are flowing into or out of the margin account at a rate different from that expected when the hedge was put on, the tailing factor for the hedge may need to be changed and the number of futures contracts adjusted accordingly.

Finally, and most importantly, the hedger will have to monitor basis risk. After all, by using the futures contract, the hedger has accepted basis risk in place of price risk; thus, it behooves the hedger to manage this basis risk as much as possible. Hence, the hedge may need to be rebalanced occasionally as the relation between the prices of the assets being hedged and the assets underlying the futures contract changes. Or the hedge may need to be rebalanced as the relation between the spot and futures prices changes.

PART IV

Swaps

9

Evolution of the Swap Contract

In one of its advertisements, Bankers Trust extolled the swap as "a tool no financial manager can ignore."[1] Although this statement has the ring of hyperbolic Madison Avenue prose, support for this view is provided by the volumes in the swap market. In Figure 9-1, we have provided volume estimates (notional principal outstanding) for currency and interest rate swaps for the period 1981–87. As this figure indicates, the volume of swaps has increased dramatically, particularly for interest rate swaps, since the introduction of the instrument in 1981.

However, this dramatic growth of the swap market is one of the few agreed-upon "facts" about the swap market. The rapid growth of the market has contributed to much confusion/misinformation/folklore about the "hows" and the "whys" of swaps.

---

1. Bankers Trust Company, "The International Swap Market," advertising supplement to *Euromoney Corporate Finance* (September 1985).

In the development of the chapters on swaps, we are particularly indebted to Lee Macdonald Wakeman. Much of the material we used is taken from three papers Cliff and Charles co-authored with Lee: "The Evolving Market for Swaps," *Midland Corporate Finance Journal* 3, no. 4 (Winter 1986): pp. 20–32; "Credit Risk and the Scope of Regulation of Swaps," *Proceedings of the Conference on Bank Structure and Competition,* Federal Reserve Bank of Chicago, 1987: pp. 166–185; and "The Market for Interest Rate Swaps," *Financial Management* 17, no. 4 (Winter 1988): 34–44. Moreover, much of our thinking—indeed, much of the thinking of the swaps market in general—on pricing and hedging swaps is based on Lee's work on the zero-coupon yield curve and hedging a book of swaps.

Figure 9-1. "Guesstimates" of Swap Volume Notional Principal Outstanding, 1981–87 (billion U.S. dollars).

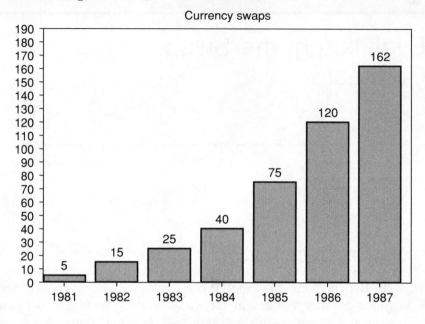

Currency swaps

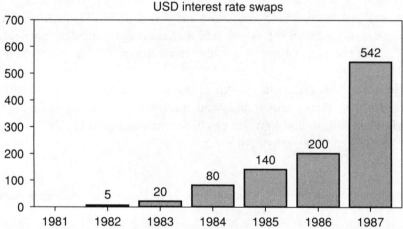

USD interest rate swaps

The 1981–85 volume estimates are taken from Ronald Layard-Leisching, *Euromoney* (January 1986). (A similar series for interest rate swaps is provided by Jane Fant Nelson in the June 1986 issue of *United States Banker*.) The 1986 estimates were obtained in releases from the International Swaps Dealers Association. The 1987 estimates were reported in *Swaps Monitor* (July 25, 1988). There is at present no series of consistent swap volume estimates. A swap might go through several intermediaries before reaching the final counterparty, and each intermediary could report the swap in its volume. Thus, the aggregation of private estimates is likely to result in significant overstatement.

From Parallel Loans to Currency Swaps

As we described in Chapter 1, the 1970s brought increased foreign exchange risk to multinational companies due to the breakdown of the Bretton Woods accord in 1973. With elimination of the fixed exchange rates, the volatility of foreign exchange rates increased dramatically. Coupled with the prevailing accounting treatment of foreign-denominated assets and liabilities (SFAS 8), the increase in foreign exchange volatility produced massive swings in reported earnings. Indeed, these changes in reported earnings due to changes in the exchange rates were frequently greater than the changes resulting from operations. Hence, for firms with significant overseas operations, the effects of financial changes swamped the effects of real changes.

Consider, for example, the case of a U.S. company with a United Kingdom subsidiary. If the pound became more valuable (i.e., if the dollar price of a pound rose), the dollar value of the assets in the United Kingdom rose; thus, the U.S. parent was better off. The opposite would be true for a decline in the dollar price of a pound. This risk is summarized in Figure 9-2.

For a U.S. parent with a foreign subsidiary, this exposure to foreign exchange movements could be hedged through *parallel loan agreements*. In our example, the U.S. company and its U.K. subsidiary would be matched with a U.K. company that has a U.S. subsidiary. The U.S. company would make a dollar-denominated loan to the U.S. subsidiary of the U.K. company. Simultaneously, the U.K. company makes a pound-denominated loan of equal current value to the U.K. subsidiary of the U.S. firm.[2] As illustrated in Figure 9-3, the loans have parallel interest and principal repayment schedules.

This parallel loan would hedge the U.S. parent's exposure to dollar/pound movements. If the value of the pound should rise, the U.S. parent would suffer a loss on its pound-denominated loan, since it has a pound

---

2. The motivation for the U.S. firm to enter into this parallel loan agreement was to reduce the volatility of reported income (under SFAS 8). The U.K. firm was attracted to this transaction because the British government had (as had other governments) imposed controls on capital movements, in effect taxing the export of capital. These "capital controls" made it difficult for the U.K. parent to fund expansions in its U.S. subsidiary. By entering into the parallel loan agreement, the U.K. parent was able to bypass the capital controls and get funds to its U.S. subsidiary.

Figure 9-2. Risk Profile for a U.S. Company with a U.K. Subsidiary.

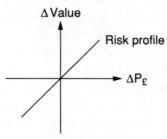

If a U.S. parent has assets in the United Kingdom, it faces risks due to movements in the price of the pound. If the dollar price of a pound ($P_£$) rises, the value of the assets in the United Kingdom rises. This raises the value of the U.S. parent through the increased reported earnings.

liability. Hence, the change in the value of the pound-denominated loan would move opposite that of the firm's inherent position. This relation is summarized in Figure 9-4.

There are, however, two major problems involved with the use of parallel loans:

1. Default risk: The loans are independent instruments, so default by one party does not release the counterparty from contractually obligated payments.

2. Balance sheet impact: If the balance sheets of the parent and its subsidiary have to be consolidated, the parallel loans will inflate the balance sheet (which leads to potential problems with financial covenants). Although the two loans effectively cancel each other out, they remain on the balance sheets for accounting and regulatory purposes.

The first problem can be managed simply by changing the structure from two independent instruments to a single instrument. Put another way, we

Figure 9-3. Cash Flows from a Parallel Loan Agreement.

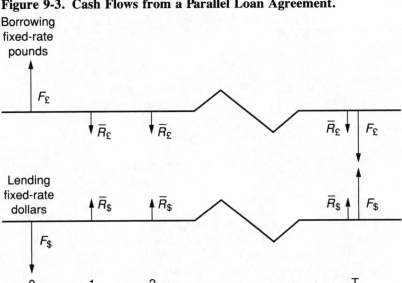

At a time 0, the U.S. firm, through its U.K. subsidiary, borrows pounds ($F_\pounds$) at the prevailing T-period pound rate. At the same time, the U.S. firm loans to the U.S. subsidiary of the U.K. firm an equivalent current amount denominated in dollars at the T-period dollar rate. During the term of the loan, the U.S. firm makes interest payments in pounds ($R_\pounds$) to the U.K. firm, which in turn makes interest payments in dollars ($R_\$$) to the U.S. firm. At maturity (time T) the two firms make their final interest payments and return the principals; the U.S. firm returns pounds and the U.K. firm returns dollars.

Note that inflows are denoted by upward arrows and outflows by downward arrows. The magnitude of the cash flow is indicated by the arrow's length.

"staple the two contracts together." The result is that the two sets of cash flows illustrated in Figure 9-3 become the single set of cash flows illustrated in Figure 9-5. The resulting instrument is a *currency swap*. As Figure 9-5 indicates, the counterparties to the swap contract have agreed to exchange—to swap—cash flows. The party illustrated in Figure 9-5 has agreed to pay a series of cash flows based on a fixed sterling interest rate in order to receive a series of cash flows based on a fixed dollar interest rate. The counterparty takes the reverse position.

By combining the parallel loans into a single legal document called a swap, the default risk has been reduced substantially. Default risk can further be reduced by *netting* the payments: At each of the *settlement*

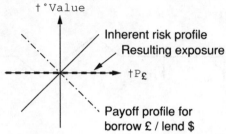

Figure 9-4. Hedging a Foreign Exchange Exposure with a Parallel Loan.

The inherent risk profile is that for the U.S. parent in Figure 9-2. The payoff profile for borrow pounds/lend dollars is that which results from the parallel loan cash flows illustrated in Figure 9-3. If the U.S. parent matches the size of the parallel loan to the size of the inherent exposure, the dollar/pound exposure could be eliminated.

dates 1, 2, . . . , *T*, it is not necessary for the party illustrated in Figure 9-5 to pay $\overline{R}_£$ and receive $\overline{R}_\$$. Instead, the two parties can exchange a *difference check*. If the value of sterling rises, the party illustrated in Figure 9-5 pays a difference check to the counterparty; if the value of sterling falls, the party illustrated in Figure 9-5 receives a difference check.

The second problem, the impact on the balance sheet, is handled even more simply: Current accounting and regulatory practices treat swaps as off-balance-sheet instruments. Therefore, the swap will not "blow up" the firm's balance sheet.

Thus, the currency swap evolved directly from the parallel loan agreement. Although privately arranged swaps existed in the mid-1970s, the public introduction of swaps is normally marked with the currency swap between IBM and the World Bank in 1981.

From Currency Swaps to . . .

From the currency swap evolved other kinds of swaps. As we have seen, the currency swap involves the exchange of a fixed-rate cash flow in one

Figure 9-5. Making a Parallel Loan Agreement into a Single Instrument: Creating a Currency Swap.

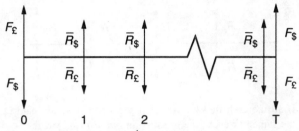

The two sets of cash flows illustrated in Figure 9-3 have been combined. The resulting cash flows are those for a *currency swap*.

currency for a fixed-rate cash flow in another. As shown in Figure 9-6, it is a simple matter to replace one of the fixed-rate cash flows with a floating-rate cash flow. The resulting instrument is referred to as a *currency coupon swap*.[3]

A special case of a currency coupon swap occurs when both currencies are the same. As illustrated in Figure 9-7, the result is an *interest rate swap*. As noted previously, the initial principal exchange in a swap is

3. Alternatively, this construction is known as a *cross-currency interest rate swap*.

Figure 9-6. A Currency Swap Converted to a Currency Coupon Swap.

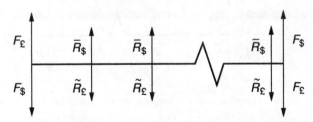

A swap of a fixed-rate cash flow ($\overline{R}_\$$) in one currency for a floating-rate cash flow ($\tilde{R}_\pounds$) in another currency is called a *currency coupon swap*.

Figure 9-7. A Currency Coupon Swap Converted to an Interest Rate Swap.

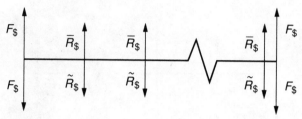

If all the cash flows in a currency coupon swap are paid in the same currency, the result is an *interest rate swap*.

not necessary. For an interest rate swap, all of the principal amounts are expressed in the same currency units. This means that the re-exchange at maturity is also not necessary. Therefore, we can illustrate the interest rate swap as in Figure 9-8.

In an interest rate swap, the cash flows are determined by one fixed interest rate and one floating interest rate (both in the same currency). In a *basis-rate swap,* both interest rates are floating (again, both in the same currency). Thus, the basis swap permits floating-rate cash flows calculated on one basis to be exchanged for floating-rate cash flows calculated on another. For example, it permits firms to convert from six-month LIBOR (London Inter Bank Offer Rate) to one-month U.S.

Figure 9-8. An Interest Rate Swap: Cash Flows for a Floating-Rate Payor.

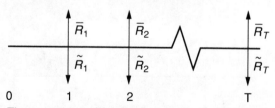

The counterparty illustrated receives a series of cash flows determined by the T-period fixed interest rate ($\bar{R}_t$) at origination, in return paying a series of cash flows ($\tilde{R}_t$) determined by the relevant floating interest rate, reset at the beginning of every period.

Figure 9-9. A Basis Swap: LIBOR to U.S. Commercial Paper.

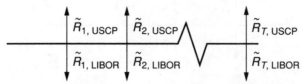

The party illustrated receives semiannual cash flows based on the compounded one-month U.S. commercial paper rates, while paying cash flows determined by six-month LIBOR rates.

commercial paper rates. Such a swap is illustrated in Figure 9-9, which suggests that a basis-rate swap is equivalent to pairing two simple interest rate swaps. The flows are converted from floating to fixed, and then converted from fixed to floating (but on a different basis).

A swap is, in effect, an exchange of cash flows calculated to reflect changes in designated prices. So far, we have considered only two prices: interest rates and exchange rates. However, swaps defined in prices other than interest rates and foreign exchange rates are also possible. Once a principal amount is determined and that principal is contractually converted to a flow, any set of prices can be used to calculate the cash flows.

Consider, for example, the possibility of swaps denoted in commodities such as wheat. The counterparties could agree to exchange a stipulated number of dollars for a specified number of bushels of wheat on specified dates. Such a swap is analytically no different from a fixed currency swap where prices of wheat replace the currency prices. In addition, neither firm need be in the wheat business; the difference checks are paid in dollars, not wheat. Moreover, in a swap in which the firm elects to pay with wheat, it can receive either fixed or floating rates in any currency or commodity.

Although wheat swaps have not yet appeared, oil swaps have. Figure 9-10 illustrates the cash flows for a party who receives cash flows based on a fixed U.S. dollar interest rate and pays cash flows determined by the price of oil. Note again that while the cash flows are expressed in terms of oil, no physical quantities of oil need be involved. At the settlement date, the difference check paid or received would reflect the

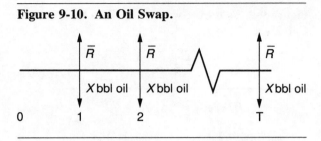

Figure 9-10. An Oil Swap.

price of oil. If oil prices have risen since contract origination, the party illustrated in Figure 9-10 would pay a net difference check; if oil prices have fallen, he or she would receive the check.

Note also that the commodity swap can, like any of the other swaps, be decomposed into long and short positions in loans (i.e., lending and borrowing). For example, the oil swap illustrated in Figure 9-10 can be decomposed into lending with standard fixed-rate coupon payments and simultaneously borrowing the same amount where the coupon payments are expressed in terms of oil. Figure 9-11 illustrates this situation.

Given the range of swaps we have described, it is not surprising to hear market participants assert that "the future potential structures . . . are limited only by the imagination and ingenuity of those participating in the market."[4]

4. Bankers Trust Company, *op. cit.* p. 2.

Figure 9-11. Decomposing an Oil Swap into Two Loan Products.

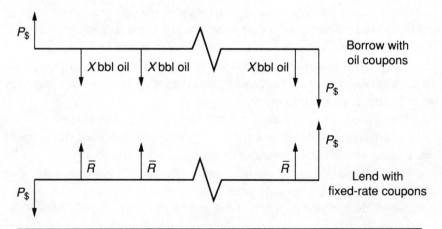

Development of the Swap Market

A picture of the historical development of the swap market can be obtained by looking either at the evolution of the products or at changes in the market's participants. Both tell the same story. We first look at the products.

As we noted, currency swaps were the first to appear. The earliest swaps were done on a one-off basis, which involved a search for matching counterparties—matching not only in the currencies, but also in the principal amounts and timing desired. These early swaps were custom-tailored products. Because the deals were all one-off, they involved a great deal of work by the financial institution arranging the swap. However—and this is a crucial point—they involved virtually no direct exposure for the broker. In the language of the market participants, the early swaps required "creative problem solving" rather than capital commitment from the intermediary.

As interest rate swaps began to appear, the movement toward a more standardized product began. With the U.S. dollar interest rate swaps, there were fewer areas in which counterparties had to match than was the case for currency swaps. The product had become more homogeneous, so there was less demand for one-off deals. Instead of looking for one exactly matching counterparty, the intermediary could look for a number of counterparties that together matched the notional principal.

With the move toward homogeneity and the reduced reliance on an identifiable counterparty, markets for swaps—in particular, interest rate swaps—began to look more and more like markets for commodities. Increased competition forced down the spreads. And with the increased competition, an extensive search for a counterparty or group of counterparties proved unprofitable for the intermediary. Instead, the intermediaries began to accept swap contracts without a counterparty, taking the interest rate risk into their own books and hedging it with interest rate futures or U.S. treasuries until it could be matched with an offsetting position.

Hence, the evolution of the products offered in the swaps market paralleled that of most markets. Swaps evolved from a customized, client-specific product to a standardized product. With the customized product, the role of the intermediary had been one of problem solving. As the product became more standardized, the role of the intermediary changed considerably, with less emphasis on arranging the deal and more on transactional efficiency and capital commitment.

As for the participants in the swaps market, the dominant intermediaries in the early stage of development were investment banks. As the market evolved, the entrants into this market changed to more highly capitalized firms, in particular commercial banks. The evolution of the role of the intermediary mirrors the change in the products. In the early stages, the emphasis was on the intermediary arranging the transaction rather than accepting risk from the transaction; thus, investment banks were the natural intermediaries. But as the swaps became more standardized, it became essential for the intermediary to be willing and able to accept part or all of a potential transaction into its books. Hence, commercial banks, with their greater capitalization, became a more significant factor.

One way of illustrating the dominance of commercial banks for U.S. dollar interest rate swaps is to look at the size of their swap books. Table 9-1 provides the notional principal outstanding for the ten largest interest rate swap dealers. Although aggregation necessarily involves some double-counting, it is useful to note that the aggregate notional

Table 9-1. Notional Principal Outstanding for Interest Rate Swaps (as of September 30, 1988).

Ranks by Swaps Notional Principal		Notional Principal Outstanding ($ billions)	Total Assets ($ billions)	Rank by Assets
1	Chemical Bank	148.5	69.8	7
2	Citicorp	130.3	209.2	1
3	Bankers Trust	108.5	57.9	9
4	Manufacturers Hanover	86.2	74.0	6
5	Chase Manhattan	75.7	97.4	2
6	J.P. Morgan	64.8	82.1	4
7	Security Pacific	62.4	78.9	5
8	First Chicago	27.6	45.1	10
9	BankAmerica	23.7	95.2	3
10	First Interstate	19.3	58.0	8

Sources: Notional Value of Swaps Outstanding from BankBase One database, Newport Associates, Ltd. Bank Holding Company Ranking by Asset Sizes printed with permission of Shesnunoff Information Services, Inc. Copyright © 1988 by Shesnunoff Information Services, Inc., Austin, Texas. The foregone information appears in Cd/Banking, a One Source Product of Lotus Development Coporation.

Table 9-2. *Euromoney* Survey of Swap Users.

Keenest Pricing on Straight Dollar Interest Rate Swap	Best Overall	Keenest Pricing on Cross-Currency Swaps
1 Citicorp	1 Security Pacific	1 Citicorp
2 Security Pacific	2 Bankers Trust	2 Bankers Trust
3 Bankers Trust	3 Citicorp	3 Morgan Guaranty
4 Chase Manhattan	4 Morgan Guaranty	4 Banque Paribus
5 Morgan Guaranty	5 Banque Paribus	5 Chase Manhattan
6 Chemical Bank	6 Chemical Bank	6 Credit Suisse First Boston
7 CIBC	7 Chase Manhattan	7 Salomon Brothers
8 = Credit Suisse First Boston	8 = Deutsche Bank	8 SBCI
8 = Banque Paribus	8 = Salomon Brothers	9 Union Bank of Switzerland
10 Merrill Lynch	10 SBCI	10 Manufacturers Hanover

Source: "Sepac Graduates Into the Big Time," *Euromoney* (September 1988): p. 216. Used with permission.

principal outstanding of these ten commercial banks amounts to $677.4 billion. Another way of ascertaining the dominance of commercial banks in swaps is to solicit the opinions of swaps users. On an annual basis, *Euromoney* surveys the views of some 100 of the largest users of swaps worldwide. The results of the most recent survey, reproduced in Table 9-2 on page 211, support the notion that the commercial banks have become dominant in this market.

Standardization has played a large part in the growth of swaps. One market observer put it well by noting that "swaps have become a high volume, lower margin business, rather than the personalized, corporate financial deal of the past."[5] As we have pointed out, the standardization has been easier for interest rate swaps, which may go a long way toward explaining why this market has grown more rapidly than that for currency swaps.

The growth of the swap market also corresponds to the expanding liquidity available through the secondary market. Swap positions can be traded (i.e., the swap contract is "assigned" to a third party), and this market is growing. However, much of the secondary market in swaps involves the reversing (unwinding) of a position. The simplest method for unwinding a swap involves a cancellation of the agreement, with a final difference check determined by the remaining value of the contract. Alternatively, the swap can be unwound by writing a "mirror" swap to cancel out the original. Most market observers indicate that the secondary market is sufficiently deep to decrease risks in the primary market, particularly for short-term swaps.

In the primary swaps market, the most liquid market is for U.S. dollar interest rate swaps. According to the International Swap Dealers Association, the average interest rate swap has a maturity of three to five years with a notional principal of $25 million. However, a market now exists for dollar interest rate swaps of up to ten-year maturities and amounts to $1 billion.

---

5. K. Henderson Schuyler, "The Constraints on Trading Swaps," *Euromoney* (May 1985): 63–64.

10

The Growth of the Swap Market

In Chapter 9 we noted that one of the few claims on which there is general agreement is that the swap market has grown dramatically. The conventional wisdom is that the growth of swaps is due to their ability to take advantage of some kind of "arbitrage opportunity." This view was articulated by Mr. Robin Leigh-Pemberton, governor of the Bank of England, when he argued that swaps permit a borrower to "arbitrage" the credit markets, allowing "a good credit rating in one part of the currency/maturity matrix to be translated into relatively cheap borrowing in another."[1]

An often-cited example of this "credit arbitrage" is the case of an interest rate swap between an AAA-rated borrower and a borrower with a BBB rating.[2] As illustrated in Table 10-1, a borrower rated AAA would be expected to be able to borrow more cheaply than one rated BBB regardless of whether rates are fixed or floating. However, note in Table 10-2 that the credit spread between the AAA and the BBB is higher for fixed than for floating rates.

The assertion is that the swap "arbitrages the credit spread differential" of $120 - 50 = 70$ basis points. As illustrated in Table 10-3, suppose the AAA firm borrows fixed and the BBB firm borrows floating. Then, if the two firms enter into an interest rate swap, both firms can end up with lower borrowing costs. Indeed, in this case, where there is no financial intermediary, the firms end up splitting the credit spread differential.

---

1. Merril Stevenson, "The Risk Game: A Survey of International Banking," *The Economist* 302, no. 7490 (March 21, 1987): 60.
2. The specific example we use is adapted from "The International Swap Market," an advertising supplement by Bankers Trust Company to *Corporate Finance* (September 1985). However, the arguments contained in this example are used widely in the swaps market.

Table 10-1. Illustrative Borrowing Costs for AAA and BBB Borrowers.

	AAA	BBB
Borrow fixed	10.8%	12.0%
Borrow floating	LIBOR + $\frac{1}{4}$%	LIBOR + $\frac{3}{4}$%

Source: Bankers Trust.

The preceding illustration is consistent with the available data:

1. Quality differentials exist between fixed and floating borrowing, referred to as "quality spreads," and these quality spreads are generally observed to increase with maturity.[3]
2. The fixed-rate payor in a swap is predominantly the less creditworthy party.
3. Firms have been able to lower their nominal funding costs by using swaps in conjunction with these quality spreads.

However, it is less clear that this kind of behavior has anything to do with classic financial arbitrage. First, financial arbitrage should lead to decreasing, not increasing, swap volumes. As the quality spread is arbitraged, the rate differences would be eliminated, and this rationale for interest rate swaps should disappear. Second, this simplistic "credit arbitrage" story ignores the underlying reason for the quality spread.

---

3. For a discussion of the quality spread in the context of swaps, see Larry D. Wall and John J. Pringle, "Interest Rate Swaps: A Review of the Issues," *Economic Review,* Federal Reserve Bank of Atlanta (November/December 1988); and "Alternative Explanations of Interest Rate Swaps: A Theoretical and Empirical Analysis," working paper, University of North Carolina (November 1988).

Table 10-2. Illustrative Credit Spreads.

	BBB − AAA Borrowing Rates	Credit Spread
Fixed	12.0% − 10.8%	= 120 basis points
Floating	(LIBOR + $\frac{3}{4}$%) − (LIBOR + $\frac{1}{4}$%)	= 50 basis points

Source: Bankers Trust.

Table 10-3. The "Savings" from a Swap.

	AAA	BBB
Fund:		
AAA borrows fixed	(10.8%)	
BBB borrows floating		(LIBOR $+ \frac{3}{4}$%)
Swap:		
AAA receives fixed,	10.9%	
pays floating	(LIBOR)	
BBB receives floating,		LIBOR
pays fixed		(10.9%)
Overall cost of funding	LIBOR $- \frac{1}{10}$%	11.65%
Savings	0.35%	0.35%

Source: Bankers Trust.

Comparative Advantage

We have heard many market participants assert—and these assertions have been picked up by the trade publications—that the quality spreads result from firms having a "comparative advantage" in one of the credit markets. According to this view, the AAA-rated company borrows in the fixed-rate market, where it has a comparative advantage. The BBB-rated company borrows in the floating-rate market, where it has a comparative advantage. Then the firms use an interest rate swap to exploit their comparative advantages and produce interest rate savings.

While this argument is appealing, it neglects arbitrage. With no barriers to capital flows, the comparative-advantage argument from elementary trade theory cannot hold. Arbitrage eliminates any comparative advantage.

Aside

Comparative advantage

The concept of comparative advantage is used in international trade theory to explain why countries trade. As you should remember from your economics courses, this concept was based on *factor immobility:*

> The United States has a comparative advantage in wheat because the
> United States has wheat-producing acreage not available in Japan. If

land could be moved—if land in Kansas could be relocated outside Tokyo—the comparative advantage would disappear.

For the concept of comparative advantage to make sense as a rationale for swaps, immobility would have to exist in the financial markets. And this assumption of immobility does not square with observations of the financial markets. The integrated capital markets will provide the BBB access to fixed-rate markets, either directly or indirectly by AAA-rated firms borrowing fixed and relending it to BBB-rated firms.

Given the weakness in the theory of comparative advantage, a number of alternative explanations have been proposed.

Underpriced Credit Risk or Risk Shifting

Some have suggested that the quality spread results because the market for fixed-rate funding prices risk differently than does the market for floating-rate funding. Specifically, it has been argued that credit risk is underpriced in floating-rate loans.[4] Underpriced credit risk for floating-rate loans would certainly explain the growth of the interest rate swap market: the gain from the swap would be at the expense of the party underpricing credit risk in the floating-rate debt market. However, the expansion of the swap market effectively increases the demand for floating-rate debt by lower-rated companies and the demand for fixed-rate debt by higher-rated companies, thereby eliminating the supposed differential pricing. So, like the comparative advantage argument, this rationale would be self-eliminating and therefore could not explain the continuing growth of the swap market.

Along a similar line, Jan Loeys suggests that the quality spread is the result of risk being shifted from the lenders to the shareholders.[5] To the extent that lenders have the right to refuse to roll over debt, more default risk is shifted from the lender to the shareholders as the maturity of the debt decreases. With this explanation, the "gains" from a swap would instead be transfers from the shareholders of the lower-rated firm to the shareholders of the higher-rated firm.

---

4. For example, in "The Valuation of Floating Rate Instruments: Theory and Evidence," *Journal of Financial Economics* 17, no. 2 (December 1986): 251–272, Krishna Ramaswamy and Suresh M. Sundaresan looked at the market for floating-rate loans and argued that the default premiums are lower than would be predicted.
5. Jan Loeys, "Interest Rate Swaps: A New Tool for Managing Risk," *Business Review,* Federal Reserve Bank of Philadelphia (May/June 1985): 17–25.

Information Asymmetries

Why does a firm choose to issue short-term floating-rate debt and then swap this floating-rate payment into a fixed-rate payment, rather than using one of the alternatives: keep the short-term debt unswapped, issue long-term fixed-rate debt, or issue long-term floating-rate debt? Marcelle Arak, Arturo Estrella, Laurie Goodman, and Andrew Silver (all of Citicorp) argue that the "issue short-term–swap to fixed" combination would be preferred if the firm

- has information that would lead it to expect its own credit spread to be lower in the future than the market expectation
- is less risk-averse to changes in its credit spread than is the market
- expects higher risk-free interest rates than does the market
- is more risk-averse to changes in the risk-free rate than is the market[6]

For example, suppose the firm desired fixed-rate funding for a project, but the company had inside information indicating that its credit rating would improve in the future. By issuing short-term debt, the firm would be able to exploit its information asymmetry; and, by swapping the debt into fixed-rate, the firm is able to eliminate its exposure to interest rate risk.

As Arak and her colleagues point out, firms that are pessimistic about future risk-free rates but optimistic about their own credit standing are drawn to the swaps market—that is, issue short-term, and swap to fixed. The expected savings would be divided between this firm and the counterparty based on prevailing demand and supply conditions.

Differential Prepayment Options

The savings in nominal—stated—borrowing cost obtained via a swap can also be understood by considering options available to the borrower. Most fixed-rate debt includes a prepayment option. If interest rates decline, the borrower can put the loan back to the lender and obtain lower-cost financing by paying the prepayment fee and the origination

---

6. Marcelle Arak, Arturo Estrella, Laurie Goodman, and Andrew Silver, "Interest Rate Swaps: An Alternative Explanation," *Financial Management* 17 (Summer 1988): 12–18.

fees on the new financing. Indeed, in standard corporate bond issues, this is simply the call provision.

In contrast, interest rate swaps contain no such prepayment option. According to the standards proposed by the International Swap Dealers Association (1986), early termination of a swap agreement requires that the remaining contract be marked to market and paid in full.

Hence, the positions of the firm that has borrowed fixed directly and the firm that has borrowed floating and swapped to fixed are quite different. The former owns a put option on interest rates; the latter does not.

Example

The value of the right to prepay

Consider the BBB-rated firm described earlier. It can obtain fixed-rate funding in two ways:

1. Borrow fixed directly at 12%.
2. Borrow floating and swap to fixed at 11.65%.

If capital markets are efficient—and the available evidence says they are—the fact that method 1 costs more than method 2 implies that it offers something method 2 does not. Included in that "something" may be the right to repay the loan early. When would the firm want to exercise this right? Clearly, the firm would want to exercise the right if rates fall.

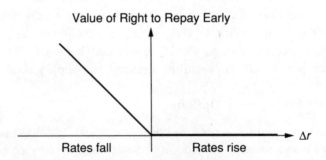

If rates fall, the firm could pay off this loan and refinance at the lower rate. And, as illustrated, the further rates fall, the more valuable is this right.

This illustration of the value of the right to repay early is the payoff profile for owning an interest rate option—specifically, a put option on interest rates. Hence, it is not surprising that method 1 costs more than method 2, since it contains an option not contained in method 2.

In this context, the transaction between the AAA-rated firm and the firm rated BBB looks less like financial arbitrage and more like an option transaction. The BBB-rated firm can borrow at a fixed rate more cheaply by swapping from floating because the "borrow floating–swap to fixed" alternative does not include the interest rate option contained in the "borrow fixed" alternative. The BBB firm, in effect, has sold an interest rate option. At least a portion of the funding cost "savings" obtained by the BBB firm (as well as the cost savings gained by the AAA firm) come from the premium on this option.

Tax and Regulatory Arbitrage

In contrast to the classic arbitrage considered previously (where the firm would earn a riskless profit by exploiting pricing differences for the same instrument), tax and regulatory arbitrage is a situation in which the firm can earn a risk-free profit by exploiting differences in tax and/or regulatory environments.

A firm issuing dollar-denominated, fixed-rate bonds in the U.S. capital markets has to comply with the requirements of the U.S. Securities and Exchange Commission. In the less-regulated Eurobond market, the costs of issue could be considerably less—as much as 80 basis points less.[7] However, not all firms have direct access to the Eurobond market. The swap contract provides firms with access and permits more firms to take advantage of this regulatory arbitrage.

Moreover, firms issuing in the U.S. capital markets, as well as the security purchasers, have generally been faced with the provisions of the U.S. tax code. The introduction of the swap market allows an "unbundling," in effect, of currency and interest rate exposure from the tax rules in some very creative ways.

For example, with the introduction of swaps, a U.S. firm can issue a yen-denominated debt in the Eurobond market, structure the issue so as to receive favorable tax treatment under the Japanese tax code, avoid much of the U.S. securities regulation, and yet still manage its currency exposure by swapping the transaction back into dollars. Unlike the classic financial arbitrage we have described, there is no reason for opportunities for tax or regulatory arbitrage to disappear (barring changes, of course, in the various tax and regulatory codes).

---

7. Jan G. Loeys, *op. cit.*

To illustrate the manner in which tax and regulatory arbitrage induces swaps, consider the way one U.S. firm used swaps to take advantage of special tax and regulatory conditions in Japan.

Example

Arbitraging Japan's tax and regulatory authorities

In 1984, *Business Week* reported that U.S. firms had discovered a way to make "free money."[8] As it turns out, this "free money" was being given away by the Japanese tax authorities. In 1984, zero-coupon bonds received particularly favorable tax treatment in Japan. The income earned from holding the zero-coupon bond (the difference between the face value of the bond and the price at which the bond was purchased) was treated as a capital gain; and, since capital gains were untaxed, the effect was to make the interest income or the zero coupon nontaxable for the Japanese investor. The result was that a zero-coupon bond sold to Japanese investors would carry a below-market interest rate.

In contrast, the U.S. tax authorities regarded the zero-coupon bond like any other debt instrument. Any U.S. firm issuing such a bond was permitted to deduct the imputed interest payments from income, thereby maintaining its tax shield.

Hence, there existed a tax arbitrage opportunity; the two tax authorities treated the same instrument differently. Not surprisingly, a number of U.S. firms—Exxon and General Mills among them—issued zero-coupon yen bonds, illustrated below.

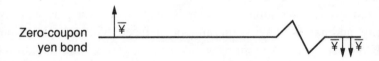

The U.S. firm issuing the zero coupon bond was no doubt pleased with the savings it achieved in interest expense. However, most U.S. issuers were much less pleased with the yen exposure that came with this zero-coupon yen bond. Hence, the assignment to the merchant/investment bank was relatively straightforward: Eliminate the yen exposure while keeping as much of the savings in interest expense as possible.

As should be clear, the exposure profile for this U.S. issuer of a zero-coupon yen bond is as illustrated below. Such an exposure could be managed via a forward yen-dollar contract, but the maturity of these bonds—five to ten years—

---

8. "A Way for U.S. Companies to make 'Free Money'," *Business Week* (October 29, 1984): 58.

eliminated forward contracts as a possibility, since the bid-offer spread on a ten-year forward contract was unacceptably high.

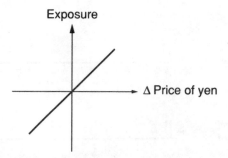

Futures contracts were also eliminated as a means of managing this exposure, since five- and ten-year futures contracts were not available. (Five- and ten-year strips of f_x futures are still not available. The longest available futures contract on foreign exchange is about twelve months.)

Hence, the best available financial instrument for neutralizing this yen exposure was (and still is) a swap. To minimize the cost of the swap (the bid-offer spread), we would want to use a standard, at-market-rate currency swap. However, when we combine such a currency swap with our zero-coupon bond, we see in the following diagram that the job is not done: there are still some yen cash flows.

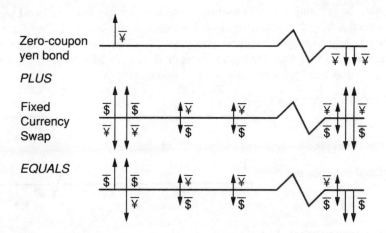

The remaining yen cash flows could be eliminated by adding a simple loan with a sinking fund. As the following figure illustrates, the amortizing yen loan would eliminate the remaining yen cash flows, and the U.S. issuer would end up with a set of cash flows identical to those for a dollar bond with below-market coupons.

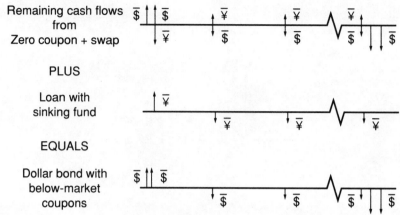

However, there was a way to structure the package that would result in a still lower realized interest rate for the U.S. issuer. In addition to the tax arbitrage, a regulatory arbitrage was available: The Ministry of Finance limited the amount a pension fund could invest in non-yen-dominated bonds issued by foreign corporations to at most 10% of their portfolio. However, the Ministry of Finance ruled that dual-currency bonds qualified as a yen issue for purposes of the 10% rule, even though the dual-currency bond has embedded within it a dollar-denominated zero. Hence, by issuing the dual currency bond, the U.S. firm was able to capitalize on the desire of Japanese pension fund managers to diversify their portfolios internationally, while at the same time adhering to the regulation imposed by the Ministry of Finance.

Hence, the remaining yen cash flows from the zero-coupon yen bond would be absorbed not by the amortizing loan but rather by the combination of a dual-currency bond and a spot currency transaction, as illustrated below. Moreover, this figure illustrates that the resulting cash flows are like those for a deep-discount dollar bond with below-market coupons.

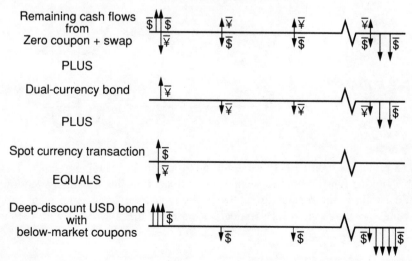

The U.S. firm will:

(1) Issue a zero-coupon yen bond in the amount of X yen

(2) Issue a dual-currency bond for $2X$ yen

(3) Enter into a currency swap with a principal of $2X$ yen

(4) Use a spot currency transaction to convert X yen to dollars

To end up with a set of cash flows that are like a deep-discount dollar bond with below-market coupons

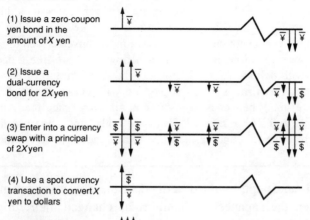

¥10,000,000,000

Zero-Coupon Yen Bonds

¥20,000,000,000

Dual-Currency Bonds

¥20,000,000,000

Yen-Dollar Currency Swap

The entire process can be summarized as follows: The U.S. firm will (1) issue a zero-coupon yen bond in the amount of X yen, (2) issue a dual-currency bond in the amount of $2X$ yen, (3) enter into a currency swap with a principal of $2X$ yen, and (4) use a spot currency transaction to convert X yen to dollars. The result of these transactions is a set of cash flows that are like a deep-discount dollar bond with below-market coupons as shown at the top of page 223.

The CFO of this firm is happy to end up with below-market funding. The merchant/investment banker is happy to end up with a nice fee. And *The Wall Street Journal* and *The Financial Times* are both happy because they got the advertising revenue for running the three tombstones depicted at the bottom of page 223.

The arbitrage opportunity described in the preceding example disappeared when the Japanese tax authorities changed their ruling on yen zeros. However, other tax and regulatory opportunities have existed, and some continue to exist. For example, in many European countries, the purchasers of zero-coupon bonds do not escape taxes (as was the case in our example); however, the tax is deferred until the maturity of the bond, and the tax rate paid is the lower, capital gains rate. Also, there are sometimes regulatory barriers limiting entry of potential issuers and thereby reducing the cost of borrowing in that market. For example, by gaining access to the restricted Swedish bond market and then swapping the proceeds, the World Bank was able to effectively borrow at a below-market rate.[9]

Exposure Management

Since swaps can be used to manage a corporation's exposure to interest rate, foreign exchange, and commodity price risk, part of the growth in interest rate swaps simply reflects general corporate hedging activities. Corresponding to the growth in the swaps market, the available market data suggest that the use of the other off-balance-sheet hedging instruments is also increasing:[10]

- Treasury bond futures contract (CBOT) volume grew from 32,000 contracts in 1977 to 67 million contracts in 1987.

---

9. This example is taken from "Techniques and Products," The Globecon Group, December 1988.

10. Data on volume of futures contracts are taken from "Volume of Futures Trading, 1960–1988," Futures Industry Association, Washington, D.C.

- Eurodollar futures contract (CME) volume grew from 15,000 contracts when the contract began in 1981 to 20 million contracts in 1987.
- Deutsche mark futures contract (CME) volume grew from 134,000 contracts in 1977 to 6 million contracts in 1987.
- Crude oil futures contract (NYME) volume grew from 323,000 contracts in 1983 to 15 million contracts in 1987.
- The number of options contracts traded grew from 2.6 million in 1983 to approximately 46.2 million in 1987.

Hence, another way of asking why swaps have grown so dramatically is to ask why more and more firms have decided to manage their exposures to financial prices—i.e., to exchange rates, interest rates and commodity prices.

One reason firms have been hedging more is obvious. As pointed out in Chapter 1, firms are more likely to manage risks in the 1980s because the world is riskier today than it was in the 1960s and early 1970s. The 1970s ushered in increases in volatility for exchange rates, interest rates, and commodity prices.

However, the mere fact that the financial environment is more risky is not in and of itself sufficient for the firm to decide to manage this risk. Although a complete discussion of the rationale for hedging will be deferred until Chapter 17, let us note here that in addition to the risk aversion rationale for the owner of a closely held corporation, there are several reasons for widely held corporations to undertake hedging programs. Value-maximizing firms may elect to hedge using swaps or some other financial instrument if this hedging

- reduces the expected tax to be paid by the firm,
- reduces the expected cost of financial distress, or
- reduces agency costs, that is, the costs of conflict between shareholders and bondholders or between shareholders and managers.

We will return to the effect of risk management on expected future tax liabilities and on the expected cost of financial distress in Chapter 17. However, at this point it is useful to note that Larry Wall looked specifically at the agency costs issue in the context of swap contracts.[11]

---

11. Larry Wall, "Interest Rate Swaps in an Agency Theoretic Model with Uncertain Interest Rates," *Journal of Banking and Finance* (in press).

He noted that long-term, fixed-rate debt can increase agency costs between shareholders and bondholders: If the firm issues long-term debt, shareholders have the incentive to underinvest (i.e., pass up positive-net-present-value projects) or to shift from low-risk to high-risk projects.[12] Recognizing this incentive, bondholders demand a large premium on long-term debt. However, this "opportunistic behavior premium" is lower for higher-rated firms, presumably because they have an established reputation. Clearly, this opportunistic behavior—and the corresponding premium—can be avoided by issuing short-term debt, but short-term debt exposes the firm to interest rate risk. Wall notes that by issuing short-term and swapping to fixed, the lower-rated firm is able to control the agency problem, while at the same time avoiding interest rate risk.

To put this theoretical argument into perspective, let's look at an example.

Example

Hedging and investment incentives

To illustrate how hedging can control the under-investment problem in a firm with uncertain cash flows, consider a firm subject to oil price risk: if oil prices rise, the value of the firm in period 1 will be higher than it will be if oil prices fall. For simplicity, let's suppose only two outcomes with a 50–50 probability:

Outcome	Probability	Value of Firm in Period 1
Price of oil rises	.5	1,000
Price of oil falls	.5	200

The firm has a riskless investment opportunity: an outlay of $600 in period 1 will result in an income of $800 in period 2 with certainty.

The firm plans to issue in period 1 bonds with a *face value* of $500 and pass on the proceeds to the shareholders. Again, for simplicity, assume: (1) no transaction costs, (2) no taxes, and (3) a risk-free interest rate equal to zero.

As shown in Table 10-4, if the price of oil falls, this firm will pass up a positive NPV project; that is, if the value of the firm in period 1 is $200, the shareholders will not undertake the investment project. Note that although the

---

12. For a discussion of the underinvestment issue, see Steward C. Myers, "Determinants of Corporate Borrowing," *Journal of Financial Economics* 5 (November 1977): 147–176. The risk shifting issue is described in Zvi Bodie and Robert A. Taggart, "Future Investment Opportunities and the Value of the Call Provision on a Bond," *Journal of Finance* 33 (September 1978): 1187–1200.

The Growth of the Swap Market **227**

Table 10-4. Uncertainty and the Investment Decision.

Period 1		Period 2			
Value of Firm		Value of Firm	Value of Debt	Value of Equity	Undertake positive NPV project?
1,000	Undertake project	1,200	500	700	Yes
	Do not undertake	1,000	500	500	
200	Undertake project	400	500	−100	No
	Do not undertake	200	200	0	

face value of the debt is $500, the market value of the debt is equal to the expected value of the debt:

$$\tfrac{1}{2}(500) + \tfrac{1}{2}(200) = \$350$$

The expected value of the shareholder's equity in the firm is $\tfrac{1}{2}(700) + \tfrac{1}{2}(0) = \$350$. Hence, the total value of the shareholder's holdings—the value of their equity in the firm plus the monies they received from the debt issue—is $350 + $350 = $700.

However, suppose the firm could enter into a simplified commodity swap agreement:

Price of oil rises: firm pays $400

Price of oil falls: firm receives $400

Now the value of the firm is hedged against oil prices: regardless of what happens to oil prices, the value of the firm is $600. Would the shareholders want to enter into this swap?

As Table 10-5 indicates, with the value of the firm hedged against oil prices, the positive NPV project will always be undertaken. And, with the hedge against oil prices, the total value of the shareholder's wealth is $500 (the proceeds of the debt issue) plus $300 (the value of their equity). That is, by hedging, the value of the shareholder's wealth has increased by $100.

Table 10-5. Hedging and the Investment Decision.

Period 1		Period 2			
Value of Firm		Value of Firm	Value of Debt	Value of Equity	Undertake positive NPV project?
600	Undertake project	800	500	300	Yes
	Do not undertake	600	500	100	

Synthetic Instruments

Still another reason for the growth of the swap market is the usefulness of swaps in the synthetic creation of new financial instruments. For example, consider long-dated interest rate forward contracts, historically a very illiquid market. Since interest rate swaps can be viewed as portfolios of forward interest rate contracts, long-term swaps have been stripped to synthesize long-dated forwards and thereby increase liquidity in the market for long-dated forward rate agreements.

Less obvious is the manner in which currency and interest rate swaps have been used to fill gaps in the international financial markets. For example, there is no Swiss treasury bill market. Currency and interest rate swaps, however, can be used to create this market synthetically.

Furthermore, swaps can be combined with existing products to create new financial instruments. As will be described in Chapter 18, the combination of a conventional fixed-rate loan and an interest rate swap, where the party pays fixed, results in a "reverse floating-rate loan."

Liquidity

A final factor explaining the observed growth in the swap market is the substantial reduction in bid-ask spreads. In 1982, these spreads exceeded 200 basis points; by 1987 they were frequently less than 10. Thus, the dramatic increase in volume has been accompanied by an equally dramatic increase in the liquidity of the swaps market.

11

Pricing Swaps

In Chapter 9 we demonstrated that a swap can be decomposed into either a portfolio of loans or a portfolio of forward contracts. In Chapter 12 we will make use of the concept of a swap as a portfolio of forwards to gain insights into the default risk of a swap. In this chapter, we use the concept of a swap as a portfolio of loans to provide insights into the pricing of a swap.

Pricing an At-Market Swap

Figure 11-1 again illustrates the equivalence of an interest rate swap and a pair of loans. The implication of this figure is that if you can value (price) loans, you should be able to value a swap contract. Put another way, if you know the mechanics of pricing loans, you should be able to determine the appropriate fixed rate in the swap illustrated in Figure 11-1.

And that is indeed the case. The loans are both zero-expected-NPV (net present value) projects.[1] Consequently, since the swap is nothing more than a long and a short position in loans, the expected NPV of the swap must also be zero. Hence, if the actual or expected floating-rate payments at time periods 1, 2, . . . , T can be determined and if the term structure of interest rates is known, the NPV of the swap can be set equal to zero, and we can solve for the fixed rate. Perhaps the best way to explain this is to go directly to an example.

---

1. We again presume here that the capital markets are efficient.

Figure 11-1. Decomposition of an Interest Rate Swap into a Portfolio of Loans.

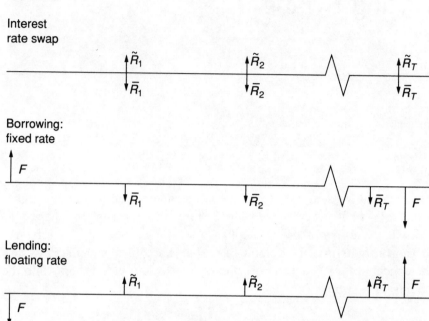

The cash flows from an interest rate swap where the party pays fixed is equivalent to the cash flows of a portfolio of two loan contracts, where borrowing is at a T-period fixed rate ($\bar{R}_t$), lending is at a floating rate ($\tilde{R}_t$), and F is the face value of the loan.

Example

Pricing an interest rate swap

Galactic Industries (GI) wishes to enter into a swap in which GI will pay cash flows based on a floating rate and receive cash flows based on a fixed rate. In the jargon of the swap market, Galactic—the floating rate payor—is referred to as the seller of the swap (or as being short the swap).

Market convention is to quote the terms of interest rate swaps as the floating-rate index (normally LIBOR) flat against some fixed rate; that is, Galactic will pay cash flows based on the floating rate flat and will receive cash flows based on a fixed rate of $X\%$. The question is: "What is the appropriate fixed rate— what is X?"

To keep our calculations at a minimum, suppose GI requested a quote from the Dead Solid Perfect Bank (DSPB) on the following simple swap:

Notional principal amount	$100
Maturity	One year
Floating index	Six-month LIBOR
Fixed coupon	_____%
Payment frequency	Semiannual
Day count	30/360[2]

From these terms, we know what Galactic will pay: At the six-month settlement, GI pays a "coupon" determined by the six-month LIBOR rate in effect at contract origination. At the twelve-month settlement, GI's "coupon" payment is determined by the six-month LIBOR rate prevailing at month 6. What is missing is how much Galactic will receive—how much DSPB will pay.

Suppose that the LIBOR yield curve (the spot yield curve) prevailing at origination of this swap is the simplified yield curve shown below.

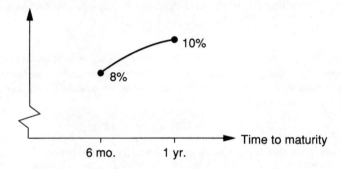

To determine the appropriate fixed rate, the managers of DSPB must consider the contractual/expected cash flows from this swap.

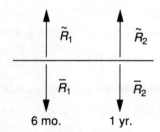

The first floating-rate inflow, $\tilde{R}_1$, is the easy one. The floating-rate cash flow DSPB will receive at the first settlement date is determined by the six-month

---

2. We use the 30/360 convention for convenience in our example. In truth, the day count convention for LIBOR is Actual/360, as is the case for commercial paper and bankers acceptances.

rate in effect at contract origination: 8%. Hence, at the six-month settlement, DSPB expects to receive

$$\tilde{R}_1 = \$100[(180/360)0.08] = \$100 \times \tfrac{1}{2}(0.08) = \$4.00$$

Note that in this calculation and all that follow, we use the bond method for calculating interest payments.[3]

To obtain the expected floating-rate inflow at the one-year settlement, we need to know the six-month rate in six months. As we know from our discussions in Part II, this rate—the rate from $t = 6$ months to $t = 1$ year—is the *forward rate*. Arbitrage guarantees that[4]

$$(1 + r_{12}) = \left[1 + \tfrac{1}{2}(r_6)\right] \times \left[1 + \tfrac{1}{2}(_6r_{12})\right]$$

where r_{12} and r_6 are, respectively, the current twelve-month and six-month *zero* (spot) rates. Using this arbitrage condition, the six-month and one-year rates of

---

3. For maturities less than one year, prevailing market practice is to quote interest rates with compounding already imbedded in the rate. Hence, if the annualized six-month rate is 8%, the amount that will be received at the end of six months on an investment of $100 can be calculated simply as

$$\$100 \times (180/360) \times 0.08 = \$4.00$$

using the convention that compounding occurs annually but the periodicity of the rate is monthly.

In contrast, the convention used by most finance textbooks is to treat the interest rate as *subject to compounding*. The common method of compounding is *discrete compounding*. Using this method, if the annualized six-month rate is 8%, the amount that will be received at the end of six months on the $100 investment is

$$\$100 \times (1.08)^{180/360} - \$100 = \$3.92$$

where the periodicity is again monthly but the rate is now compounded monthly. Put another way, to yield the $4.00 at the end of six months, the stated interest rate using the method of discrete monthly compounding would be 8.16%:

$$\$100 \times (1.0816)^{180/360} - \$100 = \$4.00$$

Although the different conventions are sometimes confusing, they cause no problem as long as the user knows which convention is being used.

4. In footnote 3, we noted the various ways in which interest rates can be quoted and the coupons calculated. Had the interest rates been quoted subject to monthly compounding, the arbitrage condition would have had to take the compounding into consideration. If we denote the annualized rate subject to compounding as $\imath$, the arbitrage condition would become

$$(1 + \imath_{12}) = (1 + \imath_6)^{\frac{1}{2}}(1 +_6 \imath_{12})^{\frac{1}{2}}$$

8% and 10%, respectively, require that the forward rate $_6r_{12}$—the six-month rate in six months—be 11.5%. Therefore,

$$\tilde{R}_2 = \$100 \times \tfrac{1}{2} \times 0.115 = \$5.75$$

Hence, the contractual/expected floating-rate inflows to DSPB are as illustrated below.

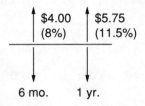

What DSPB needs to determine are the outflows, the appropriate fixed-rate payments. At origination, the expected net present value of this at-market swap is zero. That is,

$$\frac{\$4.00 - \overline{R}_1}{1 + \tfrac{1}{2}(0.08)} + \frac{\$5.75 - \overline{R}_2}{1.10} = 0$$

where $\overline{R}_1 = \overline{R}_2$. Solving this equation, $\overline{R}_1 = \overline{R}_2 = \$4.85$. Hence, the appropriate fixed rate is 9.70%.

From looking at the term structure of interest rates, it might seem that the appropriate fixed, one-year interest rate is 10%, in which case the fixed-rate outflows would be

$$\overline{R}_1 = \overline{R}_2 = \$100 \times \tfrac{1}{2}(0.10) = \$5.00$$

However, if $\overline{R}_1 = \overline{R}_2 = \$5.00$:

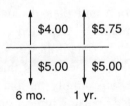

the present value of the swap to DSPB would be negative:

$$\frac{-1.00}{1 + \tfrac{1}{2}(0.08)} + \frac{0.75}{1.10} = -0.28$$

The problem is that 10% is a zero-coupon rate. As should be clear from Figure 11-1, $\overline{R}$ is associated with a coupon-bearing instrument (loan). What we need is

the market coupon interest rate—the *par* rate. The par rate is that coupon rate that would put the bond trade at par. In our case, that means the compounded annualized par rate $r_{1\,yr.}$ is given by

$$100 = \frac{\frac{1}{2}\bar{r} \times 100}{1 + \frac{1}{2}(0.08)} + \frac{\frac{1}{2}\bar{r} \times 100}{1.10} + \frac{100}{1.10}$$

Solving, the one-year par rate, $\bar{r}_{1\,yr.}$, is 9.70%, precisely the rate we determined earlier.

Hence, in the case of this simple, at-market swap, the appropriate fixed rate is the one-year par rate—9.70%. The terms of this swap can now be completed:

Notional principal amount	$100
Maturity	One year
Floating index	Six-month LIBOR
Fixed coupon	9.70%
Payment frequency	Semiannual
Day count	30/360

The expected cash flows for DSPB are as illustrated below.

As our example illustrates, pricing an interest rate swap requires that the cash flows be identified and then discounted by the zero-coupon (spot) interest rate. To obtain the expected cash flows for the floating payments, it was necessary to obtain the forward interest rates from the forward yield curve. Finally, in the case of this simple, at-market swap, the appropriate fixed rate was simply the par rate. Hence, to price an interest rate swap, we ended up using three yield curves: the zero-coupon yield curve, the forward yield curve, and the par yield curve.

Swap Pricing Conventions

The swap described in the preceding example and illustrated in Figure 11-1 is referred to (almost condescendingly) as a *plain vanilla* interest

rate swap. For this simple one-year swap, we ended up with a quote of six-month LIBOR (the spot rate) against the one-year par rate.

The market convention has come to be to price these plain vanilla swaps as LIBOR *flat* against the U.S. treasury (par) rate *plus*. An illustration of market-style quotations for at-market interest rate swaps at origination is provided in Figure 11-2. On Monday, September 12, 1988, the market was pricing a three-year interest rate swap in the interbank market such that:

If you want to receive the fixed rate, you will pay LIBOR and receive the three-year treasury par rate plus 74 basis points.

If you want to pay the fixed rate, you will receive LIBOR and pay the three-year treasury par rate plus 77 basis points.

The difference between the receive treasuries and pay treasuries, 3 basis points, was the bid-ask spread.

Valuing a Swap: Marking the Swap to Market

The market convention of LIBOR versus treasuries plus spread works well if all you want to do is price at-market swaps, at origination. However, this par rate convention does not work if you need to value a swap after origination or if you need to value (price) an off-market swap.

**Figure 11-2. U.S. Dollar
Interest Rate Swap Quotes.**

U.S. Dollar Rate Swap Quotes
[Treasury–LIBOR]

2 Yr.	T +70	T +74
3 Yr.	T +74	T +77
4 Yr.	T +74	T +78
5 Yr.	T +74	T +79
7 Yr.	T +73	T +79
10 Yr.	T +73	T +78

Source: Telerate, Fulton Prebon USA, Inc. (September 12, 1988). ©Telerate, Inc. All Rights Reserved. Reproduced with permission.

After origination, the only way to value a swap is to employ the zero-coupon yield curve. Once the swap has been contracted, its value depends on what happens to the market price on which the swap is based. The value of a dollar/sterling currency swap to the party paying dollars rises (falls) as the value of sterling rises (falls). The value of a commodity swap varies with the market price of the commodity. And, as we illustrate in the continuation of our example, the value of an interest rate swap depends on what happens to market interest rates.

Example

Valuing an interest rate swap

Galactic Industries (GI) and the Dead Solid Perfect Bank (DSPB) contracted to the interest rate swap outlined in the preceding example on the afternoon of July 23.

On the morning of July 24, the LIBOR yield curve (zero-coupon curve) shifted up by 1%, as illustrated below.

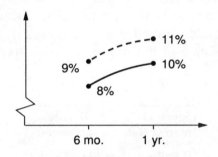

The terms of the swap contract specified that DSPB will pay at an annual rate of 9.70%. DSPB's first floating-rate receipt was determined at origination, so the $4.00 DSPB will receive in six months is unchanged. For this one-year swap, the only cash flow that will be changed is the expected floating-rate inflow at one year. With the new term structure, the forward rate, $_6r_{12}$, is 12.4%:

$$(1 + 0.11) = [1 + \tfrac{1}{2}(0.09)][1 + \tfrac{1}{2}(_6r_{12})]$$

Thus, the expected floating-rate inflow in one year is

$$\tilde{R}_2 = \$100 \times \tfrac{1}{2}(0.124) = \$6.22$$

and DSPB's expected cash flows are as illustrated below.

$$
\begin{array}{c|c}
\uparrow\ \$4.00 & \uparrow\ \$6.22 \\
\ \ (8\%) & \ \ (12.4\%) \\
\hline
\ \ \$4.85 & \$4.85 \\
\downarrow\ (9.7\%) & \downarrow\ (9.7\%) \\
\end{array}
$$

6 mo.　　　1 yr.

Calculating DSPB's expected net cash inflows,

6 mo.	1 yr.
−$0.85	+$1.37

and discounting these expected net cash inflows by the corresponding zero rates from the *current* zero-coupon yield curve,

6 mo.	1 yr.
9%	11%

the value of the swap to DSPB has risen from zero at origination to 42 cents:

$$
\frac{-\$0.85}{1 + \frac{1}{2}(0.09)} + \frac{\$1.37}{1.11} = \$0.42
$$

In the preceding example we have *marked the swap to market*. If we calculate the value of the swap for different changes in the yield curve, that is, if we mark the swap to market for different shifts in the yield curve, we can obtain a *payoff profile* for the swap. For example, if we look at the value of the preceding swap for shifts in the treasury zero curve of $+2\%$, $+3\%$, -1%, -2%, and -3%, the average change in the value of the swap contract per 1% change in the yield curve— Δ (Value of swap)/Δr—is 42 cents. Hence, we can sketch the payoff profile for this swap as in Figure 11-3.[5]

The lesson from all this is simple. To price an at-market interest rate swap, you can use the par yield curve. But to value a swap after origination, it is necessary to use the zero-coupon yield curve rather than the par yield curve.

---

5. Although the value of the swap contract is, in truth, a nonlinear function of interest rates, we continue to use a linear approximation.

Figure 11-3. Value of Swap to DSPB.

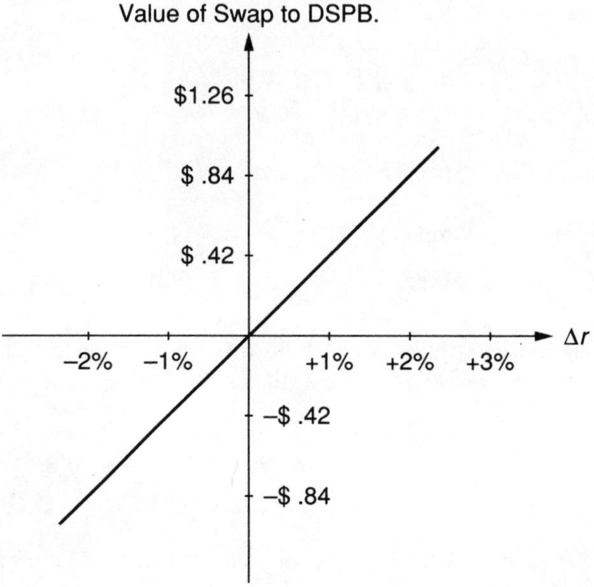

Value of Swap to DSPB.

Pricing an Off-Market Swap

As with valuing a swap after origination, it is necessary to use the zero-coupon yield curve—not the par yield—to price an off-market swap.

Figure 11-4 illustrates an off-market swap. In the case illustrated, the fixed rate paid by this party is higher than the prevailing market fixed rate: the fixed-rate payor is paying above-market "coupons." Consequently, at contract origination, a payment will have to be made from the floating-rate payor to this fixed-rate payor. The question is: How large should this initial payment be?

As Figure 11-4 indicates, the size of the initial payment from the floating-rate payor to the fixed-rate payor is determined by the difference between the market value of a bond that carries the above-market interest rate and the notional principal of the swap.

To make this more concrete, let's look at an example of an off-market swap. Consider a *delayed LIBOR reset swap* (also called a *LIBOR in arrears* swap).[6]

---

6. The delayed reset swap is discussed by Krystyna Krzyzak in "Don't Take Swaps at Face Value," *Risk* 1, no. 11 (November 1988): 28–31.

Figure 11-4. An Off-Market-Rate Swap.

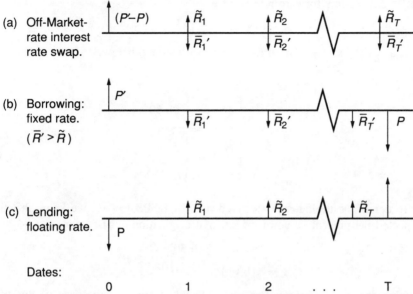

(a) Off-Market-rate interest rate swap.

(b) Borrowing: fixed rate. $(\bar{R}' > \tilde{R})$

(c) Lending: floating rate.

Dates: 0   1   2   . . .   T

The party pays cash flows $(\tilde{R}_t{}')$ determined by a fixed interest rate above the current market rate and receives cash flows $(\tilde{R}_t)$ determined by the relevant floating interest rate. In part a, a principal exchange $(P' - P)$ occurs at origination, with P' equal to the market value of a bond with coupons $\bar{R}_t'$ and a principal repayment of P. In part b this swap is decomposed into two loan contracts: borrowing at a fixed rate higher than the prevailing market rate, and lending at the market floating rate.

Example

A delayed LIBOR reset swap

In the normal (plain vanilla) swap, the rate paid at month 6 is the six-month rate in effect at month 0, and the rate paid at month 12 is the six-month rate in effect at month 6.

In a delayed reset or in-arrears swap, the rate paid at month 6 is the six-month rate in effect at month 6 and the rate paid at month 12 is the six-month rate in effect at month 12.

Let's change our swap between Galactic Industries and the Dead Solid Perfect Bank to a delayed LIBOR reset swap. With this structure, at origination, the rate DSPB *expects* to receive at month 6 is not the six-month spot rate at origination, 8%, but the forward rate—the six-month rate in six months—11.5%. Hence,

$$\tilde{R}_1 = (\$100)\tfrac{1}{2}(0.115) = \$5.75$$

Likewise, in an in-arrears swap, the rate DSPB expects to receive at month 6 is not the six-month rate in six months but the six-month rate in twelve months. Let's suppose this forward rate is 13%.

$$\tilde{R}_2 = (\$100)\tfrac{1}{2}(0.13) = \$6.50$$

Hence, DSPB's expected outflows are as illustrated below.

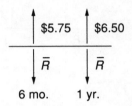

To determine the appropriate fixed rate for DSPB to pay, we know that the expected net present value of the swap at origination must be zero, so

$$\frac{5.75 - \overline{R}}{1 + \tfrac{1}{2}(0.08)} + \frac{6.50 - \overline{R}}{1.10} = 0$$

Solving the preceding equation, $\overline{R} = \$6.11$. Hence, in the case of this off-market swap, the appropriate fixed rate is 12.22%, not the par rate of 9.70%.

12

The Default Risk of Swaps[1]

The magnitude of the default risk in a swap has been a concern of both the market participants and the regulatory authorities. Indeed, the position taken by the Federal Reserve System is that the credit risks from intermediating swaps and other off-balance-sheet instruments "now constitute a significant element of the risk profiles of . . . the large multinational banking organizations that act as intermediaries between end-users of these contracts."[2] This concern has led the Basle Committee on Banking Regulations and Supervisory Practices—representatives of the central banks of Belgium, Canada, France, Germany, Italy, Japan, the Netherlands, Sweden, the United Kingdom, and the United States (the Group of Ten countries) plus Switzerland and Luxembourg—to propose capital adequacy requirements on the off-balance-sheet instruments intermediated by commercial banks.[3]

For a swap (or any other transaction), any measure of risk based on the potential default-induced loss to the intermediary is a function of two determinants:

1. *Exposure*—the amount at risk
2. *Probability of default*—the likelihood of a loss

---

1. This chapter draws heavily from Clifford W. Smith, Jr., Charles W. Smithson, and Lee Macdonald Wakeman, "The Market for Interest Rate Swaps," *Financial Management* 17, no. 4 (Winter 1988): 34–44.
2. Federal Reserve System, "Uses of Interest Rate and Exchange Rate Contracts by U.S. Banking Organizations," Appendix C to "Treatment of Interest Rate and Exchange Rate Contracts in the Risk Asset Ratio," a staff report prepared by Messrs. Taylor, Spillenkothen, Parkinson, Spindler, and Ms. White, March 2, 1987.
3. These proposals are described in two publications of the Bank for International Settlements: *Proposals for International Convergence of Capital Measurement and Capital Standards*, December 1987; and *International Convergence of Measurement and Capital Standards*, July 1988.

Using a simple mathematical expression, we can denote the potential default-induced loss from a swap as

Potential default-induced loss = Exposure × Probability of default

Aside

The approach of the Basle Committee

It is important to note that the approach proposed here has much in common with the approach of the Basle Committee. In its capital adequacy guidelines, the Federal Reserve System proposed an exposure measure weighted by the probability of default—that "applies credit conversion factors to the face value, or notional principal, amounts of off-balance sheet exposures and then assigns the resulting credit equivalent amounts to the appropriate risk category in a manner generally similar to balance sheet assets."[4] To make this cryptic description more clear, the following flowchart describes the manner in which the process is accomplished.[5]

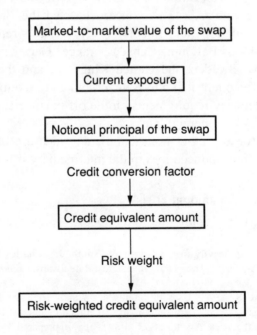

4. Federal Reserve System, *Capital Maintenance: Revisions to Capital Adequacy Guidelines,* 12 CFR part 225, Appendix A (Regulation Y), January 24, 1988, pp. 61–62.
5. Ibid., pp. 103–106.

The process begins with the *marked-to-market value of the swap*. From this measure, the *current exposure* of the financial institution to default on the swap is defined as the positive portion of the marked-to-market value:

$$\text{max } [0, \text{ marked-to-market value}] = \text{Current exposure}$$

Next, the current exposure is combined with the *notional principal amount* of the swap and a *credit conversion factor* to define the *credit equivalent amount* for the swap:

$$
\begin{array}{ccccccc}
\text{Current} & & \text{Notional} & & \text{Credit} & & \text{Credit} \\
\text{exposure} & + & \text{principal} & \times & \text{conversion} & = & \text{equivalent} \\
& & \text{of swap} & & \text{factor} & & \text{amount}
\end{array}
$$

which is equivalent to the "exposure" measure described earlier.

To get from this "exposure" measure to some measure of potential default-induced loss, the credit equivalent amount is multiplied by a *risk weight* to yield a *risk-weighted credit equivalent amount*,

$$
\begin{array}{ccccc}
\text{Credit} & & & & \text{Risk-weighted} \\
\text{equivalent} & \times & \text{Risk} & = & \text{credit} \\
\text{amount} & & \text{weight} & & \text{equivalent} \\
& & & & \text{amount}
\end{array}
$$

in much the same way as the exposure is multiplied by probability of default in our earlier equation.

It is with the two subcomponents, probability of default for a swap and the exposure generated by a swap, that this chapter will deal. We begin by looking at the probability of default for a swap.

Probability of Default for a Swap versus that for a Loan

Unfortunately, the similarity between loans and swaps, which was so useful in examining the evolution and pricing of swaps in Chapters 9 and 11, proves counterproductive when we look at default risk. Indeed, viewing swaps as "like loans" has led some to argue that the default risk in swaps is underpriced. For example, Patrick de Saint-Aignan (chairman of the International Swap Dealers Association at the time) summarized the views of many market participants when he asserted: "The credit aspect of swaps is not being adequately renumerated in the market. There's a credit spread of 150 basis points in the loan market but of

only 5 to 10 basis points in swaps. The weakest credits are getting a terrific deal."[6]

Mr. Saint-Aignan's position can be summarized in terms of the "quality spreads" we introduced in Chapter 10. In Figure 12-1, we have illustrated the quality spreads between the rates charged firms with credit ratings of AAA versus those of firms rated BBB for both loan and swap contracts. The quote from Mr. Saint-Aignan indicated that this "credit spread" was in the neighborhood of 150 basis points for loans but virtually nonexistent for swaps. Figure 12-1 suggests that there must be important differences between the default implications of loans and those of swaps. We believe that there are three primary differences.

First, the principal in a swap is not at risk; as we have described, the principal in a swap is only notional. In contrast, a significant component of the default risk of a loan has to do with the potential failure to repay the principal.

Second, for a swap, the periodic net cash flows to be paid/received (i.e., at a settlement date) are proportional to the difference in rates (e.g., in an interest rate swap, payments are made or received on the basis of the difference between a fixed interest rate and a floating rate). In a loan, the periodic cash flows to be paid/received (i.e., at the coupon payment dates) are determined by the level of rates (e.g., for a floating-

6. David Shirreff, "The Fearsome Growth of Swaps," *Euromoney* (October 1985): 247–61.

Figure 12-1. Quality Spreads for Loans and Swaps.

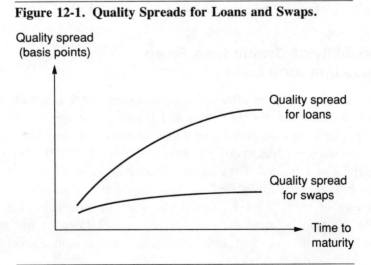

rate loan, payments are determined on the basis of the level of a floating interest rate). Hence, the periodic cash flows from a swap must be smaller than those from a comparable loan.

The third difference is that default on swaps requires that *two* conditions exist simultaneously, whereas default on a loan requires the presence of only *one*. Default on a loan requires only that the firm be in financial distress. Default on a swap requires both that the party to the swap be in financial distress and that the remaining value of the contract to that party be negative. Hence, the probability of default on a swap is a joint probability: the probability of the value of the swap being negative and the probability of the party being in financial distress. Therefore, this joint probability (on a swap) will be less than would be the simple probability (for a loan).

Probability of Default for a Swap versus that for Forwards and Futures

To examine the appropriate default premium for swaps, it is more instructive to look at the relation of swaps to forward and futures contracts than the relation of swaps to loan contracts. Figure 12-2 indicates

Figure 12-2. An Interest Rate Swap as a Portfolio of Forwards.

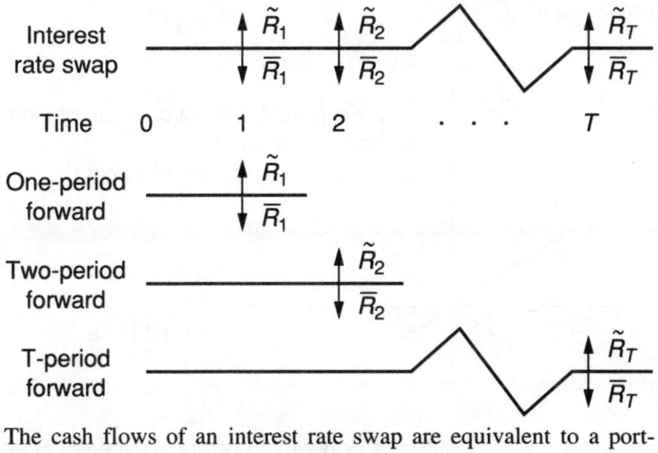

The cash flows of an interest rate swap are equivalent to a portfolio of T forward contracts. The party illustrated has agreed at origination to pay at period t a known amount $(\bar{R}_t)$ and to receive an amount determined by the prevailing single-period interest rate $(\tilde{R}_t)$.

again that a swap contract—in this case, an interest rate swap—can be decomposed into a portfolio of forward contracts. At each settlement date, the party to this swap contract has an implicit forward contract on interest rates—the obligation to sell a fixed-rate cash flow for an amount agreed on at contract origination. Hence, the swap contract is like a portfolio of forward contracts, one corresponding to each settlement date.

Aside

Swaps versus portfolios of forwards

There are two important differences between an interest rate swap and an explicit portfolio of forward contracts: (1) The exercise price for the forward contracts embedded in a swap is the par rate and not the forward rate, as would be the case for an explicit portfolio of forwards. (2) In a swap, the forward contracts are not independent, in the sense that default on any settlement check accelerates the maturity of the remaining embedded forwards.

A swap contract is thus more closely related to a futures contract, since both are like a portfolio of forward contracts. As illustrated in the case of interest rate movements in Figure 12-3, the payoff profiles for each of these three instruments are identical.

Figure 12-3. Payoff Profiles for Forwards, Futures, and Swaps.

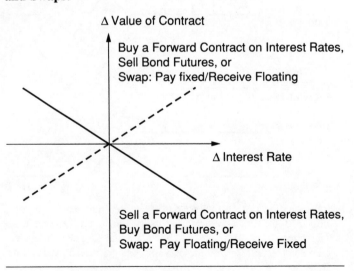

△ Value of Contract

Buy a Forward Contract on Interest Rates,
Sell Bond Futures, or
Swap: Pay fixed/Receive Floating

△ Interest Rate

Sell a Forward Contract on Interest Rates,
Buy Bond Futures, or
Swap: Pay Floating/Receive Fixed

Forwards, futures and swaps have two other important similarities. First, for all of these off-balance-sheet instruments, default risk is two-sided. In the instance illustrated in Figure 12-3, if interest rates rise, the owner of the contract is required to make a payment; conversely, if interest rates fall, the owner of the contract receives a payment.

Second, default risk depends on the use to which the instrument is put. Figure 12-4 illustrates the value of an individual settlement check for a swap, but it could also illustrate the value of a forward contract or the daily settlement of a futures contract. In any case, this payoff profile could be used either to speculate on or to hedge against changes in the interest rate. Clearly, the credit risk (the risk of default on the

---

Figure 12-4. Payoff Profile for a Swap at a Representative Settlement Date.

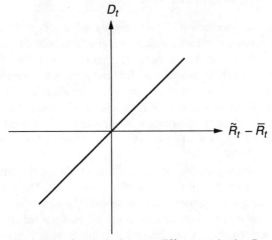

The value of a typical swap difference check, D_t, received by the party paying fixed and receiving floating. The value of the check increases as the realized floating rate, $\tilde{R}_t$, exceeds the fixed rate at origination, $\bar{R}_t$. This figure also can be used to illustrate the relations between swap, forward, and futures contracts. The value to the seller of a forward contract behaves similarly, but the fixed rate is replaced by the forward rate. The value of the day T settlement to the seller for a futures contract also behaves similarly but the rate difference is between the futures rate calculated on day t and that from $t - 1$.

---

contract) is influenced by the use of the instrument. A firm with fixed obligations faces some probability of financial distress and bankruptcy. If the firm's cash flows are sensitive to interest rate changes, and if it enters into a forward, futures, or swap contract as a hedge, the probability of bankruptcy is actually reduced. In establishing a hedge, an outflow is required only when the contract owner's core business produces net inflows.

Given the preceding similarities, the primary difference among forwards, futures, and swaps is the amount of default risk each instrument imposes on counterparties to the contract. As we described in our examination of forward and futures contracts in Parts II and III, forwards and futures represent the extreme cases for credit risk.

Aside

Forwards and futures revisited

Consider again the mechanisms guaranteeing contract performance. At one extreme is the futures contract, which contains mechanisms designed specifically to deal with the threat of nonperformance. First, the futures contract is marked-to-market and cash-settled daily, reducing the performance period to one day. Second, futures contracts require an explicit performance bond to be posted in the form of margin. With these mechanisms in place and functioning, the threat of nonperformance is substantially reduced. Thus, the futures contract involves virtually no extension of credit from one party to the other.

At the other extreme is the forward contract. No payments are made at contract origination or during the term of the contract. The total value of the contract is at risk for the entire contract term. The threat of nonperformance exists and becomes more severe as the length of the forward contract increases, since contract performance is not guaranteed, either by a bond or by any other mechanism. Thus, the forward contract is essentially a pure credit instrument; each party has extended credit to the other.

Between the extremes of forward contracts and futures contracts is the swap contract. For a swap contract, the passing of the difference check provides a periodic partial settlement of the contract; thus, the performance period for the swap is shorter than the maturity of the contract period, and the default risk for a swap is consequently less than the default risk for a comparable forward contract.

However, the default risk of a swap is strictly greater than that for a comparable futures contract. First, since only the maturing embedded

forward contract is settled at each settlement date, the value of the swap contract does not return to zero after the difference check is passed,[7] which would be the case for a futures contract. Second, swaps do not normally involve the posting of bond (margin).

These relations among the default risk characteristics of forwards, futures, and swaps are summarized in Figure 12-5.

Probability of Default for a Swap: Summary

Probability of Default for an Individual Swap

In sum, the probability of default for an individual swap contract of a given maturity lies between that of a forward contract and that of a futures contract[8] and is dramatically less than that for a comparable loan.

This theoretical assessment is borne out by market experience. For example, the results from the April 1987 Touche Ross survey of the International Swap Dealers Association members indicates that the default record for swaps is more like that for AAA corporate bonds than

---

7. For more on this, see Smith, Smithson, and Wakeman, *op. cit.*

8. Note that the contracts typically must be adjusted in size before they can be compared directly. Since a swap is like a portfolio of forwards, one corresponding to each difference check, a $10 million two-year swap with semiannual difference checks would have a smaller default risk than a $40 million two-year forward contract, but it would have a larger default than a $40 million two-year futures contract.

Figure 12-5. Default Risk Characteristics of Forwards, Futures, and Swaps.

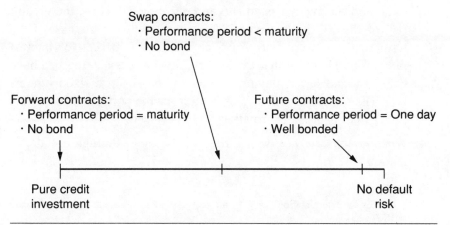

a portfolio of loans. This should not be surprising since bank loan portfolios include loans to small firms and individual consumers; however, the counterparties in swap contracts are generally limited to large banks, financial institutions, and those investment-grade firms with independent access to the capital markets.[9] Therefore, from both a theoretical and an empirical view, the probability of default associated with a portfolio of swaps is significantly less than that for a comparable portfolio of loans.

The probability of default, and therefore the appropriate credit premium, for an individual swap contract is determined primarily by four factors:

1. *The creditworthiness of the counterparty.*

2. *The counterparty's inherent exposure to movements in the financial price on which the swap is based* (i.e., interest rates, exchange rates, or commodity prices). Whether or not the firm is using the swap as a hedge will have a significant effect; a swap used as a hedge has a lower probability of default. Although for more creditworthy counterparties the financial institution is less concerned with the use to which the swap is put, for the lower-rated counterparties it is clearly in the financial institution's interest to know the use of the swap.

3. *For interest rate swaps, the shape of the term structure.* If the term structure is upward-sloping (as it has been over most of the history of the interest rate swap), the probability of default is reduced if the counterparty pays fixed and receives floating. If the term structure is upward-sloping, expectations are that the party paying fixed and receiving floating will pay difference checks early in the term of the swap and receive net payments in later periods. Thus, the default risk of the fixed-rate payor is less than would be the case if the term structure were flat. An overview of the market for interest rate swaps indicates that the less creditworthy counterparties have been, by and large, paying cash flows based on a fixed interest rate. Hence, the probability of default for the portfolio of swaps is lower than if the counterparties were reversed.

4. *Whether the contract is bonded*—for example, through collateralization.

---

9. Note that by collateralization, or posting margins, riskier counterparties can gain access to the swaps market.

Probability of Default for a Portfolio of Swaps

So far, we have considered single swaps. But many of the market participants (notably financial intermediaries) hold portfolios of swaps. As with loans, portfolio effects exist such that the exposure of the sum is less than the sum of the individual exposures. However, there are features that reduce the exposure of a portfolio of swaps more than a corresponding portfolio of loans.

One difference between a portfolio of swaps and a portfolio of loans recognized by all observers of this market is the netting arrangements that exist for swaps. As noted by the Federal Reserve and the Bank of England, these arrangements effectively reduce the notional principal of swap contracts and must therefore reduce both the current replacement cost and the potential credit exposure of a swap.[10]

Moreover, defaults on swaps should be more idiosyncratic than defaults on loans. As has been noted, default on a swap requires the simultaneous occurrence of two conditions: (1) The value of the contract to the financial intermediary's counterparty must be negative, and (2) the counterparty must be in financial distress. In contrast, the value of a loan contract to the borrower (the financial intermediary's counterparty) is always negative; thus, only one condition need be present. Therefore, since default on swaps will be more idiosyncratic, the portfolio effect should be more pronounced for swaps than for loans.

Exposure

The Federal Reserve System and the Bank of England noted that, when the swap counterparties evaluate their exposures, they should be asking about *two* exposure measures:[11]

---

10. However, the Basle capital framework did not recognize netting other than wit novation. It was felt that the legal effectiveness of net contracts subject to closeout has not yet been tested in the courts and therefore requires further consideration. Bank of International Settlements, July 1988, *op cit*.

11. The staffs of the Federal Reserve System and the Bank of England expressed these two questions as: (1) What is the *average* replacement cost over the life of a *matched pair* of swaps? (2) What is the *maximum* replacement cost over the life of a *single* swap? See "Potential Credit Exposure on Interest Rate and Foreign Exchange Rate Related Instruments," a joint working paper between the Board of Governors of the Federal Reserve System and the Bank of England, March 1987; and Mark Muffett (a mathematician at the Bank of England), "Modelling Credit Exposure on Swaps," *Proceedings of a Conference on Bank Structure and Competition*, Federal Reserve Bank of Chicago, 1986, pp. 473–96.

1. What is my *maximum exposure* if my counterparty to this contract defaults?
2. What additional exposure do I accept by entering into this contract; that is, what is the *expected exposure* generated by this contract?

Note that in the case of a loan contract, the same value—the loan principal—answers both questions. Consequently, since commercial banks have become the dominant intermediaries for swaps and since commercial banks are used to dealing with the credit risk of loans, the two-fold nature of the exposure question has become veiled.

In this section we will attempt to provide insights into the magnitude of the exposure using interest rate swaps as the example. In the exposure measures, we use the methodology for marking an interest rate swap contract to market that was introduced in Chapter 11.[12] At origination, the value of an at-market swap is zero. However, if interest rates change, the expected present value of the inflows change.

For instance, consider a fixed-rate payor: If interest rates rise, the expected present value of the inflows becomes larger than that for the outflows so the value of the swap becomes positive. Conversely, if rates fall, the value of the swap to this fixed-rate payor becomes negative. This straightforward relation is illustrated in part (*a*) of Figure 12-6. Part (*b*) illustrates the reverse: the value of a swap to the party receiving fixed and paying floating.

Expected Exposure

Expected exposure measures the likely future overall exposure to a swap portfolio of intermediating an additional swap. This exposure measure is the one the banking regulators have focused on in determining how much capital a bank should be required to hold against the swap. This exposure measure is useful to the individual bank because it provides an estimate of "the likely profitability of their swap transactions and the margins they need to charge on them to provide similar rates of return to those on other activities."[13] Consequently, expected exposure can be

---

12. Other methods of valuing (marking to market) an interest rate swap are presented in Muffett, *op. cit.*, and in Federal Reserve System, March 2 1987, *op. cit.*
13. Muffett, *op. cit.* p. 477.

Figure 12-6. Marking a Swap Contract to Market. (*a*) **The value of a swap in which the party illustrated pays fixed, receive floating.** (*b*) **The value of a swap in which the party illustrated pays floating, receives fixed.**

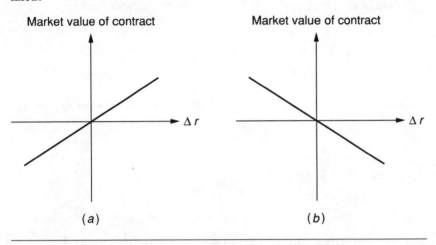

(*a*)   (*b*)

viewed as an ex ante measure of how much, on average, will be lost if the counterparty defaults.

The current replacement cost of a swap—the current exposure of the swap—is obtained directly from the market value of the swap contract. In Figure 12-6(*a*), if rates have fallen since origination, there will be no loss if the counterparty defaults since the fixed-rate payor is making payments to the counterparty. For the fixed-rate payor, a default-induced loss will occur only if rates rise. Hence, the current cost of replacing the counterparty in a swap contract is given by the positive segment of the market value profile for the swap contract. This is illustrated in Figure 12-7.

Although it is an essential element, market value (current replacement costs) alone does not accurately portray the credit risk faced. As noted by the staff of the Federal Reserve, "the cost to a banking organization of a counterparty default on an interest rate . . . contract is the cost of replacing the cash flows specified by the contract."[14] As noted earlier, the Fed characterized this *total* exposure as the sum of the current replacement cost and "a measure of the potential future credit exposure

---

14. "Potential Credit Exposure on Interest Rate and Foreign Exchange Related Instruments," *op. cit.*

Figure 12-7. Current Replacement Cost. (*a*) The current cost of replacing a floating cash flow. (*b*) The current cost of replacing a fixed cash flow.

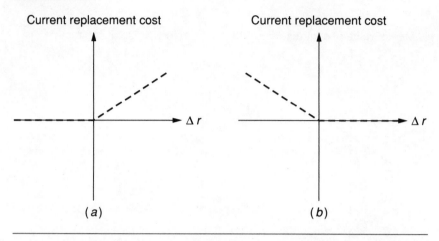

that may arise from further movements over the remaining life of the instrument."[15] Put another way, the current replacement cost indicates the cost of replacing the swap counterparty if the counterparty defaults *today*. However, the counterparty may default not today but rather at some date in the future, at which time the interest rate may differ from what it is today.

For example, consider default by a floating-rate payor. Figure 12-7(*a*) is reproduced as Figure 12-8. Suppose today's interest rates are lower than those that prevailed at contract origination: $\Delta r_t < 0$, a situation illustrated by point A in Figure 12-8. In this case, the *current* replacement cost is zero. However, since the issue is the magnitude of the total exposure to loss today of default that may occur in the future, we need to know the current replacement cost *plus* the potential credit exposure illustrated by point B in Figure 12-8.

What determines this potential credit exposure? In the context of Figure 12-8, the exposure to default-induced loss depends on potential interest rate movements. For a default-induced loss to occur, the interest rate at some future default date must exceed the rate that prevailed at contract origination (r_0). Clearly, the likelihood of this increase in rates

---

15. *Ibid.*

Figure 12-8. Potential Credit Exposure.

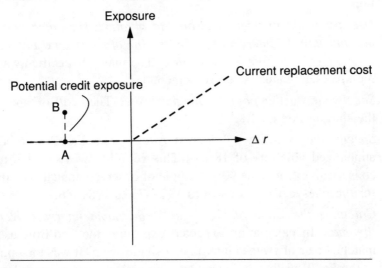

depends on the volatility of interest rates, σ_r, and on the remaining life of the contract, T. Since the exposure is the result of lost cash flows in *some future periods*, we also require a discount factor $D(r, T)$, where r is the relevant discount rate and T is the time remaining to contract maturity. Thus, five parameters go into the determination of the exposure to default-induced losses:

1. the interest rate at the evaluation date, r_t
2. the interest rate at origination, r_0
3. the volatility of interest rates, σ_r
4. the discount rate, r
5. the time remaining to contract maturity, T

However, there are at least two different ways to estimate this potential exposure.

The Simulation Approach. The methodology employed by the Federal Reserve Bank and the Bank of England (and later adopted by the Basle Committee) was a simulation approach, commonly referred to as a "Monte Carlo" simulation. For exposition, we have broken down the Fed/BoE simulation process into six steps:

1. *Specify the manner in which interest rates behave.* The Fed/BoE

assumed that interest rates follow a lognormal probability distribution.[16]

2. *Use a random number generator to obtain a simulated path for movement in the interest rate over the life of the swap (i.e., specify random walks for the interest rate).* The interval specified was six months (semiannual swap settlements).

3. *Specify the starting point for the fixed rate.* The Fed/BoE specified the starting rate as 9%.

4. *Specify the volatility of interest rates.* The Fed/BoE used an annualized volatility of 18.2%. This volatility was selected to be conservative:[17] it is the 90% quantile of observed annual volatilities for the five-year intervals from 1970–75 to 1981–86.

5. *Calculate the value of the swap at the same intervals over its lifetime.* In calculating expected exposure, the Fed/BoE used a matched pair of swaps rather than a single swap. It was the opinion of the Fed/BoE that "to a first approximation, a swap portfolio can be considered as a collection of matched pairs of swaps with equal but opposite cash flows."[18] Consequently, the valuation obtained was the value for the pair of swaps.

6. *Combine the individual estimates to obtain a probability distribution for expected exposure.*

The distribution for expected exposure obtained by the Fed/BoE is summarized in Table 12-1.[19]

To move from this distribution of exposures to an implementable rule, the Federal Reserve System determined the "credit conversion factor" as follows:

---

16. Although this is a commonly employed assumption, it does ignore some evidence that (1) the distribution for interest rates has fatter tails than does a lognormal distribution, and (2) the distribution for interest rates exhibits some evidence of mean reversion.

17. Indeed, many of the comments in response to the Fed/BoE proposal dealt with the "overly conservative" nature of this volatility estimate.

18. Muffett, *op. cit.*, p. 478.

19. Keep in mind that the exposure was calculated in terms of a matched pair of swaps. The 90% confidence limit for exposure on a matched pair is roughly equal to half the average of the 95% confidence limits for exposure on either side (*ibid.*, p. 496). Hence, in the context of Table 12-1, the 95% confidence level for expected eposure on a two-year swap is equal to twice the 90% confidence limits for a matched pair of swaps = $2 \times 0.8 = 1.6$.

Table 12-1. Federal Reserve System/Bank of England Estimates of Expected Exposures for Interest Rate Swaps. (Estimates Are Expressed as a Percentage of the Notional Principal. Volatility = 0.182, Initial Rate = 9.0%)

	Length of Swap (years)											
	1	2	3	4	5	6	7	8	9	10	11	12
99% confidence limit	0.4	1.3	2.3	3.6	5.0	6.5	8.0	9.6	11.2	12.7	14.3	15.8
95% confidence limit	0.3	0.9	1.7	2.6	3.6	4.6	5.7	6.8	7.9	9.1	10.2	11.3
90% confidence limit	0.2	0.8	1.4	2.1	3.0	3.8	4.7	5.6	6.5	7.4	8.4	9.4
80% confidence limit	0.2	0.6	1.1	1.7	2.3	3.0	3.7	4.4	5.1	5.8	6.6	7.3
70% confidence limit	0.1	0.5	0.9	1.4	1.9	2.4	3.0	3.6	4.2	4.9	5.5	6.1
60% confidence limit	0.1	0.4	0.8	1.2	1.6	2.1	2.6	3.1	3.6	4.1	4.6	5.2
50% confidence limit	0.1	0.3	0.7	1.0	1.4	1.8	2.2	2.6	3.1	3.5	4.0	4.5
Mean	0.1	0.4	0.8	1.2	1.7	2.1	2.5	3.2	3.7	4.2	4.8	5.3

Maturity of Swap	Credit Conversion Factor
Less than one year	0.000
Greater than or equal to one year	0.005

Using this credit conversion factor, the potential credit exposure is determined as

$$\begin{array}{c}\text{Notional} \\ \text{principal}\end{array} \times \begin{array}{c}\text{Credit} \\ \text{conversion} \\ \text{factor}\end{array} = \begin{array}{c}\text{Potential} \\ \text{exposure}\end{array}$$

As illustrated in part (a) of Figure 12-9, the resulting potential credit exposure is invariant to the prevailing interest rate. The potential credit exposure varies as the size of the notional principal varies or as the time to maturity changes, but it does not vary as the interest rate changes.

To obtain the total credit equivalent exposure, this constant potential credit exposure is added to the current replacement cost (shown in part (b) of Figure 12-9). However, there is one additional methodological feature: If the current replacement cost is negative, it is treated as zero. The resulting credit equivalent exposure can be summarized by the mathematical expression

Credit equivalent exposure =
            Potential credit exposure + max[0, market value of swap]

and is illustrated in part (c) of Figure 12-9.

The Federal Reserve System and the Bank of England were not the only ones to use a simulation approach to measure expected exposure. Mark Ferron and George Handjinicolaou used much the same approach in obtaining their estimates.[20] Like the Fed/BoE, Ferron and Handjinicolaou use:

- a lognormal distribution for interest rates
- 9% as the initial fixed rate
- six months as the settlement period

However, Ferron and Handjinicolaou suggest that the 18.2% used by the Fed/BoE as an estimate of interest rate volatility could be overly

---

20. Mark Ferran and George Handjinicolaou, "Understanding Swap Credit Risk: The Simulation Approach," *Journal of International Securities Markets* 1 (Winter 1987): 135–148.

Figure 12-9. The Federal Reserve/Bank of England Approach.

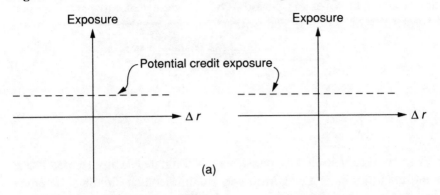

(a)

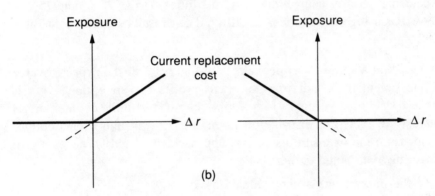

(b)

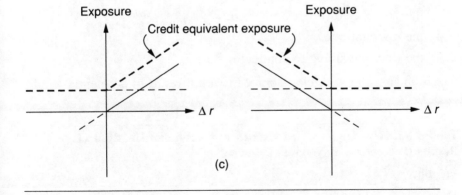

(c)

conservative. They noted that average annual volatilities for U.S. treasury bond yields over the period 1981–86 were generally smaller than the volatility used by the Fed/BoE:

Maturity	Average Historical Volatility
1 year	19.5%
3 years	16.6%
5 years	16.0%
7 years	14.8%
10 years	14.2%

Then, to demonstrate how sensitive the simulated exposure measure is to the volatility estimate, Ferron and Handjinicolaou simulated average expected exposures using a range of volatilities—15%, 20%, and 25%— as well as using the historical volatility. Their results are shown in Table 12-2.

The Option Valuation Approach.   In Figure 12-8, the expected value of the potential default resembles the profile for an option. This is because default is voluntary and occurs only if it is in the counterparty's interest. In fact, the distribution in Figure 12-8 is like a call option. To measure the exposure using this approach, it would be necessary to obtain the data noted earlier:

1. the interest rate at the evaluation date, r_t
2. the interest rate at origination, r_0
3. the volatility of interest rates, σ_r
4. the discount rate, r
5. the time remaining to contract maturity, T

A standard option pricing approach would result in a potential credit

Table 12-2. Average Expected Exposure: Ferron and Handjinicolaou Results (Percentage of Notional Principal).

Volatility	1	3	5	7	10
15%	0.09	0.57	1.12	1.64	2.37
20%	0.12	0.76	1.49	2.18	3.13
25%	0.13	0.93	1.86	2.76	3.87
Historical	0.10	0.50	1.40	1.70	2.20

exposure profile like that illustrated in Figure 12-10.[21] For an "at the money" swap (one where the prevailing interest rate is the same as the origination rate), the current replacement cost—the option's intrinsic value—is zero. But the swap contract does embody some potential credit exposure—the option has a positive time value. For an "out-of-the-money" swap (one where the market value of the swap is negative due to a decline in rates), the current replacement cost is still zero and, as the swap moves further and further out of the money, the potential credit exposure declines as time value decreases. For an "in-the-money" swap (one where the market value of the swap is positive due to an increase in rates), the current replacement cost rises as the swap moves further and further into the money; but, at the same time, the potential credit exposure declines as time value decreases.

This approach to measuring the exposure of a swap was used by J.

---

21. We treat the exposure to default-induced losses as a simple option. In fact, the valuation of this optionlike contruction is complicated by the fact that the default loss depends on two factors: (1) the value of the swap contract and (2) the financial health of the counterparty. Hence the exposure to default-induced losses is more correctly written as

$$\text{Exposure} = f(r_t, r_0, r, T, \sigma_r, \sigma_{\text{firm}}, \sigma_{r.\text{firm}})$$

where

$$\sigma_{\text{firm}} = \text{the volatility of returns for the firm}$$

and

$$\sigma_{r.\text{firm}} = \text{the covariance between movements in the interest rate and the movements in the returns to the firm}$$

Figure 12-10. Credit Equivalent Exposure as an Option.

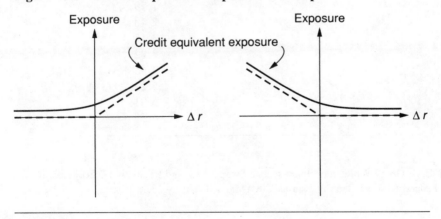

Gregg Whittaker.[22] As did the Fed/BoE and Ferron and Handjinicolaou, Whittaker assumed a lognormal distribution for interest rates. However, Whittaker assumed a much larger volatility for interest rates:

- 22% for maturities from one to seven years
- 23% for maturities in excess of seven years

Whittaker's exposure estimates are as reported in Table 12-3.

Comparison of the Two Approaches. Not surprisingly, the two approaches give similar results. The expected exposures from the three studies noted for swaps of maturities of one, three, five, seven, and ten years are summarized in Table 12-4. However, the exposures simulated or obtained from an option pricing approach differ substantially from those obtained from the Fed/BoE "rule of thumb." A comparison of the credit equivalent exposure profile from the Federal Reserve/Bank of England approach and that of an option pricing model is provided in Figure 12-11. As this figure indicates, the approach suggested by the regulators overestimates the exposures for swaps that are further in or further out of the money.

Table 12-3. Expected Exposures from an Option Pricing Model (Percentage of Notional Principal).

Maturity of Swap (in Years)	Expected Exposure
1	0.43
2	1.13
3	1.79
4	2.48
5	3.15
6	3.82
7	4.45
8	5.22
9	5.91
10	6.57

---

22. J. Gregg Whittaker, "Interest Rate Swaps: Risk and Regulation," *Economic Review,* Federal Reserve Bank of Kansas City (March 1987): 3–13.

Table 12-4. Expected Exposures (Percentage of Notional Principal).

		Maturity of the Swap				
	Volatility	**1**	**3**	**5**	**7**	**10**
Fed/BoE	18.2%	0.1	0.8	1.7	2.6	4.2
Ferron and Handjinicolaou	20%	0.12	00.76	1.49	2.18	3.13
Whittaker	22–23%	0.43	1.79	3.15	4.45	6.74

To get some idea about the magnitude of the differences between the option valuation approach and the rule proposed by the regulatory authorities, let's return to the example we began in Chapter 11.

Example

Evaluating swap exposure

We previously plotted the market value of the swap Dead Solid Perfect Bank entered into with Galactic Industries; we marked the swap to market. This valuation is reproduced at the top of page 264.

Figure 12-11. Comparison of the Option Approach and the Fed/BoE Approach.

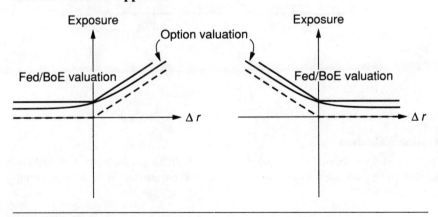

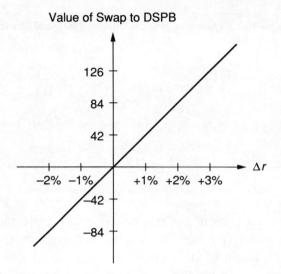

From this figure, it follows that DSPB's "default loss profile" is:

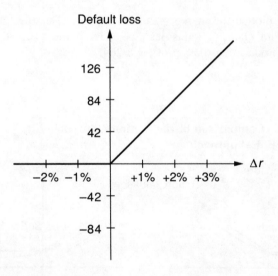

Option Valuation

To use a simple option pricing model to value DSPB's credit equivalent exposure to this swap, we need to obtain values for the parameters that go into valuing an option:

Exercise price: The value of the swap to the bank rises as the spot interest rate rises. Hence, from the perspective of the bank, the "option" gets "exercised"

if the one-year spot rate rises above the 10% rate in existence at contract origination: the "exercise price" is 10%.

Time to expiration: This is a one-year swap, so the "option" has one year to maturity.

Risk-free interest rate: Let's use a one-year rate of 10%.

Volatility: Based on data from 1987, we use an estimate of the (annualized) volatility of T-bill rates of 16%.

Using these parameters and noting that for every 1% change in the interest rate the expected potential exposure to the swap changes by 42 cents, we value the credit equivalent exposure as an option.[23] The option-based credit equivalent exposures are displayed in the following table.

One-Year Spot Rate	DSPB's Credit Equivalent Exposure
8%	$0.07
9%	0.23
10%	0.50
11%	0.86
12%	1.25

The Regulatory Rule

For one-year interest rate swaps, the proposed credit conversion factor is 0.05% of notional principal. Using this measure of potential exposure with our current exposure measures (marked-to-market values), the regulatory valuation of credit equivalent exposure would be as follows.

One-Year Rate	Marked-to-Market	Potential Exposure	Credit Equivalent Exposure
8%	−0.84	0.50	0.50
9%	−0.42	0.50	0.50
10%	0	0.50	0.50
11%	0.42	0.50	0.92
12%	0.84	0.50	1.34

The two valuations—the option valuation and the regulatory valuation—of DSPB's exposure to this swap are displayed in the following graph. As suggested in Figure 12-11, the regulatory valuation overestimates the exposure when the interest rate moves so as to put the swap further in or out of the money.

---

23. For purposes of demonstration, we used a simple Black-Scholes model. Hence, we ignored the parameters σ_{firm} and $\sigma_{r.firm}$ noted in footnote 21.

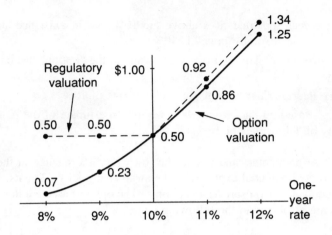

Maximum Exposure

Staff of the Bank of England have argued that the maximum exposure—a measure of the greatest amount that the party to the swap is likely to lose—is the appropriate measure for the credit allocation decision. In this view, maximum exposure is of interest "in considering individual counterparty exposure limits and how much to charge for swaps against general counterparty lines of credit."[24]

However, the optimal allocation of credit requires a marginal benefit/marginal cost rule, so there must exist some expected loss function. Look again at the "potential default-induced loss"[25] calculation, which forms the basis for our analysis (and the analysis of the Fed/BoE):

Potential default-induced loss = Exposure × Probability of default

For this measure to be used as an estimate of expected loss, the appropriate exposure measure would be expected, not maximum, exposure.

Maximum exposure would be particularly useful in the control function—that is, in the management accounting system. Maximum exposure sets some "alarm" level. If the actual exposure (the mark-to-market exposure) ever exceeds the exposure defined as the maximum at contract origination, "the alarm goes off." Once the alarm sounds, the duty of management is to determine whether the alarm was set off due to (1) a random draw from the interest rate distribution or (2) a change in the structure of interest rates. If the alarm sounded due to (1), no "response" is necessary; all we know is that an unlikely event occurred. If, however, the alarm rang due to (2), policies with respect to the next swap transaction must be reexamined.

---

24. Muffett, *op. cit.*, pp. 477–478.
25. Or, the "risk-weighted credit equivalent amount" measure proposed by the Fed/ BoE.

The feature that makes evaluating the maximum exposure to a swap so difficult is that interest rates are stochastic: there is a probability distribution for interest rates. And the distribution for interest rates requires that there be a distribution for the market value of a swap.

Consequently, there can be no true *maximum* value for the swap; in the context of the probability distribution, the value of the swap can vary between positive and negative infinity. Hence, one must talk about some value that will be the maximum with probability $X-75\%$, 90%, 95%, or 99%.

The Worst-Case Approach. As noted by Ferron and Handjinicolaou, early measures of the credit risk of swaps were based on "worst-case" assumptions about market risk and default.

> Conservative high and low projections for the future level of replacement interest rates were specified. These extreme cases were used to calculate the maximum cost of replacing all cash flows associated with a single swap. The "worst-case" procedures generally result in overly conservative assessments of swap risk. These procedures implicitly assume that default occurs immediately after inception of the swap, since all future payments are assumed to be lost.[26]

Most of these worst-case measures are proprietary. However, Marcelle Arak, Laurie S. Goodman, and Arthur Rones of Citicorp proposed a manner of simulating the maximum exposure for a single interest rate swap that has some of the worst-case flavor.[27] They assume that short-term rates follow a random walk with no drift. Then, after the swap is originated, they assume that the floating rate moves one standard deviation each year in the direction of the maximum credit exposure. The estimates of maximum exposure obtained using this conservative approach are presented in Table 12-5.

The Simulation Approach. When the Federal Reserve System/Bank of England performed their simulations, they recorded not only expected (average) exposures but also maximum exposures. Remember, they used a Monte Carlo simulation where a random number generator produced

---

26. Ferron and Handjinicolaou, *op. cit,* p. 137.
27. Marcelle Arak, Laurie S. Goodman, and Arthur Rones. "Credit Lines for New Instruments: Swaps, Over-the-Counter Options, Forwards, and Floor-Ceiling Agreements," *Proceedings of a Conference on Bank Structure and Competition,* Federal Reserve Bank of Chicago, 1986, pp. 437–456.

Table 12-5. Estimates of Maximum Exposure Calculated by Arak, Goodman, and Rones (1986) (Expressed as a Percentage of the Notional Principal, Assumes Six-month Settlements).

	Maturity of Swap					
	2	3	4	5	7	10
Bank pays floating	1.93	3.39	4.69	5.63	7.76	11.45
Bank pays fixed	1.43	2.69	4.17	5.94	9.51	15.08

the interest rate series—random walks for the interest rate. For each random walk of interest rates generated, "figures for the replacement cost of the swap . . . are calculated, and these are used to find the average or maximum replacement cost over the entire random walk."[28] The resulting maximum exposures calculated by the Fed/BoE are reported in Table 12-6.

As was the case with expected exposure, the Fed/BoE were not the only ones to use a simulation approach. Kathleen Neal and Katerina Simmons simulated the total credit exposure of a portfolio of twenty matched pairs of interest rate swaps.[29] They began with an initial portfolio generated by originating, at prevailing interest rates, one pair of five-year swaps per quarter from 1981I through 1986IV. Then, for 1987 through 1991, interest rates were generated randomly using historical volatilities. At each quarter 1987I through 1991IV, the maturing five-year swap is dropped and a new at-market swap is added. The results of "several thousand" simulations resulted in the maximum exposures presented in Table 12-7.

Comparison of the Approaches.   In the case of expected exposure, the various estimates were all similar. However, this is not the case for the estimates of maximum exposure. Table 12-8 provides a summary of the estimates.

---

28. Muffett, *op. cit.*, p. 484.
29. Kathleen Neal and Katerina Simmons, "Interest Rate Swaps, Currency Swaps & Credit Risk," *Issues in Bank Regulation*, 11, no. 4 (Spring 1988): 26–29.

Table 12-6. Federal Reserve System/Bank of England Estimates of Maximum Exposures for Interest Rate Swaps. (Estimates Are Expressed as a Percentage of the Notional Principal. Volatility = 0.182, Initial Rate = 9.0%)

| | \multicolumn{12}{c}{Length of swap (years)} |
	1	2	3	4	5	6	7	8	9	10	11	12
99% confidence limit	0.7	2.3	4.4	6.8	9.5	12.3	15.1	18.0	20.7	23.3	25.8	28.2
95% confidence limit	0.5	1.7	3.3	5.1	7.1	9.2	11.4	13.5	15.7	17.9	20.2	22.2
90% confidence limit	0.5	1.5	2.8	4.3	6.0	7.8	9.6	11.5	13.4	15.3	17.1	18.9
80% confidence limit	0.4	1.2	2.3	3.5	4.9	6.4	7.9	9.5	11.1	12.6	14.2	15.8
70% confidence limit	0.3	1.0	2.0	3.1	4.2	5.5	6.9	8.2	9.6	11.1	12.5	13.9
60% confidence limit	0.2	0.9	1.7	2.7	3.7	4.9	6.1	7.3	8.6	9.8	11.1	12.4
50% confidence limit	0.2	0.7	1.5	2.4	3.3	4.4	5.4	6.5	7.7	8.8	10.0	11.1
Mean	0.2	0.8	1.7	2.5	3.7	4.8	6.0	7.2	8.5	9.7	10.9	12.2

Table 12-7. Maximum Exposures Generated by Neal and Simmons (1988) (Expressed as a Percentage of Notional Principal).

	5-Year Swap
90% confidence level	2.89
Mean	1.85

The Impact of the Capital Adequacy Regulation

Since banks can fully capture the benefits of adequately bonding themselves, the argument that additional bonding increases social welfare must be based on the existence of some unspecified externality or market impediment. In a functioning marketplace, financial intermediaries will be forced to provide the optimal bond (the optimal level of capital reserves). It follows, then, that in a functioning market, any additional reserve requirement imposed by a regulatory authority must have the effect of lowering social welfare.

Indeed, if the capital requirement is effective—if the capital requirement is set higher than the market-determined optimum—the resulting regulatory tax will lead to reallocations in the swap market. These reallocations should be expected to occur in three primary dimensions:

Volume. The regulatory tax would raise costs and thereby lower volume. And, as swaps become more expensive, firms would be

Table 12-8. Estimates of Maximum Exposure (Expressed as a Percentage of the Notional Principal, Assumes Six-month Settlements).

	Maturity of Swap					
	2	3	4	5	7	10
Arak, Goodman and Rones	1.93	3.39	4.69	5.94	9.51	15.08
Fed/BoE (mean)	0.8	1.7	2.6	3.7	6.0	9.7
Neal and Simmons (mean)				1.85		

restricted in their ability to manage their exposure to financial price risks.

Location. If an effective capital requirement is imposed, the booking of swap business would move from the regulated institutions to unregulated institutions (financial intermediaries in other countries and financial intermediaries not covered by the regulation, e.g., investment banks in the United States). Note the perverse outcome of the proposed regulation: The very reason for the proposed capital adequacy requirements—the fact that intermediation of swaps imposes a claim on the intermediary's capital—is the reason that commercial banks are supplementing investment banks as the principal arrangers of swaps. If imposed, the capital adequacy requirement will block this movement and will, ceterius paribus, locate more of the swap business in those financial intermediaries that have less, not more, capital.

Credit quality. The imposition of a regulatory tax will affect the pricing of credit risk and therefore the composition of the users of swaps. As the "default risk price" for swaps increases, more creditworthy users will opt to switch to other markets and the effect of the regulation may well be opposite that desired: the regulation could increase rather than decrease the average default rate in the swaps market.

PART V

Options

13

A Primer on Options

An option contract conveys from one contracting party to another a *right*—the right to buy or to sell a specified asset at a specified price on (or before) a specified date. To flesh out this definition, let's look closely at the parties and the contract.

The Contracting Parties. In an option contract, one party grants to the other the right to buy from or sell to him or her. The party granting the right is referred to as the *option seller* (or the *option writer* or *option maker*). The counterparty, the party receiving the right, is referred to as the *option buyer*. Alternatively, the option buyer is said to be *long* the option position. It follows that the option seller is said to have a *short* position in the option.

The Right to Buy or to Sell. An option giving the right to buy an asset at a specified price is known as a *call* option on the asset; the call buyer has the right to purchase the asset. The right to sell an asset at a specified price is known as a *put* option on the asset; the put buyer has the right to sell. On the reverse side, the call option seller has the obligation to sell, and the put seller has the obligation to buy.

The Specified Asset. Options are available on a wide range of assets. Our purpose is to consider those options that can be used to manage financial risks. Hence, we are concerned with interest rates options (or options on a bond), foreign exchange rate options, and commodity options (e.g., options on a barrel of oil). However, to understand how options work, we will begin with those options about which the most has been written: options on shares of stock. Table 13-1 provides a

description of the exchange-traded stock and stock index option contracts listed on world financial markets.[1]

___

1. In Chapter 16 we will provide a comparable table of exchange-traded interest rate, foreign exchange, and commodity option contracts.

___

Table 13-1. Exchange-Traded Stock and Stock Index Options

United States

American Stock Exchange

Commodity	Size	Months	Hours	Delivery
Major Market stock index[*]	$100 × index	Nearest 3 and Mar Jun Sep Dec	9.30–16.15	Cash
Institutional stock index	$100 × index	Nearest 3 and Mar Jun Sep Dec	9.30–16.15	Cash
Computer stock index	$100 × index	Nearest 3 and Jan Apr Jul Oct	9.30–16.10	Cash
Oil stock index	$100 × index	Nearest 3 and Jan Apr Jul Oct	9.30–16.10	Cash
Amex also lists options on 155 equities:				
Equity Options	100 Shares	2 nearest and 2 others (varies)	9.30–16.10	Physical

*The Amex MMI stock index contract is also listed at the European Options Exchange in Amsterdam.

Chicago Board Options Exchange

S&P 100 stock index	$100 × index	Nearest 1 and Mar Jun Sep Dec	8.30–15.15	Cash
S&P 500 stock index	$100 × index	Nearest 2 and Mar Jun Sep Dec cycle. Also lists 2 year out option	8.30–15.15	Cash
Chicago Board Options Exchange also lists options of 178 equities:				
Equity options	100 shares	Nearest 2 and quarterly cycles	8.30–15.10	Physical

Chicago Mercantile Exchange

S&P 500 stock index		Mar Jun Sep Dec & serial month	8.30–15.15	Futures

New York Futures Exchange

NYSE Composite stock index	$500 × index	Mar Jun Sep Dec	9.30–16.15	Futures

Table 13-1. (Continued)

New York Stock Exchange

Commodity	Size	Months	Hours	Delivery
NYSE Composite stock index	$100 × index	Mar Jun Sep Dec	9.30–16.15	Cash
NYSE Beta stock index	$100 × index	Mar Jun Sep Dec	9.30–16.15	Cash
The New York Stock Exchange also lists options on 13 equities:				
Equity options	100 shares	Quarterly	9.30–16.10	Physical

Pacific Stock Exchange

FNCI stock index	$100 × index	Mar cycle	6.30–13.15	Cash
The Pacific Stock Exchange also lists options on 102 equities:				
Equity options	100 shares	Jan Feb Mar Sep	6.30–13.10	Physical

Philadelphia Stock Exchange

National OTC stock index	$100 × index	Nearest 2 and Mar Jun Sep	9.30–16.15	Cash
Value Line stock index	$100 × index	Nearest 2 and Mar Jun Sep	9.30–16.15	Cash
Gold/silver stock index	$100 × index	Nearest 2 and Mar Jun Sep	9.30–16.10	Cash
Utility stock index	$100 × index	Nearest 2 and Mar Jun Sep	9.30–16.10	Cash
The Philadelphia Stock Exchange also lists options on 109 equities:				
Equity options	100 shares	Jan Feb Mar	9.30–16.10	Physical

Canada

Montreal Exchange

The Montreal Exchange lists options on 25 equities:				
Equity options	100 shares	3&5 mo. cycles	9.00–16.00	Physical

Toronto Futures Exchange

Commodity	Size	Months	Hours	Cash
TSE 35 stock	$100 × index	Nearest 3 mo.	9.15–16.15	Cash
The TSE also lists options on 43 equities:				
Equities	100 shares	Varies	9.30–4.00	Physical

The Toronto Futures Exchange is a subsidiary of the Toronto Stock Exchange.

Table 13-1. (Continued)

International Stock Exchange

Commodity	Size	Months	Hours	Delivery
FTSE	£10 × index	Nearest 4 mo.	9.05–15.40	Cash
Equity options	1,000 shares	Up to 9 months out	9.05–15.40	Physical

The International Stock Exchange lists option on the following equities:

Allied Lyons	Britod	Ladbroke	Sears
Amstrad	Cable & Wireless	Land Securities	Shell Transport and Trading
BAA	Cadbury Schweppes	London & Scottish Marine Oil	Storehouse
Bass	Commercial Union	Lonsho	STC
Barclays Bank	Consolidated Goldhelds	Marks & Spencer	Tesco
BAT Industries	Courtaulds	Midland Bank	Thorn EMI
Beecham	Downs	Peugeot (100 shares)	Trafalgar House
Blue Circle Industries	Elf Aquitaine (100 shares)	P&O	Trustee Savings Bank
Boots	General Electric	Pilkington	Trusthouse Forte
BTR	Glaxo	Plessey	Unilever
British Aerospace	Grand Metropolitan	Prudential	Vaal Keer (100 shares)
British Airways	Guest Keen & Nettlefolds	Racal Electronics	Wellcome
British & Commonwealth	Guinness	Rio Tinto–Zinc	Woolworth
British Gas	Hanson Trust	Rolls Royce	
British Petroleum	ICI	Sansbury	
British Telcom	Jaguar	St. Gobain (100 shares)	

Netherlands

European Options Exchange

EOE stock index	Dfl 100 × index	1,2,3,6,9,12 month series	10.30–16.30	Cash
MMI[†] US stock index	$100 × index	Nearest 3 months	12.30–4.30	Cash
Equity options	100 shares	Jan Apr Jul Oct	10.00–16.30	Physical

The European Options Exchange lists options on the following equities:

Algemene Bank Nederland	Hoogovens
Aegon	Koninklijke Luchtvaart Mij
Ahold	Koninklijke Nedlloyd
Akzo	Koninklijke Nederlandse Papierfabrieken
Amev	Nationale Nederlanden
Amsterdam–Rotterdam Bank	Petronna
Buhrmann Tetterode	Philips
Elsevier	Kon. Ned. Petroleum Mij.
Gist–Brocades	Robeco
Heineken	Unilever

[†]The Major Market stock index option (MMI) is also listed at the American Stock Exchange.

Table 13-1. (Continued)

Sweden

Stockholm Options Market

Commodity	Size	Months	Hours	Delivery
OMX 30 stock index[*]	Kr 100 × index	2 and 4 months out	10.00–16.00	Cash or Physical
Equity options (calls only)	100 shares	3 and 6 months out	10.00–16.00	Physical

The Stockholm Options Market lists options on the following equities:

Astra	SE Bank
Atlas Copco A	Skandia (unrestricted)
Electrolux B	Skandia Int
Ericsson B	SKF B
Pharmacia B	Volvo B (restricted)
SCA B	Volvo B (unrestricted)

*The exchange also lists forward contracts (margins settled daily) on Swedish T-bonds and the OMX 30 stock index.

Australia

Sydney Futures Exchange

All-Ordinaries stock index	A$100 × index	Nearest 2 and Mar Jun Sep Dec	9.30–12.30 and 14.00–15.45	Futures

Note: The Swedish Options and Futures Exchange (SOFE) ceased trading operations on February 22, 1989.

This table is adapted from tables which appeared in *Global Investor,* a *Euromoney* publication, March 1988. Used with permission.

The Specified Price.   The price at which the option buyer can buy or sell the asset is called the *exercise* or *strike* price.

The Specified Date.   The date on or before which the option owner can buy or sell the asset is known as the *expiration* or *maturity* date. An option that can be exercised only on the expiration date is referred to as

a *European* option. An *American* option can be exercised on or before the expiration date.[2]

Aside

Reading the options quotes

Listed Options Quotations

Thursday, March 9, 1989

Options closing prices. Sales unit usually is 100 shares.
Stock close is New York or American exchange final price.

Chicago Board

Option & NY Close	Strike Price	Calls–Last Mar	Calls–Last Apr	Calls–Last May	Puts–Last Mar	Puts–Last Apr	Puts–Last May
Amdahl	$17\frac{1}{2}$	r	r	$1\frac{1}{4}$	r	r	r
$17\frac{1}{2}$	20	$\frac{1}{16}$	r	$\frac{3}{8}$	r	r	$2\frac{5}{8}$
AlnGrp	75	r	r	r	r	r	$1\frac{1}{2}$
Amoco	75	$5\frac{5}{8}$	r	$6\frac{3}{4}$	r	r	$\frac{1}{2}$
$80\frac{3}{4}$	80	$1\frac{1}{8}$	$2\frac{3}{8}$	$2\frac{7}{8}$	$\frac{1}{2}$	$1\frac{3}{16}$	r
$80\frac{3}{4}$	85	$\frac{1}{16}$	r	1	r	r	r
A M P	45	$\frac{3}{8}$	$1\frac{5}{8}$	2	r	$1\frac{1}{2}$	r
Anadrk	30	r	r	$\frac{5}{8}$	r	r	r
Baxter	20	$\frac{1}{8}$	$\frac{1}{2}$	$\frac{13}{16}$	$\frac{7}{8}$	1	$1\frac{1}{8}$
$19\frac{1}{4}$	$22\frac{1}{2}$	r	$\frac{1}{8}$	$\frac{1}{4}$	r	r	$3\frac{1}{8}$
Blk Dk	$22\frac{1}{2}$	r	r	r	r	r	$\frac{1}{4}$
$23\frac{7}{8}$	25	$\frac{1}{16}$	$\frac{1}{2}$	$\frac{3}{4}$	1	r	r
Boeing	60	$5\frac{1}{4}$	r	$6\frac{1}{8}$	$\frac{1}{16}$	r	$\frac{5}{8}$
$65\frac{1}{8}$	65	$\frac{3}{4}$	$2\frac{3}{8}$	3	$\frac{3}{4}$	$1\frac{1}{2}$	$2\frac{1}{4}$
$65\frac{1}{8}$	70	s	$\frac{1}{2}$	$\frac{15}{16}$	s	r	r
Brunos	$12\frac{1}{2}$	r	r	$\frac{1}{4}$	r	r	r
C B S	165	r	r	r	$\frac{1}{8}$	r	$2\frac{1}{4}$
$172\frac{1}{4}$	170	$2\frac{5}{8}$	$5\frac{1}{2}$	$7\frac{1}{4}$	r	r	r
$172\frac{1}{4}$	175	r	$3\frac{1}{4}$	5	r	r	r
CapCit	360	r	r	r	$\frac{1}{8}$	r	$3\frac{5}{8}$
$379\frac{1}{2}$	370	10	r	r	1	r	r
$379\frac{1}{2}$	380	$2\frac{7}{8}$	$9\frac{1}{2}$	r	5	r	r
$379\frac{1}{2}$	390	$\frac{3}{8}$	s	r	r	s	r
Coke	45	r	r	$5\frac{1}{8}$	$\frac{1}{16}$	r	$\frac{3}{8}$
49	50	$\frac{1}{2}$	$1\frac{1}{4}$	$1\frac{7}{8}$	$1\frac{3}{8}$	$1\frac{7}{8}$	$2\frac{3}{8}$

Option & NY Close	Strike Price	Calls–Last Mar	Calls–Last Apr	Calls–Last Jul	Puts–Last Mar	Puts–Last Apr	Puts–Last Jul
$15\frac{3}{8}$	15	$\frac{3}{8}$	$\frac{3}{4}$	$1\frac{1}{8}$	r	r	r
$15\frac{3}{8}$	$17\frac{1}{2}$	r	r	$\frac{1}{4}$	r	r	r
BellAtl	70	r	$4\frac{3}{4}$	$6\frac{1}{8}$	r	r	r
$74\frac{3}{4}$	75	$\frac{1}{2}$	r	$2\frac{5}{8}$	r	r	r
$74\frac{3}{4}$	80	r	r	$\frac{3}{4}$	r	r	r
Beth S	$17\frac{1}{2}$	s	r	r	s	$\frac{1}{16}$	r
$25\frac{1}{8}$	20	s	r	r	s	r	$\frac{5}{16}$
$25\frac{1}{8}$	$22\frac{1}{2}$	r	$3\frac{1}{8}$	r	r	r	$\frac{9}{16}$
$25\frac{1}{8}$	25	$\frac{9}{16}$	$1\frac{3}{8}$	$2\frac{3}{8}$	$\frac{5}{16}$	$\frac{13}{16}$	$1\frac{3}{8}$
$25\frac{1}{8}$	30	r	$\frac{3}{16}$	$\frac{5}{8}$	r	r	r
Bolar	$17\frac{1}{2}$	s	$7\frac{1}{4}$	r	s	r	r
$24\frac{1}{2}$	$22\frac{1}{2}$	r	$2\frac{1}{2}$	r	r	$\frac{1}{4}$	r
$24\frac{1}{2}$	25	r	1	$1\frac{13}{16}$	r	r	$1\frac{3}{4}$
BurlN	25	r	$\frac{9}{16}$	r	r	r	$1\frac{5}{8}$
24	30	r	r	$\frac{3}{16}$	r	r	r
C N W	25	r	r	r	r	r	$\frac{1}{4}$
$37\frac{1}{8}$	30	7	8	$8\frac{3}{4}$	r	r	1
$37\frac{1}{8}$	35	$2\frac{9}{16}$	4	$5\frac{3}{8}$	$\frac{1}{2}$	$1\frac{1}{2}$	$2\frac{3}{4}$
$37\frac{1}{8}$	40	s	$1\frac{3}{4}$	3	s	r	$5\frac{3}{4}$
ChrisC	$22\frac{1}{2}$	$10\frac{1}{4}$	r	r	r	r	r
$31\frac{7}{8}$	25	r	$7\frac{7}{8}$	r	r	$\frac{3}{16}$	r
$31\frac{7}{8}$	30	$2\frac{1}{8}$	$2\frac{7}{8}$	$4\frac{1}{2}$	$\frac{1}{4}$	1	r
$31\frac{7}{8}$	35	s	1	$2\frac{1}{2}$	s	r	r
Chryslr	$22\frac{1}{2}$	r	$3\frac{5}{8}$	r	r	$\frac{1}{16}$	$\frac{5}{16}$
$25\frac{3}{4}$	25	$1\frac{1}{16}$	$1\frac{5}{8}$	$2\frac{1}{2}$	$\frac{1}{8}$	$\frac{9}{16}$	$1\frac{1}{8}$
$25\frac{3}{4}$	30	r	$\frac{1}{8}$	$\frac{11}{16}$	$4\frac{1}{8}$	$4\frac{1}{4}$	$4\frac{3}{8}$
$25\frac{3}{4}$	35	r	r	$\frac{1}{8}$	r	r	r

Source: Reprinted by permission of *The Wall Street Journal*, ©Dow Jones & Company Inc. (1989). All Rights Reserved Worldwide.

We have reproduced the quotes from the Chicago Board Options Exchange (CBOE) as they appeared in *The Wall Street Journal* on March 10, 1989. The first column lists the name of the stock and the closing price on the stock exchange. On March 9, *Boeing* closed at $65\frac{1}{8}$.

The second column lists the exercise prices. *Boeing has options listed with exercise prices of 60, 65 and 70.*

2. Note that the terms *European* and *American* refer only to the style of the option—whether or not it can be exercised before the expiration date. The fact that an option is European or American says nothing about where the option is traded; for example, options traded on the Amsterdam Exchange are American-style options, not European-style.

The next three columns are closing call prices for March, April and May expirations; the three final columns are closing put prices for March, April and May expirations. *A Boeing call with an exercise price of 65 and a May maturity closed at 3.*

Option contracts traded on the CBOE are for 100 shares of stock. *The one May 65 Boeing call contract noted above would cost $300 plus commissions.*

The symbol *s* indicates that the exchange has not authorized trading an option for a given exercise price. The symbol *r* indicates that no trading has taken place on an authorized contract.

The Graphics of Options

The simplest way to understand how options work is with an illustration. Let's begin by considering the value at expiration of a European-style call option for a share of stock, using the following notation:

$$S = \text{Share price, the price of the asset}$$

$$X = \text{Exercise price for the option}$$

$$C = \text{Value of the call option}$$

If, at expiration, the share price is less than the exercise price ($S < X$), the option to purchase the asset for the exercise price is worthless ($C = 0$). In other words, since the share could be purchased in the share market for less than X, the right to buy it for X is worthless. However, if the share price is greater than the exercise price at expiration of the option ($S > X$), the value of the right to buy the share at the exercise price is equal to the difference between the share price and the exercise price ($C = S - X$). That is, if $S > X$ at expiration, the call owner would purchase the share for a price of X and then sell it in the share market at S, pocketing $S - X$ as profit. The value of a European-style call option at expiration is summarized in the mathematical expression

$$C = \max[0, (S - X)] \tag{13-1}$$

and is summarized graphically in Figure 13-1. As illustrated, if at expiration the share price is higher than the exercise price, the owner of the call option benefits at the expense of the seller of the call option: the payoff to the option owner is $S - X$, and the payoff (expense) to the party that sold the option is the reverse, $X - S$. If, however, the share price at expiration is less than the exercise price, the call option is worthless, so the payoff to both parties is zero.

Figure 13-1. The Value at Expiration of a European-Style Call Option. (*a*) **The Payoff Profile for the Call Buyer.** (*b*) **The Payoff Profile for the Call Seller.**

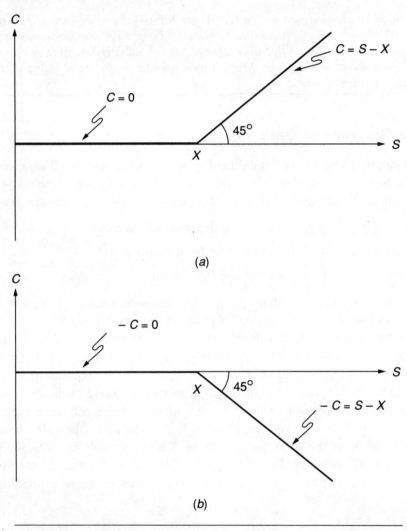

(a)

(b)

Given the preceding explanation of the value of the call option, the valuation at expiration of a put option (P) on a share of stock follows directly. The put option—the right to sell the share of stock at a price of X—is worthless ($P = 0$) when the price of the share in the asset market is greater than the exercise price ($S > X$). (Why exercise the option and sell the asset for a price of X when it could be sold in the

share market for more than that?) If, however, the price of the share at expiration is less than the exercise price, the right to sell the share at a price of X is valuable; the value of the option is the difference between the price at which the share can be sold by exercising the option and the price it could be sold for in the asset market directly, $X - S$.[3] Hence, the value of the European-style put option at expiration can be summarized mathematically as

$$P = \max[0, (X - S)] \qquad (13\text{-}2)$$

or graphically as in Figure 13-2. As illustrated, value is conveyed from the seller of the put option to the buyer of the put option only if at expiration the price of the share in the asset market is less than the exercise price.

To the reader with any experience in markets, Figures 13-1 and 13-2 should provoke a question: Since the writer of the option can only lose, why would anyone write an option? Clearly, the answer to this question is something not included in these figures: the *option premium*. At origination, the buyer of the option pays to the writer of the option a premium. As illustrated in Figure 13-3 for the call option, the option premium shifts the payoff profile for the option buyer down and that for the option writer up. Precisely the same is true for the put option.

Hence, we know that, at origination and during the life of the option, the option has some value—the option premium. But how can we determine this value? It is to this question we now turn.

Put-Call Parity

The preceding discussion suggests that we have to derive two option premiums: call premiums and put premiums. Luckily, there is a relation between puts and calls that requires us to derive only one of the premiums; if we know the premium for a call, we can solve for the premium for a put, and vice versa. This useful relation is referred to as *put-call parity*.

To see how this relation works, consider two portfolios. Portfolio 1 is made up of a call option on a share of stock and the discounted exercise price for this option. (Remember that the option can be exercised only

---

3. Put another way, if $S < X$, the owner of the put option could purchase the share for S and sell it at X, thereby profiting in the amount of $X - S$.

Figure 13-2. The Value at Expiration of a European-Style Put Option. (*a*) The Payoff Profile for the Put Buyer. (*b*) The Payoff Profile for the Put Seller.

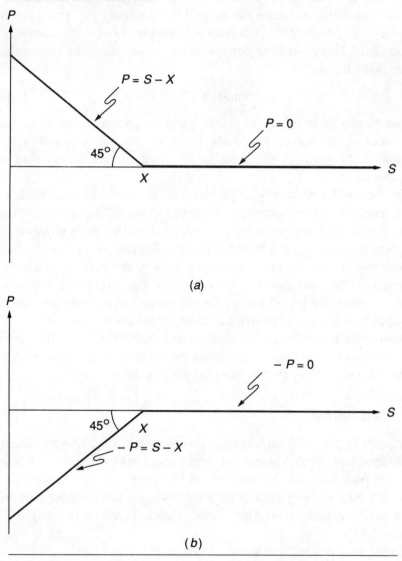

(a)

(b)

at maturity, in T days. Hence, today, the party doesn't need to hold the exercise price, X, but only the discounted value of the exercise price, XD, where the discount, D, is a function of the time to maturity, T, and the prevailing treasury bill rate for that maturity, r.)

**Figure 13-3. The Value at Expiration of a European-Style
Call Option, Including the Option Premium.** (*a*) **The Profit
Profile for the Call Buyer.** (*b*) **The Profit Profile for the
Call Writer.**

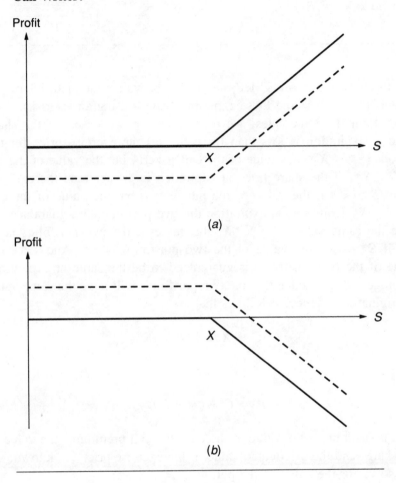

(*a*)

(*b*)

Portfolio 1: $C + XD$

The second portfolio is made up of a put option on the share of stock,
which has the same exercise price and time to maturity as the call option
in portfolio 1, and a share of the stock:

Portfolio 2: $P + S$

Table 13-2. The Arbitrage Relations for Put-Call Parity.

	$S^* < X$	$S^* > X$
Portfolio 1: $V_1 = C + XD$	$0 + X$	$(S^* - X) + X$
Portfolio 2: $V_2 = P + S$	$(X - S^*) + S^*$	$0 + S^*$
	$V_1^* = V_2^*$	$V_1^* = V_2^*$

For these two portfolios, let's consider the values at maturity of the options (we will denote these expiration values using an asterisk).

As Table 13-2 indicates, we must consider two cases. If the share price at expiration is less than (or equal to) the exercise price for the options ($S^* < X$), the value of the call is zero, but the value of the put is $X - S^*$. If the share price at expiration is greater than the exercise price ($S^* > X$), the value of the put is zero but the value of the call is $S^* - X$. However, at expiration the two portfolios are guaranteed to have the same value: if $S^* < X$, the value of the two portfolios is X, and if $S^* > X$, the value of the two portfolios is S^*. And since the value of the two portfolios is guaranteed to be the same at expiration, arbitrage will guarantee that the two portfolios will have the same value at origination. Hence, it follows that

$$C + XD = P + S \qquad (13\text{-}3)$$

or

$$P = C - (S - XD) \qquad (13\text{-}4)$$

That is, as long as the value of the call (the call premium), the value of the share, and the discounted value of the exercise price are known, we can solve for the value of the put.

To make this relation more formal, note that $S - XD$ is the value of a forward contract with an exercise price of X. Hence, a common way to remember the put-call parity relations is as follows:

The combination of long a call and short a put is equivalent to being long a forward position:
$$C - P = F$$

The combination of long a put and short a call is equivalent to being short a forward position:

$$P - C = -F$$

These relations are illustrated graphically in Figure 13-4.[4]

Bounding the Value of the Option[5]

Given the preceding relations, we need only consider one type of option; if we know the value of a call, we can solve for the value of a put, and vice versa. Again using T to denote the time remaining until expiration of the option, we know that for $T = 0$ (i.e., at expiration), the value of the call option is

$$C^* = \max[0, (S^* - X)] \tag{13-5}$$

However, what is important to the buyer and seller of the option is not how much the option will be worth in the future (at expiration) but how much the option is worth today.

We take up the explicit valuation of such a call in Chapters 14 and 15. But, before we tackle that problem, let's build up some intuition by looking at the bounds on the value of a call option.

Bounds on Option Values

In order to bound the value of an option, it is necessary to assume only that markets will price assets so that no asset is "dominated."

> For asset A to "dominate" asset B over some period, the rate of return to A must be at least as great as the rate of return to B for all possible outcomes, and the rate of return to A must be strictly greater than the rate of return to B for some outcomes.

---

4. In Figure 13-4 we do not illustrate the option premium. However, since the option premiums would cancel out, this exclusion does not affect the conclusions drawn from the figure.

5. The bounds for the value of an option were first discussed in Robert Merton, "Theory of Rational Option Pricing," *Bell Journal of Economics and Management Science* 4 (Spring 1973): 141–183.

Figure 13-4. Put-Call Parity Relations. (*a*) **Long a Call + Short a Put = Long a Forward.** (*b*) **Long a Put + Short a Call = Short a Forward.**

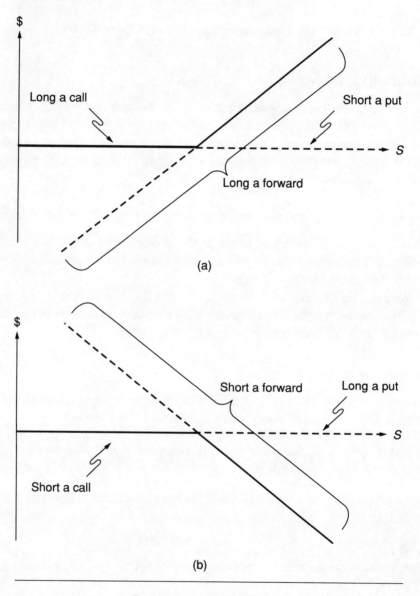

In a well-functioning market, dominated securities should not exist. No one would want to hold a dominated security, so its price would be bid down until the domination was eliminated.

Call prices are nonnegative. From the definition of call option, exercise is voluntary. Since exercise will only be undertaken when it is in the best interests of the option holder,

$$c(S,T;X) \geq 0 \text{ [European call]} \tag{13-6}$$

$$C(S,T;X) \geq 0 \text{ [American call]} \tag{13-7}$$

At any date prior to the maturity date (t*) *an American call must sell for at least the difference between the stock price and the exercise price.* An American call can be exercised at any time before the expiration date; therefore,

$$C(S,T;X) \geq \max[0, S - X] \tag{13-8}$$

If two options differ only in expiration date, then the one with the longer term to maturity, T_1, *must sell for no less than that with the shorter term to maturity,* T_2. At the expiration date of the shorter-term option, its price will be equal to the maximum of zero and the difference between the stock price and the exercise price, from Equation (13-5), and this is the minimum price of the longer-term option, by Equation (13-8). Thus, to prevent dominance

$$c(S,T_1;X) \geq c(S,T_2;X) \tag{13-9}$$

If two options differ only in exercise price, then the option with the lower exercise price must sell for a price that is no less than that of the option with the higher exercise price. This can be demonstrated by constructing two portfolios: portfolio A contains one call with exercise price X_2, $c(S,T;X_2)$, and portfolio B contains one call with exercise price X_1, $c(S,T;X_1)$, where $X_1 > X_2$. Table 13-3 illustrates that if

Table 13-3. A Call with a Lower Exercise Price, X_2, Will Have Dollar Payoffs Greater than or Equal to a Call with a Higher Exercise Price, X_1.

	Current	Stock Price at t^*		
Portfolio	Value	$S^* \leq X_2$	$X_2 < S^* < X_1$	$X_1 \leq S^*$
A	$c(S,T;X_2)$	0	$S^* - X_2$	$S^* - X_2$
B	$c(S,T;X_1)$	0	0	$S^* - X_1$
		$V_a^* = V_b^*$	$V_a^* > V_b^*$	$V_a^* > V_b^*$

at t^* stock prices are above the lower exercise price, X_2, the terminal value of portfolio A, V_a^*, is greater than that of portfolio B, V_b^*. Thus, the current price of A must be no less than the current price of B. If the two prices were equal, then the rate of return to A would exceed the rate of return for B whenever the stock price exceeds X_2, and B would be a dominated portfolio. Therefore,

$$c(S,T;X_1) \leq c(S,T;X_2) \tag{13-10}$$

where $X_1 > X_2$.

An American call must be priced no lower than an identical European call. Since an American call confers all the rights of the European call plus the privilege of early exercise,

$$C(S,T;X) \geq c(S,T;X) \tag{13-11}$$

The underlying stock is at least as valuable as a perpetual call $(T = \infty)$ with a zero exercise price. Thus, from Equations (13-8), (13-9), and (13-10) it follows that

$$S \geq C(S,\infty; 0) \geq C(S,T;X) \tag{13-12}$$

(S may exceed $C(S,\infty;0)$ because of dividends, voting rights, etc.)

A call on a non-dividend-paying stock must sell for at least the stock price minus the discounted exercise price. Let $B(T)$ be the price of a risk-free, pure discount bond that pays \$1 T years from now. Consider two portfolios: In portfolio A purchase one European call, $c(S,T;X)$, plus X bonds, $XB(T)$; in portfolio B purchase the stock, S. Table 13-4 demonstrates that the terminal value of portfolio A, V_a^*, is not less than V_b^*. Therefore, the current value of A, V_a, must be greater than or equal

---

Table 13-4. A Call Plus Discount Bonds with a Face Value of X Yield a Terminal Value Greater than or Equal to That of the Respective Stock if the Stock Pays No Dividends.

Portfolio	Current Value	Stock Price at t^*	
		$S^* \leq X$	$X \leq S^*$
A	$c(S,T;X) + XB(T)$	$0 + X$	$(S^* - X) + X$
B	S	S^*	S^*
		$V_a^* > V_b^*$	$V_a^* = V_b^*$

Figure 13-5. Bounds on the Price of a Call Option.

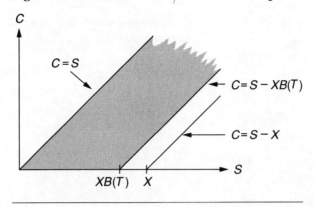

to that of B to avoid dominance. This restriction can be rearranged to yield,

$$c(S,T;X) \geq \max[0, S - XB(T)] \qquad (13\text{-}13)$$

Figure 13-5 summarizes these restrictions on rational bounds on call option prices. The call must be no less than zero, from Equation (13-6); it must be no greater than the stock price, from Equation (13-12); and it must be no less than the stock price minus the discounted exercise price, from Equation (13-13).

14

Valuing Options: A Simplified Approach

In Chapter 13 we specified the value of an option *at maturity*. However, the question facing the buyer and seller of the option is not the value at maturity but rather the value *today*. This question bedeviled the finance profession from the time option pricing was first addressed in 1900[1] until the question was finally successfully answered in 1973 by Fischer Black and Myron Scholes.[2] The Black-Scholes option pricing model, the topic of discussion in the next chapter, is of necessity somewhat mathematical. So let's first look at a simplified approach to option pricing that was provided by William F. Sharpe[3] and expanded by John C. Cox, Stephen A. Ross, and Mark Rubinstein.[4] This approach is referred to as the *binomial option pricing model*.[5] We will present the binomial pricing model by looking at the pricing of an European-style option. Once this is complete, we will look briefly at the pricing of an American-style option.

---

1. Among the first to address the question of option pricing was Louis Bachelier in his dissertation *Theorie de la Speculation* at the Sorbonne in 1900.
2. Fischer Black and Myron Scholes, "The Pricing of Options and Corporate Liabilities," *Journal of Political Economy* 81, no. 3 (May–June 1973): 637.
3. This simplified exposition of option pricing appeared in William F. Sharpe, *Investments* (Englewood Cliffs, N.J.: Prentice-Hall, 1978).
4. John C. Cox, Stephen A. Ross, and Mark Rubinstein, "Options Pricing: A Simplified Approach," *Journal of Financial Economics*, (September 1979): 229–263.
5. Alternatively, the model is referred to as the Cox, Ross, Rubinstein (C-R-R) Approach.

The Binomial Pricing Model

In this simplified approach to option pricing, we look at our continuous-process world as a series of snapshots—in much the same way that a movie is a series of still pictures. Let's suppose that today, on day 0, the price of a particular share of stock is $100. Let's suppose further that tomorrow it could rise or fall by 5%:

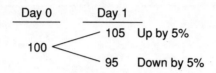

Aside

At first glance, the preceding model looks too simple to have any connection to the real world. However, it is simple only because we have let the share price move only once per day. How about if we let the share price move up or down by 5% every twelve hours,

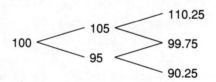

or every six hours, or....

If we make the intervals shorter, this simple binomial model becomes more realistic.

Let's consider a one-day call option on this share of stock. For simplicity, let's set the exercise price of this one-day call option at $100. Hence, the value of the call option *at maturity*—day 1—is:

Share Price at Expiration	Value of Call at Expiration
$105	$5
95	0

However, a party thinking about selling (or buying) this call option is not as interested in its value at maturity as in its value today. A number

of very smart people have tried to find this value directly . . . and failed. The approach we are going to follow is modeled on the approach of Black and Scholes. We will value the option by valuing an *arbitrage portfolio* that contains the option.

An arbitrage portfolio is one that earns a riskless return. The object is to form such a portfolio out of the two risky assets—the share of stock and the call option on the share of stock—so that the gains made on one of the assets would be exactly offset by losses on the other. As the following table indicates, for the case in point, such a portfolio could be formed by creating a portfolio that is *long* one share of stock and *short* two call options:

S	C	2C	S−2C
105	5	10	95
95	0	0	95

As indicated, the value of the portfolio—$S - 2C$—will be \$95, regardless of the value of the share of stock. Hence, we have formed a portfolio that has no risk.

Aside

Calculating the hedge ratio

In the preceding illustration, it was pretty easy to see that two calls would exactly hedge the movement in one share of stock. However, we need a more general rule when we encounter more complex situations. Not surprisingly, such a rule involves nothing more than a little algebra. For the case in point, we want to find the number of call options that will make the value of the portfolio when the share price is 105,

$$105 - N \times 5$$

equal to the value of the portfolio when the share price is 95,

$$95 - N \times 0$$

Hence, if

$$105 - N \times 5 = 95 - N \times 0$$

it follows that $N = 2$.

Generalizing, let's follow Cox, Ross, and Rubenstein by defining the high share price as $SU = uS$ and the low share price as $SD = dS$. For the case

we are examining, $u = 1.05$ and $d = 0.95$. Continuing to follow Cox, Ross, and Rubenstein, we define the value of the call option when share price is high as $CU = C[uS, T]$ and the value of the call when share price is low as $CD = C[dS, T]$. Then, the number of calls necessary to form the arbitrage portfolio (N) is

$$N = (SH - SL)/(CU - CD)$$
$$= [uS - dS]/\{C[uS, T] - C[dS, T]\}$$

In the remainder of this discussion, we will refer to the *hedge ratio* (Δ) as the *inverse* of the number of calls necessary to form the arbitrage portfolio,

$$\Delta = 1/N$$

Hence, for the case in point, the hedge ratio is $\Delta = 1/2$.

On day 0, the value of the share is $100 so we can express the value of the arbitrage portfolio, $S - 2C$, as $100 - 2C$. What we want to find out is the value of the call option, C, on day 0—a value that is so far unknown. We do know, however, that on day 1, the value of the portfolio is 95. Hence, we know that

$$(100 - 2C)_{\text{day 0}} \rightarrow (95)_{\text{day 1}}$$

In order to turn this into an equality and thus solve for C, the value of the call option on day 0, it is necessary to take the present value of the $95 to be received in one day:

$$100 - 2C = 95/(1 + r)$$

where r is a one-day interest rate. Since the arbitrage portfolio is riskless, the interest rate used is the *risk-free interest rate*. Continuing our example, if the annualized one-day risk-free rate—the treasury bill rate for one-day bills—is 7.5%, the rate for one day is $(1/365) \times 0.075 = 0.0002$, and the preceding equation becomes

$$100 - 2C = 95/1.0002$$

Hence, for our example, the value of the one-day call option *on day 0* with a prevailing share price of $100 is $2.51 (see Figure 14-1).

Figure 14-1. Valuing a One-Day Option.

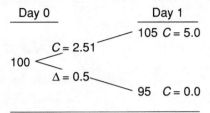

Aside

An option payoff diagram

The tree diagram in Figure 14-1 provides the value of the call for a *particular* share price on day 0—in this instance, a share price of $100. To transform this tree diagram to a more familiar option diagram, we need to think about the value of the call on day 0 for *various* share prices.

To accomplish this, we need the general expression for the value of this one-period call option as provided by Cox, Ross, and Rubinstein[6]

$$C = \frac{\left(\frac{(1+r)-d}{u-d}\right)CU + \left(\frac{u-(1+r)}{u-d}\right)CD}{(1+r)}$$

Using this general equation, consider three cases:[7]

1. *If on day 0, the share price is less than or equal to* X/u, *the value of the call option is zero.* For the case in point, if the share price on day 0 is less than or equal to 95.23, the value of the call is zero.

2. *If on day 0, the share price is greater than or equal to* X/d, *the value of the call option is* S − X/(1 + r). For the case in point, if the share price on day 0 is greater than or equal to 105.26, the value of the call is S − 99.98.

3. *If, on day 0, the share price is greater than* X/u *but less than* X/d, *the value of the call option is:*

$$\left[\frac{(1+r)-d}{u-d}\right]\left[\frac{uS-X}{(1+r)}\right]$$

6. Cox, Ross, and Rubinstein, *op. cit.*
7. This is taken from John C. Cox and Mark Rubinstein, *Options Markets* (Englewood Cliffs, N.J.: Prentice-Hall, 1985), p. 173.

For the one-period option we have been looking at:

Share Price on Day 0	Value of Call
101	3.04
100	2.51
99	1.98

The payoff diagram for the specific option we have been examining can then be drawn as follows:

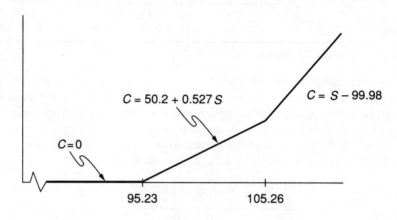

Or, more generally, the payoff diagram for a one-period option can be illustrated as:

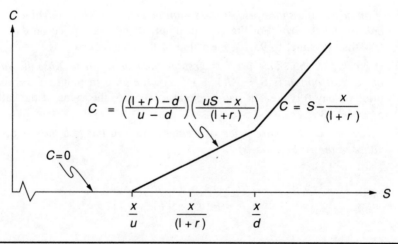

At this point, you may be saying that this is all very well and good, but not very relevant since it is unlikely we will encounter many one-

day option contracts. So let's see what happens when we let the option run for two days. Continuing to assume that the share price can move up or down by 5% every day, the distribution of share prices over the three days and the value of the call option at expiration are as follows:

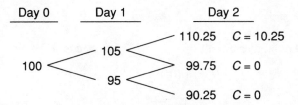

Day 0	Day 1	Day 2	
		110.25	$C = 10.25$
	105		
100		99.75	$C = 0$
	95		
		90.25	$C = 0$

Again, we want to know the value of the call option at day 0. To find this out, we must first determine the values of the option on day 1 and then use these values to determine what the option will be worth on day 0:

Day 1

If the value of the share is 105: The arbitrage portfolio would be $S - (1.025)C$. That is, the number of shares necessary to hedge one share of stock would be

$$N = (110.25 - 99.75)/(10.25 - 0)$$

$$= 10.50/10.25$$

$$= 1.025$$

(The hedge ratio is $1/N = 0.976$.) So,

$$(105 - 1.025C)_{day\ 1} \rightarrow (99.75)_{day\ 2}$$

Therefore,

$$(105 - 1.025C) = (99.75)/(1.0002)$$

The value of the call would be $5.14.

If the value of the share is 95, the value of the call is 0. The value of the call will be zero regardless of whether the value of the share rises to $99.75 or falls to $90.25.[8]

---

8. Put another way, since the number of shares necessary to hedge one share of stock is, in the limit, positive infinity,

$$N = (99.75 - 90.25)/(0 - 0)$$
$$= 9.50/0$$

the value of the call option must approach zero as a limit.

Day 0

The relevant distribution has become

$$100 \begin{array}{c} \diagup \; 105 \quad C = 5.14 \\ \diagdown \; 95 \quad\;\; C = 0 \end{array}$$

Hence, the number of call options needed to hedge one share of stock is

$$N = (105 - 95)/(5.14 - 0)$$

$$= 10/5.14$$

$$= 1.95$$

(The hedge ratio is 0.514.) Thus, the arbitrage portfolio is $S - 1.95C$:

$$(100 - 1.95C)_{\text{day } 0} \rightarrow (95)_{\text{day } 1}$$

Continuing to use 7.5% as the relevant annualized rate for a one-day treasury bill,

$$(100 - 1.95C) = 95/1.0002$$

The value of the call option would be 2.579—i.e., \$2.58.

This valuation is summarized in Figure 14-2. And if we can value a two-day option, we can value a three-day, four-day, or n-day option. The logic is exactly the same: we solve iteratively from expiration to time period 0. The only thing that changes is the size of the problem.

Figure 14-2. Valuing a Two-Day Option.

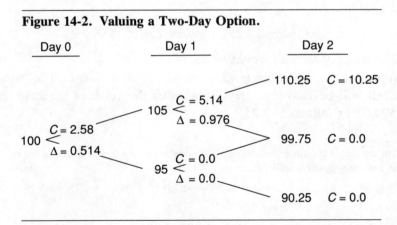

The preceding discussion has had two objectives. The first is obvious: *to demonstrate to you that the pricing of an option is not as difficult as it might otherwise seem.* The second objective of this discussion of pricing is much more subtle: to show you the five variables that determine the value of an option. To see these variables, look again at the examples. The variables we employed to value the option were:

The prevailing share price, S. In our example, the share price on day 0, the date of origination of the option contract, was $100.

The exercise price of the option, X. In our example, we used $100 as the exercise price.

The time to expiration of the option, T. We considered both one day and two days.

The risk-free interest rate corresponding to the time remaining on the option, r. In our example, the annualized rate for a one-day T-bill was 7.5%, so the one-day interest rate was 0.0002.

The volatility in the share price, σ. In the form of the binomial pricing model we have been using, the value of the call option was determined in part by the magnitude of the movements in the share price. In our example, we have used price movements of 5% up or down per day. This magnitude could be summarized by the variance in the distribution of share prices.

Hence, we could write an implicit function for the value of a call option as

$$C = C(S, X, T, r, \sigma) \tag{14-1}$$

where the following relationships hold:

Increases in the share price increase the value of the call option. If we increase the original share price by $10 in our example,

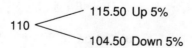

while leaving the exercise price at $100 and the other determinants unchanged, the value of the call option will rise from $2.51 to $5.52.

Increases in the exercise price decrease the value of the call option. If we change our example by increasing the exercise price from $100 to $101, the value of the one-day call option would fall from $2.51 to $2.01.

Increases in the time to expiration increase the value of the call option. As noted, increasing the time to maturity from one to two days increased the value of the call option from $2.51 to $2.58.

Increases in the risk-free interest rate increase the value of the call option. If the annualized rate on a one-day T-bill rose from 7.5% to 15%, the daily risk-free interest rate would rise from 0.0002 to 0.0004, and the value of the one-day call option would rise from $2.51 to $2.52.

Increases in the volatility of share price increase the value of the call option. Suppose that instead of 5% up or down each day, share prices could move up or down by 10% each day:

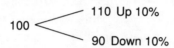

With no other changes in the determinants of the option value, the value of our one-day call option would rise from $2.51 to $5.01.

The preceding relationships can be summarized as

$$C = C(\overset{+}{S}, \overset{-}{X}, \overset{+}{T}, \overset{+}{r}, \overset{+}{\sigma}) \tag{14-2}$$

Then, using the put-call parity relations defined in the preceding section, the value of a European-style put option can be expressed as:

$$P = C - S + XD = P(\overset{-}{S}, \overset{+}{X}, \overset{?}{T}, \overset{-}{r}, \overset{+}{\sigma}) \tag{14-3}$$

From the definition of a put option it follows that the right to sell an asset at price X becomes more valuable as the market price of the asset (*S*) falls or the exercise price (*X*) rises. From the put-call parity relation, the effect of *T* on the value of a put is indeterminate because it increases the value of the call (*C*) but decreases the discounted exercise

price (*XD*). In the case of r, the decrease in the discounted exercise price exceeds the increase in the value of the call; so, an increase in r decreases the value of the put. Finally, since an increase in volatility (σ) increases *C* but has no effect on *S* or *XD*, it follows directly that an increase in volatility will increase the value of the put option.

A Note on American Options

An American option gives its owner all of the rights contained in a European option *plus* the right to *early exercise*; that is, the owner of the American option has the right to exercise the option prior to maturity. It follows, then, that the value of the American option is always at least that of the European option. Whether the American option is worth more than the European option[9] depends on whether or not the option would ever be exercised early.

Hence, the question of the value of an American option depends on yet another question: Will an American option ever be exercised early? As with so many other questions, the answer is: *it depends*.

American Calls

If the share of stock pays no dividend, it is never optimal to exercise the American call option early. Suppose that, at some time prior to expiration, the American call option is "in the money"; that is, the prevailing share price (*S*) is greater than the exercise price for the call option (*X*). If the option is exercised, the owner will receive a gain equal to the difference between the prevailing share price and the exercise price for the option. However, if instead the owner of the option sells the option, we know from the preceding discussion that the market value of the option is equal to the difference between the prevailing share price and the *discounted exercise price* plus the remaining time value of the option. The strategies are detailed in Table 14-1.

As long as there is time remaining to maturity of the option, $D < 1$ (and Time value > 0); thus, it follows that $(S - XD) > (S - X)$ and

$$S - XD + \text{Time value} > S - X \qquad (14\text{-}4)$$

---

9. And, consequently, whether it will be necessary to use a valuation model other than the Black-Scholes model or the binomial model outlined in this chapter.

Table 14-1. Strategies for Realizing an In-the-Money American Option.

Strategy	Gain
Exercise the option early	$S - X$
Sell the option	$S - XD + \text{Time value}$

Hence, for a non-dividend-paying stock, early exercise of an American call option will never occur. (Therefore, in this case, the value of an American call option is identical to that of a European call option.)

For an American call option on a dividend-paying share of stock, early exercise will be optimal if the dividend is sufficiently large; and early exercise will occur on the last day before the ex-dividend day, if at all. Since shares purchased on or after the ex-dividend day do not receive the next dividend, the share price will fall on the ex-dividend day by an amount equal to the dividend. It is this drop in price that can provide the incentive for early exercise of the American call option. The party who exercises the option just before the ex-dividend date will receive a dividend payment that will not be received if the option is not exercised. Hence, the question becomes whether the amount received from exercising the option,

$$S - X + \text{Dividend}$$

is greater or less than the value of the call option if it were to be sold:

$$S - XD + \text{Time value}$$

It follows that the American call option would be exercised early if

$$\text{Dividend} > X(1 - D) + \text{Time value} \qquad (14\text{-}5)$$

To value the American call option, the value of this early exercise provision would have to be determined for each of the ex-dividend dates that occur during the life of the option.

American Puts

Early exercise of an American put option will be optimal if the price of the stock falls sufficiently below the exercise price. This rather complex concept is most easily seen via an example. Let's consider an American

put option that has the following characteristics:

$$X = \$100$$
$$T = 1 \text{ year}$$
$$r = 20\%$$

Suppose the price of the share falls to $10. The person exercising the option early will receive $X - S = \$100 - \$10 = \$90$ today. And, if that $90 is held in a T-bill, he or she will have at maturity $90 \times (1.2) = \$108$. On the other hand, if the option is held to maturity, the most the option would be worth is $100—*and this only if the share price fell to zero*. In this case, since $108 > \$100$, it is clear that the American put option would be exercised early.

If, however, the share price only falls to $20, the situation is more complex. Early exercise of the option will bring $80 today and $80 × $(1.2) = \$96$ at the end of one year. As before, the option could be worth at maturity as much as $100 so it may not be optimal to exercise early. However, the option is worth $100 only if the value of the share drops to zero. If instead the share price falls to $5 at expiration, the value of the option would be $95, and it would be optimal to exercise the option early. Hence, in this case, it may or may not be optimal to exercise the American put option early, depending on the probability distribution of share prices.

The point is that to determine the value of an American put option on a non-dividend-paying stock, it is necessary to determine whether it would be optimal to exercise the option early on any of the days prior to expiration. Since there is no closed-form equation that will provide the solution, this involves a large, iterative, numerical approximation problem: we first check to see if early exercise could be optimal on the day prior to expiration, then on the day before that, then on the day before that, and so on.

Interestingly, while dividends make it more difficult to value American call options (because they make it possible for early exercise to be optimal), the existence of dividends makes it less difficult to value American put options. As illustrated, American puts are exercised early only if there is a sufficiently large drop in the share price. For non-dividend-paying stocks, we would have to check this relation for each

trading day prior to expiration. However, for dividend-paying stocks, the predictable share price drop on the ex-dividend dates makes the probability of optimal early exercise highest on ex-dividend dates. Hence, for American put options on dividend paying stocks, the value can be closely approximated by considering early exercise only for the remaining ex-dividend dates.

15

The Black-Scholes Option Pricing Model

In the preceding chapter, we presented a simplified approach to the valuation of an option, the so-called "binomial method." Although the binomial method is widely used for valuing options,[1] the most well known option pricing model is that proposed by Fischer Black and Myron Scholes in 1973.[2] The Black-Scholes model was the first successful model for valuing options, and it spawned a number of variations.

Indeed, the Black-Scholes approach lies behind the development of the binomial method. The paradigm that makes the binomial model work is the concept of the *arbitrage portfolio:* options and shares can be combined to form a portfolio that is *riskless.* This paradigm is the central feature of the Black-Scholes approach. Black and Scholes noted that a riskless hedge can be created out of positions in the option and shares of underlying stock. Because the hedge is [instantaneously] riskless, arbitrage ensures that the return to the hedge is the riskless rate. By combining this equilibrium condition with the appropriate boundary conditions, Black and Scholes were able to derive a specific option pricing model.

---

1. The Black-Scholes method is based on the assumptions that the underlying distribution of asset prices at maturity is lognormal and the option is European. It follows that the binomial method is particularly useful when a lognormal distribution is not appropriate for the underlying asset price and/or when the option is American and there is the possibility of an early exercise. As we will indicate in Chapter 16, the binomial model is widely used in valuing interest rate options.

2. Fischer Black and Myron Scholes, "The Pricing of Options and Corporate Liabilities," *Journal of Political Economy,* 81, no.3 (May–June 1973): 637.

Because the Black-Scholes model is by nature mathematical, this chapter is more analytical than those that precede or follow it. However, keep in mind that our purpose is not to turn you into some kind of rocket scientist but to provide you with some insights into this crucial pricing relation. Hence, in the discussion that follows, we have attempted to hold the mathematics to a minimum. The reader interested in a more mathematical approach is invited to examine the sources provided.

Valuing a European Call Option

Like any other mathematical model, the Black-Scholes model for valuing a European option is based on a set of assumptions. The first three assumptions are straightforward:

1. Transaction costs and taxes are zero, and there are no penalties for short sales.

2. The riskless interest rate is known and constant.

3. The stock pays no dividends.

The fourth assumption is a little more complicated:

4. The market operates continuously, and the stock price follows what is referred to as a *continuous Ito process*.

For those of you for whom the "continuous Ito process" is foreign, we provide the following aside.

Aside

A continuous Ito process

Were this a mathematics text, we could define an Ito process simply as "a Markov process in continuous time." Since this is not a math text, a little more detail is in order.

A *Markov process* is one in which the observation in time period t depends only on the preceding observation. For example, if a stock price follows a Markov process, the stock price S in period t could be defined as

$$S_t = X(S_{t-1}) + E_t$$

where X is a constant and E_t is a random error term.

A process is *continuous* if it can be drawn without picking the pen up from the paper.

Combining the preceding conditions, the following figure provides an illustrative path of a random variable S that follows an Ito process through time.

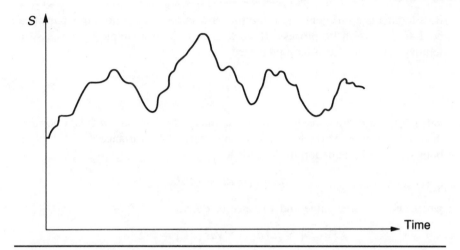

In general, the hedge portfolio—the arbitrage portfolio—is formed by combining both stock and call options. The value of the hedge portfolio, V_H, can be expressed as:

$$V_H = Q_S S + Q_C C \tag{15-1}$$

where S is the price of a share of the stock, C is the price of a European call option to purchase one share of the stock, Q_S is the quantity of stock in the hedge, and Q_C is the quantity of call options in the hedge.

The change in the value of the hedge, that is, the derivative of the value of the hedge, dV_H, is simply

$$dV_H = Q_S dS + Q_C dC \tag{15-2}$$

Note in Equation (15-2) that, since at some point in time the quantities of options and stock are given, the change in the value of the hedge results simply from the change in the prices of the assets, dS and dC.

As we have noted, the stock price is assumed to follow a continuous Ito process, so there exists a specific mathematical expression for dS. We know that the call price is a function of the stock price and the time remaining to expiration of the option. What we need is a mathematical expression for dC. This is provided by *Ito's lemma*. As indicated in the following aside, Ito's lemma provides an expression for the differential of functions of variables that follow an Ito process.

Aside

Ito's lemma

Ito's lemma is a differentiation rule for random variables whose movement can be described as an Ito process. If stock price follows a simple Ito process, the returns to the stock can be represented by

$$\frac{dS}{S} = \mu dt + \sigma dZ$$

Where μ and σ are constants, dt is the change in time, and dZ is a normally distributed random variable with a mean of zero and a variance dt. Multiplying both sides of the equation by S leads to

$$dS = \mu S \, dt + \sigma S \, dZ$$

where the expected value and variance of dS are

$$E[dS] = \mu S \, dt \qquad Var[dS] = \sigma^2 S^2 dt$$

As noted earlier, the value of a call option written on the stock is a function of the stock price and the time remaining to expiration of the option:

$$C = C(S, t)$$

What we want to know is the effect of incremental changes in S and t on the value of the call option, $C(S + \Delta S, t + \Delta t) - c(S,t)$. To obtain $C(S + \Delta S, t + \Delta t)$, we use a second-order Taylor series approximation:

$$C(S + \Delta S, t + \Delta t) = C(S, t) + \frac{\partial C}{\partial t}\Delta t + \frac{\partial C}{\partial S}\Delta S + \frac{1}{2}\frac{\partial^2 C}{\partial S^2}(\Delta S)^2$$

Then

$$dC = C(S + \Delta S, t + \Delta t) - C(S,t) = \frac{\partial C}{\partial t}\Delta t + \frac{\partial C}{\partial S}\Delta S + \frac{1}{2}\frac{\partial^2 C}{\partial S^2}(\Delta S)^2$$

Interpreting $(\Delta S)^2$ as the variance of dS, we can express dC as

$$dC = \frac{\partial C}{\partial S}dS + \left(\frac{\partial C}{\partial t} + \frac{1}{2}\frac{\partial^2 C}{\partial S^2}S^2\sigma^2\right)dt$$

A crucial insight of the preceding analysis is that the change in the call price, dC, can be expressed as the sum of two terms, one related to the change in the stock price and the other related to the change in the time to maturity:

Figure 15-1. The Change in the Call Price, *dC*, from a Change in the Stock Price, *dS*, is the Slope of the Tangent, $\partial C / \partial S$, Times the Stock Price Change, *dS*.

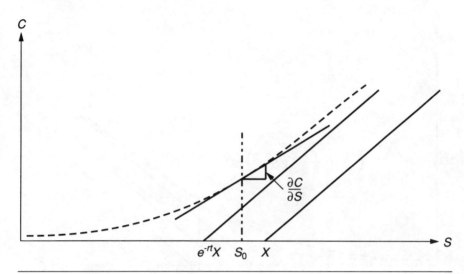

$$dC = \frac{\partial C}{\partial S} dS + \left(\frac{\partial C}{\partial t} + \frac{1}{2} \frac{\partial^2 C}{\partial S^2} s^2 \sigma^2 \right) dt \qquad (15\text{-}3)$$

It is helpful to look at this decomposition of the change in the call price graphically. Figure 15-1 illustrates the first term in Equation (15-3). For small changes in the stock price, the associated change in the call price is given by the slope of the tangent, $\frac{\partial C}{\partial S}$, times the stock price change, dS. The second term in Equation (15-3), the component related to the change in the time to maturity, is illustrated in Figure 15-2. Given the prevailing stock price, S_0, a decrease in the time to maturity decreases the present value of the exercise price. Thus, from Equation (15-3), decreasing the time remaining to maturity decreases the value of the call. Note that on the right-hand side of the equation, only the first term, $(\partial C/\partial S)dS$ is stochastic; the rest of the terms are deterministic.

If Equation (15-3) is substituted into Equation (15-2), we obtain the following expression for the change in the value of the hedge portfolio:

$$dV_H = Q_S dS + Q_C \left[\frac{\partial C}{\partial S} dS + \left(\frac{\partial C}{\partial t} + \frac{1}{2} \frac{\partial^2 C}{\partial S^2} S^2 \sigma^2 \right) dt \right] \qquad (15\text{-}4)$$

Figure 15-2. The Change in the Value of the Call, dC, from a Change in the Time to Maturity, dt, is the Shift in the Curve When the Present Value of the Exercise Price Changes from e^{-rT} X to $e^{-rT'}$ X.

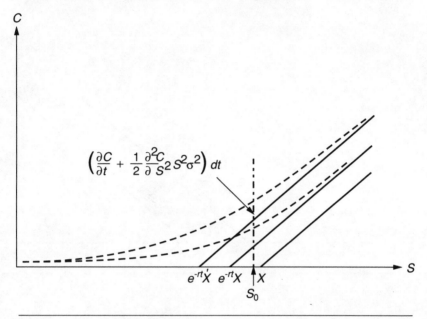

If the quantities of stock and of call options in the hedge portfolio are chosen so that Q_S/Q_C equals $-\partial C/\partial S$, the first two terms on the right-hand side of Equation (15-4) sum to zero. And, since these are the only stochastic terms, it follows that if Q_S/Q_C is equal to $(-\partial C/\partial S)$, the change in the value of the hedge becomes deterministic; that is, the hedge portfolio becomes riskless.

This means that, with the appropriate long position in the stock and short position in the call, an increase in the price of the stock will be offset by the decrease in the value of the short position in the call, and vice versa.[3] This can be illustrated graphically by returning to Figures 15-1 and 15-2. By setting Q_S/Q_C equal to $-\partial C/\partial S$ the unanticipated change in the call price due to stock price change (illustrated in Figure 15-1) is hedged by the stock price change itself, so that the predictable

---

3. The riskless hedge could also be created with a short position in the stock and a long position in the call. Note that the restriction is placed on the ratio Q_S/Q_C; it makes no difference which asset is short.

change in the call price from the reduction in the time to maturity, illustrated in Figure 15-2, is all that remains.

Hence, the insight provided by Black and Scholes is that, if the quantities of the stock and of the call option in the hedge portfolio are continuously adjusted in the appropriate manner as asset prices change over time, then the return to the portfolio becomes riskless. Setting $Q_C = -1$ and $Q_S = (\partial C / \partial S)$ in Equation (15-4) yields

$$dV_H = -\left\{ \frac{\partial C}{\partial t} + \frac{1}{2} \frac{\partial^2 C}{\partial S^2} S^2 \sigma^2 \right\} dt \qquad (15\text{-}5)$$

Thus, we have mathematically eliminated all the stochastic terms (since dt is deterministic, dV_H is deterministic), so this hedge portfolio is riskless. Hence, the return to the hedge portfolio must equal the riskless rate:

$$\frac{dV_H}{V_H} = (r)dt \qquad (15\text{-}6)$$

We are now ready to do some arithmetic to derive an explicit expression for the change in the call price. Imposing $Q_C = -1$ and $Q_S = (\partial C / \partial S)$ on Equation (15-1),

$$V_H = \left(\frac{\partial C}{\partial S} \right) S - C \qquad (15\text{-}7)$$

Then, using Equation (15-7) in Equation (15-6),

$$dV_H = \left(r \frac{\partial C}{\partial S} S \right) dt - (rC)dt \qquad (15\text{-}8)$$

and setting the right-hand sides of Equations (15-5) and (15-8) equal to one another, we obtain

$$\frac{\partial C}{\partial t} = rC - r \frac{\partial C}{\partial S} S - \frac{1}{2} \frac{\partial^2 C}{\partial S^2} (S^2 \sigma^2) \qquad (15\text{-}9)$$

We are now close to our objective: an expression for the value of the call. We have in Equation (15-9) an expression for the change in the value of the call—what mathematicians call a differential equation. We need to get from the differential equation to an equation for the value of the call; that is, given Equation (15-9), we want to solve for the value of the call.

Aside

Differential equations

A differential equation is simply an equation that contains derivatives. If there is a single independent variable, the derivatives are ordinary derivatives and the equation is an ordinary differential equation. For example, an ordinary differential equation would be $dy/dx = 0.8$. If there are two or more independent variables, the derivatives are partial derivatives and the equation is called a partial differential equation. Note that Equation (15-9) is a partial differential equation since it involves both $\partial C/\partial S$ and $\partial C/\partial t$.

To gain some intuition, consider again the simple ordinary differential equation above, $dy/dx = 0.8$. Since the differential equation is equal to a constant, 0.8, the equation is telling us that the slope of y plotted against x would be a constant 0.8. In other words, this differential equation implies that the function linking y and x is a straight line with a slope of 0.8. But there are an infinite number of straight lines with a slope of 0.8 — which one is the correct one? To identify a single line, we also need a "boundary condition," a fixed point to tie down the function. Hence, also knowing that if $x = 0$, $y = 2$ tells us that the unique solution we seek is $y = 2 + 0.8x$.

As noted in the preceding aside, to derive an expression for the call value, we must have a boundary condition, something to tie down our expression for the change in call value. The required boundary condition for the solution of this differential equation is the condition we outlined in Chapter 13: At expiration of the option, the option value must equal the maximum of either the difference between the stock price and the exercise price, $S^* - X$, or zero:[4]

$$C^* = \max[S^* - X, 0] \qquad (15\text{-}10)$$

Thus, the value of the call option will be obtained by solving Equation (15-9) subject to Equation (15-10).

Before proceeding to the solution to our problem, we should note that whatever the form of the solution, it must be a function only of five

---

4. In general, for the solution of a partial differential equation (a differential equation that is a function of more than one variable), one boundary equation is required for each dimension. Equation (15-10) is the boundary condition in the time dimension. In the stock price dimension, the boundary condition is that the call price is zero if the stock price is zero. However, because it is explicitly assumed that the call price is lognormally distributed, the stock price cannot be zero. Therefore the boundary condition will never be binding and, in this special case, can be ignored.

variables: the stock price, S; the exercise price, X; the variance rate, σ^2; time, t; and the riskless interest rate, r. This is because these are the only variables that appear in the problem.

To obtain the solution to the differential equation Black and Scholes noted that Equation (15-9) could be transformed into an equation that is familar to physicists: the "heat exchange equation." However, since we anticipate that few readers are familiar with the heat exchange equation, a more intuitive solution technique is likely to be more useful and informative.[5]

Note that when we described the equilibrium return to the hedge portfolio, the only assumption we made about the preferences of the market participants is that two assets that are perfect substitutes must earn the same rate of return; because the hedge portfolio has zero risk, it must earn the riskless rate of return. Hence, the pricing model implied by Equation (15-9) must be invariant to preferences since no assumptions involving the risk preferences of the economic agents have been made. It follows, then, that if we can find a solution to the problem for a particular preference structure, it must also be the solution to the differential equation for any other preference structure that permits a solution.

Therefore, to solve Equation (15-9), we choose the preference structure that most simplifies the mathematics: We assume a preference structure where all agents are risk-neutral. In a risk-neutral world, the expected rate of return on all assets is equal. Hence, the current call price is the present value of the expected call price at expiration of the contract, $E[C^*]$, discounted by the market-wide discount rate, r. That is,

$$C = e^{-rT}E[C^*] \qquad (15\text{-}11)$$

where T is the amount of time remaining until expiration. If we assume further that the distribution of stock prices at any future date will be lognormal, Equation (15-11) can be expressed as

$$C = e^{-rT}\int_x^\infty (S^* - X)L'(S^*)dS^* \qquad (15\text{-}12)$$

where $L'(S^*)$ is the lognormal density function.

---

5. See Avner Friedman, *Stochastic Differential Equations and Applications* (New York): Academic Press, 1975, p. 148, for a mathematical proof of the solution technique.

Equation (15-12) is integrated using a theorem from Smith.[6] The result of this integration is the Black-Scholes solution to the European call pricing problem:

$$C = S \times N \left\{ \frac{\ln(S/X) + (r + \sigma^2/2)T}{\sigma\sqrt{T}} \right\}$$

$$-e^{-rT} \times N \left\{ \frac{\ln(S/X) + (r - \sigma^2/2)T}{\sigma\sqrt{T}} \right\}$$

(15-13)

where $N\{\cdot\}$ denotes the cumulative standard nornmal. The payoff function for the call option and the lognormal density function for the stock prices are presented in Figure 15-3. Figure 15-4 illustrates graphically the relation between the Black-Scholes valuation of the call and the stock price, given the exercise price, the time to maturity, and the riskless rate.

Interpreting the Black-Scholes Pricing Model

As we anticipated, the solution to Equation (15-9)—the Black-Scholes option pricing model—involves only five variables:

$$\overset{+ \ - \ + \ + \ +}{C = C(S, X, T, r, \sigma)}$$

(15-14)

In Equation (15-14), the signs above the variables represent their partial derivatives. The partial effects again have intuitive interpretations:

- As the stock price increases, the expected payoff of the option increases.
- With a higher exercise price, the expected payoff decreases.
- With a longer time to maturity, the present value of the exercise payment is lower, thus increasing the value of the option.

---

6. Clifford W. Smith, Jr., "Option Pricing: A Review," *Journal of Financial Economics* 3 (January–March 1976): 3–51.

Figure 15-3. (*a*) **Dollar Payoff to Call as a Function of Stock Price,** $C^* = \max [0, S^*- X]$, (*b*) **Lognormal Density Function of Stock Prices at** $t^*, L'(S^*)$.

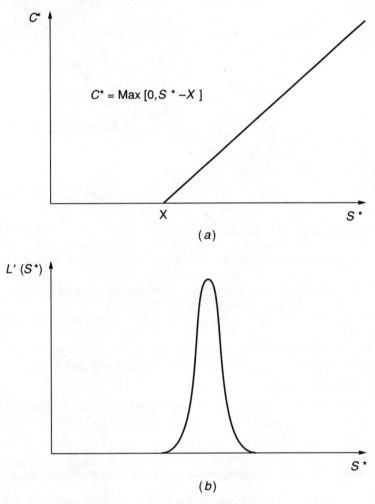

$C^* = \text{Max} [0, S^* - X]$

(*a*)

(*b*)

- With a higher interest rate, the present value of the exercise payment is lower, thus increasing the value of the option.
- With a larger variance for the underlying stock price (or with a longer time to maturity), the probability of a large stock price change during the life of the option is greater. Since the call

---

Figure 15-4. Black-Scholes Call Option Price for Different Stock Prices, with a Given Interest Rate, Variance Rate, and Time to Maturity.

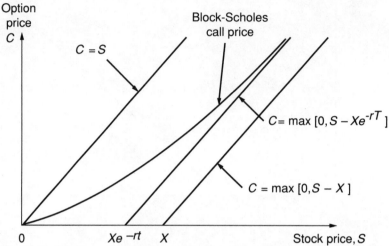

The Black-Scholes call option prices lies below the maximum possible value, $C = S$ (except where $S = 0$), and above the minimum value, $C = \max[0, S - X e^{-rT}]$. Note that the curve relating to the Black-Scholes call price to the stock price asymptotically approaches the $C = \max[0, S - X e^{-rT}]$ line.

---

price cannot be negative, a larger range of possible stock prices increases the maximum value of the option without lowering the minimum value.

Additional understanding of the Black-Scholes model is obtained by going a little deeper into the risk-neutral pricing outlined in Equations (15-11) and (15-12). With risk neutrality, Equation (15-12) can be rewritten to express the value of the call in terms of conditional expected values:

$$C = e^{-rT} E(S^* \mid S^* > X) \, \text{prob}(S^* > X) - e^{-rT} X \, \text{prob}(S^* > X)$$

(15-15)

The two terms in Equation (15-15) have natural interpretations: The first term is the product of (1) the discounted expected value of the stock price at contract maturity, conditional on the terminal stock price exceeding the exercise price, and (2) the probability that the stock price at contract maturity is greater than the exercise price. The second term is the product

of (1) the discounted exercise price and (2) the probability that the stock price at contract maturity exceeds the exercise price.

Let's examine the Black-Scholes solution in Equation (15-13), by considering two extreme cases:

1. *An extremely out-of-the-money call* $(S * << X)$. For the extremely out-of-the money-call, the ratio of stock price to exercise price is significantly less than 1: $S/X << 1$. Thus, the natural logarithm of that ratio is negative $—\ln(S/X) < 0)—$so, the area under a standard normal from negative infinity to that point is very small: $N[\ln(S/X)] \to 0$. Therefore, the value of an extremely out-of-the-money call is approximately zero.

2. *An extremely in-the-money call* $(S * >> X)$. For the extremely in-the-money call, the ratio of stock to exercise price is significantly greater than 1: $S/X >> 1$. Thus, the natural logarithm of that ratio is positive $—\ln(S/X) > 0—$so the area under a standard normal from negative infinity to that point is close to one, $N[\ln(S/X)] \to 1$. Therefore, the value of an extremely in-the-money call is approximately $S - e^{-rT}X$.

The derivative of the Black-Scholes call price with respect to change in the stock price—the option's delta—is the first cumulative standard normal term:

$$\frac{\partial C}{\partial S} = N \left\{ \frac{\ln(S/X) + (r + \sigma^2/2)T}{\sigma\sqrt{T}} \right\} \qquad (15\text{-}16)$$

For an out-of-the-money call, the delta is virtually 0. For an extremely in-the-money call, the delta is virtually 1. And, for an at-the-money call, the delta is approximately $\frac{1}{2}$.

Aside

Fraternity Row

Understanding the changes in the value of an option, which result from changes in the price of the underlying asset, in the time to expiration, and in the volatility of the asset price, is essential to managing a portfolio of options. On the street, these derivatives have been given Greek (or pseudo-Greek) names.

Delta is $\partial C/\partial S$, the expected change in the option premium for a small change in the price of the underlying asset, other variables constant. Delta varies from 0 to 1 for long calls and from 0 to -1 for long puts.

Gamma is $\partial^2 C/\partial S^2$, the expected change in delta for a small change in the price of the underlying asset, other variables constant. Gamma measures the convexity of the option pricing function, or the stability of delta. (If delta is like velocity, then gamma is like acceleration.) Because convexity benefits long option holders, long-option gammas are positive and short-option gammas are negative.

Theta is $\partial C/\partial T$, the expected change in the option premium for a small change in time to expiration, other variables constant. The theta of a long option is negative.

Vega is $\partial C/\partial \sigma$, the expected change in the option premium for a small change in volatility, other variables constant. (We presume that this term was coined because there is no Greek letter beginning with V—for volatility.) Vegas of long positions are positive.

Employing the Formula: Implied Volatilities

The Black-Scholes option pricing model of equation (15-13) involves only five variables: the asset price, the exercise price, time to maturity, the riskless rate, and the volatility of the asset price. In applying the formula, the first four values are simple to obtain. The exercise price and the maturity date are stated in the contract, the asset price is quoted in the market, and the riskless rate can be derived from quoted bond prices. It is volatility that causes the difficulties, since this variable is not directly observable. If it can be assumed that the historical volatility provides an accurate indicator of future volatility, then the simple standard deviation of the log of the rate of return, $\hat{\sigma}$, can be employed to calculate the call price.

Another method is to recognize that for listed options, the market's assessment of the value of the call is available as well as stock prices and interest rates. With that information, one can calculate the implied volatility, which, when plugged into the Black-Scholes formula along with the current stock price, interest rate, exercise price, and time to maturity, yields the observed call price.

In calculating implied volatilities, a few caveats are in order. First, the average variance rate expected over the next one month is not necessarily the same as that over the next ten months; there can be a term structure of volatility just as there is a term structure of interest

rates. Therefore, when pricing a given option, employ a measure of implied volatility obtained from other options of comparable maturity. Second, the Black-Scholes model assumes no transaction costs yet bid-ask spreads in options markets can be substantial. To reduce the impact of this problem, use the midpoint of the bid-ask spread for call, stock, and interest rate inputs in calculating implied volatilities. Third, any error in the Black-Scholes pricing model will be translated into the implied volatility. For example, if the stock is expected to pay a dividend prior to the maturity of the option, there is a substantial probability of early exercise.

Relaxing the Black-Scholes Assumptions

Although restrictive assumptions have been employed in this derivation, there has been much work done concerning the effect of their relaxation. Generally, the model seems quite robust to relaxing the basic assumptions.

Restrictions on Short Sales

There are restrictions on the ability of some traders to engage in short sales. For example, there are restrictions on the use of short sale proceeds, as well as the "up-tick" rule (which requires short sales to be executed only after a price increase). Some have worried that this constrains individuals from establishing a riskless hedge with a long position in the call and a short position in the stock. However, if the individual begins with a well-diversified portfolio, the economic effect of the addition of a short position in the stock can be alternatively achieved by reducing an existing long stock position (rather than selling short), thus avoiding the restrictions.

Variable Interest Rates

If interest rates are variable, the basic results of the option pricing model are unaffected as long as zero-coupon riskless bonds of the same maturity as the call are used in establishing the hedge. However, the volatility of the call price will now have two components, one from stock price volatility (σ_S^2) and the other from bond price volatility (σ_B^2). By employing comparable-maturity T-bills to hedge, the interest rate

uncertainty cancels out over the life of the hedge, since we know the bond price goes to par at maturity. The price of the option becomes:

$$C = S \times N \left\{ \frac{\ln(S/X) - \ln B(T) + (\sigma^2/2)T}{\sigma\sqrt{T}} \right\}$$

$$-B(T) \times N \left\{ \frac{\ln(S/X) - \ln B(T) - (\sigma^2/2)T}{\sigma\sqrt{T}} \right\} \tag{15-17}$$

where $B(T)$ is the price of a default risk-free bond that matures in T periods and pays \$1.

Dividend Payments

As noted in Chapter 14, since the option holder only has a claim on the capital gain component of the stock return, higher expected dividends over the life of the option reduce the value of the call. Assuming that the dividend is paid continuously and that the dividend yield, $\delta = D/S$, is constant, Robert C. Merton showed that the pricing equation for a European call on a stock with continuous proportional dividends is[7]

$$C = e^{-\delta T} S \times N \left\{ \frac{\ln(S/X) + [r - \delta + (\sigma^2/2)]T}{\sigma\sqrt{T}} \right\}$$

$$-e^{-rT} X \times N \left\{ \frac{\ln(S/X) + [r - \delta - (\sigma^2/2)]T}{\sigma\sqrt{T}} \right\} \tag{15-18}$$

---

7. Robert C. Merton, "Theory of Rational Option Pricing," *Bell Journal of Economics and Management Science* 4 (Spring 1973): 141–183.
8. For a discussion of the valuation of American call options on dividend-paying stocks, see Richard Roll, "An Analytic Valuation Formula for Unprotected American Call Options on Stocks with Known Dividends," *Journal of Financial Economics* 5 (November 1977): 251–258; Robert Geske, "A Note on an Analytic Valuation Formula for Unprotected American Call Options on Stocks with Known Dividends," *Journal of Financial Economics* 7 (December 1979): 375–380; and Robert E. Whaley, "On the Valuation of American Call Options on Stocks with Known Dividends," *Journal of Financial Economics* 9 (June 1981): 207–212.

For American calls, the valuation of call options on dividend-paying stocks is more complicated, since there is a positive probability of premature exercise of such calls.[8]

Discontinuous Share Price: Pricing with Jumps

In Chapter 14 we saw that if the stock price can take only one of two values at each point, we can derive the binomial pricing model. Here we have seen that with a lognormal diffusion process, we can obtain the Black-Scholes price options. But what if the stock price contains both a diffusion component and a jump component? Robert C. Merton[9] examines this case and demonstrates that, in general, no riskless hedge can be formed that simultaneously hedges against the two components of the price change. However, if the jumps are uncorrelated across securities, then jump risk is unsystematic; so jump risk is diversifiable and a security's expected return is determined by its nondiversifiable risk. If the jumps are also lognormally distributed, Merton shows that the option price will be a weighted average of Black-Scholes solutions, conditional on the number of jumps.

---

9. Robert C. Merton, "Option Pricing When Underlying Stock Returns are Discontinuous," *Journal of Financial Economics* 3 (January–March 1976): 125–144.

16

Options on Foreign Exchange, Interest Rates, and Commodity Prices

Throughout this book, our focus has been on the manner in which a firm can manage its exposure to volatile foreign exchange rates, interest rates, and commodity prices. However, to this point, our discussion of options has focused on share options because these are simpler and more familiar. In this chapter, we consider options on foreign exchange, interest rates, and commodities. Our goal is to show that the techniques for valuing and using these options follow directly from those we have developed for share options.

Options on foreign exchange and interest rates are available both over the counter (from commercial banks and other financial institutions) and on organized exchanges. Options on commodities are usually obtained from an exchange. The over-the-counter option contracts are by nature not standardized, but we can describe the range of exchange-traded contracts available. Table 16-1 summarizes the option contracts on foreign exchange, interest rates (i.e., on the debt instruments), and commodities that are listed on exchanges throughout the world.

Foreign Exchange Options

It is useful to note from Table 16-1 that foreign exchange options are available in two forms. In one, the deliverable is the underlying currency itself. In the other, the deliverable is a futures contract on the currency. We begin by looking at options where the physical asset is delivered.

The Philadelphia, Montreal, Vancouver, London International, and European Options Exchanges all trade options that specify delivery in terms of the underlying physical currency.

Table 16-1. Exchange-Traded Exchange Rate, Interest Rate, and Commodity Options.

United States

Chicago Board of Trade

Commodity	Size	Months	Hours	Delivery
Corn	5,000 bu	Mar May Jul Sep Dec	9.30–13.15	Futures
Soyabeans	5,000 bu	Jan Mar May Jul Aug Sep Nov	9.30–13.15	Futures
Soyabean Meal	100 tons	Jan Mar May Jul Aug Sep Oct Dec	9.30–13.25	Futures
Soyabean Oil	60,000 lbs	Jan Mar May Jul Aug Sep Oct Dec	9.30–13.15	Futures
Wheat	5,000 bu	Jul Sep Dec Mar May	9.15–13.15	Futures
Silver	1,000 troz	Feb Apr Jun Aug Oct Dec	7.25–13.25	Futures
US T-notes	$100,000	Mar Jun Sep Dec	8.00–14.00	Futures
US T-bonds	$100,000	Mar Jun Sep Dec	8.00–14.00 and (Sun– Thur only) 17.30–20.30	Futures
Muni bond index	$100,000 × index	Mar Jun Sep Dec	8.00–14.00	Futures

Chicago Board Options Exchange

US T-notes	$100,000	Mar Jun Sep Dec	8.00–14.00	Physical
US T-bonds	$100,000	Mar Jun Sep Dec	8.00–14.00	Physical

This table is adapted from tables which appeared in *Global Investor,* a *Euromoney* publication, March 1988. Used with permission.

Table 16-1. (Continued)

Chicago Mercantile Exchange

Commodity	Size	Months	Hours	Delivery
Feeder cattle		Jan Mar Apr May Sep Oct Nov	9.05–13.00	Futures
Live cattle		Feb and alt months	9.05–13.00	Futures
Live hogs		Feb Apr Jun Jul Aug Oct Dec	9.10–13.00	Futures
Pork bellies		Feb Mar May Jul Aug	9.10–13.00	Futures
Random lumber		Jan Mar May Jul Sep Nov	9.00–13.00	Futures
Eurodollars		Mar Jun Sep Dec	7.20–14.00	Futures
US T-bills		Mar Jun Sep Dec	7.20–14.00	Futures
Swiss Francs		Mar Jun Sep Dec & serial month	7.20–13.16	Futures
Deutsche marks		Mar Jun Sep Dec & serial month	7.20–13.20	Futures
British pounds		Mar Jun Sep Dec & serial month	7.20–13.24	Futures
Japanese yen		Mar Jun Sep Dec & serial month	7.20–13.22	Futures
Canadian dollars		Mar Jun Sep Dec & serial month	7.20–13.26	Futures

Coffee, Sugar, and Cocoa Exchange

Coffee C	37,500 lbs	Mar May Jul Sep Dec	9.45–14.43	Futures
Cocoa	10 tons	Mar May Jul Sep Dec	9.30–15.00	Futures
No. 11 Sugar	50 tons	Jan Mar May Jul Sep Oct	10.00–13.43	Futures

Kansas City Board of Trade

No 2. Red wheat	5,000 bu	Mar May Jul Sep	9.30–13.20	Futures

Table 16-1. (Continued)

Mid-America Commodity Exchange

Commodity	Size	Months	Hours	Delivery
Soyabeans	1,000 bu	Jan Mar May Jul Aug Sep Nov	9.30–13.30	Futures
Wheat	1,000 bu	Mar May Jul Sep Dec	9.30–13.30	Futures
Gold	33.2 troz	Feb Apr Jun Aug Oct Dec	7.20–13.40	Futures

Minneapolis Grain Exchange

Hard Red spring wheat	5,000 bu	Mar May Jul Sep Dec	9.35–13.25	Futures

COMEX

Copper	25,000 lbs	Jan Mar May Jul Sep Dec	9.25–14.00	Futures
Gold	100 troz	Feb Apr Jun Aug Oct Dec	8.20–14.30	Futures
Silver	5,000 troz	Jan Mar May Jul Sep Dec	8.25–14.25	Futures

New York Cotton Exchange

US Dollar index	$500 × index	Mar Jun Sep Dec	8.20–14.40	Futures
Orange juice	15,000 lbs	Jan Mar May Jul Sep Nov	10.15–14.45	Futures
Cotton	50,000 lbs	Mar May Jul Oct Dec	10.30–15.00	Futures

New York Mercantile Exchange

Heating oil	42,000 gals	Nearest 6 months	9.50–15.05	Futures
WTI Crude	1,000 bbl	Nearest 6 months	9.45–15.10	Futures

Table 16-1. (Continued)

Philadelphia Stock Exchange

Commodity	Size	Months	Hours	Delivery
Australian dollars	A$50,000	Mar Jun Sep Dec	8.00–14.30 and (Sun–Thur only) 19.00–23.00	Physical
British pounds	£12,500	Mar Jun Sep Dec	8.00–14.20	Physical
Canadian dollars	C$50,000	Mar Jun Sep Dec	8.00–14.30	Physical
Deutsche marks	DM62,500	Mar Jun Sep Dec	8.00–14.30 and (Sun–Thur only) 19.00–23.00	Physical
French francs	Ffr125,000	Mar Jun Sep Dec	8.00–14.30	Physical
Japanese yen	¥6,250,000	Mar Jun Sep Dec	8.00–14.30 and (Sun–Thur only) 19.00–23.00	Physical
Swiss francs	Sfr62,500	Mar Jun Sep Dec	8.00–14.30	Physical
Ecu	Ecu62,500	Mar Jun Sep Dec	8.00–14.30	Physical

Canada

Montreal Exchange

Gold*	10 troz	Feb May Aug Nov	9.00–14.30	Physical
Platinum*	10 troz	Mar Jun Sep Dec	9.30–14.30	Physical
Canadian T-bills	C$250,000	Nearest 3 and Mar Jun Sep Dec	8.30–15.00	Cash
Canadian T-bonds	C$25,000	Nearest 3 and Mar Jun Sep Dec	9.00–16.00	Physical
Canadian dollars*	CS$50,000	Nearest 3 and Mar Jun Sep Dec	8.00–14.30	Physical

*The precious metal options are listed on a mutual offset link with the Vancouver and Australian stock exchanges and the European Options Exchange in Amsterdam, and the Canadian dollar option with Vancouver.

Table 16-1. (Continued)

Toronto Futures Exchange

Commodity	Size	Months	Hours	Delivery
Canadian T-bonds	C$25,000	Mar Jun Sep Dec	9.00–16.00	Physical
Silver	100 troz	Mar Jun Sep Dec	9.05–16.00	Physical

Vancouver Stock Exchange

Gold*	10 troz	Feb May Aug Nov	11.30–16.00	Physical
Silver*	250 troz	Mar Jun Sep Dec	7.30–16.00	Physical
Platinum*	10 troz	Mar Jun Sep Dec	11.30–16.00	Physical
Canadian dollars*	C$50,000	Mar Jun Sep Dec	11.30–16.00	Physical

Winnipeg Commodity Exchange

Gold	20 troz	Mar Jun Sep Dec	10.00–13.25	Futures

United Kingdom

International Petroleum Exchange

Gasoil	100 tonnes	Current and 9 consecutive	9.15–12.24 and 14.30–17.24	Physical

International Stock Exchange

Long gilts	£50,000	Feb May Aug Nov	9.05–15.40	Physical
Short gilts	£50,000	Feb May Aug Nov	9.05–15.40	Physical
British pounds	$12,500	2 nearest and Mar Jun Sep Dec	9.05–15.40	Physical
Deutsche marks	DM62,500	2 nearest and Mar Jun Sep Dec	9.05–15.40	Physical

*The precious metal options are listed on a mutual offset link with the Montreal and Australian stock exchanges and the European Options Exchange in Amsterdam, and the Canadian dollar option with the Montreal Exchange. The VSE also lists options on 14 equities.

Table 16-1. **(Continued)**

London Futures and Options Exchange

Commodity	Size	Months	Hours	Delivery
Robusta coffee	5 tonnes	Jan Mar May Jul Sep Nov	9.45–12.30 and 14.30–17.00	Futures
No. 6 Cocoa	10 tonnes	Mar May Jul Sep Dec	10.00–13.00 and 14.30–17.00	Futures
No. 6 Sugar	50 tonnes	Mar May Aug Oct Dec	10.30–12.30 and 14.30–19.00	Futures

London International Financial Futures Exchange

Long gilt	£50,000	Mar Jun Sep Dec	9.02–16.15	Futures
US T-bonds	$100,000	Mar Jun Sep Dec	8.17–16.10	Futures
Eurodollars	$1,000,000	Mar Jun Sep Dec	8.32–16.00	Futures
3-month Sterling	£500,000	Mar Jun Sep Dec	8.22–16.02	Futures
British pounds	£25,000	Nearest 3 and Mar Jun Sep Dec	8.34–16.02	Physical
$/Deutsche marks	$50,000/DM	Nearest 3 and Mar Jun Sep Dec	8.36–16.04	Physical

France

Compagnie des Commissionnaires Agrees

No.2 Sugar (white)	50 tonnes	Mar May Aug Oct	11.00–13.00 and 15.00–18.45	Futures

Marché à Terme des Instruments Financiers (MATIF)

French T-bonds	Ffr500,000	Jun Sep Dec Mar	10.05–15.00	Futures

Table 16-1. (Continued)

Netherlands

European Options Exchange

Commodity	Size	Months	Hours	Delivery
Gold*	10 troz	Feb May Aug Nov	10.30–16.30	Physical
Silver*	250 troz	Mar Jun Sep Dec	10.30–16.30	Physical
Platinum*	10 troz	Mar Jun Sep Dec	10.30–16.30	Physical
Guilders	$10,000	1,2,3,6,9,12 month series	10.00–16.30	Physical
£/Guilders	£10,000	1,2,3,6,9,12 month series	10.00–16.30	Physical
Dutch T-bonds	Dfl10,000	Feb May Aug Nov	10.00–16.30	Physical

Sweden

Stockholm Options Market

Swedish T-bond**	Kr1,000,000	3 and 6 months out	9.00–15.00	Cash or physical

Australia

Sydney Futures Exchange

90-day bank bills	A$500,000	Mar Jun Sep Dec	9.00–12.30 and 14.00–16.30	Futures
Commonwealth T-bonds	A$100,000	Mar Jun Sep Dec	9.05–12.30 and 14.00–16.30	Futures

*The precious metal options are listed on a mutual offset link with the Montreal, Vancouver, and Australian stock exchanges.
**The exchange also lists forward contracts (margins settled daily) on Swedish T-bonds.

Table 16-1. (Continued)

Australian Stock Exchange

Commodity	Size	Months	Hours	Delivery
Gold*	10 troz	Feb May Aug Nov	11.00–13.00 and 14.30–16.30	Physical
Silver*	10 troz	Mar Jun Sep Dec	11.00–13.00 and 14.30–16.30	Physical
Platinum*	10 troz	Mar Jun Sep Dec	11.00–13.00 and 14.30–16.30	Physical

Singapore

Singapore International Monetary Exchange

Eurodollars	US$1,000,000	Mar Jun Sep Dec	8.30–17.20	Futures
Deutsche marks	DM125,000	Mar Jun Sep Dec	8.20–17.10	Futures
Japanese yen	¥12,500,000	Mar Jun Sep Dec	8.15–17.05	Futures

*The precious metals options are listed on a mutual offset link with the Montreal and Vancouver stock exchanges and the European Options Exchange in Amsterdam.

Aside

Reading quotes on currency options

OPTIONS
Philadelphia Exchange

Thursday, Mar. 9

Option & Strike Underlying Price		Calls–Last			Puts–Last	
		Mar	Apr	Jun	Mar	Apr	Jun

We have reproduced the quotes from the Philadelphia Exchange for March 9, 1989, as they appeared in *The Wall Street Journal*. To better understand these quotes, let's use the contract on the British pound as an example. Each contract is for 31,250 pounds sterling.

The first column indicates that the closing spot price was 172.1, that is, 172.1 U.S. cents per pound sterling, or 1.7210 U.S. dollars per pound. The second column lists the available exercise prices offered on the exchange, from $1.675 to $1.750 per pound.

The next three columns provide the prices for call options on sterling for the available contracts, that is, for contracts expiring in March, April, and June.[*] For example, an April call on the pound with an exercise price of $1.725 traded for 1.75 cents per pound. The final three columns provide put prices.

As with the share options we looked at in Chapter 13, an *r* means that there were no trades, and an *s* indicates that the exchange has not auhorized trading in the contract.

50,000 Australian Dollars–cents per unit.

Option & Strike Underlying Price		Mar	Apr	Jun	Mar	Apr	Jun
Adollr	...70	r	r	r	r	r	0.04
81.86	...76	r	r	r	r	r	0.48
81.86	...77	r	4.72	r	r	r	r
81.86	...78	r	r	r	r	r	0.96
81.86	...80	r	1.92	r	r	0.70	r
81.86	...81	0.85	r	r	0.13	r	r
81.86	...82	0.15	0.96	1.35	0.26	r	r
81.86	...83	0.02	r	0.95	r	r	r
81.86	...84	r	0.38	r	r	r	r
81.86	...85	r	r	0.55	r	r	r

50,000 Australian Dollars–European Style.

		Mar	Apr	Jun	Mar	Apr	Jun
81.86	...88	r	r	r	6.20	r	r

31.250 British Pounds–cents per unit.

		Mar	Apr	Jun	Mar	Apr	Jun
BPound	167½	r	r	r	0.04	r	r
172.10	.170	r	r	r	0.10	1.42	r
172.10	172½	0.23	1.75	r	0.77	r	r
172.10	.175	0.03	r	2.16	3.26	r	r

50,000 Canadian Dollars–cents per unit.

		Mar	Apr	Jun	Mar	Apr	Jun
CDollr	...81	2.26	r	r	r	r	r
83.34	.81½	1.71	r	r	r	r	r
83.34	...82	r	r	r	r	r	0.60
83.34	.82½	1.71	r	1.14	r	0.30	r
83.34	...83	0.31	r	0.90	r	0.45	1.02
83.34	.83½	0.01	r	r	0.28	0.74	r
83.34	...84	r	0.26	0.47	0.70	r	1.58
83.34	.84½	r	r	r	1.17	r	r

50,000 Canadian Dollars–European Style.

		Mar	Apr	Jun	Mar	Apr	Jun
CDollr	...83	r	0.53	r	r	0.47	r
83.34	.83½	0.05	r	r	0.29	r	r
83.34	...84	r	r	r	0.77	r	r

62,500 West German Marks–cents per unit.

		Mar	Apr	Jun	Mar	Apr	Jun
DMark	...50	r	r	r	r	r	0.10
53.82	...52	r	r	r	r	0.10	r
53.82	...53	0.75	1.18	r	0.02	0.30	0.75
53.82	...54	0.06	0.58	r	0.23	0.69	1.08
53.82	...55	r	0.29	r	1.18	1.36	r
53.82	...56	r	0.10	0.48	r	r	r
53.82	...57	r	r	0.30	r	r	r
53.82	...58	r	r	r	r	r	4.28
53.82	...59	r	r	0.11	r	r	r
53.82	...60	r	r	0.06	r	r	r

250,000 French Francs–10ths of a cent per unit.

		Mar	Apr	Jun	Mar	Apr	Jun
Ffranc	...16	r	1.54	r	r	r	r

6,250,000 Japanese Yen–100ths of a cent per unit.

		Mar	Apr	Jun	Mar	Apr	Jun
JYen	...76	r	r	r	0.02	0.25	r
77.47	...77	r	r	r	0.05	0.45	r
77.47	...78	0.09	0.80	r	0.62	0.89	1.17
77.47	...79	0.01	0.44	r	1.46	1.60	r
77.47	...80	r	0.18	r	2.52	r	r

6,250,000 Japanese Yen–European Style.

		Mar	Apr	Jun	Mar	Apr	Jun
77.47	...79	r	r	r	1.46	r	r
77.47	...85	r	s	r	7.48	s	r

62,500 Swiss Francs–cents per unit.

		Mar	Apr	Jun	Mar	Apr	Jun
SFranc	...58	4.95	r	r	r	r	r
63.01	...60	r	r	r	r	0.08	r
63.01	...62	r	r	r	r	0.32	r
63.01	...63	0.15	r	1.74	0.18	r	r
63.01	...64	r	0.48	1.18	1.10	r	r
63.01	...65	r	r	r	r	2.10	r
63.01	...66	r	0.08	r	3.11	r	r
63.01	...67	r	r	r	4.02	r	r
63.01	...69	r	r	r	6.00	r	r

62,500 Swiss Francs–European Style.

		Mar	Apr	Jun	Mar	Apr	Jun
63.01	...63	0.13	r	r	0.18	r	r

Total call vol.	12,198		Call open int.		370,652
Total put vol.	15,638		Put open int.		383,899

r–Not traded. s–No option offered.
Last is premium (purchase price).

---

[*] As with the quotes for options on shares, the prices listed are the "last trade" prices. Consequently, there is no guarantee that the time mark for the option price corresponds to the time mark on the spot price.

If we assume that interest rates in both the domestic and foreign countries are constant and that changes in the foreign exchange rate follow a lognormal probability distribution, the mathematics of the pricing of a European-style foreign currency option follow directly from the pricing of a European option on a stock that pays a continuous dividend.[1] In a foreign exchange option, the foreign interest rate (r_f) has the same role as the continuous-dividend yield (δ) in the share option: If the share of stock is held, the dividend is received; if a deposit denominated in a foreign currency is held, an interest payment determined by the foreign interest rate is received. Hence, to value a European-style foreign currency call option, we need only replace δ with r_f in the continuous-dividend model we provided in Chapter 15:[2]

$$
C = e^{-\overset{r_f}{\delta}T} S \times N \left\{ \frac{\ln(S/X) + [r - \overset{r_f}{\delta} + (\sigma^2/2)]T}{\sigma\sqrt{T}} \right\}
$$

$$
- e^{-rT} X \times N \left\{ \frac{\ln(S/X) + [r - \overset{r_f}{\delta}(\sigma^2/2)]T}{\sigma\sqrt{T}} \right\} \tag{16-1}
$$

For our foreign exchange option:

S is the exchange rate (domestic/foreign), rather than the share price

r_f is the foreign risk-free interest rate

r is the domestic risk-free interest rate

σ is the volatility of the exchange rate.

Hence, the value of a foreign currency call option depends on six variables:

$$
C = C(\overset{+}{S},\ \overset{-}{X},\ \overset{?}{T},\ \overset{+}{\sigma^2},\ \overset{-}{r_f},\ \overset{+}{r}\ ) \tag{16-2}
$$

---

1. The pricing of an option on a share of stock that pays a continuous dividend was discussed in Chapter 15.
2. This model was proposed in Mark B. Garman and Steven W. Kohlhagen, "Foreign Currency Option Values," *Journal of International Money and Finance* 2 (1983): 231–237.

The logic of the partial effects indicated in Equation (16-2) follows precisely the same line as that derived when we valued stock options:

The higher the current spot rate, the higher the expected payoff of the call.

With a higher exercise price, the expected payoff decreases.

With a higher domestic interest rate, the present value of the exercise price is lower, thereby increasing the value of the option.

With greater volatility in the exchange rate, the probability of a large exchange rate change over the life of the option becomes higher. Since the call price cannot be negative, an increase in volatility increases the range of possible positive payoffs to the option without lowering the minimum value.

The higher the foreign interest rate, the lower the expected increase in the exchange rate and, consequently, the lower the value of the call.

Time to maturity operates through three terms: $\sigma^2 T$, rT, and $r_f T$. Since the effects do not reinforce each other, the impact on time to maturity is ambiguous.

The put-call parity relation described in Chapter 13 allows us to express the value of a European put on foreign exchange as:

$$P = e^{-r_f T} S \times N \left\{ \frac{-\ln(S/X) - (r - r_f + \sigma^2/2)T}{\sigma \sqrt{T}} \right\}$$

$$+ e^{-rT} X \times N \left\{ \frac{-\ln(S/X) - (r - r_f - \sigma^2/2)T}{\sigma \sqrt{T}} \right\} \qquad (16\text{-}3)$$

Again, the value of the foreign currency put depends on six variables:

$$\begin{array}{ccccccc} & - & + & ? & + & + & - \\ P = P\,(& S, & X, & T, & \sigma^2, & r_f, & r\ ) \end{array} \qquad (16\text{-}4)$$

The higher the exchange rate, the lower the expected payoff of the put.

The higher the exercise price, the higher the expected payoff to the put.

As volatility increases, the expected option payoff increases.

A higher domestic interest rate lowers the discounted exercise price and thereby lowers the expected payoff.

Higher foreign interest rates reduce the expected increase in the exchange rate and thus raise the value of the put.

For time to maturity, volatility and the foreign interest rate have an effect on the value of the put opposite that of the present value of the exercise price. Hence, the value of the European put is ambiguous.

Obviously, for American puts or calls, an increase in the time to maturity cannot make the option less valuable. To value American puts and calls, the binomial pricing model described in Chapter 14 is generally employed to account for the probability of early exercise.

The deliverable for currency options traded on the International Monetary Market of the Chicago Mercantile Exchange (IMM/CME) and the Singapore International Monetary Exchange (SIMEX) is a futures contract on the currency rather than the physical currency.[3]

Aside

Reading quotes on currency futures options

The quotes from the Chicago Mercantile Exchange (IMM) for March 9, 1989, are reproduced as they appeared in *The Wall Street Journal*. Let's again look at the British pound.

On the CME, each contract represents an option on one CME futures contract on British pounds. Thus, each option contract relates to 62,500 pounds sterling.

The available exercise prices are listed in the first column. The sterling option has exercise prices from $1.650 to $1.775 per pound.

The next three columns provide the prices for call options on sterling futures for the available contracts, that is, for contracts expiring in April, May, and June. For example, an April call with an exercise price of $1.725 traded for 1.26 cents per pound.[*] The final three columns provide last-trade put prices.

---

[*] In contrast to 1.75 cents for the option on the currency itself on the Philadelphia exchange.

---

3. This is also now the case for sterling options on the London International Financial Futures Exchange (LIFFE).

FUTURES OPTIONS

JAPANESE YEN (IMM) 12,500,000 yen; cents per 100 yen

Strike	Calls – Settle			Puts – Settle		
Price	Apr-c	May-c	Jun-c	Apr-p	May-p	Jun-p
77	1.98	....	2.41	0.19	0.40	0.65
78	1.22	1.51	1.77	0.42	0.71	0.98
79	0.65	0.95	1.23	0.85	1.15	1.43
80	0.31	0.58	0.84	1.50	1.77	2.00
81	0.13	0.34	0.55	2.32	....	2.70
82	0.06	0.18	0.35	....	....	3.48

Est. vol. 6,471, Wed vol. 4,035 calls, 9,307 puts
Open interest Wed; 29,301 calls, 49,410 puts

W. GERMAN MARK (IMM) 125,000 marks; cents per mark

Strike	Calls – Settle			Puts – Settle		
Price	Apr-c	May-c	Jun-c	Apr-p	May-p	Jun-p
52	....	....	2.61	0.05	0.16	0.32
53	1.47	....	1.88	0.15	0.34	0.57
54	0.75	1.00	1.26	0.72	0.67	0.93
55	0.31	0.55	0.79	0.98	1.22	1.46
56	0.11	0.28	0.47	1.77	1.93	2.12
57	0.04	0.13	0.28	....	....	2.90

Est. vol. 8,127, Wed vol. 3,909 calls, 5,317 puts
Open interest Wed; 38,816 calls, 44,889 puts

CANADIAN DOLLAR (IMM) 100,000 Can.$, cents per Can.$

Strike	Calls – Settle			Puts – Settle		
Price	Apr-c	May-c	Jun-c	Apr-p	May-p	Jun-p
820	....	....	1.39	0.17	0.33	0.48
825	0.72	....	1.09	0.30	0.50	0.67
830	0.43	0.65	0.83	0.51	0.72	0.90
835	0.24	0.44	0.61	0.81	1.00	1.18
840	0.13	0.29	0.45	1.20	1.34	1.49
845	0.07	0.19	0.32	1.63	....	1.85

Est. vol. 1,429, Wed vol. 403 calls, 719 puts
Open interest Wed; 10,937 calls, 7,298 puts

BRITISH POUND (IMM) 62,500 pounds; cents per pound

Strike	Calls – Settle			Puts – Settle		
Price	Apr-c	May-c	Jun-c	Apr-p	May-p	Jun-p
1650	....	....	7.10	0.26	0.74	1.26
1675	4.08	....	5.42	0.68	1.34	2.00
1700	2.42	3.18	3.98	1.50	2.26	3.00
1725	1.26	2.02	2.80	2.82	....	4.28
1750	0.58	1.22	1.88	4.62	5.20	5.80
1775	0.24	0.70	1.22	6.78	....	7.58

Est. vol. 695, Wed vol. 188 calls, 226 puts
Open interest Wed; 3,766 calls, 5,672 puts

SWISS FRANC (IMM) 125,000 francs; cents per franc

Strike	Calls – Settle			Puts – Settle		
Price	Apr-c	May-c	Jun-c	Apr-p	May-p	Jun-p
62	....	....	2.33	0.16	0.37	0.63
63	1.12	1.42	1.70	0.39	0.70	0.98
64	0.57	0.87	1.17	0.84	1.14	1.43
65	0.25	0.51	0.79	1.52	1.78	2.04
66	0.10	0.27	0.52	2.37	....	2.75
67	0.05	0.15	0.33	....	....	3.55

Est. vol. 2,900, Wed vol. 1,361 calls, 2,436 puts
Open interest Wed; 11,534 calls, 14,548 puts

OTHER FUTURES OPTIONS

Final or settlement prices of selected contracts. Volume and open interest are totals in all contract months.

U.S. Dollar Index (FINEX) 500 times index

Strike	Jun-c	Sep-c	Dec-c	Jun-p	Sep-p	Dec-p
96	2.10	....	....	....	....	....

Est. vol. 1. Wed vol. 2. Op. Int. 41.

Australian Dollar (IMM) $100,000; $ per $

Strike	Apr-c	May-c	Jun-c	Apr-p	May-p	Jun-p
81	1.47	....	2.32	0.97	....	1.83

Est. vol. 5. Wed vol. 41. Op. Int. 1,171.

Sterling (LIFFE) £250,000, pts. of 100%

Strike	Mar-c	Apr-c	May-c	Mar-p	Apr-p	May-p
165	6.95	6.96	6.95	0.00	0.25	0.75

Act. vol. Thur. vol. 0. Op. Int. 3,885.

FINEX – Financial Instrument Exchange, a division of the New York Cotton Exchange. IMM-International Monetary Market at Chicago Mercantile Exchange. LIFFE-London International Financing Futures Exchange.

A futures option contract is similar to an option on a stock in the sense that a call allows its owner to purchase the underlying asset (the futures contract) at the exercise price of the option. However, unlike the stock option, exercise of the futures option does not involve the payment of cash equal to the exercise price. Rather, upon exercise, the owner of the futures option merely acquires a long or short futures position with the futures price equal to the exercise price of the option.[4] Exercise of a call option on futures results in a long futures contract at the call's exercise price (generally effective on the next trading day). Conversely, exercise of a put option on a futures results in a short futures position. When the futures position thereby acquired is marked to market at the close of the day, the option holder is free to liquidate the position.

For valuing currency futures options, recall the foreign exchange forward/futures pricing relation introduced in Chapter 4.[5] The key relation is referred to as *interest rate parity*.

Aside

Interest rate parity revisited

The simplest way to express the interest rate parity relation is to visualize the relation between dollars in the future and some other currency in the future as a "box." Let's continue to think about dollars and sterling.

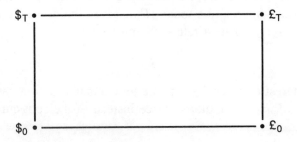

At the lower left corner, put dollars today ($\$_0$); at the lower right, put pounds

---

4. At exercise, no payment is required. However, when the option owner exercises the option and takes the futures position, the standard margin deposit for a futures contract is required.

5. See the section in the chapter entitled "The Forward Exchange Rate."

today ($£_0$). At the upper left corner is future dollars ($\$_T$), and at the upper right corner is future pounds ($£_T$).

There are four markets linking these magnitudes: (1) Dollars today ($\$_0$) and dollars in the future ($\$_T$) are related by the U.S. credit market, which determines the domestic interest rate (r_{US}). (2) Similarly, U.K. credit markets link pounds today ($£_0$) with future pounds ($£_T$), through the interest rate in the U.K. (r_{UK}). (3) Dollars today and pounds today are linked by the spot currency market (S). (4) Future pounds and future dollars are linked through the forward/futures market (F).

We can get from future dollars to future pounds via the forward/futures currency market—across the top of the box. But we can also get from future dollars to future pounds by going around the box the other way:

1. Borrow dollars today in the U.S. credit market.
2. Trade the current dollars received for current pounds in the spot FX market.
3. Lend the pounds today in the U.K. credit market for future pounds.

Since the same result can be achieved in two ways, arbitrage forces the prices for the two ways to be the same. Therefore, spot, futures/forward, and credit market prices must be mutually consistent. The forward price must be related to the spot price via the domestic and foreign interest rates.

Using interest rate parity, the relation between the spot rate today (S_0) and the forward/futures rate today (F_0), given the domestic interest rate (r) and the foreign interest rate (r_f), must be:[6]

$$F_0 = S_0 e^{(r-r_f)T} \tag{16-5}$$

Given interest rate parity, our foreign exchange option can be valued in terms of a forward or futures price instead of the spot currency rate.

---

6. In Equation (16-5), we employ the continuous-compounding assumption common to option pricing models. In Chapter 4, we assumed discrete-period (annual) compounding, so we expressed the interest rate parity relation as

$$F_0 = S_0 \left(\frac{1+r}{1+r_f} \right)$$

the expressions differ only with respect to the compounding conventions.

Substituting Equation (16-5) into Equation (16-1) yields[7]

$$C = e^{-r_f T}\left[F \times N\left\{ \frac{\ln(F/X) + (\sigma^2/2)T}{\sigma\sqrt{T}} \right\} \right.$$

$$\left. - X \times N\left\{ \frac{\ln(F/X) - (\sigma^2/2)T}{\sigma\sqrt{T}} \right\} \right] \qquad (16\text{-}6)$$

Hence, the value of a European foreign currency futures option depends on only five separate variables:

$$\overset{+\ -\ ?\ +\ -}{C = C\,(\,F, X, T, \sigma^2, r_f\,)} \qquad (16\text{-}7)$$

In Equation (16-7) most of the partial effects have their expected signs. However, it is useful to elaborate on the effect of time to maturity. Consider a market where the futures price is greater than the current spot price. For example, suppose the foreign interest rate were 6% and the domestic interest rate 9%; interest rate parity, Equation (16-5), would imply that $F > S$. We also know that at the expiration of the futures contract, the spot and futures prices must be equal. Thus, even though the domestic interest rate has been substituted out of this expression, its impact still enters through the forward/futures price.

So far, we have presented the valuation of European-style options on foreign exchange futures; we have no closed-form solution for valuing an American currency futures option. Here again, the binomial pricing techniques are useful in simulating an optimal exercise strategy and deriving the valuation implications for the option.

Interest Rate Options: Options on Debt Instruments

Interest rate protection in the form of an option could be quoted using any one of a number of different conventions. We could talk about an

---

7. This kind of approach to value options on futures contracts was first dicussed in Fischer Black, "The Pricing of Commodity Contracts," *Journal of Financial Economics* 3 (March 1976):167–179.

option on an interest rate or an option on the price of the corresponding bond. And, we could talk about an option on the bond itself or an option on a futures contract on the bond. One of the things that make interest rate options more difficult to deal with is the fact that *instead of a single convention, all of these conventions are employed.*

By and large, the exchanges quote options on bond prices—either options on the bond itself or options on a futures contract on the bond. It is with these exchange-traded contracts that we will begin. However, a large and growing market is the market for over-the-counter interest rate options from commercial banks. The convention of this market is to quote the option as an option on an interest rate:

A call option on an interest rate = A *Cap*.

A put option on an interest rate = A *Floor*.

Aside

Reading quotes on bond options

Thursday, March 9, 1989
For Notes and Bonds, decimals in closing prices represent 32nds; 1.01 means 1¹⁄₃₂. For Bills, decimals in closing prices represent basis points; $25 per .01.

OPTIONS
Chicago Board Options Exchange

U.S. TREASURY BOND—$100,000 principal value

Underlying Issue	Strike Price	Calls–Last			Puts–Last		
		Mar	Apr	Jun	Mar	Apr	Jun
8⅞% (yba)	97½	....	....	....	....	1.04	....
due 2/2019		....	....	....	....	....	....
9% (ybk)	100	0.10	....	....	....	....	....
due 11/2018		....	....	....	....	....	....
9⅛% (ybl)	100	....	....	....	....	1.12	....
due 5/2018	102	0.04	....	....	....	....	....

Total call vol. 28   Call open Int. 3,865
Total put vol. 201   Put open Int. 4,341
5-YEAR U.S. TREASURY NOTE–$100,000 principal value
Total call vol. 0   Call open limit Int. 0
Total put vol. 0   Put open Int. 102
3 p.m. prices of underlying Issues supplied by the Chicago Corp.: T-Bonds 8⅞% 98.03; 8⅞% 98.24;9% 99.09; 9⅛% 100.12. T-Notes 8⅛% 97.31; 9% 98.17; 9½% 100.19.

We have reproduced the quotes on bond and note options from the Chicago Board Options Exchange for March 9, 1989, as they appeared in *The Wall Street Journal.*

Look at the quotes for the U.S. treasury bond options. As indicated in the first column, there were option contracts available on three Treasury bonds—the 8 7/8s of 2/2019, the 9s of 11/2018 and the 9 1/8s of 5/2018.* For the 9s of 11/2018 with an exercise price of 100 and a March expiration, the option price is 10 "ticks," or 1/32. Since the bond option contract is denominated in $100,000 units, the price of this option is 10 ticks × $31.25 per tick = $312.50.

The low volume in the market for options on the physical bond is clear from these quotes. Volume has been low in these contracts over their entire history.

---

* Unlike futures contracts on treasury bonds, the CBOE option contract does not permit a choice of which instrument can be delivered.

As noted in Table 16-1, several exchanges trade options on physical bonds: the Chicago Board Options Exchange, the Montreal Exchange, the Toronto Futures Exchange, the International Stock Exchange, the European Options Exchange, and the Stockholm Options Market.

Table 16-1 indicates that options on futures contracts on bonds are traded on the Chicago Board of Trade, the Chicago Mercantile Exchange, the London International Financial Futures Exchange, the Sydney Futures Exchange, and the Singapore International Monetary Exchange.

The valuation of bond options—whether on the physical bond or on a futures contract on the bond—is generally more difficult than the valuation of options on stock described in Chapters 14 and 15 or the valuation of foreign exchange options discussed earlier in this chapter. The primary source of the difficulty is that the time series behavior of interest rates is more difficult to model than the time series of stock prices or foreign exchange rates. Although the assumption of a random walk appears a reasonable approximation for stock prices and spot foreign exchange rates, the dynamics of bond price movements are generally more complicated.

Current information about interest rates is normally summarized using a *term structure of interest rates*. We discussed the basics of the term structure of interest rates in Chapter 4, noting that interest rates should not be expected to be constant over time. We often see an upward-sloping term structure, indicating higher expected future rates, but we have also seen downward-sloping term structures, indicating lower expected future rates; and in 1989 we again saw a humped term structure, indicating first higher then lower expected future rates. In fact, virtually any pattern of expected rates is feasible.

Since the whole term's structure is required to summarize market interest rates, potentially important information is lost in the effort to parameterize the structure of rates.[8] The fewer the parameters used, the more information is lost. Indeed, we can distinguish the approaches to valuing debt options by looking at the number of parameters employed to represent the stochastic process that generates the bond prices.

---

8. When we speak of parameterizing the term structure, we are referring to attempts to summarize the term structure with (1) a limited number of points from the term structure or (2) a mathematical function (e.g., the function for a straight line).

Aside

Reading quotes on options on bond futures

FUTURES OPTIONS

T–BONDS (CBT) $100,000; points and 64ths of 100%

Strike	Calls–Last			Puts–Last		
Price	Jun–c	Sep–c	Dec–c	Jun–p	Sep–p	Dec–p
84	4–59	5–22	....	0–20	0–51	1–16
86	3–17	3–58	....	0–40	1–21	1–56
88	1–57	2–44	3–15	1–14	2–02	2–36
90	0–61	1–47	2–23	2–16	3–02	....
92	0–26	1–04	1–42	3–44	4–18	....
94	0–11	0–42	1–10	5–27	....	....

Est. vol. 63,000, Wed vol. 39,355 calls, 30,989 puts
Open Interest Wed; 167,954 calls, 193,372 puts

T–NOTES (CBT) $100,000; points and 64ths of 100%

Strike	Calls–Last			Puts–Last		
Price	Jun–c	Sep–c	Dec–c	Jun–p	Sep–p	Dec–p
90	2–41	....	....	0–24	....	....
91	1–57	....	....	0–38	1–04	....
92	1–15	1–55	....	0–60	1–29	....
93	0–49	....	....	1–29	1–61	....
94	0–27	0–62	....	2–06	2–33	....
95	0–15	0–43	....	2–57	3–13	....

Est. vol. 4,300, Wed vol. 1,947 calls, 1,067 puts
Open Interest Wed; 15,818 calls, 17,596 puts

MUNICIPAL BOND INDEX (CBT) $100,000; pts & 64ths of 100%

Strike	Calls–Settle			Puts–Settle		
Price	Mar–c	Jun–c	Sep–c	Mar–p	Jun–p	Sep–p
86	4–36	....	....	0–01	0–30	....
88	2–37	2–35	....	0–02	0–63	....
90	0–50	1–23	....	0–14	1–45	....
92	0–06	0–41	....	1–34	3–03	....
94	0–01	0–19	....	3–28	....	....
96	0–01	....	....	....	....	....

Est. vol, Wed vol. 265 calls, 394 puts
Open Interest Wed; 7,164 calls, 8,411 puts

EURODOLLAR (CME) $ million; pts. of 100%

Strike	Calls–Settle			Puts–Settle		
Price	Mar–c	Jun–c	Sep–c	Mar–p	Jun–p	Sep–p
8950	0.38	0.33	0.51	0.01	0.28	0.40
8975	0.14	0.22	0.35	0.02	0.41	0.51
9000	0.02	0.14	0.29	0.15	0.57	0.64
9025	.0004	0.08	0.21	0.38	0.75	0.79
9050	.0004	0.05	0.14	0.63	0.96	0.97
9075	.0004	0.03	0.10	0.88	1.19	1.16

Est. vol. 13,808, Wed vol. 7,140 calls, 8,938 puts
Open Interest Wed; 177,546 calls, 144,931 puts

EURODOLLAR (LIFFE) $1 million; pts. of 100%

Strike	Calls–Settle			Puts–Settle		
Price	Mar–c	Jun–c	Sep–c	Mar–p	Jun–p	Sep–p
8925	0.61	0.51	0.70	0.00	0.19	0.33
8950	0.37	0.36	0.55	0.01	0.29	0.43
8975	0.14	0.22	0.42	0.03	0.40	0.55
9000	0.02	0.14	0.31	0.16	0.57	0.69
9025	0.01	0.08	0.22	0.40	0.76	0.85
9050	0.00	0.04	0.15	0.64	0.97	1.03

Est. vol. Thur, 0 Calls, 75 Puts.
Open Interest Wed. 6,950 Calls, 6,866 Puts.

LONG GILT (LIFFE)—b–å50,000; 64ths of 100%

Strike	Calls–Settle			Puts–Settle		
Price	Jun–c	Sep–c	Dec–c	Jun–p	Sep–p	Dec–p
94	4.16	5.28	....	0.10	0.20	....
96	3.25	4.38	....	0.19	0.30	....
98	2.37	3.52	....	0.31	0.44	....
100	1.55	3.07	....	0.49	0.63	....
102	1.17	2.31	....	1.11	1.23	....
104	0.53	1.60	....	1.47	1.52	....

Est. Vol. Thurs, 920 Calls, 331 Puts.
Open Interest Wed 21,572, Calls, 12,635 Puts.

We have reproduced the quotes on options on futures contracts on U.S. treasury bonds and notes, municipal bonds, Eurodollar deposits, and long gilts for March 9, 1989, as they appeared in *The Wall Street Journal*.

As with many other option contracts, the first column lists the available exercise prices. The next three columns provide quotes on the available call options, and the final three columns provide the quotes for available put options.

Since we previously looked at the options on physical treasury bonds (CBOE), let's look at the quotes for the options on futures contracts on U.S. treasury bonds (CBT). For a September futures contract, a strike price of 88 is almost at the money (September T-bond futures were trading at 88 22/32). The price of the call option on a September futures contract is listed as 2-44, that is, 2 44/64%. (In this market, a "tick" is 1/64%.) Since the bond option contract is denominated in $100,000 units, the price of this option is 2.6875% of $100,000, or $2,687.50.

One-Parameter Models

A number of researchers and practitioners started off by trying to apply the Black-Scholes model. Indeed, John Hull suggests that, even today, for options on zero-coupon bonds (or options on bonds short enough that no coupon payments are to be received during the life of the option), the Black-Scholes model is the most widely used.[9]

Hull also suggests that the model for valuing options on futures, which we described in Equation (16-6), is often used to value interest rate caps and floors.[10] Using this model for pricing interest rate options, the discount rate, r, is the riskless rate for the period covered by the option; the forward price, F, is the forward interest rate obtained from the term structure of interest rates;[11] and the exercise price, X, is the cap rate for the interest rate option:

$$C = e^{-rT} \left[F \times N \left\{ \frac{\ln(F/X) + (\sigma^2/2)T}{\sigma\sqrt{T}} \right\} - X \times N \left\{ \frac{\ln(F/X) - (\sigma^2/2)T}{\sigma\sqrt{T}} \right\} \right]$$

$$(16\text{-}8)$$

For coupon-paying bonds it was noted that, in the context of an option pricing model, the coupon payment on a bond is much like the dividend payment on a share of stock in pricing options on shares (or the foreign interest in pricing foreign exchange options). Hence, an apparent way of valuing debt options is to use the continuous-dividend model we described in Chapter 15, replacing the dividend yield (δ) with the coupon rate on the bond (c),

$$C = e^{-\frac{c}{b}T} S \times N \left\{ \frac{\ln(S/X) + [r - \frac{c}{b} + (\sigma^2/2)]T}{\sigma\sqrt{T}} \right\}$$

$$(16\text{-}9)$$

$$- e^{-rT} X \times N \left\{ \frac{\ln(S/X) + (r - \frac{c}{b} - \sigma^2/2)T}{\sigma\sqrt{T}} \right\}$$

9. John Hull, *Options, Futures, and Other Derivative Securities* (Englewood Cliffs: N.J. Prentice-Hall, 1989), p. 260.
10. *Ibid.*, p. 263.
11. In Chapter 4 we described the manner in which forward interest rates can be obtained from the zero-coupon yield curve.

where, in this case, the current price of the asset (S) is equal to the current bond price (B). In this approach, the value of this European debt option depends on six variables:

$$\overset{+\ -\ ?\ +\ -\ +}{C = C(\,B,\,X,\,T,\,\sigma^2,\,c,\,r\,\,)} \tag{16-10}$$

where the partial effects have their expected signs.

This technique works best in the valuation of a short-term option on a long-term bond. However, if the life of the option covers a substantial fraction of the life of the bond, the assumption of constant bond price volatility becomes untenable. This is because as a bond approaches maturity, the volatility of the bond price goes to zero.

Since we have suggested that coupon payments can be viewed as equivalent to dividend payments in the context of option pricing, you have probably already noted that it may be optimal to exercise an American option on a coupon-paying bond prior to maturity. Again, to simultaneously evaluate the optimal exercise strategy and price the option, binomial techniques are typically employed.

A Two-Parameter Model

In valuing debt options, some researchers and practitioners focus on interest rates rather than bond prices. They argue that the process generating interest rates is, in some sense, better behaved than the process generating bond prices. One example is the model developed by Richard J. Rendleman, Jr., and Brit J. Bartter.[12] They describe the process generating changes in the interest rate as a function of three parameters: the expected growth rate of the interest rate, m; the market price of risk, λ; and the volatility of interest rates, σ.[13] They assumed that all three of these were constants, which implies that the interest rate has a constant growth rate $(m - \lambda\sigma)$ and a constant variance, σ^2.

---

12. Richard J. Rendleman, Jr., and Brit J. Bartter, "The Pricing of Options on Debt Securities," *Journal of Financial and Quantitative Analysis* 15 (March 1980):11–24.

13. Specifically, Rendleman and Bartter assumed that the change in the interest rate can be described as

$$dr = (m - \lambda\sigma)r\,dt + r\,\sigma dz$$

where r is the interest rate, σ is the standard deviation of r, m is the expected growth rate of r, λ is the market price of the risk of r, t is time, and dz is a Weiner process (i.e., a process that follows geometric Brownian motion).

This simple model is then used to generate a "tree" of future bond prices, assuming that the bond price in period T is

$$B(T) = e^{-R_T T} \qquad (16\text{-}11)$$

where R_T is the continually compounded interest rate for the period 0 to T. The result is a "tree" of bond prices much like the share price trees we looked at in Chapter 14. Given the lattice of bond prices, option prices can be derived using the techniques discussed in Chapter 14.

In employing the Rendleman-Bartter model, it is important to remember that the term structure of interest rates is identified by only two parameters: $(m - \lambda \sigma)$ and σ. This severely limits the nature of the future changes in the structure of rates that can be examined.

A widely known (and, apparently, widely used) model for valuing interest rate options is that developed by Thomas S. Y. Ho and S. B. Lee.[14] Like Rendleman and Bartter, Ho and Lee use a binomial approach to model future interest rates/bond prices. Beginning with the current term structure, they use estimates of (1) the probability of a term structure shift and (2) term structure uncertainty to build a "tree" of future discounts.[15] Like Rendleman-Bartter, the Ho-Lee model uses only two parameters. However, the Ho-Lee functional specification is more flexible than the one assumed by Rendleman-Bartter; therefore, their procedure is able to capture more of the information in the current term structure.

The Ho-Lee model is widely praised for its ability to incorporate information from the yield curve and as a system of pricing that eliminates arbitrage. However, their model is criticized because it implies that all interest rates have the same variance.

A Three-Parameter Model

The model of the term structure developed by John C. Cox, Jonathan E. Ingersoll, Jr., and Stephen A. Ross[16] has received a great deal of

---

14. Thomas S. Y. Ho and S. B. Lee, "Term Structure Movements and Pricing Interest Rate Contingent Claims," *Journal of Finance* 41 (1986):1011–1029.
15. The future discounts are inverse functions of the future interest rates.
16. John C. Cox, Jonathan E. Ingersoll, Jr., and Stephen A. Ross, "A Theory of the Term Structure of Interest Rates," *Econometrica* 53 (March 1985):385–407.

attention from researchers and practitioners because it was one of the first models to assume that there is *mean reversion* in the interest rate process.

Aside

Mean reversion

Mean reversion implies that there is some long-run average value for the interest rate. Thus, if the current rate were above this long-term average, the probability of an increase in rates would be somewhat lower while the probability of a rate reduction would be somewhat higher. The opposite would be true if rates were below the long-run average.

Mean reversion is one of those concepts that just seems to "ring true." We have run into a number of people who take the position that mean reversion is obvious. However, the scientific evidence with respect to mean reversion is less obvious and is currently mixed with respect to issues such as the periods over which mean reversion occurs.[17]

Although we are not aware of published debt option pricing models using the Cox-Ingersoll-Ross approach, the concepts in this model have received a great deal of attention in the practitioners' arena.[18]

Commodity Options

Options exercisable into the physical commodity are traded for certain commodities (primarily precious metals) on the Montreal, Toronto, Vancouver, International Petroleum, European Options, and Australian stock exchanges. However, in the United States commodity options are typically exercisable into a futures contract on the commodity rather than the physical commodity itself. Table 16-1 indicates that options on commod-

---

17. See, for example, Eugene F. Fama and Robert R. Bliss, "The Information in Long-Maturity Forward Rates," *American Economic Review* 77 (September 1987):680–692. They report some evidence of mean reversion for rates longer than one-year but much less evidence of mean reversion for shorter rates.

18. John Hull *(op. cit.)* did note that George Courtadon's model that incorporated a mean-reverting drift that is the same as for the Cox-Ingersoll-Ross model. See George Courtadon, "The Pricing of Options on Default-Free Bonds," *Journal of Financial and Quantitative Analysis* 17 (March 1982):75–100. Also, it is fair to note that the practitioners are less sanguine about the implication of the Cox-Ingersoll-Ross model that the volatility of long-term rates is zero.

ity futures are traded on the Chicago Board of Trade; the Chicago Mercantile Exchange; the Coffee, Sugar, and Cocoa Exchange; the Kansas City Board of Trade; the Mid-America Commodity Exchange; the Minneapolis Grain Exchange; the COMEX; the New York Cotton Exchange; and the New York Mercantile Exchange; as well as on the Winnipeg Commodity Exchange, the London Futures and Options Exchange, and the Compagnie Des Commissionnaires Agrees.

Aside

Reading quotes on options on commodity futures

We have reproduced the data for options on futures contracts on agricultural commodities, oil, livestock, and metals for March 9, 1989, as they appeared in *The Wall Street Journal*.

As with many other option contracts, the first column lists the available exercise prices. The next three columns provide quotes on the available call options, and the final three columns provide the quotes for available put options.

One of the authors, being a Texan, insisted that we look at the options on crude oil futures traded on the New York Mercantile Exchange. For a May futures contract, a strike price of 18 is almost at the money (May oil futures

COMMODITY FUTURES OPTIONS

Thursday March 9, 1989

—AGRICULTURAL—

CORN (CBT) 5,000 bu.; cents per bu.

Strike	Calls–Settle			Puts–Settle		
Price	May–c	Jly–c	Sep–c	May–p	Jly–p	Sep–p
260	22½	28¼	28½	¾	3¾	13
270	14	21¾	24	2⅝	6⅝	17½
280	7½	15¾	19½	5¾	10¾	23½
290	4	11½	16	12¼	15¾	29
300	1¾	8¼	13	19½	23	....
310	1	6	10½	29½	30½	....

Est. vol. 4,000, Wed vol. 1,765 calls, 1,158 puts
Open interest Wed 52,734 calls, 30,613 puts

SOYBEANS (CBT) 5,000 bu.; cents per bu.

Strike	Calls–Settle			Puts–Settle		
Price	May–c	Jly–c	Aug–c	May–p	Jly–p	Aug–p
725	55½	74	80	4½	15½	27
750	37½	58	66	11	23½	36
775	24½	46	55	22½	35½	....
800	14⅜	36	46	38½	50	....
825	8½	28	37½	56	66½	....
850	4¾	22¼	30½	77½	85	....

Est. vol. 12,000, Wed vol. 4,293 calls, 2,965 puts
Open interest Wed 61,597 calls, 24,485 puts

SOYBEAN MEAL (CBT) 100 tons; $ per ton

Strike	Calls–Settle			Puts–Settle		
Price	May–c	Jly–c	Aug–c	May–p	Jly–p	Aug–p
230	13.00	16.50	17.50	2.85	8.50	....
235	9.70	....	....	4.70	....	....
240	7.25	12.00	....	6.90	13.60	....
245	5.20	....	....	10.00	....	....
250	3.75	8.50	....	13.50	....	....
255	2.70	....	....	17.30	....	....

Est. vol. 300, Wed vol 318 calls, 72 puts
Open interest Wed 5,807 calls, 2.024 puts

—OIL—

CRUDE OIL (NYM) 1,000 bbls.; $ per bbl.

Strike	Calls–Settle			Puts–Settle		
Price	Apr–c	May–c	Jun–c	Apr–p	May–p	Jun–p
17	1.52	1.26	1.19	0.01	0.18	0.44
18	0.54	0.60	0.66	0.02	0.52	0.89
19	0.02	0.20	0.32	0.50	1.11	1.55
20	0.01	0.05	0.14	1.48	1.95	....
21	0.01	....	0.06	....	....	....
22	....	....	....	....	....	....

Est. vol. 23,432; Wed vol. 9,229 calls; 12,508 puts
Open interest Wed; 116,438 calls; 157,678 puts

HEATING OIL No.2 (NYM) 42,000 gal.; $ per gal.

Strike	Calls–Settle			Puts–Settle		
Price	Apr–c	May–c	Jun–c	Apr–p	May–p	Jun–p
4600	.0440	.0300	.0255	.0001	.0060	.0145
4800	.0240	.0160	.0140	.0001	.0120	.0230
5000	.0055	.0080	.0080	.0015	.0240	....
5200	.0005	.0040	....	.0165	....	....
5400	.0001	....	....	....	....	....
5600	.0001	....	....	....	....	....

Est. vol. 275; Wed vol. 101 calls; 97 puts
Open interest Wed; 2,021 calls; 1,670 puts

—LIVESTOCK—

CATTLE-FEEDER (CME) 44,000 lbs.; cents per lb.

Strike	Calls–Settle			Puts–Settle		
Price	Mar–c	Apr–c	May–c	Mar–p	Apr–p	May–p
76	4.87	....	....	0.00	0.20	0.40
78	2.90	....	3.07	0.02	0.47	0.85
80	1.12	1.55	1.87	0.25	1.15	1.65
82	0.12	0.70	0.92	1.20	2.30	2.70
84	0.00	0.20	0.45	3.12	3.80	4.22
86	0.00	0.10	0.20	5.12	....	....

Est. vol. 793, Wed vol. 117 calls, 236 puts
Open interest Wed; 5,700 calls, 9,726 puts

SOYBEAN OIL (CBT) 60,000 lbs.; cents per lb.

Strike	Calls–Settle			Puts–Settle		
Price	May–c	Jly–c	Aug–c	May–p	Jly–p	Aug–p
21	2.500	....	....	.060	.250	....
22	1.600	2.400	....	.150	.450	.530
23	.900	1.850	....	.400	.800	....
24	.500	1.450	1.650	1.00	1.200	....
25	.250	1.000	1.300	....	....	....
26	.110	.680	....	....	2.600	....

Est, vol. 200, Wed vol. 292 calls, 118 puts
Open interest Wed 6,091 calls, 2,324 puts

WHEAT (CBT) 5,000 bu.; cents per bu.

Strike	Calls–Settle			Puts–Settle		
Price	May–c	Jly–c	Sep–c	May–p	Jly–p	Sep–p
420	20	15⅛	26	3½	22½	26½
430	12	12¼	22	7	29	....
440	7⅞	9¾	18	12½	....	....
450	5	6¾	14½	18½	....	....
460	3½	5	12½	....	....	....
470	2	4⅛	....	35	....	....

Est. vol. 2,000, Wed vol. 689 calls, 120 puts
Open interest Wed 17,988 calls, 7,784 puts

WHEAT (KC) 5,000 bu.; cents per bu.

Strike	Calls–Settle			Puts–Settle		
Price	May–c	Jly–c	Sep–c	May–p	Jly–p	Sep–p
410	23¼	25	34	2½	14½	17¼
420	16	21¼	28¼	5½	18½	20½
430	10¼	15¼	25	9¾	23	26
440	6	12½	19	15¾	....	....
450	2½	8½	15½	....	....	....
460	1½	7	....	....	....	....

Est. vol. 316, Wed vol. 689 calls, 120 puts
Open interest Wed 1,738 calls, 597 puts

—OIL—

COTTON (CTN) 50,000 lbs.; cents per lb.

Strike	Calls–Settle			Puts–Settle		
Price	May–c	Jly–c	Oc–c	May–p	Jly–p	Oct–p
60	2.08	3.30	....	0.40	0.80	....
61	1.38	2.70	....	0.70	1.20	1.30
62	0.98	2.05	2.85	....	1.55	1.80
63	0.60	1.55	....	....	....	....
64	0.30	....	....	....	....	....
65	0.20	0.85	....	....	....	....

Est. vol. 700; Wed vol. 339 calls, 419 puts
Open interest Wed; 7,567 calls, 12,537 puts

COFFEE (CSCE) 37,500 lbs.; cents per lb.

Strike	Calls–Settle			Puts–Settle		
Price	May–c	Jly–c	Sep–c	May–p	Jly–p	Sep–p
120	12.73	10.09	10.07	0.55	3.25	6.75
125	8.25	7.80	8.00	1.25	5.50	9.68
130	4.80	5.80	6.50	2.85	9.04	13.18
135	2.63	4.03	5.13	5.50	11.50	16.81
140	1.18	3.00	4.00	9.00	16.16	20.68
145	0.63	2.13	3.38	13.45	20.29	....

Est. vol. 202; Wed vol. 204 calls, 186 puts
Open interest Wed; 4,327 calls, 3,493 puts

SUGAR—WORLD (CSCE) 112,000 lbs.; cents per lb.

Strike	Calls–Settle			Puts–Settle		
Price	May–c	Jly–c	Oct–c	May–p	Jly–p	Oct–p
10.00	1.88	2.00	2.24	0.07	0.13	0.52
11.00	1.10	1.39	1.62	0.25	0.60	1.00
12.00	0.60	0.97	1.32	0.72	1.10	1.55
13.00	0.30	0.65	0.99	1.32	1.78	2.27
14.00	0.17	0.46	0.85	....	....	....
15.00	0.09	0.33	....	....	....	....

Est. vol. 12,473; Wed vol. 7,174 calls, 2,245 puts
Open interest Wed; 54,051 calls; 22,521 puts

COCOA (CSCE) 10 metric tons; cents per ton

Strike	Calls–Settle			Puts–Settle		
Price	May–c	Jly–c	Sep–c	May–p	Jly–p	Sep–p
1200	218	199	228	6	12	35
1300	131	124	148	10	37	55
1400	61	75	96	49	75	113
1500	28	43	48	116	142	155
1600	9	20	35	197	223	242
1700	3	13	26	291	326	....

Est. vol. 303; Wed vol. 569 calls, 70 puts
Open interest Wed; 9,048 calls; 7,144 puts

CATTLE–LIVE (CME) 40,000 lbs.; cents per lb.

Strike	Calls–Settle			Puts–Settle		
Price	Apr–c	Jun–c	Aug–c	Apr–p	Jun–p	Aug–p
74	3.17	1.55	0.92	0.07	1.57	3.00
76	1.40	0.77	0.47	0.32	2.77	4.57
78	0.37	0.35	0.20	1.30	4.30	....
80	0.07	0.15	0.10	3.00	....	....
82	0.00	0.05	....	4.92	....	....
84	0.00	0.02	....	....	....	....

Est. vol. 3,531, Wed vol. 1,604 calls, 1,426 puts
Open interest Wed; 34,288 calls, 33,819

HOGS–LIVE (CME) 30,000 lbs.; cents per lb.

Strike	Calls–Settle			Puts–Settle		
Price	Apr–c	Jun–c	Jly–c	Apr–p	Jun–p	Jly–p
40	3.77	....	....	0.05	0.05	....
42	1.87	....	....	0.15	0.17	0.30
44	0.50	....	....	0.80	0.35	0.55
46	0.07	3.20	3.40	2.35	0.85	1.05
48	0.02	1.97	2.40	4.30	1.60	1.90
50	0.02	1.10	1.50	....	2.65	2.90

Est. vol. 473, Wed vol. 215 calls, 425 puts
Open interest Wed; 6,042 calls, 5,457 puts

—METALS—

COPPER (CMX) 25,000 lbs.; cents per lb.

Strike	Calls–Last			Puts–Last		
Price	May–c	Jly–c	Sep–c	May–p	Jly–p	Sep–p
130	11.55	10.20	9.00	3.10	8.70	13.50
135	8.15	8.00	7.30	4.70	11.35	16.55
140	5.50	6.05	5.85	6.95	14.25	19.85
145	3.60	4.40	4.65	10.05	17.50	23.40
150	2.30	3.25	3.65	13.60	21.15	27.15
155	1.40	2.30	....	17.70	25.10	....

Est. vol. 1,250, Wed vol. 825 calls, 494 puts
Open interest Wed; 6,495 calls, 7,626 puts

Strike	Calls–Last			Puts–Last		
Price	Apr–c	Jun–c	Aug–c	Apr–p	Jun–p	Aug–p
380	17.40	24.60	31.90	0.10	2.70	4.60
390	7.50	16.90	24.30	0.20	4.90	7.30
400	0.70	10.30	17.80	3.40	8.30	10.50
410	0.10	6.20	12.90	12.80	14.20	15.50
420	0.10	3.50	9.10	22.70	21.40	21.20
430	0.10	1.80	6.20	32.70	29.90	28.10

Est. vol. 4,200, Wed vol. 5,524 calls, 3,453 puts
Open interest Wed; 65,970 calls, 39,846 puts

SILVER (CMX) 5,000 troy ounces; cents per troy ounce

Strike	Calls–Last			Puts–Last		
Price	May–c	Jly–c	Sep–c	May–p	Jly–p	Sep–p
550	60.0	72.0	86.0	1.5	4.0	7.5
575	37.5	52.0	67.5	3.5	9.2	13.0
600	19.5	36.0	51.5	10.5	16.5	21.5
625	8.5	26.0	40.0	24.5	30.0	34.0
650	5.3	18.0	31.5	46.0	46.5	49.0
675	2.8	12.0	23.5	68.5	65.5	67.0

Est. vol. 2,700, Wed vol. 1,657 calls, 530 puts
Open interest Wed; 23,897 calls, 10,010 puts

—OTHER FUTURES OPTIONS—

Final or settlement prices of selected contracts. Volume and open interest are totals in all contract months.

Pork Bellies (CME) 40,000 lbs.; cents per lb.

Strike	May–c	Jly–c	Aug–c	May–p	Jly–p	Aug–p
38	2.35	3.70	3.85	2.15	3.30	4.40

Est. vol. 40. Wed vol. 64. Op. Int. 1,543.

Lumber (CME) 150,000 bd.ft., $ per 1,000 bd.ft.

Strike	May–c	Jly–c	Sep–c	May–p	Jly–p	Sep–p
185	3.50	....	....	4.90	....	....

Est. vol. 47. Wed vol. 326. Op. Int. 608.

Silver (CBT) 1,000 oz.; cents per oz.

Strike	Apr–c	Jun–c	Aug–c	Apr–p	Jun–p	Aug–p
600	12.0	30.0	46.0	8.0	15.0	....

Est. vol. 20. Wed vol. 4. Op. Int. 732.

Soybeans (MCE) 1,000 bu.; cents per bu.

Strike	May–c	Jly–c	Aug–c	May–p	Jly–p	Aug–p
775	24½	46	55	22½	35½	....

Est. vol. 65. Wed vol. 59. Op. Int. 3,311.

settled at 18.08). The price of the call option on a May futures contract is listed as 0.60 (i.e., $0.60 per barrel). Since the oil option contract is denominated in 1,000 barrels, the price of this option is $600.

Fischer Black has shown that as long as the volatility of the underlying asset return is constant and the cost of carry for the commodity is at most a function of time, then the value of a commodity futures call (like that of a currency futures call) is[19]

$$C = e^{-rT}\left[F \times N\left\{ \frac{\ln(F/X) + (\sigma^2/2)T}{\sigma\sqrt{T}} \right\} \right.$$

$$\left. - X \times N\left\{ \frac{\ln(F/X) - (\sigma^2/2)T}{\sigma\sqrt{T}} \right\} \right]$$

(16-12)

Thus, the value of a commodities futures call is a function of five variables,

$$\begin{array}{ccccc} + & - & ? & + & - \\ C = C(\ F, & X, & T, & \sigma^2, & r\ ) \end{array}$$

(16-13)

all of which have their expected signs.

---

19. Black, *op. cit.*

PART VI

Using the Instruments

17

The Rationale for Risk Management

Let's see where we stand. In Part I (particularly Chapter 1), we saw clear evidence that the financial environment in which the modern corporation operates has become more volatile: firms are subject to more financial price risk today than in the past. And, as illustrated in Figure 17-1, this financial price risk translates into risk with respect to the value of the firm. In Parts II through IV, we examined the various off-balance-sheet instruments that can be used to manage this financial price risk. The effect of managing financial price risk is illustrated in Figure 17-2.

A tantalizing conclusion is that, since firms are subject to financial price risk, and since the off-balance-sheet instruments are available, firms with exposures to interest rates, foreign exchange rates, or commodity prices will all naturally use forwards, futures, swaps, or options to manage their financial price risk. Albeit tantalizing, this conclusion is incorrect. That a firm is confronted with financial price risk is a *necessary* but not a *sufficient* condition for the firm to manage that risk.

To understand the rationale for a firm to manage financial price risk, begin by defining the overall objective to be the maximization of the expected value of the firm. As in texts in corporate finance, we express the expected value of the firm, $E(V_j)$, as

$$E(V_j) = \sum_{t=0}^{T} \frac{E(\text{NCF}_{j,t})}{(1 + r_j)^t} \qquad (17\text{-}1)$$

where $E(\text{NCF}_{j,t})$ is the expected net cash flow for the firm in period t and r_j is the appropriate discount rate for this firm. The *sufficient* condition for a firm to manage financial price risk is that the risk management strategy increases the expected value of the firm. As is clear in Equation

Figure 17-1. Financial Price Volatility Translates into Risk in the Value of the Firm.

Financial prices have become more volatile:

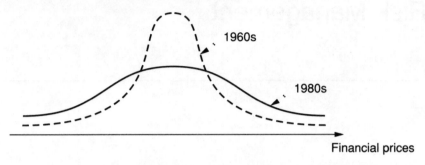

Firms are exposed to these financial prices, for example:

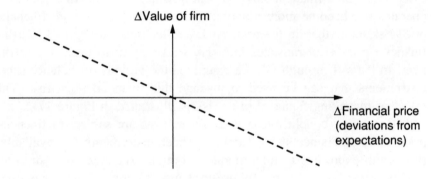

Therefore, firms are facing risk with respect to their value:

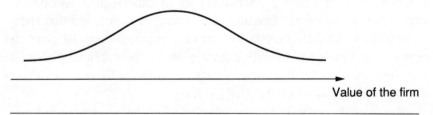

(17-1), if the expected value of the firm is to increase, it must be via either an increase in expected net cash flows or a decrease in the discount rate.

Since we are talking about risk, the first, most logical place to look for an effect is through a decrease in the discount rate. But, as we will describe in the next section, portfolio theory implies that such an

Figure 17-2. The Impact of Risk Management—Hedging—Is to Reduce the Variance in the Distribution of Firm Value.

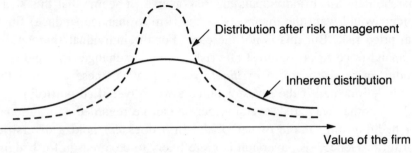

The Impact of Risk Management–hedging–Is to
Reduce the Variance in the Distribution of Firm Value.

Distribution after risk management

Inherent distribution

Value of the firm

effect will not occur: because financial price risks are *diversifiable* risks, managing the financial price risk will have no impact on the discount rate for the firm.

If, then, the effect of hedging does not enter through the discount rate, it must enter through the expected net cash flows. As will be shown in the third section of this chapter, the Modligliani-Miller (M&M) proposition provides some guidance here. If financial policies—one of which is the risk management policy—affect the value of the firm, they must do so through their impact on *taxes, transaction costs*, or the firm's *investment decision*.

Using the M&M proposition as a guide, we then identify some characteristics of firms that will be more likely to manage financial price risk. We conclude this chapter with a survey of the available empirical evidence on this issue. From these studies, we can gain some insights into the characteristics of firms that do and firms that do not use risk management instruments.

Not Managing Risk Might Be Best: Portfolio Theory

What makes the incorrect conclusion noted earlier so tantalizing is that we tend to think about firms as if they are somehow like individuals: Individuals want to manage (reduce) risk because they are risk averse; so, relying on a presumption of risk aversion, firms would also want to manage (reduce) the risks they face. However, firms are not like individuals. Indeed, firms might best be viewed as "legal fictions which serve as a

nexus for a set of contracting relationships among individuals."[1] Consequently, it is more productive to think of a firm not as an entity but rather as the creature of the individuals who hold claims upon it.

Let's begin with the ultimate owner of the firm: the individual shareholder. Since individuals are risk-averse, it seems that this shareholder would want the managers of the firm to manage (reduce) financial price risk. But this is not the case. For the individual shareholder, financial price risks—interest rate risk, foreign exchange risk, and commodity price risk—are *diversifiable* risks. That is, these are risks that can be eliminated if the investor holds a well-diversified portfolio.

Put another way, risk aversion per se can be regarded as a rationale for hedging only if the owner of the firm does *not* hold a diversified portfolio. Hence, risk aversion is more likely to be a reason for hedging if the firm is a proprietorship or a closely held corporation.

The position that risk can be reduced by holding a well-diversified portfolio has come to be referred to as *portfolio theory*.[2] As illustrated in Figure 17-3, when more securities are added to the investor's portfolio, the unique risk associated with a particular security is diversified away, leaving the investor with only market risk: the risks faced due to economy-wide changes. Hence, as more and more securities are added to the investor's portfolio, the level of total portfolio risk declines toward market risk, the risk associated with a portfolio that contains some of all of the securities available in the market.[3]

Aside

The math of portfolio theory

At its core, portfolio theory is based on a simple statistical relation: The variance of a combination of random variables involves not only the variances of the random variables but also the covariance,

$$\text{var}(A + B) = \text{var}(A) + \text{var}(B) + 2\text{cov}(A, B)$$

1. Michael C. Jensen and Wiliam H. Meckling, "Theory of the Firm: Managerial Behavior, Agency Costs and Ownership Structure," *Journal of Financial Economics* 3 (1976): 310.

2. This insight was due to Harry M. Markowitz and first appeared in "Portfolio Selection," *Journal of Finance* 7 (March 1952):77–91.

3. For an excellent exposition of portfolio theory, see Richard Brealey and Stewart Myers, *Principles of Corporate Finance* (New York: McGraw-Hill, 1984), Chaps. 7 and 8.

Figure 17-3. The Impact of Diversification on an Individual Investor's Portfolio Risk.

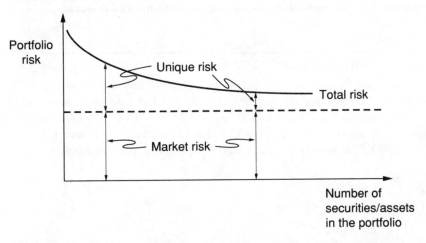

Define the risk for security A as the standard deviation of its returns, σ_A. Likewise, define the risk for security B as σ_B. Then consider a simple portfolio made up of one of security A and one of B. If risk were additive, the variance for this portfolio would be given by:

$$(\sigma_A + \sigma_B)^2 = \sigma_A^2 + \sigma_B^2 + 2\sigma_A\sigma_B$$

However, using the variance formula noted above, the variance of the portfolio is given by

$$\sigma_P^2 = \sigma_A^2 + \sigma_B^2 + 2\rho_{AB}\sigma_A\sigma_B$$

where ρ_{AB} is the correlation between the returns of securities A and B, and the product $\rho_{AB}\sigma_A\sigma_B$ is $\text{cov}(A,B)$. Comparing these two equations, we see that the riskiness of the portfolio is less than the linear combination of the risks for the individual securities,

$$\sigma_P < \sigma_A + \sigma_B$$

unless the two securities are perfectly positively correlated, that is, unless $\rho_{AB} = 1$.[4]

The basic idea of portfolio theory is very simple: If assets are combined in a portfolio, "something funny happens." More precisely, if assets are combined in a portfolio, the riskiness of the resulting portfolio is less than the linear combination of the risks for the assets (unless the

---

4. Note that if $\rho_{AB} = 1$, securities A and B are effectively the same security.

assets are perfectly positively correlated). The preceding mathematical exposition may have been helpful to some readers, but, for others, a numerical example will be useful for solidifying this concept.

Example

Benefits of diversification[5]

Suppose that, during the first quarter of 1986, an investor wanted to hold a portfolio of shares. Suppose first that the investor had held only one stock. For example, suppose that the investor had bought one share of Chase Manhattan Bank stock on December 27, 1985, and held the share until March 29, 1986 (13 weeks). The weekly returns would have been as illustrated below.

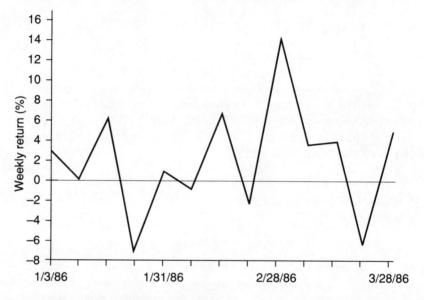

Suppose next that the investor had held a portfolio made up of one share of Chase and one share of General Motors. The returns for the two shares and for the portfolio are illustrated at the top of page 361. Note that, by diversifying, the investor would have reduced the variability of returns. Holding the portfolio made up of one share of stock in each firm results in a lower level of risk (as measured by the standard deviation of returns) than would result if either of the shares were held individually:

$$\sigma_{CHASE} = 5.58\%, \quad \sigma_{GM} = 2.88\%, \quad \sigma_{(CHASE + GM)} = 2.57\%$$

---

5. This example is taken from S. Charles Maurice and Charles W. Smithson, *Managerial Economics* (Homewood, Ill.: Richard D. Irwin, 1988): 594–7.

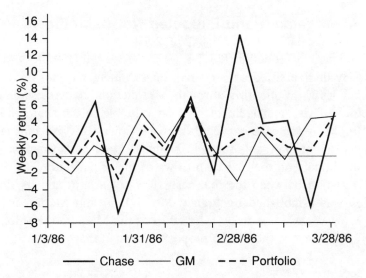

The volatility of the portfolio is lower than the average of the volatilities of the individual shares.

The investor can further reduce the riskiness of the portfolio by further diversifying. Indeed, if the investor holds a *market portfolio* containing shares of all available securities and assets, the risk of the portfolio would be reduced to only market risk. To approximate this, suppose the investor had held the S&P 500 portfolio. The weekly returns for the S&P 500 portfolio and the (1 Chase + 1 GM) portfolio are displayed below. The standard deviation of the S&P 500 returns was only 1.84%, as compared with 2.57% for the (1 Chase + 1 GM) portfolio.

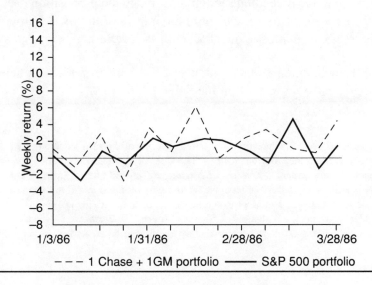

Risk Management and Expected Net Cash Flows

In the context of equation (17-1), we have seen that (unless the firm is held by undiversified owners) risk management will not increase the expected value of the firm through a reduction in the discount rate. Therefore, if risk management is to be valuable to the shareholders, it must somehow increase expected net cash flows. But risk management is simply one of the firm's financial policies. How can a financial policy have any impact on the real cash flows of the organization?

The relation between the real cash flows of a firm and its financial policies was established by Franco Modligliani and Merton Miller in 1958 in what has come to be referred to as the M&M proposition I.[6] In its original version, the M&M proposition stated that:

If there are no taxes,

If there are no transaction costs, and

If the investment policy of the firm is fixed,

Then the financial policies of the firm are irrelevant.

Risk management—hedging—is one of the firm's financial policies. The M&M proposition indicates that in a world with no taxes, no transaction costs, and fixed investment policies, investors can create their own risk management by holding diversified portfolios (precisely the conclusion we came to in the preceding section). Although the proposition itself is of extreme importance to an academic, the impact of the M&M proposition to a practitioner is most evident when it is inverted:

If financial policies matter, that is, if risk management policies are going to have an impact on the value of the firm,

---

6. The original M&M proposition was stated in terms of the firm's debt equity ratio: see Franco Modligliani and Merton Miller, "The Cost of Capital, Corporation Finance and the Theory of Investment," *American Economic Review* 48 (June 1958): 261–197. The rational is that, since individual leverage is possible, an investor will not pay the firm for corporate leverage. The M&M proposition was extended to dividends in 1961: "Divided Policy, Growth and the Valuaion of Shares," *Journal of Business* 34 (October 1961): 411–433, which argued that "homemade" dividends can be created as the investor sells the firm's stock.

Then it must be that the financial policies impact taxes or *transaction costs* or the firm's *investment policies*.

Hence, the M&M propostion tells us the general headings under which we will find the impact of risk management on the firm's expected net cash flows. A firm's likelihood of using a financial risk management strategy increases with increases in the benefits achievable with respect to its expected taxes, transaction costs, and its investment decision.

To actually identify the kind of firm that will use risk management, it is necessary to look a little deeper into each of these categories.

Taxes

To see how a risk management strategy can reduce expected taxes, let's begin by looking at a naive example.

Example

Hedging and expected taxes

Consider the naive case of a firm that has an equal probability of a pretax income of either -400 or $+600$. The simple probability distribution, illustrated below, will result in an expected pretax income of 100:

$$E(\text{PTI}) = 1/2(-400) + 1/2(600)$$

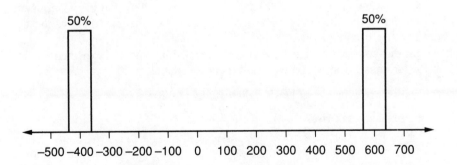

We are concentrating on the tax effect, so we assume that there are no transaction costs and that the investment decision is fixed. For simplicity, we also assume a zero interest rate.

Example

Tax code 1

Suppose that the tax rate on pretax income is 20% and that the government will refund to the firm 20% of its losses.[7] The resulting tax schedule is illustrated below.

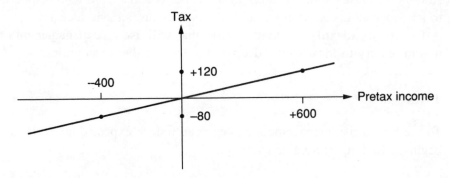

With this tax code, the tax on expected income,

$$T[E(\text{PTI})] = T[100] = 20$$

is the same as expected tax,

$$E(T) = \tfrac{1}{2}[T(-400)] + \tfrac{1}{2}[T(600)] = \tfrac{1}{2}(-80) + \tfrac{1}{2}(120) = 20$$

Consequently, there is no benefit to the firm from hedging.

Tax code 2

Suppose that the tax rate on pretax income remains at 20%, but the government will refund to the firm only 10% of its losses.[8] As illustrated below, the tax schedule has become *convex*.

With this convex tax schedule, tax on expected income and expected tax are no longer equal. The tax on expected income remains at 20,

$$T[E(\text{PTI})] = T[100] = 20$$

but the expected tax rises to 40:

$$E(T) = \tfrac{1}{2}[T(-400)] + \tfrac{1}{2}[T(600)] = \tfrac{1}{2}(-40) + \tfrac{1}{2}(120) = 40$$

---

7. In a multiperiod world, this is equivalent to a 100% tax loss carryforward.

8. In a multiperiod world, this is equivalent to a 50% tax loss carryforward. Note, however, that the same asymmetry of the tax schedule could be generated simply by having a positive interest rate.

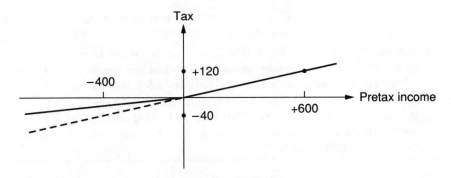

Clearly, the firm would prefer the tax: on expected income to the expected tax: the firm would prefer to pay 20 rather than 40. As illustrated below, this is done by completely hedging the firm: instead of a 50–50 probability of a pretax profit of 600 or loss of 400, the firm would have a 100% probability of a pretax income of 100.

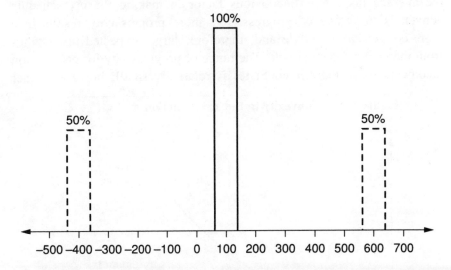

With the convex tax schedule, hedging has provided a tax benefit to the firm. In the case in point, the benefit is 20. However, this example can be expanded to see that:

- **The tax benefit of hedging is a positive function of the volatility of pretax income.** If we reduce the range of pretax income to (−200, +400) instead of (−400, +600), the tax benefit falls from 20 to 10.
- **The tax benefit of hedging is a positive function of the convexity of the tax schedule.** Let's make the tax schedule more convex.

Suppose the tax rate on profits is 20% and that none of the losses are refunded.[9] In this case, the tax benefit rises from 20 to 40.

- *The tax benefit of hedging is a positive function of the percentage of the distribution of pretax income that lies in the convex region of the tax schedule.* Let's keep the volatility of pretax income the same but move the distribution to the right: Instead of (−400, 600), let the distribution be (−200, 800). Now less of the distribution lies around the "kink" in the tax schedule, and the tax benefit of hedging declines from 20 to 10.

The preceding example illustrates that there are two conditions necessary for a risk management strategy to produce tax benefits. First, the tax schedule must be convex; the more convex the tax schedule, the greater the tax benefits. As illustrated in Figure 17-4, convexity of the tax schedule means simply that the marginal tax rate exceeds the average tax rate. The obvious factor in making the tax schedule convex is the range of progressivity: more progressivity results in a more convex tax schedule and, therefore, larger expected tax savings from managing financial risk. The range of progressivity for corporation income taxes in the United States is relatively small; however, other

Figure 17-4. Convexity in the Tax Function.

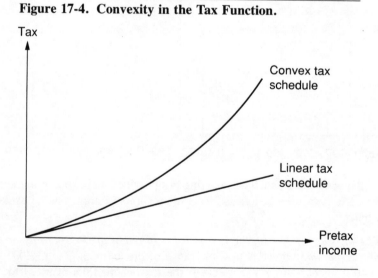

---

9. In the multiperiod world, the tax loss carryforward declines to 0%.

factors such as tax loss carryforwards and investment tax credits (ITCs) also make the tax schedule more convex. Moreover, since the alternate minimum tax (AMT) gives the tax authorities a claim that is similar to a call option on the pretax income of the firm, the AMT also makes the tax schedule more convex.[10]

Consequently, the tax benefit of risk management is increased by increases in the progressivity of the tax code, tax loss carryforwards, and investment tax credits. The tax benefit of risk management is also increased by the introduction of the alternate minimum tax.

Our simple example indicated that the second condition necessary for a risk management strategy to reduce expected taxes is that some portion of the range for pretax income lies within the convex section of the tax schedule. And the more of the range of pretax income in the convex section, the greater the tax benefit of risk mangement. Define the range of pretax income to be a 95% confidence interval for the firm's expected income as Range = Expected income $\pm$ 2 (σ_{income}), where σ_{income} is the standard deviation for the firm's pretax income. Then, from the preceding discussion, the important value is the percentage of the range of pretax income that lies in the convex portion of the tax schedule. It follows that, as the percentage of the range of pretax income lying in the convex portion of the tax schedule increases, the tax benefit from managing risk will also increase.

To summarize, the tax benefit from risk management increases as:

the tax code becomes more progressive

the firm has more tax loss carryforwards

the firm has more investment tax credits

the alternate minimum tax rules are in effect

more of the range of the firm's pretax income is in the convex region of the tax schedule.

---

10. There exists a substantial body of evidence on the convexity of the tax function and the factors that make it convex, including J. J. Siegfried, "Effective Average U.S. Corporation Income Tax Rates," *National Tax Journal* (June 1974): 245–259; J. L. Zimmerman, "Taxes and Firm Size," *Journal of Accounting and Economics* (August 1983): 119–149; and P. J. Wilkie, "Corporate Average Effectve Tax Rates and Inferences About Relative Tax Preferences," *Journal of American Taxation Association* (Fall 1988): 75–88.

Transaction Costs: Expected Costs of Financial Distress

As illustrated in Figure 17-5, risk management reduces the probability of a firm's encountering financial distress by reducing the variance in the distribution of the value of the firm. Consequently, risk management reduces the firm's expected costs—those costs it would face should it encounters financial distress.

In the framework laid earlier, we referred to the benefits from managing risk in terms of reduction in transaction costs. Let's continue that pattern by considering the positive benefits of hedging in terms of reduction in the firm's expected costs due to financial distress.

The magnitude of the reduction in cost depends on two obvious factors: (1) the probability that the firm will encounter financial distress if it does not hedge and (2) the costs it will face if it does encounter financial distress. The reduction in costs—the benefit from risk management—will be greater, the greater the probability of financial distress if the firm does not hedge and the greater the cost of this financial distress.

Two factors determine the probability of default. First, since default results when a firm is unable to service its fixed claims, the larger the ratio of service on fixed claims to cash inflows, the higher the probability of default. Second, since default is triggered when the firm's

Figure 17-5. The Impact of Hedging on the Probability of Financial Distress.

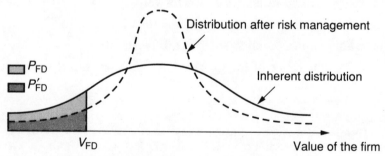

Define V_{FD} as that value of the firm below which financial distress is encountered. Risk management reduces the probability of V_{FD} from P_{FD} to P'_{FD}.

income is too low to pay its fixed claims, the more volatile the firm's income, the more likely the firm is to face default.

The cost of financial distress itself depends on a number of factors. Financial distress can certainly lead to bankruptcy and then to reorganization or liquidation, situations in which the firm would face substantial direct legal and accounting costs. The accounting and legal costs of bankruptcy tend to have a substantial fixed component: it doesn't take many more accountants and lawyers to reorganize a large firm than it does to reorganize a small one. Hence, the costs per share per dollar of equity are higher for small firms than for large firms so small firms should be more likely to hedge to avoid financial distress.

Even if financial distress does not lead to bankruptcy, the firm will encounter a number of indirect costs.[11] The indirect costs of financial distress result from higher contracting costs of the firm with its customers, its employees, and its suppliers.

Customers. Firms that provide service agreements or warranties have a higher degree of contracting with their customers, so these firms would face higher costs if the firm shoud encounter financial distress. The value consumers place on the service agreements and warranties is dependent on the financial viability of the firm. If the firm is less viable, consumers will place less value on the service agreements and warranties. In the same way, contracting costs are higher for firms that produce *credence* goods: goods for which quality is important but whose quality cannot be judged prior to consumption.[12] Consumers of credence goods must use other characteristics of the firm as indicators of the quality of the product. If the firm is in financial distress, the concern of the consumer focuses on reduced quality of the product.

---

11. The work of Jerry Warner suggests that the direct costs of bankruptcy are small in relation to the value of the firm; see "Bankruptcy, Absolute Priority, and the Pricing of Risky Debt Claims," *Journal of Financial Economics* 13 (May 1977): 239–276. However, the indirect costs are significant; see "Bankruptcy Costs: Some Evidence," *Journal of Finance* 32 (May 1977): 337–347.

12. Examples of credence goods include medications and air travel—quality is of extreme importance, but there is no way to judge quality ex ante. (You don't know whether the drug is effective or the airline is safe and on time until the drug is taken or the flight is over). Goods whose quality can be judged before consumption are called *experience* goods.

Employees. Contracting costs of the firm with its employees increase as the firm uses more specialized labor or as the firm spends more time and money training its workers. Moreover, if the firm is perceived to be in financial distress, it will experience more turnover of its employees so the cost of financial distress rises further.

Suppliers. Contracting costs of the firm with its suppliers increase as the firm requires more customization from its suppliers or as the firm has fewer potential suppliers. As the firm encounters financial distress, it may receive unfavorable credit terms, delivery schedules, and service. Moreover, its suppliers may be less willing to tailor their production facilities to meet customization requirements.

Combining the preceding points, we can say that the firm will be more likely to hedge to reduce the expected costs of financial distress if:

>   the probability of financial distress is higher, that is, if:
>
>>   the ratio of fixed claims to total cash inflows is larger
>>
>>   the volatility in the firm's income is higher
>
>   the costs of financial distress are higher, that is, if:
>
>>   the firm is smaller
>>
>>   the firm offers service agreements or warranties
>>
>>   the firm produces a credence good
>>
>>>   the firm uses specialized labor or must provide specialized training for its workers
>>
>>   the firm requires customization from its suppliers
>>
>>   the firm has few potential suppliers

The Investment Decision

Modligliani and Miller assume a world in which the firm's investment policy is fixed. If the objective is to maximize shareholder value, the optimal fixed investment policy is simple: *Accept all positive NPV projects and reject all negative NPV projects.*

However, we saw in Chapter 10 an instance in which a firm will turn down a positive NPV project. Let's look again at that example.

Example

Rejection of a positive NPV project

Consider again the firm subject to oil price risk.

Outcome	Probability	Value of Firm in Period 1
Price of oil rises	.5	1,000
Price of oil falls	.5	200

The firm has available a positive NPV project. An outlay of $600 in period 1 will result in an income of $800 in period 2 with certainty.

The firm plans to issue bonds with *face value* of $500 in Period 1 and pass on the proceeds to the shareholders in the form of a special dividend. For simplicity, assume: (1) no transaction costs, (2) no taxes, and (3) risk-free interest rate equal to zero.

As shown in the following table, if the price of oil falls, this firm will pass up the positive NPV project; that is, if the value of the firm in Period 1 is $200, the shareholders would not undertake the investment project.

Period 1		Period 2			
Value of Firm		**Value of Firm**	**Value of Debt**	**Value of Equity**	**Undertake positive NPV project?**
1,000	Undertake project	1,200	500	700	Yes
	Do not undertake	1,000	500	500	
Value of Firm		**Value of Firm**	**Value of Debt**	**Value of Equity**	**Undertake positive NPV project?**
200	Undertake project	400	500	−100	No
	Do not undertake	200	200	0	

As noted when we first presented this example, the debt will sell for $350, not $500, and the proceeds will be distributed to the shareholders. The expected value of the equity is $350; so the total value to the shareholders including the dividends is $700.

The preceding example illustrates a classic conflict between the shareholder and bondholders that economists call *the underinvestment problem*.[13] In the example, if the value of the firm is low, the shareholders will opt not to undertake the positive NPV project because the gains accrue to the bondholders. The problem is the amount of debt the firm has in its capital structure. As illustrated below, if the firm reduces the debt/equity ratio, the underinvestment problem disappears.

Example

Controlling the underinvestment problem via lower debt

Look again at the preceding example, but this time suppose that the firm issued debt with a face value of $350 instead of $500.

Period 1		Period 2			
Value of Firm		Value of Firm	Value of Debt	Value of Equity	Undertake Positive NPV Project?
1,000	Undertake project	1,200	350	850	Yes
	Do not undertake	1,000	350	650	

Period 1		Period 2			
Value of Firm		Value of Firm	Value of Debt	Value of Equity	Undertake Positive NPV Project?
200	Undertake project	400	350	50	Yes
	Do not undertake	200	200	0	

As illustrated, with less debt in the capital structure, the positive NPV project will always be undertaken. The debt sells at its face value of $350, the proceeds of which go to the shareholders. The expected value of the equity is $450;

---

13. The underinvestment problem was introduced by S. C. Myers, "The Determinants of Corporate Borrowing," *Journal of Financial Economics* 5 (November 1977): 147–175.

the total value of the shareholders' position including the dividends is $450 + $350 = $800, rather than the $700 when the face value of the debt was $500. That is, by reducing the face value of the debt, the shareholders have gained $100.

As an alternative to altering the debt/equity ratio, the underinvestment problem can be controlled by hedging—by using risk management techniques.

Example

Controlling the underinvestment problem via hedging

Suppose the firm could hedge its exposure to oil prices so that, regardless of what happens to oil prices, the value of the firm is $600. With the value of the firm hedged against oil prices, the positive NPV project will always be undertaken:

Period 1		Period 2			
Value of Firm		Value of Firm	Value of Debt	Value of Equity	Undertake Positive NPV Project?
600	Undertake project	800	500	300	Yes
	Do not undertake	600	500	100	

With the hedge against oil prices, the firm can issue debt with a face value of $500 and still avoid the underinvestment problem. In this case, the total value of the shareholder's wealth is $800: the dividend paid from the proceeds of the debt issue ($500) plus the value of their equity ($300).

The preceding example illustrates that the more debt the firm has in its capital structure, the greater the benefit from using risk management to control the underinvestment problem. The larger the firm's debt/equity ratio (D/E), the greater the benefit of hedging with respect to the firm's investment decision.

Underinvestment is but one problem resulting from the conflict between the bondholders and the shareholders, a conflict that is a special

case of the *agency problem*.[14] The conflict is the result of the difference in the claims held by the bondholders and the shareholders. The bondholders hold fixed claims, while the shareholders hold claims that are equivalent to a call option on the value of the firm.

We have already seen that an increase in the debt/equity ratio increases the probability of conflict between shareholders and bondholders—and it thereby increases the value of a hedging strategy to reduce the cost of this conflict. Another determinant of the conflict between shareholders and bondholders (and, consequently, of the value of a hedging strategy) is the range of investment projects available to the firm. Like any other option, the value of the shareholders' equity rises as the variance in the returns to the underlying asset increases. If the shareholders can switch from low-variance investment projects to high-variance projects, they can transfer wealth from the bondholders to themselves.[15] But since the bondholders realize that this opportunistic behavior could occur, they will protect themselves against the shareholders' temptation to select high-variance projects by lowering the price they are willing to pay for the firm's bonds. To get the bondholders to pay more for the bonds, the shareholders must assure the bondholders that the wealth transfers will not take place. This assurance can take the form of restrictive covenants or hedging.

It follows, then, that the value of a risk management program to a firm depends on the range of investment projects it has available, in addition to the level of debt in the firm's capital structure. The wider the range of investment projects available (i.e., the greater the variance in the returns for the available projects), the greater the potential for conflict between the shareholders and bondholders; so, the greater the benefit of a hedging program that will reduce the conflict.

---

14. The agency problem refers to the conflicts of interest that occur in virtually all cooperative activities among self-interested individuals. The agency problem was introduced in Michael C. Jensen and William H. Meckling, "Theory of the Firm: Managerial Behavior, Agency Costs and Ownership Structure," *Journal of Financial Economics* 3 (1976): 305–360.

15. The problem referred to as *asset substitution* is a case in point. A firm can increase the wealth of its shareholders at the expense of its bondholders by (1) issuing debt with the promise of investing in low-risk projects and (2) then investing the proceeds in high-risk projects.

Hence, the benefit of a risk management program to the firm's investment decision increases as:

the firm's debt/equity ratio increases

the firm has access to a wider range of investment projects

The Determinants of Hedging

We have discussed various benefits of hedging. We first talked about the risk-averse investor who is holding an ill-diversified portfolio. We then talked about the tax benefits of hedging, the transaction cost benefits of hedging, and the benefits of hedging in terms of the firm's investment policies. We have seen that a firm is more likely to use the financial instruments to manage its financial risk:

due to risk-averse owners if:
the firm is owned by ill-diversified investors
to reduce expected tax liabilities if:
the tax code becomes more progressive
the firm has more tax loss carryforwards
the firm has more investment tax credits
the alternate minimum tax rules are in effect
more of the range of the firm's pretax income is in the convex
region of the tax schedule
to reduce expected costs associated with financial distress if:
the probability of financial distress is higher, that is, if:
the ratio of fixed claims to cash inflows is higher
the volatility of the firm's income is higher
the costs of financial distress are higher, that is, if:
the firm is smaller
the firm provides more warranties or service agreements
the firm produces a credence good
the firm uses specialized labor or must provide specialized
training for its workers
the firm requires more customized service from its suppliers
or has fewer suppliers

to reduce agency costs if:

the firm has a larger debt/equity ratio

the firm has available a wider range of potential investment projects

Some Empirical Evidence

The question that must be asked is whether the theoretical relations we have described can be observed empirically. The problem is that, since we are dealing with off-balance-sheet financial instruments (forwards, futures, swaps, and options) data about firms' use of hedging techniques are severely limited. Consequently, the empirical studies have had to resort to surveys.

In 1982 banks and savings and loan associations were surveyed by James R. Booth, Richard L. Smith, and Richard W. Stolz regarding their use of interest rate futures.[16] The survey indicated that 30.7% of S&Ls used interest rate futures whereas only 10.4% of banks did. The researchers suggested two reasons for this difference: (1) The S&Ls were larger. (2) The S&Ls had greater maturity mismatches on assets and liabilities; that is, the S&Ls had a higher probability of encountering interest rate–induced financial distress.

In July 1985 the Fortune 500 firms were surveyed about their use of interest rate futures and options by Stanley B. Block and Timothy J. Gallagher.[17] Again, size appeared significant: 23.7% of the larger firms reported using interest rate futures and options whereas only 5.4% of the smaller firms did. The researchers also looked at the firms' debt/equity ratios and found that although the firms with higher debt/equity ratios were more likely to use interest rate futures and options, the relationship was not statistically significant.

The difficulty with the two preceding studies is that they did not address the theoretical relation discussed above. Instead of relating hedging activity with characteristics of the firm, they tended to ask the firm, "Why did (or didn't) you hedge?"

---

16. J. R. Booth, R. L. Smith, and R. W. Stolz, "The Use of Interest Futures by Financial Institutions," *Journal of Bank Research* (Spring 1984): 15–20.

17. S. B. Block and T. J. Gallagher, "The Use of Interest Rate Futures and Options by Corporate Financial Managers," *Financial Management* 15 (Autumn 1986): 73–78.

A more recent survey of the Fortune 500 firms by two of the authors of this book with Deana R. Nance[18] asked the responding firms only if, in fiscal year 1986, the firm used forwards, futures, swaps, or options. These data on whether or not the firm used the off-balance-sheet instruments were coupled with publicly-available data on characteristics of the firm. Comparing the means for the firms that used the off-balance-sheet instruments with those that did not, this study provided results that support the theoretical arguments presented here. With respect to the tax effects, the firms that hedged had larger ITCs, larger tax loss carryforwards, and more of the range of pretax income in the convex (progressive) region of the tax schedule. With respect to the transaction cost benefit from hedging, the firms that used the risk management instruments had less coverage of their fixed claims (interest expense) and tended to produce credence goods. However, the firms that hedged were larger—not smaller—than those that did not hedge. With respect to the benefit of hedging on the firm's investment decision, the firms that used the risk management instruments had larger debt/equity ratios and had a wider range of investment projects available (as proxied by the firm's R&D expenditures).

Finally, a study by Mayers and Smith[19] looked at another form of hedging: purchasing insurance. Their study of the insurance purchases of insurance companies (i.e., *reinsurance*) indicated that the firms that purchased reinsurance were owned by less diversified owners. Moreover, there was strong evidence that smaller firms were more likely to purchase the reinsurance.

This empirical evidence is summarized in Figure 17-6 and is extremely supportive of the theoretical relations presented here. In the case of firm size, the results obtained from looking at the use of newer financial instruments do not support the theoretical arguments; however, the results from looking at the more established reinsurance market are supportive, leading us to suspect that, over time, this variable will also conform to predictions.[20]

---

18. Deana R. Nance, Clifford W. Smith, Jr., and Charles W. Smithson, "The Determinants of Corporate Hedging," working paper (1989).

19. David Mayers and Clifford W. Smith, Jr., "On the Corporate Demand for Insurance: Evidence from the Reinsurance Market," *Journal of Business* (in press).

20. For more on the argument that, over time, smaller firms will be more likely to use risk management, see Nance, Smith, and Smithson, op. cit.

Figure 17-6. Summary of Empirical Evidence on Rationale for Hedging.

Theory Indicates that a Firm is More Likely to Hedge	Hypothesis Supported?			
	Booth, Smith & Stulz	Block & Gallagher	Nance, Smith & Smithson	Mayers & Smith
Due to risk-averse owners if:				
the firm is owned by ill-diversified investors	—	—	—	Yes*
To reduce expected taxes if:				
the firm has more tax loss carryforwards	—	—	Yes	—
the firm has more investment tax credits	—	—	Yes*	—
more of the range of the firm's pretax income is in the progressive region of the tax schedule	—	—	Yes*	—
To reduce expected financial distress costs if:				
The probability of financial distress is higher, that is, if:	Yes*	—	—	—
the ratio of fixed claims to cash inflows is higher	—	—	Yes	—
The costs of financial distress are higher, that is, if:				
the firm is smaller	No*	No*	No*	Yes*
the firm produces a credence good	—	—	Yes*	—
To reduce agency costs if:				
the firm has a larger debt/equity ratio	—	Yes	Yes*	—
the firm has available a wider range of potential investment projects	—	—	Yes*	—

— Hypothesis not examined

* Result deemed statistically significant by researcher

18

Assembling the Building Blocks

In Chapter 3 we introduced the building-block concept. We showed that the forward contract is the basic component out of which the other financial instruments—futures, swaps, and options—can be built and how the instruments can be built from each other. Since then, we have spent thirteen chapters describing the individual building blocks (and one chapter on the rationale for hedging).

It's time to reestablish our theme and discuss the way that forwards, futures, swaps, and options can be used to provide "financially engineered" solutions. To begin, let's look at the building blocks we have available. Figure 18-1 repeats the instruction sheet for the financial building blocks, which was first provided in Chapter 3. With these financial instrument building blocks, we can combine the traditional credit extension building blocks: bonds or loans. In Figure 18-2, we have illustrated the standard bond or loan contracts: zero coupon, level coupon, floating-rate coupon, and amortizing. Our job now is to use these building blocks to provide customized solutions.

Using the Building Blocks to Respond to Risk Management Needs

Consider a company whose value is directly related to unexpected changes in some financial price, P. The risk profile of this company is illustrated in Figure 18-3. How can we use the financial building blocks to modify this inherent exposure?

The simplest solution is to use a forward, a futures, or a swap to neutralize this exposure. This is shown in part (a) of Figure 18-4.

However, the use of a forward, a futures, or a swap eliminates possible losses by giving up the possibility of profiting from favorable outcomes.

Figure 18-1. The Financial Building Blocks.

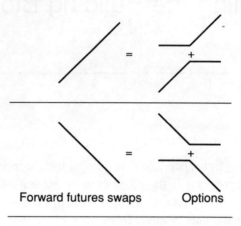

Forward futures swaps   Options

Figure 18-2. Credit Extension Instruments: Bonds or Loans.

Zero coupon

Level coupon

Floating-Rate Coupon

Amortizing

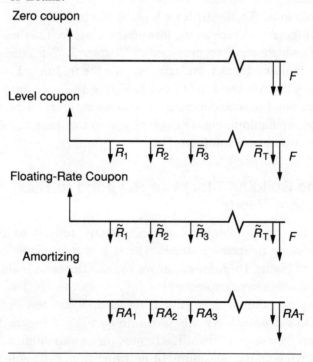

Figure 18-3. The Firm's Risk Profile.

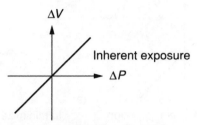

The value of the firm is directly related to financial price P(i.e., interest rates, foreign exchange rates, or commodity prices). If P rises, the value of the firm rises.

The company might want to minimize the effect of unfavorable outcomes while still allowing the possibility of gaining from favorable ones. This can be accomplished using options. The payoff profile of an at-the-money option (including the premium paid to buy the option) is shown on the left side of Figure 18-4(*b*). Snapping this building block onto the inherent exposure profile gives the resulting exposure illustrated on the right.

A common complaint about options—especially at-the-money options—is that they are too expensive. To reduce the option premium, an out-of-the-money option can be used. As part (*c*) of Figure 18-4 illustrates, the firm can thereby give up some protection from adverse outcomes in return for paying a lower premium.

However, with an out-of-the-money option, *some* premium expense remains. Part (*d*) illustrates how the out-of-pocket expense could be eliminated. The firm could sell a call option with an exercise price selected so as to generate premium income equal to the premium due on the put option it wishes to purchase. In the building-block parlance, we snap the "buy a put" option onto the inherent risk profile to reduce downside outcomes, and we snap on the "sell a call" option to fund this insurance by giving up some of the favorable outcomes.

Part (*e*) reminds us that forwards, futures, and swaps can be used in combination with options. Suppose the treasurer of the firm we have been considering makes the following request:

Figure 18-4. Using the Building Blocks to Manage the Firm's Exposure.

Use a forward or futures or swap...   to neutralize the risk

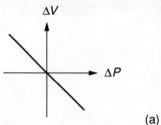 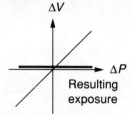

(a)

Or use an at-the-money option...   to minimize adverse outcomes

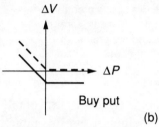 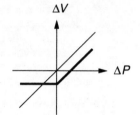

Buy put

(b)

Or use an out-of-the-money option...   to get lower cost insurance

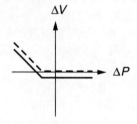 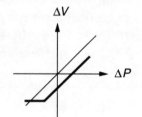

(c)

or buy and sell options   to eliminate out-of-pocket costs

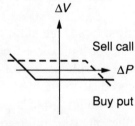 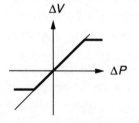

Sell call

Buy put

(d)

Or use a forward/futures/swap with options... to provide customized solutions

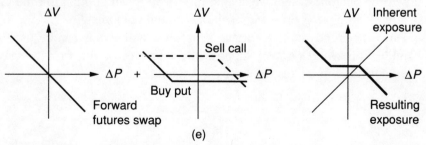

(e)

> I think that this financial price, *P*, is going to fall dramatically. And, although I know enough about financial markets to know that *P* could actually rise a little, I am sure it will not rise by much.
>
> I want some kind of financial solution that will let me benefit when my predictions come to pass. But I don't want to pay any out-of-pocket premiums; instead, I want this financial engineering product to pay me a premium.

From looking at the firm's inherent risk profile in Figure 18-3, this seems like a big request: the firm's inherent position is such that it would lose rather than gain from big decreases in *P*. The resulting exposure profile, illustrated on the right side of part (*e*), is the profile the firm wants: it would benefit from large decreases in *P*, it is protected against small increases in *P* (but not against large increases), and it receives a premium for the instrument.

How was this new profile achieved? As illustrated on the left side of part (*e*), we first snapped a forward/futures/swap position onto the original risk profile to neutralize the firm's inherent exposure. We then sold a call option and bought a put option with exercise prices set such that the income from selling the call exceeded the premium required to buy the put.

No high-level math was required. Indeed, we did this bit of financial engineering by simply looking through the box of financial building blocks until we found those that snapped together to give us the profile we wanted.

Using the Building Blocks to Redesign Financial Instruments

Now that you understand how forwards, futures, swaps, and options relate to one another, it is a relatively short step to determining how the instruments can be combined to give one financial instrument the characteristics of another. Rather than discuss this in the abstract, let's look at some examples of how this has been done in the marketplace.

Combining Forwards with Swaps

Suppose a firm is currently unexposed to interest rate movements but will, at a known date in the future, be inversely exposed to interest

rates: if rates rise, the value of the firm will decrease.[1] To manage this exposure, the firm could use a forward or a futures or a swap, but one commencing at that known future date rather than today.

Such a product is the *forward swap* (also referred to by names such as the *delayed-start swap*). A forward swap is illustrated in part (*c*) of Figure 18-5, where the party illustrated pays a fixed rate and receives floating *starting in period 5*. This instrument is a forward contract on a swap, but (not surprisingly) it can also be constructed as a package of swaps. As Figure 18-5 illustrates, the forward swap is equivalent to a package of two swaps:

Swap 1: From period 1 to period *T*, the party pays fixed and receives floating.

Swap 2: From period 1 to period 4, the party pays floating and receives fixed.

Forwards with Optionlike Characteristics

The addition of optionlike characteristics to forward contracts first appeared in the foreign exchange markets. To see how this was done, let's follow the evolution.

Begin with a standard forward contract on foreign exchange. Figure 18-6 (*a*) illustrates a stylized forward contract on sterling with the forward sterling exchange rate—the contract rate—set at $1.50 per pound sterling. If, at maturity, the spot price of sterling exceeds $1.50, the owner of this contract makes a profit (equal to the spot rate minus $1.50). Conversely, if at maturity the spot price of sterling is less than $1.50, the owner of this contract suffers a loss.

In contrast to the "standard," the owner of the forward contract might desire a contract that allows a profit if the price of sterling rises but that floors the losses if the price of sterling falls.[2] Such a contract would be

---

1. For example, the firm may know that, in one year, it will require funds that will be borrowed at a flotaing rate, thereby giving the firm the inverse exposure to interest rates. Or the firm may be adding a new product line, the demand for which is extremely sensitive to interest rate movements: as rates rise, the demand for the product decreases and cash flows to the firm decrease.

2. This discussion is adapted from Warren Edwardes and Edmond Levy, "Break Forwards: A Synthetic Option Hedging Instrument," *Midland Corporate Finance Journal* 5 (Summer 1987): 59–67.

Figure 18-5. Creating a Forward Swap.

Pay fixed, receive floating for periods 1 through T

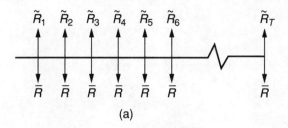

(a)

Plus Pay floating, receive fixed for periods 1 through 4

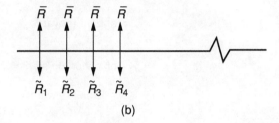

(b)

Equals A four-period forward contract on a pay fixed, receive floating swap

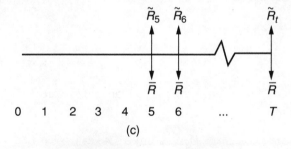

(c)

a call option on sterling, implying a premium to be paid. Illustrated in part (*b*) of Figure 18-6 is a call option on sterling with an exercise price of $1.50. In this illustration we have presumed an option premium of 5 cents (per pound sterling). However, the payoff profile illustrated in Figure 18-6(*b*) could be obtained by altering the terms of the standard forward contract in two ways:

Figure 18-6. (*a*) A Standard Forward. (*b*) A Break Forward. (*c*) A Range Forward.

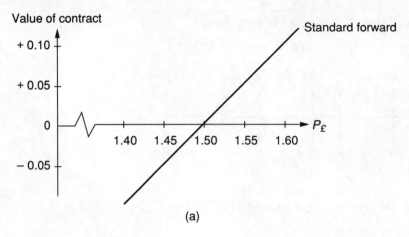

(a)

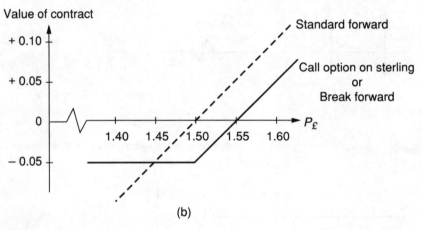

(b)

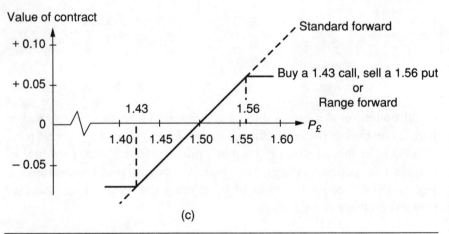

(c)

1. Change the contract price so that the exercise price of the forward contract is no longer $1.50 but is instead $1.55. The owner of the forward contract agrees to purchase sterling at contract maturity at a price of $1.55 per unit.

2. Permit the owner of the contract to break—that is, unwind—the agreement at a sterling price of $1.50.

This altered forward contract is referred to as a *break forward contract.*[3] With this new contract, if the price of sterling at expiration is greater than 1.55, the owner of the forward contract will profit in the amount of: Spot price − $1.55. If the price of expiration is less than or equal to 1.50, the owner of the forward contract will buy the sterling at a price of $1.55 per unit, suffering a loss per unit of: 1.55 − Spot price. The owner will then unwind the contract by selling the pounds at the break price of $1.50 and making a profit of: Spot price − 1.50. Combining these amounts, the owner of the break forward will suffer a loss per unit of: 1.55 − 1.50 = 0.05, which is the 5 unit cost of the option. Finally, if the sterling price at expiration is between 1.50 and 1.55, the owner of the break forward will suffer a loss equal to: 1.55 − Spot price.

The break forward construction has no explicit option premium, but a premium, is still being paid by the owner of the break forward contract in the form of the above-market contract exchange rate. From our discussion of options, we know that a call can be paid for with the proceeds from selling a put. The payoff profile for such a situation is illustrated in part (*c*) of Figure 18-6. In this illustration, we have presumed that the proceeds of a put option on sterling with an exercise price of $1.56 would carry the same premium as a call option on sterling with an exercise price of $1.43.[4] A payoff profile identical to this option payoff

---

3. According to Sam Srinivasulu in "Second-Generation Forwards: A Comparative Analysis," *Business International Money Report* (September 21, 1987):297–299,302, *break forward* is the name given to this construction by Midland Bank. It goes under other names: Boston option (Bank of Boston); FOX, or forward with optional exit (Hambros Bank); and cancelable forward (Goldman Sachs).

4. These numbers are only for purposes of illustration. To determine the exercise prices at which the values of the puts and calls are equal, one would have to use an option pricing model. Moreover, as our colleague Nicholas Warren of Chase Manhattan Bank reminded us, an additional complication is added by the language of the foreign exchange market: what we refer to as a put option on sterling would be, in the foreign exchange market, labeled a call. Likewise, the call option on sterling would be referred to as a put.

profile could, however, also be generated simply by changing the terms of a standard forward contract to the following:

> At maturity, the buyer of the forward contract agrees to purchase sterling at a price of $1.50 per pound sterling.
>
> The buyer of the forward contract has the right to break—unwind— the contract at a price of $1.43 per pound sterling.
>
> The seller of the forward contract has the right to break—unwind— the contract at a price of $1.56 per pound sterling.

Such a forward contract is referred to as a *range forward*.[5]

Swaps with Optionlike Characteristics

Given that swaps can be viewed as packages of forward contracts, it should not be surprising that swaps can also be constructed to have optionlike characteristics similar to those illustrated for forwards in Figure 18-6(*c*). For example, suppose that a firm with a floating-rate liability wanted to limit its outflows, should interest rates rise substantially, and was willing to give up some potential gains, should there instead be a dramatic decline in short-term rates. To achieve this end, the firm could modify the interest rate swap contract as follows:

> As long as the interest rate neither rises by more than 200 basis points nor falls more than 100 basis points, the firm pays a floating rate and receives a fixed rate. But if the interest is more than 200 basis points above or 100 basis points below the current rate, the firm receives and pays a fixed rate.

The resulting payoff profile for this *floating floor-ceiling swap* is illustrated in part (*a*) of Figure 18-7. Conversely, the interest rate swap contract could have been modified as follows:

> As long as the interest rate is within 200 basis points of the current rate, the firm neither makes nor receives a payment. But if the interest rate rises or falls by more than 200 basis points, the firm pays a floating rate and receives a fixed rate.

---

5. As Srinivasulu, *op. cit.*, pointed out, this construction also appears under a number of names: range forward (Salomon Brothers), collar (Midland Montagu), flexible forward (Manufacturers Hanover), cylinder option (Citicorp), option fence (Bank of America), mini-max (Goldman Sachs), and forward band (Chase Manhattan).

Figure 18-7. Payoff Profile for Floor-Ceiling Swaps.

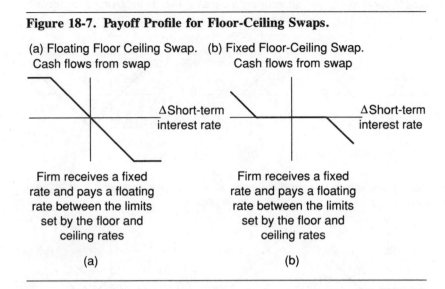

(a) Floating Floor Ceiling Swap.   (b) Fixed Floor-Ceiling Swap.
Cash flows from swap   Cash flows from swap

ΔShort-term interest rate

ΔShort-term interest rate

Firm receives a fixed
rate and pays a floating
rate between the limits
set by the floor and
ceiling rates

Firm receives a fixed
rate and pays a floating
rate between the limits
set by the floor and
ceiling rates

(a)

(b)

The payoff profile for the resulting *fixed floor-ceiling swap* is illustrated in part (*b*) of Figure 18-7.

Redesigned Options

Normally to "redesign" an option, two or more options are put together to change the payoff profile. Examples abound in the world of the option trader. Figure 18-8 illustrates how some of the more colorfully named combinations are formed: *straddles, strangles,* and *butterflies.*[6]

To see how and why such creations evolve, let's look at a hypothetical situation. Suppose a firm is confronted with the exposure illustrated in part (*a*) of Figure 18-9. Suppose further that, due perhaps to concerns about financial distress, the firm wants to establish a floor on its financial price–induced losses.

Of course, this could be done with a call option on the financial price. Purchase an out-of-the-money call option with exercise price X, paying a premium of W, as illustrated in part (*b*) of Figure 18-9. Then add the call option payoff profile to the inherent profile to end up with the floor

6. For a discussion of traditional option strategies such as straddles, strangles, and butterflies, see, for instance, Richard M. Bookstaber, *Option Pricing and Strategies in Investing* (Reading, Mass.: Addison-Wesley, 1981), Chap. 7.

Figure 18-8. Option Strategies.

Buying a call...   and buying a put at   results in buying a *straddle*
the same excercise price...

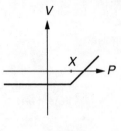 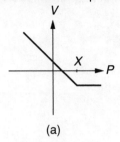 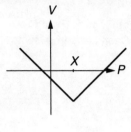

(a)

Buying a call at   and buying a put at   results in buying a *strangle*
one excercise price...   a lower excercise price...

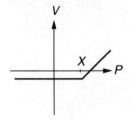 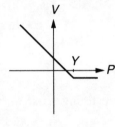 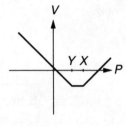

(b)

Buying a call at   and buying a put at
one excercise price...   a higher excercise price...

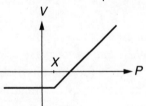 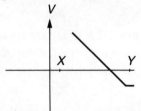

then selling a call and a put at   results in buying a *butterfly*
an excercise price in between...

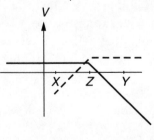 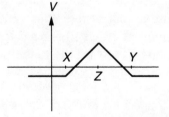

(c)

Figure 18-9. Creating a Floor with a Call Option.

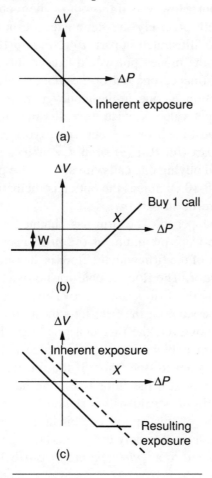

(a)

(b)

(c)

illustrated.[7] The problem with this solution is the premium the firm has to pay.

___

7. For simplicity, we have drawn the inherent risk profile in Figure 18-9 as a 45° line. Hence, one dollar's worth of the option will exactly hedge one dollar's worth of underlying exposure. In this case, the only mathematical problem is the determination of the exercise price, X, that will give the firm the precise floor it desires. In an actual setting, it is unlikely that the risk profile would be 45°; one dollar's worth of the option would either hedge more or less than one dollar's worth of the underlying exposure. In this case, the firm would also have to determine the appropriate number of call options to purchase.

Is there a way the premium can be eliminated? You have already seen that buying this out-of-the-money call could be financed by selling an out-of-the-money put. However, if this out-of-the-money call is financed by selling a put with precisely the same exercise price, the put would be in the money. As illustrated in part (*b*) of Figure 18-10, the proceeds from selling the in-the-money put would exceed the cost of the out-of-the-money call; to finance one out-of-the-money call, one would need to sell only a fraction of one in-the-money put. In part (*b*) we have presumed that the put value is twice the call value; to finance one call, the firm would need to sell only $\frac{1}{2}$ put; the payoff profile for which is also illustrated in part (*b*). Part (*c*) simply combines the payoff profiles for selling $\frac{1}{2}$ put and buying one call with an exercise price of *X*. Finally, part (*d*) of Figure 18-10 combines the option combination in part (*c*) with the inherent risk profile in part (*a*).

Note what has happened. The firm has obtained the floor it wanted, but, there is no up-front premium: at the price at which the option is exercised, the value of the firm with the floor is the same as it would have been without the floor. The floor is paid for not with a fixed premium, but with a share of the firm's gains above the floor. If the financial price rises by *X*, the value of the firm falls to the floor, and there is no premium paid. If, however, the financial price rises by less—say, *Y* — the value of the firm is higher (the loss in value is less), and the firm pays a positive premium for the floor. If the financial price falls—say, by *Z*—the price it pays for the floor rises. We have a situation where the provider of the floor is paid with a share of potential gains, thereby leading to the name of this option combination: a *participation*. This construction has been most widely used in the foreign exchange market, where they are referred to as *participating forwards*.[8]

Options on Other Financial Instruments

As we described in Chapter 16, in addition to options on shares and options on physical commodities, there are *options on futures contracts*.

---

8. As with the break and range forwards, this construction is explained in more detail in Srinivalsulu, *op. cit.* Alternatively, an excellent discussion of optionlike combinations in the currency markets is provided by Eric Briys and Michel Crouhy, "Creating and Pricing Hybrid Foreign Currency Options," *Financial Management* 17, no. 4 (Winter 1988): 59–65.

Figure 18-10. Creating a "Participation."

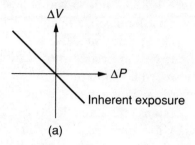

(a)

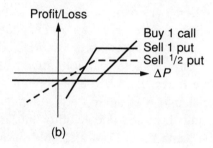

(b)

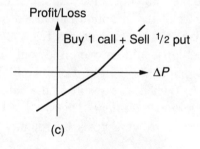

(c)

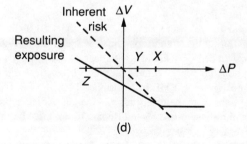

(d)

Options on futures contracts have been actively traded on the Chicago Board of Trade since 1982.[9] And, as was shown in Chapter 16, the valuation of an option on a futures is a relatively straightforward extension of the traditional option pricing models.

Given the relations we have established between futures and forwards and futures and swaps, you would probably suspect that the introduction of options on forwards and options on swaps would have followed close on the heels of the options on futures. However, options on forwards—in particular, *options on forward rate agreements*—and options on swaps— referred to as *swaptions*[10]—appeared only recently. In early 1989, the market for swaptions was particularly active as bond issuers were using swaptions to sell the interest rate option imbedded in the call provision of a bond. A case in point is Ford Motor Credit Corporation.[11] Ford issued standard ten-year notes callable after five years (by having the option to call the notes, Ford had a put option on interest rates[12]). The firm then entered into a standard "pay floating/receive fixed" interest rate swap, turning the fixed-rate liability into a floating-rate liability. However, at the same time, Ford also sold through its underwriter the right to terminate the swap after five years; that is, Ford sold a swaption. In effect, the buyer of the swaption purchased the right to pay floating and receive the fixed rate specified today for years 5 through 10. Clearly, this right is valuable (would be exercised) only if rates fall; that is, the buyer of this swaption has bought the put option on interest rates that Ford Motor Credit owned as a result of the call provision on its notes. According to *Investment Dealers' Digest*, this structure "was rumored to have cut Ford's borrowing costs by roughly 20 basis points." Put

---

9. Options on the T-bond futures were first traded on the CBOT in October 1982, followed by options on Eurodollar futures on the CME in March 1985. Options on currency futures were first traded on the CME in January 1984. Options on commodity futures appeared with options on copper futures on the COMEX in April 1985 and with options on crude oil futures on the NYME in November 1986.

10. A discussion of swaptions from the perspective of market participants is contained in Krystyna Krzyzak, "Swaptions Deciphered," and Robert Tompkins, "Behind the Mirror," both in *Risk* 2, no. 2 (February 1989).

11. This example is adapted from "First Boston Snares Ford Credit with Swaption-Linked Deal," *Investment Dealers' Digest* (January 16, 1989): 42–43.

12. We will return to the idea of the call provision as an interest rate option in the next section.

another way, the put option on interest rates sold by Ford had a value equivalent to 20 basis points on the $250 million borrowing.

For the options we have discussed so far, the reference price specified in the option contract is a "spot" price: the value of the option at expiration is determined by the difference between the exercise price and the price prevailing at expiration. Recently, however, options have appeared that specify the reference price as the average price—*average-price options*. Thus, at expiration, the value of the option would be determined by the difference between the exercise price and the average of the spot prices that have existed over the option's lifetime (or some part of this period).[13]

Even more innovative are the so-called *lookback options*. Such an option gives its owners the right to exercise the option at expiration, at the most favorable price that has occurred during the lifetime of the option. For instance, the owner of a lookback call option is able to buy an asset at expiration for the lowest price seen during the lifetime of the option. Such an option can be viewed as the combination of an at-the-money option and a second option that permits the exercise price to be changed with favorable movements in the underlying price.[14]

More complicated analytically is the valuation of an option on an option—a *compound option*.[15] These analytical difficulties notwithstanding, some options on options have begun to be traded. Compound options first appeared as *options on foreign exchange options*. These options were particularly valuable to firms bidding on contracts denominated in foreign currencies. If the firm won the bid, an option would be desired, but if the firm lost the bid, the option would not be needed; hence, what the bidding firm wanted was an option on the option. However, today the more active market for compound options is for options on interest rate options (caps). Referred to in the trade as *captions*, these compound options are becoming more widely quoted and used.

---

13. For more on this instrument, see Martin Coward and Lee Thomas, "When Average Can Be Good," *Risk* 1, no. 8 (July 1988): 42–43.

14. For more on this option, see "Optional Hindsight," *Risk* 1, no. 10 (October 1988): 48, and Mark Garman, "Recollection in Tranquility," *Risk* 2, no. 3 (March 1989): 16–19.

15. For a discussion of the compound option problem, see John C. Cox and Mark Rubenstein, *Options Markets* (Englewood Cliffs, N.J.: Prentice-Hall, 1985): pp. 412–415.

Figure 18-11. Using a Swap to Create a Reverse Floating-Rate Loan.

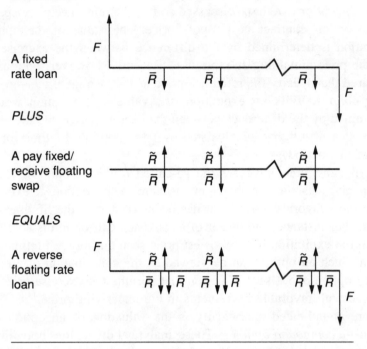

Using the Building Blocks to Design "New" Products

It's unusual to go through a day in the financial markets without hearing of at least one "new" or "hybrid" product. However, as should come as no surprise by now, our position with respect to these financial products is that there is little new under the sun. The "new" products generally involve nothing more than putting the building blocks together in a different fashion.[16]

An example of a hybrid security made up of a standard credit extension instrument and a swap is provided in Figure 18-11. If we combine a conventional fixed-rate loan and an interest rate swap where the party pays fixed and receives floating, the result is a *reverse floating-rate loan*.

---

16. In this section we describe a number of hybrid securities. The reader interested in a more encyclopedic description of hybrids is referred to John D. Finnerty, "Financial Engineering in Corporate Finance: An Overview," *Financial Management* 17, no. 4 (Winter 1988): 14–33.

The net coupon payments on the hybrid loan are equal to twice the fixed rate minus the floating rate times the principal.

$$\text{Net coupon} = 2\overline{R} - \tilde{R}$$
$$= (2\overline{r} - \tilde{r})P$$

If the floating rate rises (i.e., if $\tilde{r}$ rises), the net coupon payment falls.[17]

A hybrid security made up of a standard credit extension instrument and a forward contract is a *dual-currency bond*. The top of Figure 18-12 illustrates a dual-currency bond in which the coupons are paid in dollars but the principal is paid in yen. The remainder of Figure 18-12 illustrates that this bond is made up of a standard, level-coupon dollar bond and a dollar/yen forward contract.[18]

A "hybrid security" with which most of us are comfortable is a bond with an attached warrant—most commonly, bonds with share warrants. In the context of our building-block theme, these hybrids can be viewed as the combination of a straight bond and an option on shares of the issuing firm. The tombstone for such a bond is reproduced in Figure 18-13.

Today we are seeing more and more hybrids, extending the process begun by these simple bonds with warrants. On one dimension, the extension is simply an expansion of the kinds of warrants available. In addition to warrants linked to the firm's share price, warrants have appeared tied to foreign exchange (see Figure 18-14) and the price of gold (see Figure 18-15). And, with its June 19, 1986, issue of *oil-indexed notes*, Standard Oil gave wide coverage to the idea of bonds with oil warrants.[19] The tombstone for this bond is reproduced in Figure

---

17. In our example, we created the reverse floating-rate note from a fixed-rate loan and a swap for the same notional principal. However, the same set of cash flows can be created by combining a floating-rate loan (coupon $= \tilde{R}$) with a receive-floating swap with a notional principal equal to twice the principal of the loan (receive $2\tilde{R}$, pay $2\overline{R}$) to give the reverse floating-rate note (coupon $= \tilde{R} + 2\overline{R} - 2\tilde{R} = 2\overline{R} - \tilde{R}$). These reverse floating-rate notes—also called *bull floating-rate notes*—are discussed in Donald J. Smith, "The Pricing of Bull and Bear Floating Notes: An Application of Financial Engineering," *Financial Management* 17, no. 4 (Winter 1988): 72–81.

18. The same structure is created for bank loans via *dual-currency loans*: the loan is drawn in one currency, but the bank has the right to convert this loan principal to another currency at a specified exchange rate. [See *International Financing Review*, issue 742 (September 17, 1988) p. 2989.]

19. In an early draft of this book, we referred to the Standard Oil issue as the first time bonds had appeared with oil warrants attached. However, as our colleague James M. O'Keane of the Continental Bank pointed out, Pemex (The Mexican state oil company) issued such petro-bonds in April 1973.

Figure 18-12. A Dual Currency Bond.

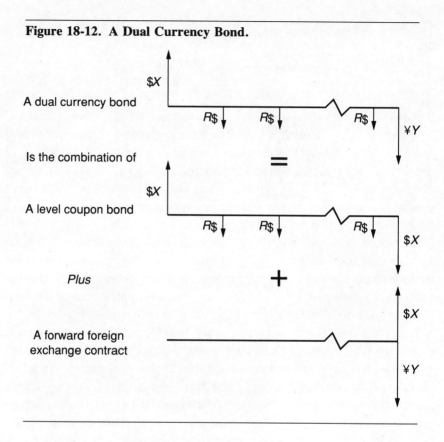

18-16. As described in the prospectus, at maturity, the holder of the oil-indexed note would receive (in addition to the principal) an amount tied to the value of crude oil. The holders of the 1990 notes would receive "the excess . . .of the Crude Oil Price . . .over $25 multiplied by 170 barrels of Light Sweet Crude Oil."[20] What this means is that the 1990 note has imbedded in it a four-year option on 170 barrels of crude oil. If, at maturity, the value of Light Sweet Oklahoma Crude Oil exceeds $25, the holder of the note would receive[21]

20. Prospectus Supplement, June 19, 1986, p. S-5 The holder of the 1992 note had the same payoff, but for 200 barrels instead of 170.
21. This issue did, however, impose a cap on he crude oil price of $40, so the maximum the holder of the bond could receive was $40 − $25 = $15 per barrel.

Figure 18-13. Bond With Share Warrant.

All of these Securities have been sold. This announcement appears as a matter of record only.

U.S. $150,000,000

General Electric Company

(Incorporated in the State of New York, U.S.A.)

2¾% Discount Notes Due 1994

and

1,785,000 Warrants Each to Purchase One Share of General Electric Company Common Stock

---

MORGAN STANLEY INTERNATIONAL

BANQUE INDOSUEZ | **BANQUE PARIBAS CAPITAL MARKETS** Limited | **CREDIT SUISSE FIRST BOSTON** Limited

DAIWA EUROPE LIMITED | **DEUTSCHE BANK CAPITAL MARKETS** Limited

IMI CAPITAL MARKETS (UK) LTD. | **KIDDER, PEABODY INTERNATIONAL** Limited

NOMURA INTERNATIONAL Limited | **J. HENRY SCHRODER WAGG & CO.** Limited

SWISS BANK CORPORATION INTERNATIONAL Limited | **SWISS VOLKSBANK**

UNION BANK OF SWITZERLAND (SECURITIES) Limited | **YAMAICHI INTERNATIONAL (EUROPE)** Limited

March, 1987

Reprinted courtesy of General Electric Company and Morgan Stanley International.

Figure 18-14. Bond With Foreign Exchange Warrant

New Issue
September 13, 1988

This announcement appears
as a matter of record only.

Finance for Danish Industry International S.A.
Luxembourg, Grand Duchy of Luxembourg

unconditionally and irrevocably guaranteed by
Finansieringsinstituttet for Industri
og Håndværk A/S
Copenhagen, Kingdom of Denmark

Can$ 50,000,000
10¾% Notes of 1988/1991 with currency warrants

Offering Price:	110,63%
Interest:	10¾% p.a., payable annually on September 13
Repayment:	September 13, 1991
Subscription Right:	each note of Can$ 10,000 will be issued with one warrant entitling the holder on May 17, 1989 to sell a total of U.S.$ 30,000 at a rate of U.S.$ 1.80 per Deutsche Mark
Listing:	Luxembourg Stock Exchange (Notes and Warrants)

Deutsche Bank Capital Markets
Limited

Privatbanken A/S

$$(Price - \$25) \times 170$$

If the value of Light Sweet Oklahoma Crude Oil is less than $25 at maturity in 1990, the option expires worthless.

So far, we have illustrated hybrids made up of a bond plus either share options, foreign exchange options, or commodity options. Not surprisingly, there also exist hybrids created by combining a standard bond and an interest rate option. The most common example is a *callable bond*, a bond that gives the issuer a put option on interest rates. If rates fall, the call provision is valuable: the issuer can call the bonds and issue new bonds at a lower rate. There are also some *extendible notes*, which permit the issuer to extend the maturity of the note at some prespecified interest rate. In this case, the issuer has a call option on interest rates; if rates rise above the specified rate, the issuer benefits from the extendibility. Both of these deal with interest rate options owned

Figure 18-15. Bond with Gold Warrants.

This announcement appears as a matter of record only. These Securities have not been registered under the United States Securities Act of 1933, the Notes may not be offered or sold in the United States or to United States persons as part of the distribution and the Warrants may not at any time be offered, sold or traded in the United States or to or with United States persons.

New Issue

25th June, 1987

U.S. $130,000,000

Eastman Kodak Company

9% Notes Due 1990
with
130,000 Gold Warrants

Issue Price 113.175%

Union Bank of Switzerland (Securities) Limited

Banque Indosuez | **Crédit Commercial de France**

Shearson Lehman Brothers International

Banque Paribas Capital Markets Limited | **DG BANK Deutsche Genossenschaftsbank**

Goldman Sachs International Corp. | **Leu Securities Limited**

Mitsubishi Trust International Limited | **Morgan Stanley International**

Salomon Brothers International Limited | **Société Générale**

Reprinted courtesy of Eastman-Kodak Company and Union Bank of Switzerland (Securities) Limited.

Figure 18-16. Bond with Oil Warrant.

This announcement is neither an offer to sell nor a solicitation of offers to buy any of these securities. The offering is made only by the Prospectus and the related Prospectus Supplement.

NEW ISSUE

June 23, 1986

The Standard Oil Company

37,500 Oil Indexed Units

Consisting of

$300,000,000 6.30% Debentures Due 2001

$37,500,000 Oil Indexed Notes Due 1990

$37,500,000 Oil Indexed Notes Due 1992

The Debentures and Notes are being offered in Units, each of which consists of eight Debentures of $1,000 principal amount each, one Oil Indexed Note Due 1990 and one Oil Indexed Note Due 1992 of $1,000 principal amount each. The Debentures and Notes will be issued only in registered form and will not be separately transferable until after July 31, 1986, or such earlier date as may be determined by the Underwriters with the concurrence of the Company.

Price $7,976 Per Unit

plus accrued interest on the Debentures from July 1, 1986

Copies of the Prospectus and the related Prospectus Supplement may be obtained in any State in which this announcement is circulated only from such of the undersigned as may legally offer these securities in such State.

The First Boston Corporation Lazard Frères & Co.

by the issuer (callable bonds = put option on interest rates; extendible notes = call option on interest rates).[22] However, *puttable notes* can provide the bondholder with a call option on interest rates. If rates rise, the bondholder can put the notes back to the issuer and invest in notes paying a higher interest rate. Moreover, these puttable notes also can provide the bondholder with an option on the creditworthiness of the issuer. If the issuer's creditworthiness declines, the bondholder can redeem the bonds at a specified price.[23]

In addition to offering options on assets other than shares, the building-block process has been extended along another dimension by modifying the timing of the options imbedded in the bond. For the traditional bond with an attached warrant, there is only one option,[24] which is exercisable at one point in time. More recent bonds have involved packages of options that are exercisable at different points in time. An example of this type of hybrid is Magma Copper Company's *copper interest-indexed senior subordinated notes*, issued in November 1988; the tombstone is illustrated in Figure 18-17. This ten-year issue pays quarterly interest payment determined by the prevailing price of copper:

Average Copper Price	Indexed Interest Rate
$ 2.00 or above	21%
1.80	20
1.60	19
1.40	18
1.30	17
1.20	16
1.10	15
1.00	14
0.90	13
0.80 or below	12

November 23, 1988, prospectus, p. 5.

---

22. The issuer pays for these options with a larger coupon rate on the bond.
23. This idea of providing the bondholder with an option on the creditworthiness of the issuer was used by Manufacturers Hanover in February 1988, when it issued *floating-rate, rating-sensitive notes*. With these notes, the spread over LIBOR automatically changed if the issuer's credit rating changed. Note that in contrast to the puttable notes, which combine an interest rate option and an option on the creditworthiness of the issuer, these floating-rate, rating-sensitive notes contain only options on Manufacturers Hanover's creditworthiness.
24. The option may, however, be exercisable into more than one share.

Figure 18-17. Bond with Multiple Commodity Options.

This announcement appears as a matter of record only.

COPPER COMPANY

$503,000,000

Recapitalization

$200,000,000 Bank Term Loan and Revolving Credit

$210,000,000 Copper Interest-Indexed
Senior Subordinated Notes

$93,000,000 Cumulative Convertible Exchangeable
Preferred Stock

*We structured and negotiated the Recapitalization, and our venture banking affiliate,
Warburg, Pincus Capital Company, L.P., purchased the Cumulative
Convertible Exchangeable Preferred Stock.*

E. M. WARBURG, PINCUS & CO., INC.

NEW YORK   LONDON   LOS ANGELES

December 1988

Reprinted courtesy of Magma Copper Company and E. M. Worburg, Pincus & Co, Inc.

Hence, at each coupon date, the holder of the debenture has an option position on copper price.[25] That is, this ten-year debenture has imbedded in it forty option positions on the price of copper—one with maturity three months, one with maturity six months, . . . , and one with maturity ten years.

To get a little fancier, consider an *oil-indexed, dual-currency bond.* In Figure 18-18, we have provided a tombstone for this issue (which,

25. In effect, the owner of the note is long a call option with an exercise price of $0.80 and is short a call with an exercise price of $2.00.

Figure 18-18. Oil-Indexed, Dual Currency Bond.

This announcement is neither an offer to sell nor a solicitation of offers to buy any of these securities. The offering is made only by the Prospectus and the related Prospectus Supplement.

NEW ISSUE   May 18, 1989

125,000,000

East Tex Oil Co.

Oil Interest Indexed, Dual Currency Notes due 1994

Price   %

Copies of the Prospectus and the related Prospectus Supplement may be obtained in any State in which this announcement is circulated only from such of the undersigned as may legally offer these securities in such State.

unlike the other hybrids discussed, has yet to be issued). Note that the only thing missing in this tombstone is the price of the issue. Let's see how it would be priced. Suppose that this five-year bond is issued in denominations of $1,000. Suppose further that the prospectus specifies that the semiannual coupon would be indexed to the price of crude oil:

> At each coupon date, the bondholder will receive the greater of $34 or the value of two barrels of Sweet Light Crude Oil.

Here we have again encountered an option: If the value of crude oil is less than $17 per barrel, the bondholder will receive $34. If the value of the reference crude is greater than $34, the bondholder will receive the value of two barrels of the crude oil. The payoff profile for the coupon is illustrated in Figure 18-19. As should be clear, the coupon is actually the sum of two components:

$$\$34 + \begin{array}{c}\text{Option on two barrels of}\\ \text{crude oil with exercise}\\ \text{price of \$17 per barrel}\end{array}$$

And, since this is a dual-currency issue, the prospectus specified that:

> At maturity, each bondholder will receive 140,000 yen in lieu of the face value of $1,000.

What we have here is a forward contract on yen. The bondholder has agreed that in five years, he will pay $1,000 (the face value of the bond) to receive 140,000 yen. Hence, as illustrated in Figure 18-20, in order to value this hybrid security, we need to:

1. Value the off-market bond. (The bond is off-market because $34 is much below the coupon EasTex oil would have to pay if it were to issue a straight bond.)
2. Value the package of ten oil options. Each option is for two barrels of oil. All of the options have the same exercise price, $17 per barrel. The first option has a maturity of six months; the second one year; and so on, with the tenth option maturing in five years.
3. Value the five-year forward contract on yen.
4. Add up the preceding three values.

An oil-indexed, dual-currency bond may sound intimidating, but this complicated-looking bond is nothing more than a package of a standard bond, a package of options, and a forward contract.

* * * * *

Financial engineering sounds like something you need a degree from MIT or CalTech to do; it sounds complicated. But building innovative financial products with the financial building blocks is easy.

Figure 18-19. The Imbedded Oil Option.

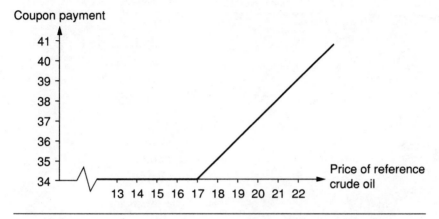

Figure 18-20. An Oil-Indexed Dual-Currency Bond.

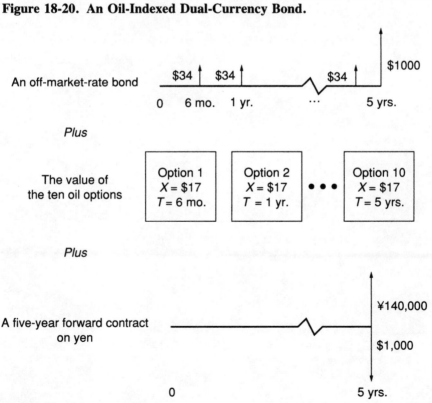

Index

About the Authors

Clifford W. Smith, Jr.,   Clarey Professor of Finance at the William E. Simon Graduate School of Business Administration at The University of Rochester, has published over forty papers, and five books in the fields of option pricing, corporate financial policy, and financial intermediation. Students gave Mr. Smith their Superior Teaching Award nine occasions and he was chosen from among the University of Rochester faculty as one of ten University Mentors in recognition of his scholarship and teaching. He is an editor of the *Journal of Financial Economics*, associate editor of the *Journal of Financial and Quantitative Analysis*, the *Journal of Accounting and Economics*, the *Journal of Real Estate Finance and Economics*, and *Financial Management*, a member of the editorial review board of the *Journal of the American Real Estate and Urban Economics Association*; and a member of the advisory board of the Continental Bank Journal of Applied Corporate Finance.

Charles W. Smithson   is a Managing Director at Continental Bank, serving as the Director of Research for Capital Markets Products. His own research has focused on a wide range of microeconomic issues including derivative instruments, regulation, production, labor markets, and natural resources. His current research is focused on financial instruments and risk management. Smithson is the author of numerous articles which have appeared in scholarly journals, the trade press, and the popular press. He is also the author of several books including *Managerial Economics* and *The Doomsday Myth*. He holds a B.A. and an M.A. from the University of Texas at Arlington, and received his Ph.D. from Tulane University.

D. Sykes Wilford,   a Managing Director of the Chase Investment Bank Ltd., is responsible for Risk Management Product Marketing for Chase

in Europe. His responsibilities include design and development as well as origination of financial and commodity price risk management solutions for Chase's global clients.

Previously he has acted as Head of International Capital Markets Research for Drexel Burnham Lambert and was an economist with the Federal Reserve Bank in New York. Wilford, whose main research interests are monetary economics and international finance, has written in both the academic and popular press. His articles have appeared in research journals such as the *American Economic Review* and the *Journal of Finance* as well as market oriented publications like *Euromoney* and *The Money Manager*. He has both authored and edited several books.

His interest is not limited to research; as an active consultant for corporations, central banks and governments, he explains and lectures about financial innovations and methodologies for analyzing international markets. He has held positions at several universities, including New York University and The University of New Orleans. Wilford holds a B.A., M.A., and Ph.D. in economics.

The Institutional Investor Series in Finance

The Institutional Investor Series in Finance has been developed specifically to bring you—the finance professional—the latest thinking and developments in investments and corporate finance. As new challenges arise in this fast-paced arena, you can count on this series to provide you with the information you need to gain the competitive edge.

Institutional Investor is the leading communications company serving the global financial community and publisher of the magazine of the same name. Institutional Investor has won 36 major awards for distinguished financial journalism—including the prestigious National Magazine Award for the best reporting of any magazine in the United States. More than 560,000 financial executives in 170 countries read Institutional Investor publications each month. Thousands more attend Institutional Investor's world wide conferences and seminars each year.